D1237770

Yavneh-Yam

T. Sippor

Or ha-ner

Tel Aviv

T. Qasile

T. Poleg

Sefunim Cave

Shiqmona

Tuleilat Batashi

Ramla

S h a r o n

Wadi Rabah

Yarkon

T. Zeror

Qafze Cave

Sepphoris

T. Rosh ha-Niqra

T. es-Safi

Shaalbim

Sorek Valley

Shuqba Cave

T. er-Ras

Samaria

Taanach

Tiberias

Yonim Cave

Kh. Shema'

Kh. el-Qom

Ramat Rahel

Shiloh

Shechem

Wadi Daliyeh

Shinjeh Cave

Ubeidiye

'Ein Feshkha

Qumran

Pella

Sha'ar ha-Golan

Tuleilat Ghassul

T. es-Sa'idiyeh

Rabbat Ammon

Alma College
Monteith Library

SIGILLUM ALMAE COLLEGII
IN NOMINE DEI, AMEN.
INCORPORATED A.D. 1886.

ENCYCLOPEDIA OF ARCHAEOLOGICAL EXCAVATIONS IN THE HOLY LAND

ENCYCLOPEDIA OF ARCHAEOLOGICAL EXCAVATIONS IN THE HOLY LAND

VOLUME IV

Editors, English Edition

Michael Avi-Yonah

Ephraim Stern

Prentice-Hall, Inc., Englewood Cliffs, N.J.

LIBRARY OF CONGRESS CATALOGING IN PUBLICATION DATA
MAIN ENTRY UNDER TITLE:
THE ENCYCLOPEDIA OF ARCHAEOLOGICAL EXCAVATIONS IN THE HOLY LAND.
1. Palestine — Antiquities — Dictionaries.
2. Bible — Antiquities — Dictionaries. I. Avi-Yonah, Michael, 1904–1974 ed.
DS111.A2E5   220.9'3   73–14997
ISBN o–13–275149–6

ALL RIGHTS RESERVED. NO PART OF THIS PUBLICATION MAY BE REPRINTED
WITHOUT THE PRIOR WRITTEN PERMISSION OF THE COPYRIGHT OWERS.

© 1978 by Prentice-Hall, Inc., Englewood Cliffs, N.J.
© 1978 by The Israel Exploration Society and Massada Press, Jerusalem

Simultaneously published in Great Britain by
Oxford University Press.

PRINTED IN ISRAEL by Peli Printing Works Ltd.

792004

LIBRARY
ALMA COLLEGE
ALMA, MICHIGAN

EDITORS, ENGLISH EDITION:
The late Michael Avi-Yonah
Ephraim Stern

EDITORIAL DIRECTOR:
Joseph Aviram

ASSISTANT EDITOR:
Essa Cindorf

ILLUSTRATIONS EDITOR:
Joseph S. Schweig

EDITORIAL BOARD
OF THE HEBREW EDITION

EDITOR-IN-CHIEF:
Benjamin Mazar

EDITORS:
the late Yohanan Aharoni
Nahman Avigad
the late Michael Avi-Yonah
the late Moshe Stekelis
Yigael Yadin

EDITORIAL DIRECTOR:
Joseph Aviram

SCIENTIFIC SECRETARY:
Magen Broshi

ILLUSTRATIONS EDITOR:
Joseph S. Schweig

PROF. YOHANAN AHARONI (deceased), Tel Aviv University — *Ramat Maṭred, Ramat Raḥel*

PROF. NAHMAN AVIGAD, Hebrew University, Jerusalem — *Samaria*

PROF. MICHAEL AVI-YONAH (deceased), Hebrew University, Jerusalem — *Rabbath-Ammon, Sepphoris, Shinjeh Cave, Synagogues*

DR. DAN BARAG, Hebrew University, Jerusalem — *Sha'albim*

PROF. OFER BAR-YOSEF, Hebrew University, Jerusalem — *Sefunim Caves, Shuqba Cave, 'Ubeidiya, Yonim Cave*

PROF. ABRAHAM BIRAN, Hebrew Union College, Jerusalem — *Tel Ṣippor*

DR. ROBERT J. BULL, Drew University, Madison N.J. — *Tell er-Ras*

R. DE VEAX O.P. (deceased), Ecole Biblique et Archéologique Française, Jerusalem — *Khirbet Qumran and 'Ein Feshkha*

DR. WILLIAM G. DEVER, University of Arizona, Tucson — *Khirbet el-Qôm*

PROF. MOSHE DOTHAN, Haifa University — *Hammat-Tiberias*

PROF. TRUDE DOTHAN, Hebrew University, Jerusalem — *Tell Qasile*

MR. IMANUEL DUNAYEVSKY (deceased), Hebrew University, Jerusalem — *Tell Qasile*

DR. YOSEF ELGAVISH, Museum of Ancient Art, Haifa — *Tel Shiqmona*

DR. GIDEON FOERSTER, Hebrew University, Jerusalem — *Tiberias*

PROF. MORDECHAI GICHON, Tel Aviv University — *Meṣad Tamar*

PROF. NELSON GLUECK, (deceased), Hebrew Union College, Jerusalem — *Khirbet et-Tannur*

DR. A. E. GLOCK, The Albright Institute, Jerusalem — *Taanach*

DR. RAM GOPHNA, Tel Aviv University — *Tel Poleg, Sharon Plain, Ḥazerim by Sharuḥen Naḥal Sorek*

MR. SHMARYAHU GUTMAN, Na'an — *Khirbet Susiya*

MRS. YAEL ISRAELI, Israel Museum, Jerusalem — *Tel Sharuḥen*

DR. JACOB KAPLAN, Museum of Antiquities, Tel Aviv–Jaffa — *Wadi Rabah. Ramla, Tel Aviv, Tuleilat Batashi, Yavneh-Yam*

DR. AHARON KEMPINSKI, Tel Aviv University — *Shiloh*

DR. MOSHE KOCHAVI, Tel Aviv University — *Khirbet Rabud, Tell Esdar, Mount Yeruḥam, Tel Zeror*

DR. JOHN R. LEE, St. John Fisher College, Rochester, N.Y. — *Tuleilat Ghassul*

DR. LEE I. LEVINE, Hebrew University, Jerusalem — *Pella*

DR. AMIHAI MAZAR, Hebrew University, Jerusalem — *Tell Qasile*

DR. ERIC M. MEYERS, Duke Univesity, Durham, N.C. — *Khirbet Shema'*

PROF. ABRAHAM NEGEV, Hebrew University, Jerusalem — *Petra, er-Ram, Subeita*

DR. EHUD NETZER, Hebrew University, Jerusalem — *Khirbet Susiya*

DR. ELIEZER D. OREN, Ben-Gurion University, Beer Sheva — *Tel Sera'*

PROF. JAMES B. PRITCHARD, University of Pennsylvania, Philadelphia, Pa. — *Tell es-Sa'idiyeh*

DR. BENNO ROTHENBERG, Institute of Mining and Metals, Tel Aviv — *Timna'*

PROF. MIRIAM ROSEN-AYALON, Hebrew University, Jerusalem — *Ramla*

PROF. MOSHE STEKELIS (deceased), Hebrew University, Jerusalem — *el-Qafza cave, Sha'ar ha-Golan, 'Ubeidiya*

DR. EPHRAIM STERN, Hebrew University, Jerusalem — *Rabbath-Ammon, Tell es-Safi*

MRS. MIRIAM TADMOR, Israel Museum, Jerusalem — *Tel Rosh ha-Niqra*

DR. YORAM TSAFRIR, Hebrew University, Jerusalem *Or ha-Ner*

PROF. G. ERNEST WRIGHT (deceased), Harvard University — *Shechem*

DR. ZEEV YEIVIN, Dept. of Antiquities and Museums, Jerusalem — *Khirbet Susiya*

LIST OF ABBREVIATIONS

Abel, GP. F. M. Abel, Géographie de la Palestine 1–2, Paris 1933–1938

Aharoni, LB. Aharoni, Y: The Land of the Bible, London 1966

Alt, KSch. A. Alt, Kleine Schriften zur Geschichte des Volkes Israel 1–3, München 1953–1959

Avi-Yonah, HL. Avi-Yonah, M.: The Holy Land, Grand Rapids 1966

Benoit et alii, Discoveries 2. P. Benoit — J. T. Milik — R. de Vaux, Discoveries in the Judaean Desert 2 (Les Grottes de Murabba'at), Oxford 1961

Bliss — Macalister, Excavations. F. J. Bliss — R. A. S. Macalister, Excavations in Palestine during the Years 1898–1900, London 1902

Brünnow — Domaszewski, Die Provincia Arabia. R.E. Brünnow — A. V. Domaszewski, Die Provincia Arabia 1–3, Strassburg 1904–1909

Clermont-Ganneau, ARP. C. Clermont-Ganneau, Archaeological Researches in Palestine 1–2, London 1896–1899

Clermont-Ganneau, RAO. C. Clermont-Ganneau,. Recueil d'archéologie orientale 1–8, Paris 1888 ss.

Conder-Kitchener, SWP. C. R. Conder–H. H. Kitchener, Survey of Western Palestine, Memoirs 1–3, London 1881–1883

Crowfoot, Early Churches J. W. Crowfoot, Early Churches in Palestine, London 1941

EI. Eretz-Israel, Jerusalem 1950 ff.

Enc. Miqr. Encyclopaedia Biblica, 6 vols, Jerusalem 1955 ff.

Frey, Corpus. J. B. Frey, Corpus Inscriptionum Iudaicarum 2, Roma 1952

Goodenough, Jewish Symbols. E. R. Goodenough, Jewish Symbols in the Greco-Roman Period 1–12, New York 1953–1965

Guérin, Galilée. V. Guérin, Description géographique, historique et archéologique de la Palestine, Galilée, Paris 1868–1880

Guérin, Galilée. V. Guérin, Description géographique historique et archéologique de la Palestine, Judée, Paris 1868–1869

Hill, BMC. G. F. Hill, Catalogue of the Greek Coins in the British Museum, Palestine, London 1914

Klein, Corpus. S. Klein, Jüdisch-palästinisches Corpus Inscriptionum, Wien-Berlin 1920

Kohl-Watzinger, Synagogen. H. Kohl — C. Watzinger, Antike Synagogen in Galilea, Leipzig 1916

Lidzbarski, Ephemeris. M. Lidzbarski, Ephemeris für semitische Epigraphik 1–3, Giessen 1902–1915

Musil, Arabia Petraea. A. Musil, Arabia Petraea 1–3, Wien 1907–1908

Pritchard, ANET. J. B. Pritchard (ed.) Ancient Near Eastern Texts Relating to the Old Testament, Princeton 1950

Robinson, Biblical Researches. E. Robinson, Biblical Researches in Palestine, London 1841

Saller-Bagatti, Town of Nebo. S. J. Saller — B. Bagatti, The Town of Nebo, Jerusalem 1949

Schürer, GJV2. E. Schürer, Geschichte des jüdischen Volkes im Zeitalter Jesu Christi, Leipzig 1907

Stern, Material Culture. E. Stern, The Material Culture of the Land of the Bible in the Persian Period, Jerusalem 1973 (Hebrew)

Sukenik, Ancient Synagogues. E. L. Sukenik, Ancient Synagogues in Palestine and Greece, London 1934

Vincent-Abel, Jérusalem Nouvelle. L. H. Vincent—F. M. Abel, Jérusalem nouvelle 1–2, Paris 1912–1926

Vincent-Steve, Jérusalem. L. H. Vincent — M. A. Steve, Jérusalem de l'Ancien Testament 1–4, Paris 1954–1956

Watzinger, DP. K. Watzinger, Denkmäler Palästinas 1–2, Leipzig 1933–1935

Wilson-Kitchener, Special Papers. Ch. Wilson — H. H. Kitchener, The Survey of Western Palestine, Special Papers, London 1881

AAA	Annals of Archaeology and Anthropology
AASOR	Annual of the American Schools of Oriental Research
ADAJ	Annual of the Department of Antiquities of Jordan
AJA	American Journal of Archaeology
AJSLL	American Journal of Semitic Languages and Literatures
'Alon	Bulletin of the Israel Department of Antiquities
APEF	Annual of the Palestine Exploration Fund
'Atiqot	Journal of the Israel Department of Antiquities
BA	Biblical Archaeologist
BASOR	Bulletin of the American Schools of Oriental Research
BBSAJ	Bulletin, British School of Archaeology in Jerusalem
BIAL	Bulletin, Institute of Archaeology, London
BIES	Bulletin of the Israel Exploration Society (1951–1962), continuing
BJPES	Bulletin of the Jewish Palestine Exploration Society
BMB	Bulletin du musée de Beyrouth
BPM	Bulletin of the Palestine Museum
BS	Bibliotheca Sacra
BZ	Biblische Zeitschrift
CRAIBL	Comptes-rendus Academie des inscriptions et belles-lettres
HUCA	Hebrew Union College Annual
IEJ	Israel Exploration Journal
ILN	The Illustrated London News
JAOS	Journal of the American Oriental Society
JBL	Journal of Biblical Literature
JCS	Journal of Cuneiform Studies
JEA	Journal of Egyptian Archaeology
JNES	Journal of Near Eastern Studies
JPOS	Journal of the Palestine Oriental Society
JRAI	Journal of the Royal Anthropological Institute
JRAS	Journal of the Royal Asiatic Society
JRS	Journal of Roman Studies
MDOG	Mitteilungen der deutschen orientalischen Gesellschaft
MUSJ	Mélanges de l'Université Saint Joseph de Beyrouth
OLZ	Orientalistische Literaturzeitung
PEFA	Palestine Exploration Fund, Annual
PEFQSt	Palestine Exploration Fund, Quarterly Statement
PEQ	Palestine Exploration Quarterly
PJB	Palästina-Jahrbuch
QDAP	Quarterly of the Department of Antiquities in Palestine
RAr	Revue Archéologique
RB	Revue biblique
RHR	Revue de l'histoire des religions
TLZ	Theologische Literaturzeitung
VT	Vetus Testamentum
Yediot	Continuation of BIES (1962–1968)
ZAW	Zeitschrift für die alttestamentliche Wissenchaft
ZDPV	Zeitschrift des deutschen Palästina-Vereins

OR HA-NER

A tomb located near Khirbet Umm Tabun (map reference 111106), south of Kibbutz Or ha-Ner, was excavated in 1941 by the late J. Ory. The tomb was built of limestone rubble and blocks of *kurkar* bonded with cement. The walls were covered with a thick layer of light plaster. The tomb consists of four vaulted burial chambers (internal measurements, about 2 by 2 meters), two on each side of an elongated central hall (about 2 by 4.5 meters). Since it had been looted in ancient times, few objects were uncovered in the excavation. Thus, the date of the tomb can be arrived at only by the style of construction and the wall paintings. These indicate a date in the fourth century A.D. The tomb was apparently built by a wealthy local family, probably pagan, which had connections with Ashkelon.

The wall paintings are situated in the central hall. On the northern wall, above the entrance to the tomb, is a Greek inscription written in red paint: Εἰσελθε Ουδις ἀθάνατος. "Enter! No one is immortal." On either side of the opening are painted swordlike forms with tassels, probably representing candlesticks or torches. On each of the side walls are three parallel friezes, separated by horizontal red stripes, and above them a single frieze, with floral designs of vine branches and leaves in green paint, running along the ceiling.

The lower frieze, a dado, contains red-colored imitations of marble panels. The middle frieze consists of a pattern of pointed leaves in red and green with groups of red dots between them. The upper frieze contains the major paintings, portraits of men and women, set inside fourteen medallions, each touching another. There are seven medallions on each wall, and in the gaps between the end medallions and the northern corners appear two more candlesticks or torches. The spaces between the medallions are filled with flowers with eight petals painted alternately in red and green. The medallions, .58–.59 meter high and .56–.57 meter wide, are almost circular. Three of the portraits are of women, and eleven are of men. The males are young and clean-shaven. They wear a red cloak over a tunic. The women (only one is well preserved) are also dressed in a cloak over a tunic and long earrings. The portraits are painted in dark

Or ha-Ner. Medallions bearing portraits of a man and a woman. From the wall painting in the Tomb — 4th century A.D.

colors (red and black) for the outlines and in light colors (red-brown and orange) for the faces. All the portraits are en face. The eyes are large and directed upward or to the side. The brows and lips are thick, giving a stern expression to the faces. The portraits resemble the later Egyptian mummy portraits of the fourth century. In the manner of representation, the paintings display some similarity with Coptic art of the fifth–sixth centuries, and allow us to regard them as an early stage in the development of Coptic art. Y. TSAFRIR

BIBLIOGRAPHY

Y. Tsafrir, *IEJ* 18 (1968), 170–80; *idem, Qadmoniot* 2 (1969), 61–65 (Hebrew).

Left, top to bottom: General view of the central room, looking northward; Row of medallions with portaits of men; View of the roof of the tomb.
Below: Interior of the tomb — isometric reconstruction.

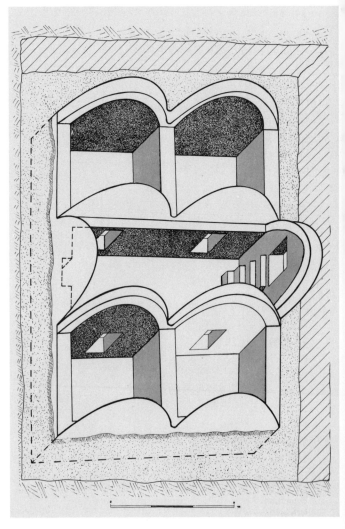

PELLA

IDENTIFICATION. Pella (in Greek Πέλλα, in Arabic Faḥl), located on the eastern side of the Jordan Valley and about 12 kilometers (7 miles) southeast of Beth-Shean, was an important city throughout much of antiquity — from the Canaanite period into the Middle Ages. The identification of the site is based on three considerations: the numerous references in ancient literary and epigraphic sources, the archaeological finds, and a similarity between the modern Arabic name and its ancient predecessor. Eusebius notes that Pella was situated on the road leading from Beth-Shean to Geresa (*Onomasticon*, ed. Klostermann, 326, 110, 13).

Pella is situated on a great mound rising some 31 meters above the surroundings on a plain about 2.5 by 1.5 kilometers. The city is rectangular in shape, measuring 300 by 200 meters within the Roman or Byzantine walls, whose outlines are still visible today. On the east, the mound is connected to the mountains by a ridge. To the north and south it towers over the Jordan Valley on the one hand and Wadi Jirm on the other. In the latter are found the springs for which Pella was famous (Pliny, *Natural History* 18, 5, 74, Palestinian Talmud, *Shevi'it* VI, 1, 36c).

Around the perimeter of the mound is a formidable wall built of impressive hewn stone. Near the valley are remnants of a Hellenistic–Roman theater and a temple-church, while in the surrounding area stand the remains of colonnaded streets and monumental gates. Toward the west, north, and east of the mound are remains of other public buildings, possibly churches and basilicas. Graves were cut into the nearby hills (see below), and remnants of sarcophagi and mausoleums were found in the plain to the west. The cliffs above the valley are pocketed by numerous artificial caves, possibly used by monks or hermits in the Byzantine period.

HISTORY

Pella is first mentioned in the Egyptian Execration Texts (nineteenth century B.C.), and in numerous documents dating from the New Kingdom (fifteenth–thirteenth century B.C.). The city appears in lists of Thutmose III and Seti I, and perhaps in those of Amenhotep, Horemheb as well as Ramses

II. Among the Amarna letters (fourteenth century B.C.), there is one from Mot-Ba'al, king of Pella. Another letter notes that Mot-Ba'al's territory bordered that of Hazor. On the stele of Seti I found in Beth-Shean, it is recorded that Pella was allied with Hamath against Rehov. During the Israelite period, Pella appears to have been of only minor importance, and it is not mentioned in the Bible. Later, in the Greco-Roman period, the city attained relative importance. It was named after Pella of Macedonia, the birthplace of Alexander. Undoubtedly some of Alexander's veteran soldiers were settled there. Antiochus III conquered the city in 218 B.C. (Polybius 5, 70–71), and the city fell to Alexander Jannaeus about the year 80 B.C. (Josephus, *War* I, 103–05; *Antiquities* XIII, 392–97). In 63 B.C., Pompey detached Pella from Judea along with other Transjordanian cities (*War* I, 133–34, 155–57, *Antiquities* XIV, 18–19, 74–76), and it was probably at this time that he founded the Decapolis, a loose federation of ten cities in the region (Pliny, *Natural History,* 5, 16, 74). Gabinius may have undertaken a major rebuilding of Pella (about 57 B.C.) as he did in many other cities in the province. According to Eusebius, the Christian community of Jerusalem escaped to Pella during the siege of the city (*Ecclesiastical History,* 3, 5, 3–4), and Pella became an important Christian center in subsequent centuries (Epiphanius, *Adversus Haereses,* 29, 7, 7–8; 30, 2, 7–8). One of the city's well-known sons was Ariston, a noted second-century Christian writer. During the Byzantine period, a number of important bishops resided in the city.

EXCAVATIONS

In 1958, preliminary excavations were carried out under the auspices of the American Schools of Oriental Research under the supervision of H. N. Richardson and R. W. Funk. Two exploratory trenches (7 by 7 meters each) were cut, one at the top of the mound (square I), the second at its base (square II). The area uncovered was thus quite restricted, and the results are at best provisional.

Square I. The earliest pottery dates from the tenth century B.C. The earliest architectural remains were the foundations of an eighth-century B.C. Israelite building. The top of an unusual wall was exposed, built of medium-sized stones and covered on both faces with bricklike material. It may belong to the Iron Age II. Above these remains

Both pages, counterclockwise from below:
Topographical map of Pella, showing the two areas
excavated in 1967; West church sanctuary and
atrium, reconstruction. Placement of windows is
conjectured; Roman or Byzantine wall on south edge
of mound; View of south flank of mound descending
to Wadi Jirm.

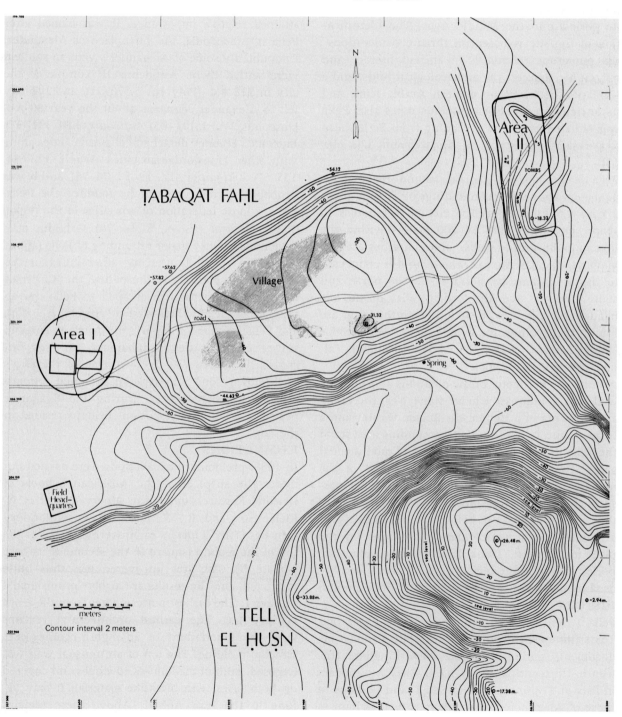

ṬABAQAT FAḤL

Village

road

Area I

Area II

TOMBS

Spring

Field Head-quarters

TELL EL ḤUṢN

meters

Contour interval 2 meters

stood a series of houses of similar plan. A later building reflecting two distinct stages was also uncoverd. The earlier stage (first century B.C.) is dated by Hellenistic pottery, and the later stage was marked by the introduction of a stone floor built on the earlier rubble. In a number of places the already existing wall was strengthened by hewn stones, and plastered and painted on the interior. A Byzantine building of the fourth–fifth century was erected atop the Roman one, and this in turn was buried under accumulation from the Middle Ages.

Square II. Near the surface was uncovered a complex of walls whose purpose remains enigmatic. Five different levels were related to these walls, and on the basis of the numerous coins, lamps, and glass vessels found, these levels can be dated from the late fourth to the late fifth century. Among the walls of this complex was an imposing Roman wall, built of hewn stone and reused in a later period. Mixed debris 1 meter deep separated the Hellenistic and Byzantine strata, and it was impossible to relate this material to specific buildings. Thirty-five coins were found, the majority Roman-Byzantine. From the Hellenistic period,

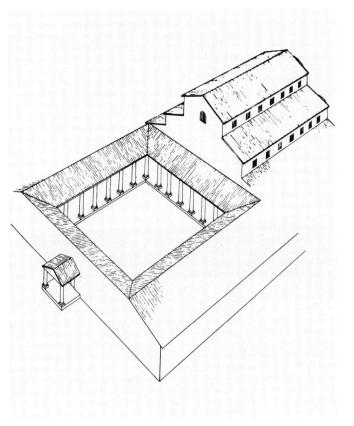

one coin was Ptolemaic, one Seleucid, and one of John Hyrcanus.

In 1967, the College of Wooster sponsored an expedition to Pella under the direction of R. H. Smith. Excavations were concentrated in two areas, the West church complex (area I) and the cemetery to the east (area II).

AREA I. The outline of a tri-apsidal church with its large colonnaded atrium was already visible just above ground in the nineteenth century. The exterior length of the sanctuary is approximately 35 meters, and the atrium to the west is 35 meters on each side. The following provisional history of the complex is offered by the excavators. Five major phases were distinguished:

PHASE I, about A.D. 530–610. The church was built on Middle Bronze Age deposits in the late fifth or sixth century, perhaps during the reign of Justinian I. The interior decorations included a dado and glass mosaic on parts of the wall and ceiling as well as a multi-colored tessellated pavement in the central aisle. Signs of a violent destruction are apparent, probably as a result of the Persian conquest in 610.

PHASE II, about 610–660. During this period the workmanship evidenced is of far inferior quality. The earlier dado which had been damaged was either plastered over or its stones slabs were used to repair the floor of the sanctuary. Several doorways were sealed, perhaps for security purposes. This stage ended in 658–660, as a result of an earthquake.

PHASE III, about 660–717. The repairs carried out did not include rebuilding of the collapsed walls of the sanctuary and atrium, and these were leveled off at a height of 3–5 meters. The remaining stones were removed as were the original piers of the sanctuary proper. Smaller columns or timbers were utilized for the roof, and the walls were replastered. This phase ended with the earthquake of 713 or that of 717.

PHASE IV, about 717–746. The building continued in use, this time unrepaired, and for different purposes. Without a roof, the sanctuary began silting up, as did the atrium. There are signs of squatters and animals. An oven was installed in a side room. Many paving stones were robbed. Again an earthquake, this time of 746, brought an end to this phase. Virtually all the remaining walls collapsed, generally falling westward. This stratum, together with the previous one, is clearly Umayyad, on the basis of the ceramic and numismatic evidence.

PHASE V, about 746 to present. The complex changed very little, aside from a slight additional silting.

One of the most interesting discoveries in this area was a sarcophagus lying in a carefully constructed vault under the northeast part of the sanctuary. Made of limestone, it measured 2.04 meters in length and 52 meters in width. Its height, excluding the gable roof with its acroteria, was .6 meter. Across the front of the sarcophagus is a highly stylized frieze depicting leaves, tendrils, and clusters of grapes in close proximity. This horror vacui, together with the winding vine throughout the frieze, is reminiscent of earlier Roman style and is best dated to the first or second century. While similarities with the Rosh ha-'Ayin

Inscribed lintel from the doorway of tomb 7 — sixth century A.D.

mausoleum are striking, a Carbon-14 dating on several small bone pieces found inside gives a date of 655. This fact suggests that the sarcophagus was probably deposited in the church during phase II, about 610–660. Stylistic considerations, parallels, and traces of an earlier phase of the north apse, on the other hand, suggest that a mausoleum had already existed on the site and that the church was later built there, and the cist was incorporated into the north apse, the prothesis, of the church. This area sometimes served as a martyrs' chapel in Byzantine churches. If this was indeed the case, the mausoleum may have been that of a venerated ancestor, perhaps one of the Jewish–Christians who fled to Pella from Jerusalem in 66, and the bones dating to the seventh century A.D. must have been a later interment.

AREA II. This area was used for thousands of years as a burial ground by the inhabitants of Pella — from the Middle Bronze Age through the Byzantine period. Six tombs were excavated, and a variety of lamps, pottery, human and animal bones were found. Within the tombs burial chambers, arcosolia, cists, loculi, and graves were cut in the floors. Personal articles included iron blades, rings, and buckles. In one tomb, an unusual tube installation was discovered, a ceramic funnel set into a vertical cylindrical cutting in the bedrock. This may have been some sort of libation tube used in rites for the dead. In another tomb a five-line Greek inscription was found. Two soldiers by the name of Johen were buried there in the year 584.

LEE I. LEVINE

BIBLIOGRAPHY

Surveys. S. Merrill, *East of the Jordan*, New York, 1881, 184 f., 442–47, 463 • G. Schumacher, *Across the Jordan*, London, 1886, 271–78; idem, *Abila, Pella and Northern 'Ajlun*, London, 1889–95: *Pella* (1895), 78 ff • J. Richmond, *PEQ*, 1934, 18–31 • W. F. Albright, *AASOR* 6 (1924–25), 39–42 • N. Glueck, *Explorations in Eastern Palestine* 4 *(AASOR* 25–28, 1945–49 [1951]); idem, *BASOR* 89 (1943), 3, 5 f.; 90 (1943), 3; 91 (1943), 16.
History. Abel, *GP* 2, 405 f. and passim • W. F. Albright, *BASOR* 81 (1941), 19; 83 (1941), 33, 36; 89 (1943), 9–13, 15, 17 • Pritchard, *ANET* 243, 253, 329, 486.
Excavations. H. N. Richardson and R. W. Funk, *BA* 26 (1958), 82–96 • H. Richardson, *RB* 67 (1960), 242–43 • R. J. Bull, *ILN*, March 16, 1968, 26–27, figs. 1–7 • R. H. Smith, *RB* 75 (1968), 105–12, pls. 12–14; idem, *Archaelogy* 21, (1968), 134–37; idem, *Wooster Alumni Magazine* 82 (1968), 4–13; idem, *PEQ*, 1969, 2–3, 55; idem, *ADAJ* 14 (1969), 5–10, pls. 1–10 • R. Houston Smith, *Pella of the Decapolis* I, London, 1973.

PETRA

IDENTIFICATION. Petra (Greek πέτρα, "rock"), the capital of the Nabataean kingdom in Edom, is situated about 80 kilometers (47.5 miles) south of the Dead Sea. The name appears for the first time in Diodorus Siculus *(Bibliotheca* XIX, 95), not as the name of a settlement, but as a term meaning "a certain rock," i.e., the place where the Nabataeans sough refuge for themselves, their goods, and their chattels, when they were attacked by Antigonus I Cyclops in 312 B.C. The identification of Petra with the biblical Selah of Edom derives from the Septuagint and was accepted by Eusebius who also identified Selah Joktheel with Petra *(Onomasticon* 36, 13; 142, 7; 144, 7), Josephus *(Antiquities* IV, 82) when speaking of the five Midianite kings (Numbers 31:8) identifies Rekem, the town named after its founder, with Petra, the capital of Arabia. This identification has been confirmed by a Nabataean inscription recently discovered at Petra, which mentions Raqmn, probably the name of the town. However, since up to now Edomite pottery (Iron Age II) has been found in Petra only on the top of the cliff (Umm el-Biyara), most scholars are still doubtful whether Selah is indeed to be identified with Petra.

History of the Site. Petra was apparently not settled prior to the Hellenistic period, as is evidenced both by the single literary source, that of Diodorus, and by the archaeological finds. In all the sections of the town area where excavations have been

Petra. City coin from the time of Hadrian (A.D. *117–138).*

conducted, no pottery or coins prior to the fourth century B.C. have been discovered thus far. The same is true in all other excavations of Nabataean sites in Palestine (see Elusa, Nessana, Eboda).

Aretas, the first known Nabataean ruler, is mentioned in II Maccabees 5:8. He is the king from whom Jason of the Tobias family requested asylum in 169 B.C. The Nabataean kingdom of Petra was apparently founded by Aretomos (Iustin. XXXIX 5, 5–6, also known as Aretas II, who reigned from approximately 100–96 B.C. Most of the Nabataean kings who reigned in Petra from that date until the abolishment of the Nabataean kingdom in A.D. 106 are known. An important event in the history of the Nabataean kingdom was the conquest of southern Syria, including Damascus, during the reign of Aretas III Philhellenos (87–62 B.C.). In his time the first attempt was made to crush the independence of the Nabataeans. The first Roman legate in Syria, Marcus Aemilius Scaurus, marched on Petra after Aretas II's intervention in Judea, and

Map of the site. 1. Spring. 2. Ed-Deir. 3. Qaṣr Bint Far'un. 4. City wall. 5. Triumphal gate. 6. Turkmaniyeh tomb. 7. Theater. 8. Round High Place. 9. Tomb of the statues. 10. High Place. 11. Urn Tomb. 12. Corinthian tomb. 13. Palace tomb. 14. Tomb of St. Florentinus. 15. The Khazneh. 16. The Sik. 17. Tunnel.

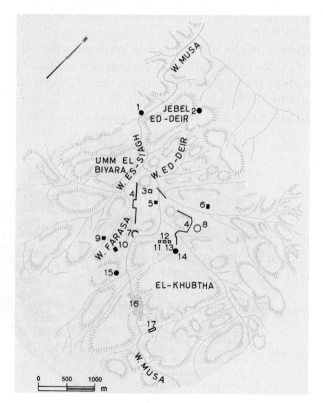

the Nabataeans were forced to pay tribute to the Romans and their kingdom became a tributary state under the suzerainty of Rome. During the reigns of Obodas II (30–9 B.C.) and Aretas IV Philodemos (9 B.C.–A.D. 40), Petra enjoyed a period of prosperity. During the reign of Obodas II, the Romans began a struggle for the control of the caravan trade, the consequences of which were not felt, however, until the second half of the first century A.D.

The history of Petra during the reign of its last two kings Malichus II (A.D. 40–70) and Rabel II (A.D. 70–106), called the Restorer and Savior of his people, is not known in detail. On the death of Rabel II in A.D. 106, the Emperor Trajan annexed the Nabataean Kingdom to the Province of Arabia with its capital at Bostra, and appointed Cornelius Palma governor. Under Roman domination, Petra was hardly more than a passing memory. In A.D. 131 the Emperor Hadrian visited Petra and granted it the name of Ἀδριανὴ Πέτρα. But the diversion of the caravan trade to new routes brought about the rise of Palmyra and the decline of Petra. During the Late Roman period, Petra served only as a religious center for towns in Transjordan and southern Syria.

In the fourth century A.D., the Province of Arabia was divided into two parts, the southern one, including the town of Petra, being incorporated in the province of Palaestina. Henceforth Bostra became the capital of the Province of Arabia and Petra that of Palaestina Tertia. In the fifth century Christianity found its way to Petra, and during the fifth and sixth centuries, it was the see of an archbishop. There is no information on the history of Petra in the first centuries of the Arab period. In later Arab sources the town appears under the name of Al Asuit. At the beginning of the twelfth century, the town was occupied by Baldwin I, King of Jerusalem. The Crusaders gave it the name Li Vaux Moyse ("the valley of Moses"). Petra is mentioned for the last time in connection with the visit of Baybars to the town.

History of Exploration. Although U. J. Seetzen was the first European traveler to reach Petra (in 1807), he had no idea what it was, and it was identified only in 1812 by J. L. Burckhardt, who is consequently considered the discoverer of the site. During the nineteenth century, numerous travelers visited Petra. Toward the close of the century, the Dominican fathers of the French School of Archaeology in Jerusalem started work at Petra and began to publish their results in 1896. Of special importance is the work of R. E. Brünnow and A. von Domaszewski who in 1897–98 explored the tombs of Petra and some of its buildings. Before World War I, G. Dalman examined the necropolis and especially the places of worship, on behalf of the German Evangelic Institute for Exploration of the Antiquities of the Holy Land in Jerusalem. H. Kohl explored the Qaṣr Bint Far'un building on behalf of the German Society for

Oriental Research. During World War I, the Committee for the Preservation of Monuments (Denkmalschutz-Kommando) of the German-Turkish Army Staff worked at Petra under the direction of T. Wiegand, mainly investigating the remains of the Roman town.

The first excavations at Petra were conducted in 1929 by the Lord Melchett Expedition under the direction of Agnes (Conway) and G. Horsfield on behalf of the Department of Antiquities of the Mandatory Government. Work was concentrated mainly in the dumps of the town, several sections

Umm el-Biyara and the tombs at its foot.

of the town wall, and a few tombs. In 1934, another season of excavations was carried out under the direction of Margaret Murray and J. C. Ellis, who uncovered a street in the center of the town and several rock-cut tombs. In 1955, excavations were renewed by the Jordanian Government in cooperation with the British School of Archaeology in Jerusalem under the direction of P. J. Parr and various American institutions. Several sections of the colonnaded street and the monumental gate were cleared and the dumps of the town and other sites were excavated in order to establish the chronology of the Nabataean pottery. In 1962–63, P. C. Hammond uncovered the large theater on behalf of the Princeton Theological Seminary and the Jordan Department of Antiquities.

Topography. Petra is situated in a valley enclosed by rugged mountains. The special formation of this region attracted the nomadic Nabataeans, who believed it to be a sufficiently secure refuge for themselves and their possessions. The valley is about 1,000 meters long from north to south and 400 meters wide from east to west, the Wadi Musa crossing it lengthwise. Steep cliffs on the east and west side of the site tower more than 300 meters above the valley. In the southwest corner rises the el-Habis rock. The mountain range to the east of the valley is cut by a narrow canyon called Wadi Siq, through which runs the easiest approach to Petra. The mountains surrounding the valley are cut by numerous wadis, into whose cliff facades were hewn tombs.

EXCAVATIONS

Prehistoric Period. Scanty remains from the Upper Paleolithic and the Neolithic periods have been found at various sites in Petra and its surroundings, especially in Wadi Beidha (q.v.) where excavations have been conducted.

Iron Age. The various surveys, carried out especially on the Umm el-Biyara mountain west of the valley, have yielded pottery identified by G. Horsfield, N. Glueck, and others as Edomite ware.

Early Nabataean (Hellenistic) Period. The literary sources and the numerous small finds from the Hellenistic period discovered at Petra, especially in the dumps of the town and on surface level, attest to the fact that the site was occupied in the third century B.C., although there is no definite proof that the inhabitants were Nabataeans. The same picture emerges from the excavations of the Naba-

taean sites Nessana and Eboda in the Negev.

In the excavations of the British School of Archaeology in Jerusalem, a trial sounding was made in the area of the town in order to establish the stratigraphy of the site. In the lowest layer, on virgin soil, were discovered remains of buildings, the foundations and walls built of rubble and pounded earth and the floors made of clay. On the basis of the pottery, especially the lamps and black-glazed ware, and of coin finds, the excavator dated the construction of these buildings to the end of the third century B.C. They continued in use, with numerous repairs, until the end of the second century B.C. Due to the restricted area of the excavations, it was impossible to ascertain the plan of the buildings. To the same occupation level belong also small incense altars and small figurines of stone in the form of human faces.

Middle Nabataean Period (Roman I). From the end of the first century B.C. to the beginning of the second century A.D.

HOUSES. Thus far few remains of buildings from this period have been encountered in the town. It seems that Petra in this period was not a city in the full sense of the word. Although the city housed the seat of the royal house, the national shrines and a national necropolis and attendants, the citizens dwelled either at neighboring Gaia, to the east of Petra, with a more favorable climate, or entirely in tents, as did their immediate predecessors. At the end of the first century B.C., probably during the reign of Aretas IV, buildings began to be erected of ashlar instead of rubble and clay. To prepare the rocky basin for the construction of a town, a fill (15 meters wide) was poured on the northern bank of the valley crossing the town, and on this fill was built the main thoroughfare that ran through the town from east to west. Between this road and the valley were erected buildings of well-dressed stone. Here, too, the excavators were unable to establish the plans of the houses due to the restricted excavation area. Typical Nabataean pottery, both painted and plain ware, was discovered under the floors of these buildings.

In the dump in the south of the valley, a house was cleared which the excavators ascribed to the first century A.D. Since it was covered with debris of the Roman II town, its walls were preserved to a height of 3 meters. The house is built of ashlar stones, and on its outer face is displayed the characteristic oblique Nabataean dressing. The inner face of the walls is merely chipped, since this side was plastered and ornamented with reliefs, remains of which have survived. The building was in continuous use for many years, and its plan was altered several times. In its final stage it consisted of a long narrow courtyard (30 meters long), entered from the town side (on the north). The short sides of the courtyard led into a series of small chambers. The southern side of the courtyard had neither windows nor doorways, and in the opinion of the excavator, the house was incorporated into the fortifications of the town. It was roofed with stone slabs resting on arches, as was common in that period in the Negev and the Nabataean Hauran. The discovery of Early Roman pottery in the foundations of the building led the

Below: Plan of the city. 1. Qaṣr Bint Far'un.
2. Small temple. 3. Bathhouse. 4. Main gate.
5. Gymnasium. 6. Large temple. 7. Palace.
8. Lower market. 9. Byzantine house. 10. Central
market. 11. Upper market. 12. North nymphaeum.
13. South nymphaeum. Right: Aqueduct in Wadi es-Sik.

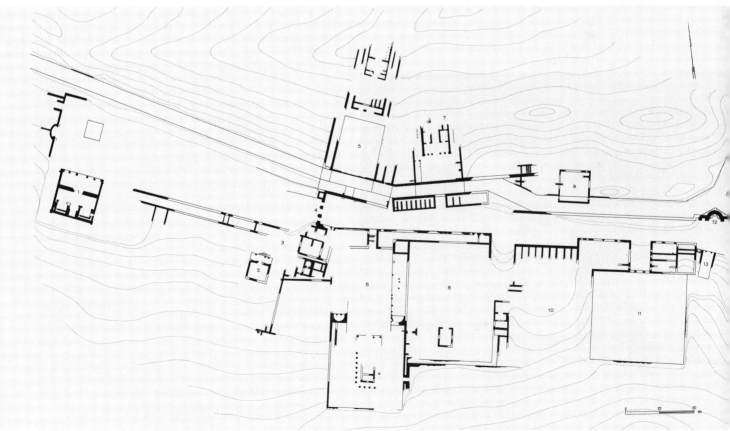

excavator to attribute its construction to the end of the first quarter of the first century A.D. The building continued in use up to the Roman conquest of Petra.

The houses of the Nabataean town were built not only in the area of the valley but on the slopes as well, where they were supported by terraces. Horsfield examined several such houses, some of which were cut into the rock, and others built in front of the rock wall. No public building has yet been uncovered in the town area which could be attributed to the Nabataean period.

THE THEATER. The road descending to the town from Wadi Siq first reaches the theater, situated above the southern bank of Wadi Musa at the point where it widens. The seats were cut in the Nubian sandstone cliff, causing the destruction of a few Nabataean tombs cut in the steep slope. The upper two tiers of seats were visible and have been described by all visitors to Petra, whereas the third tier was cleared by Hammond. The excavations showed that the *cavea* was divided by flights of stairs into six wedge-shaped groups of seats *(cunei)*. In the wings of the stage, two roofed passages were discovered. The stage itself was not a

Below: Qaṣr Bint Far'un. Opposite page, top: Qaṣr Bint Far'un — cross section of the holy of holies. Bottom: Qaṣr Bint Far'un — Plan.

building proper but a decorated *scena frons* with three entrances, the central one being a large semi-circular niche. The excavator distinguished three stages of construction in the theater, the last being the type customary in the Imperial period. In the opinion of the excavator, the theater was built during the reign of Aretas IV, re-used in Rabel II's time, and its final phase was during the Late Roman period. In the opinion of the excavator, the theater served as a place of assembly and amusement, but this, however, seems doubtful. The theater is situated in the midst of the huge, main necropolis of Petra, at a distance of more than 1 kilometer from the center of the city. A. Negev has consequently suggested that this theater, like others in the Nabataean kingdom, had a cultural function, serving in the case of Petra for the performance of funerary rites. It was apparently erected by Aretas IV, the probable builder of the Khazneh, for the performance of these rites after his own death. In any case, it is unthinkable to have a theater in the Greco-Roman sense, in the climate of Petra, in the midst of a necropolis, which was still used for burials during the existence of the theater.

THE COLONNADED STREET also ran along the southern bank of Wadi Musa. It was the main thoroughfare of the town which it bisected. To its south, the ground rises steeply, and on the slope, three terraces were built which held dwellings. The colonnade is separated from the lowest terrace by its retaining wall, preserved to a height of 5 meters. The wall extends along the entire length of the colonnade and joins the southern pier of the three-entryway gate (see below).

The colonnade-lined street is 6 meters wide and slopes sharply, .25 meter on 3 meters. The pedestals of the columns were found in situ in a 65-meter-long section of the street. On the sides of the street, there were stone sidewalks, two steps above the level of the road itself. The date of its construction is not known exactly, the excavators suggesting either immediately after the Nabataean kingdom was turned into the Province of Arabia, or later during the reign of the Antonines, which was a period of extensive building activity in the East. The first date is supported by an inscription from A.D. 114 found in debris near the colonnade. However, judging from all that is known of Nabataean history, both dates appear to be much too late; and like most of the monuments of Petra, the street probably belongs to the reigns of Obodas II and Aretas IV, although it could also have been used in subsequent periods.

THE MONUMENTAL GATEWAY. As its western extremity the street terminates in a tripartite gateway. The excavations revealed that the gateway had been built later than the street, a part of the paving having been removed during its construction. The paving was subsequently repaired and enlarged to form a small square. The gateway itself consists of four piers (the inner ones measuring 3 by 3 meters and the two outer ones 2.2 by 3 meters), which form three openings. The central opening is 3.5 meters wide and the two lateral ones 2 meters each. Both the inside and outside of the gateway are built of dressed Nubian sandstone, bound by a thin layer of mortar, unnoticeable from the outside, so that the construction seems to be of the dry mortarless type. The core of the walls is made of rubble, also laid in courses, and leveled with sandstone fragments. In front of the western side of the gateway stood four columns on high pedestals, a column in front of each pier. The east side of the gate is adorned with engaged half-columns, set on half pedestals, also attached to the wall. An arch crowned the gateway, but its upper parts were not uncovered. On the basis of its plan, the excavators ascribed the gateway to the time of the Antonines or even to the beginning of the third century A.D. Gateways with three openings — especially those with freestanding columns in front of their piers — are known in the Roman world from as early as the beginning of the first century B.C. and thus the dating of this monument appears to be much too high. Wiegand believed that the gateway formed the western entrance to the town, but the most recent excavations proved — confirming Domaszewski's opinion — that this gateway was the entrance to the area on the edge of which stood the temple Qaṣr Bint Far'un, the only freestanding structure preserved at Petra.

QAṢR BINT FAR'UN. This temple is situated west of the tripartite gateway, on the edge of a large square, which is surrounded, at least partly, by rows of columns. A road, about 200 meters long, leads from the gateway to the temple. Towering above the square is an isolated peak known as el-Habis. The building — which has been described in detail by Domaszewski, Wiegand, and Kohl — is preserved to a height of 23 meters, up to its roof.

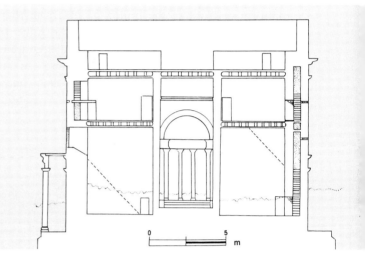

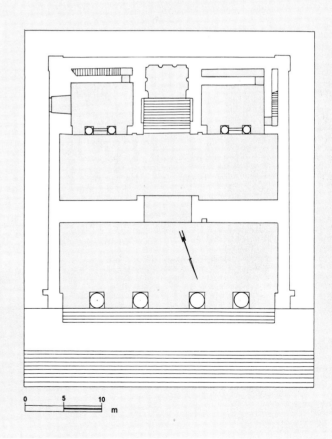

In the latest excavations, conducted by the British School of Archaeology in Jerusalem, several additional soundings were made in the building. It stands on a high podium (38 by 36 meters) and is completely faced with marble in a unique manner: marble orthostats are revetted to the wall at fixed intervals with regular wall construction between them. Nine steps ascend from the road to a narrow platform in front of the building, and from there four more steps lead up to the pronaos (28.8 by 11.2 meters). The facade of the pronaos contains four columns between antas. From here, an entrance 6.25 meters wide and as high as the pronaos itself leads into the *naos* (28.8 by 8.4 meters).

Twelve steps lead from the *naos* to the adytum situated in the southern part of the building and consisting of a central cell and two flanking ones. The front of the lateral cells is decorated with a pair of columns between antas. Their outer walls are double, and in the space between them are spiral stairways leading up to the flat roof of the building and to the exedra above the lateral cells. The walls of the temple, like those of the tripartite gate, consist of a core made of rubble set in clay mortar and sandstone slabs for leveling the courses, the whole faced inside and outside with dressed stones. In addition, wooden beams were laid inside the inner and outer sides of the walls to in-

Facade of Palace tomb. At the right, the Corinthian tomb.

crease the building's stability in case of earthquake. This system is also found in other buildings in Petra and its surroundings.

An early date for this monument could be indicated by the location of the gateway mentioned above. Nabataean temples follow two distinct plans. Temples in northern Arabia, southern Edom (see Er-Ram), and the Hauran (Seeia, Saḥir, Sur) were built of an encasing outer temple, an inner temple, and an adytum, a plan erroneously ascribed to an Iranian origin, but in fact a Nabataean adaption to specific cultural needs. In front of these temples was a court surrounded on three sides by porticoes containing benches, an arrangement called *theatron*

in Nabataean inscriptions. The temple at Sur was also provided with an actual theater in addition to the *theatron* in front of the shrine. An altar in the court completed the equipment. Temples of this type were constructed in the times of Obodas II and Aretas IV.

The temple of Qaṣr Bint Far'un, however, belongs to the second type, which was common in the Nabataean district of Moab (see Dibon). Here the traditional Bronze Age–Iron Age plan has been preserved with the tripartite division of pronaos, *naos,* and adytum placed on a longitudinal axis. The benches along the walls of the court, the altar in its center, and the staircases either in the double

Triclinium tomb.

back walls as in Qaṣr Bint Far'un, or in staircase towers on the side of the facade as in other temples in Moab, provide the necessary components of the Nabataean religious ritual, which most likely included a solemn procession and the burning of incense on the roof of the temple (hence the staircases), the sacrifice of animals and the festive meal (partaken in the *theatron*). There is no chronological difference between the two types of temple, but only a regional one.

In more recent soundings made by P. J. Parr in the temple compound, an inscription of Aretas IV was discovered engraved on a bench of the *theatron*. This inscription, found in situ, attests to the date of construction of the porticoes and indicates that the temple could have been contemporary with the *theatron,* or even earlier, from the time of Obodas II.

The Late Nabataean Period. The attribution of any of the Petraean structures to this period, save perhaps for a handful of funerary monuments, seems doubtful. In this period, which was one of decline for Petra, there could have been at the most a re-use of some monuments in the second and third centuries A.D., but even evidence for this is still lacking.

The Necropolis. Two types of tombs were discovered at Petra. The first consists of shaft tombs cut into horizontal rock platforms. Some of these tombs were excavated by Horsfield in 1929. Since all of them have been plundered, the excavator could only estimate that their dates ranged from the second century B.C. to the first century A.D. These tombs are of several forms: a shaft leading to a single burial chamber, in the bottom of which were cut several pits; a shaft leading to two burial chambers on either side thereof; or a shaft leading to a small vaulted chamber with loculi cut in its three walls.

The second type is represented by tombs dug into the vertical rock walls of the canyons around the valley. For constructing the tombs, the vertical rock walls were first smoothed and then the facades, either ornamented, flat or molded, were cut out. Most of the tombs in the necropolis of Petra belong to this type. At the end of the nineteenth century, Domaszewski classified the tomb facades according to style, from the simple to the composite, and he also attempted to arrive at a chronological classification of the tombs by topographic and stylistic criteria. He distinguished seven types of facades: 1. pylon tombs; 2. stepped tombs; 3. Proto-Hegr type; 4. Hegr type (the last two types derive their names from the Nabataean necropolis at Madayin Saliḥ el-Hege-Egra, in northern Arabia, where they were first observed); 5. arched tombs; 6. gabled tombs; 7. Roman temple-type tombs.

1. PYLON TOMBS. This type, the simplest, was subdivided by Domaszewski into several groups, according to the decorations of the facade and the entrance. The upper part of the facade has one or two rows of crenellations (like those on a city wall), the entrance is either plain or has a simple cornice or — with more developed forms — a pediment. The doorposts of the entrance are either smooth or decorated with pillars, either without capitals or with simple ones. On some facades the capitals are in typical Nabataean style, like those found mainly in the other types of facades.

2. STEPPED TOMBS. The facades of these tombs are not crenellated, but decorated by two large steps, facing each other and leading down to the center of the facade. These two steps are set above an Egyptian cornice. The entrance is decorated with only an architrave or pediment.

3. PROTO-HEGR TOMBS. These tombs, which were named by comparison with the tombs at Madayin Saliḥ, were already known in the time of Domaszewski, who saw in this type signs of the beginning of Greek influence in Petra. At the top of the facade were two steps placed above an Egyptian cornice, the latter supported by two engaged pilasters with Nabataean capitals set at the corners of the facade. The decoration of the entrance is similar to that of the above types.

4. THE HEGR TYPE is more developed than the preceding types and differs from the Proto-Hegr type by the addition of an attic and of a further architrave. As a rule the architrave rests on corner pillars crowned with Nabataean capitals. Above the architrave, there is an attic with an additional architrave terminating in a pediment, and above this a cornice and steps. Only a few entrances of these tombs were left plain. In some cases they had one entrance set within another. In more elaborate facades further decorations can be found, as, for example, small columns in the attic, two engaged half columns on the facade, and pillars with quarter columns attached to the corner pillars.

5. ARCHED TOMBS. In these tombs the upper part

General view of Ed-Deir

of the facade is constructed in the form of an arch. In some cases, a libation bowl (patera) is placed within the arch above the entrance as decoration. The entrance itself is either simple or has columns supporting an architrave.

6. GABLED TOMBS. The twelve monuments constituting this group are similar in decoration to the more developed Hegr-type tomb, except for the Egyptian cornice and the two steps crowning the facade, which are missing here and are replaced by a pediment.

7. ROMAN TEMPLE-TYPE TOMBS. In this group Domaszewski included twenty-two monuments, most of them concentrated in al-Farsa and in the northeastern wall of the Valley of Petra. These monuments differ greatly from one another, and in many cases each and every one forms a separate type. In their simpler forms, the facades show an architrave supported by two freestanding columns, between two engaged pilasters at the corners of the facade. The columns and pillars have typical Nabataean capitals. In some cases the frieze is decorated with metopes and triglyphs. More frequent is the pediment-crowned facade generally having

Petra. General view of Ed-Deir.

corner pillars with engaged quarter columns and Nabataean capitals, supporting an architrave and a pediment, decorated with acroteria. The opening is decorated with pillars topped by capitals and bearing simple or double architraves, while the frieze shows metopes and triglyphs. The tympanon of the main pediment is decorated in some cases with a Medusa or with a mask from which serpents twist out. The facades of larger tombs of this type have two engaged half columns between the corner pillars. The only tomb at Petra which can be dated with much certainty is that of Sextus Florentinus, the Roman legate in Petra in A.D. 127, but this date seems to be valid only for his burial, and the erection of the monument could have quite well taken place about a century earlier. This tomb, situated in the northeastern rock wall, belongs to the class of tombs with a pediment, but is more elaborate. In its facade are two engaged half columns flanking the opening and two corner pillars with engaged quarter columns supporting an architrave decorated with flat pilasters. Above this architrave is an attic also decorated with flat pilasters forming the continuation of the pilasters of the architrave. A semicircular arch, bearing an eagle at its top, occupies most of the area of the attic. Four short pilasters with Nabataean capitals, forming the continuation of the pilasters of the attic, support a further architrave above which the urn-crowned pediment rises.

Outstanding in their splendor are the Tomb of ed-Deir, the Palace Tomb, the Corinthian Tomb, and Khaznet Far'un. All these monuments are carved like facades of buildings with two stories or more.

ED-DEIR. The facade of this tomb is two-storied. The lower story has six engaged half columns, three on each side of the entrance, and two corner pillars with engaged quarter columns. All the columns and pillars are crowned by Nabataean capitals. The entrance is decorated with an architrave and a pediment. The main pillars and columns support an architrave above which rises the second story, also decorated with six columns and two pillars, and bearing a broken pediment, in the center of which is a tholos, crowned by an urn placed on a Nabataean capital. Between the columns are niches, which are topped in the lower story by a flat arch and in the upper story by a pediment.

KHAZNET FAR'UN is the most magnificent monument at Petra. In general plan, its facade is similar to that of ed-Deir, but the details are different. The facade consists of two Corinthian orders, placed one above the other. The lower story is detached from the rock from which it was cut, forming a temple portico supported by six columns with Corinthian capitals. To give the facade the impression of depth, the two extreme columns and the parts of the pediment supported by them project from the facade. In the portico are three entrances, one leading to the main hall and the two side entrances leading to the lateral halls. The frieze of the lower story is decorated with pairs of griffins flanking a vase with plant tendrils. The pediment, resting on the four interior columns only, is decorated with plant ornaments. The symbol of the goddess Isis is an acroterion, a fact which leaves the nature of the building open to various interpretations. In the upper order, the attic above the pediment of the lower story serves as the base for the upper complex. In its center is a tholos, apparently enclosed by six columns, and on its sides, two pavilions with two columns on their front, each pavilion bearing a broken pediment. On top of the tholos is a Corinthian capital surmounted by an urn. The capitals of the upper order are also Corinthian. In the space between the columns of the two orders are remains of reliefs probably representing female figures, the significance of which has raised considerable controversy. In general, opinion is divided as to whether Khaznet Far'un is a tomb or a temple, although scholars recently are more inclined to consider it a tomb.

Chronology and Significance of the Tomb Facades. In the tomb facades at Petra, only a single inscription has been preserved that can assist in their dating, and then only of one type. When Domaszewski dated these tombs, he assumed that the Nabataeans had first settled in Petra in the sixth century B.C., and he therefore ascribed types 1–4 to the period from the sixth or fifth century B.C. to the first century A.D. Dalman attempted to establish the dates of the last type, distinguishing three facade types as follow: 1. tombs made in Nabataean–Oriental style; 2. tombs in Hellenistic style; 3. tombs in Roman style. In Dalman's opinion, the first type is to be dated from the third to the second centuries B.C., the second from the first century B.C. to the first century A.D., and the last from the Roman conquest onward. Attempts to arrive at a conclusion on the basis of the numerous inscriptions appearing on the tomb facades at Madayin Salih proved unsuccessful. At that site, there are tombs belonging to the first four types of Domaszewski's classification. The construction of these tombs began in the year 1 B.C. The last tomb dates from A.D. 76. Thus the four types at Madayin Salih were nearly contemporaneous. Scholars accordingly assumed that at the new provincial center of Madayin Salih, the facades were built on the pattern of the tombs at Petra, where they had passed through all their stages of development. As for the absence of Roman temple tombs at Madayin Salih, two explanations were offered — either the

tombs in Petra were cut after the year A.D. 76 or this type was too expensive for a provincial center. As far as is known, the material culture of the Nabataeans did not attain its zenith prior to the second half of the first century B.C. or even later, at the end of the reign of Obodas II (30–9 B.C.) — and especially in the time of Aretas IV (9 B.C.–A.D. 40). During that period, most of the magnificent temples in the Hauran and in the south of the kingdom were built, and in those days Nabataean pottery also reached its floruit. It can therefore be assumed that the simple-type tombs, which do not contain any typical feature of Hellenistic art, were not hewn before the middle of the first century B.C. In the

Sik al-Barid. Nabataean wall painting.

second half of that century, the tombs belonging to the pylon type, stepped type, Proto-Hegr and Hegr types (1–4) made their successive appearance. Decorations of the facades were generally of Eastern style (Persian and Egyptian elements), Greek elements being always secondary. The development of relations with the Roman Empire and the Hellenized East brought about an increased importance of the Greek-Roman elements, such as the pediment, Ionic and Doric architraves, and Corinthian capitals. The temple plans probably also changed during the period. While the temples from the time of Obodas II and Aretas IV were built on an Oriental pattern, the Qaṣr Bint Far'un was built on a Greek-Syrian plan. At any rate, the year A.D. 106, when the Nabataean kingdom became the Roman Provincia Arabia, was not the year of transition from one style to another. Hellenistic-Roman elements had already appeared earlier in Petra, while typical Nabataean-Oriental elements continue to be used in facades which were hewn undoubtedly in the course of the second century A.D.

In a recent study, A. Negev has suggested that the difference in style reflects not a chronological development but rather a social division of Nabataean society. This conclusion is based on a study of seventy monuments at Egra, thirty of which bear detailed funerary inscriptions stating ownership, rank, date, etc. It was seen that the simpler pylons and stepped tombs were made by women, partnerships of women of different families, a man and a woman each representing a different family, or by men who presented the monument to their mothers. It is only in the Proto-Hegr type of monument that men of some distinction occur among the owners: a daughter of a strategus, a centurion, a Jew (merchant?). The cream of the Egraean society owned the most developed Hegr type of tombs, and among the owners were strategi, hipparchs, a doctor, a teller of omens, and rich caravaneers. At Egra, the monuments of the Proto-Hegr and Hegr types constituted more than fifty percent of the total, a situation befitting an important commercial and military center such as Egra. At Petra the division of types is entirely different: pylons and stepped tombs constitute 63.7 percent, and with the addition of arched tombs, also a simple form, this rises to 69.7 percent; Proto-Hegr, 12.3 percent; Hegr, 11 percent; gabled, 2.3 percent; temple tombs, 4 percent. This reflects a more normal division of the society of that part of Edom of which Petra was the center, with the middle class at the base of Petraean society, and the higher administrative, military, and mercantile class with 23.3 percent of the monuments. We are thus left with 6.3 percent of the monuments for which there are no parallels at Egra. These monuments Negev attributes to the royal house, members of the government, and the owners of the large commercial corporations, all naturally absent from the provincial capital of Egra. Furthermore, three of the Roman temple types of tombs are outstanding: the Khazneh, the Corinthian Tomb, and ed-Deir. Common to these is the arrangement of the two superimposed orders, the temple facade in the lower, and the tholos in pavilions in the upper. Wheras the last two monuments contain a mixture of Nabataean and Greek elements in their decoration, the Khazneh is purely Greek. Negev considers this to be an indication of a relatively early date, and attributes its construction to Aretas IV, who invited Alexandrian sculptors to make the monument in about A.D. 25. The tomb was a masterpiece and influenced the other monuments at Petra. Accordingly, the Corinthian Tomb, situated in the midst of very elaborate tombs in the necropolis, is ascribed to Malichus II possibly in about A.D. 60 and ed-Deir, to Rabel II, who may have constructed this latest funerary monument at Petra in about A.D. 100. The whole rise, development, and dissolution of Nabataean funerary art is thus compressed into the course of one century. This phenomenon is in complete accordance with the development of Nabataean pottery for which an Alexandrian origin is also sought.

There has been considerable controversy regarding the significance of the tomb facades. Some scholars considered that the decorations of the facades had no connection with actual architecture, but were merely decorative, and facades such as the Khaznet Far'un type were produced on the pattern of wall paintings like those at Pompeii. In the opinion of other scholars, however, the tomb facades were copies of contemporary buildings. They contended that the pylon tombs and the stepped tombs were imitations of the houses in which the deceased Nabataeans had lived during their lifetimes. No evidence has been found in support of this opinion. It should be noted that tombs with similar crenellations and steps have been discovered in Syria and Phoenicia and also in Roman incense altars. The controversy was especially sharp concerning the tomb facades of the Khaznet Far'un, ed-Deir, and similar ones. Even those scholars who considered the facades copies of real buildings were compelled to have recourse to the paintings of Pompeii, which in their opinion depicted building existing at that time. Other scholars held that the Khaznet Far'un tomb was built after the pattern of buildings existing in Alexandria, which have not however been preserved. According to this interpretation, the lower story of the Khaznet Far'un tomb represents a magnificent entrance to a temple area, whereas the tholos is a circular building placed within an exedra behind the entrance. According to another explanation, the tholos represents a tower on the roof of the house, used for relaxation, or a tower containing a staircase leading up to a roof garden.

Such combinations of different architectural elements are, however, frequent in this part of the Near East. Thus, for example, an Egyptian pyramid is placed on an Ionic cubic structure in the "Tomb of Zechariah", and a tholos tops a Doric frieze adorning an Ionic cubic building in the "Tomb of Absalom". Both of these tombs are contemporary or only slightly earlier than the Khaznet Far'un tomb. The

Below: Sik al-Barid.
Right: Rock-cut structure in Sik al-Barid.

closest examples, which may have inspired the later Petra monuments, are perhaps to be found in Herod's buildings at Masada, especially those at the northwestern extremity of the rock, although for constructional reasons the elements of the Khaznet Far'un tomb were built in inverse order. The main building is placed at the upper edge of the rock, the tholos in the center, and the open exedra at the foot of the rock. It can therefore probably be assumed that the Khaznet Far'un tomb is nothing more than a perspectival representation of the analogous group of buildings at Masada, adapted to the rock wall in Siq.   A. NEGEV

BIBLIOGRAPHY

J. L. Burckhardt, *Travels in Syria and the Holy Land,* London, 1822 • Brünnow-Domaszewski, *Die Provincia Arabia* 1 (contains full bibliography up to 1903) • G. Dalman, *Petra und seine Pelsheiligtümer,* Leipzig, 1908 • Musil, *Arabia Petraea* 2, 41–150 • H. Kohl, *Kasr Firaun,* Leipzig, 1910 • G. Dalman, *Khaznet Far'un,* APEF 1 (1911), 95–107; idem, *Neue Petra Forschungen,* Leipzig, 1912 • T. Wiegand et alii, *Petra,* Leipzig, 1921 • A. Kammerer, *Petra et la Nabatène,* Paris, 1929 • G. and A. Horsfield, *QDAP* 7 (1938), 1–42; 8 (1939), 87–115; 9 (1942), 105–204 • M. A. Murray and J. C. Ellis, *A Street in Petra,* London, 1940 • B. Mazar, *Tarbiz* 30 (1950), 316–19 (Hebrew) • J. Starcky, *BA* 18 (1955), 84–106 • P. J. Parr, *PEQ,* 1957, 5–16 • P. C. Hammond, *PEQ,* 1958, 12–15 • P. J. Parr, *PEQ,* 1959, 106–08 • P. C. Hammond, *BA* 23 (1960), 29–32 • D. Kirkbride, *RB* 67 (1960), 235–38 • P. J. Parr, *RB* 67 (1960), 239–42 • R. L. Cleveland, *The Excavation of the Conway High-Place (Petra),* AASOR 34–35 (1954–56), 1960, 53–83 • P. J. Parr, *PEQ,* 1960, 124–35 • D. Kirkbride, *ADAJ* 4–5 (1960), 117–22 • P. C. Hammond, *BASOR* 159 (1960), 26–31 • G. R. H. Wright, *PEQ,* 1961, 8–37, 124–35; idem, *ADAJ* 6–7 (1962), 24–54 • P. J. Parr and J. Starcky, *ADAJ* 6–7 (1962), 13–20 • C. M. Bennett, *Archaeology* 15 (1962), 277–79 • P. C. Hammond, *BASOR* 174 (1962), 59–66 • P. J. Parr, *ILN,* Nov. 10, 1962, 746–49; Nov. 17, 1962, 789–91 • P. C. Hammond, *ILN,* May 25, 1963, 804–05 • Y. Yadin, in: *Sefer Eilat,* Jerusalem, 1963, 156 ff. (Hebrew) • R. Yanait-Ben-Zvi, A. Negev, *The Rock of Edom,* Tel Aviv, 1964 (Hebrew) • J. Starcky, *RB* 62 (1965), 95–97; 72 (1965), 95–97; idem, Petra et la Nabatène, *Suppl. au Dictionnaire de la Bible* VII, Paris, 1966, 886–1018 • J. Starcky and J. Strugnell, *RB* 73 (1966), 236–47 • G. R. H. Wright, *RB* 73 (1966), 404–19 • P. J. Parr, *PEQ,* 1968, 5–15 • P. J. Parr, G. R. H. Wright, J. Starcky, C. M. Bennett, *Syria* 45 (1968), 1–66 • P. J. Parr, *ADAJ* 12–13 (1968), 30–50 • G. R. H. Wright, *PEQ,* 1969, 113–16 • H. J. Kellner, ed., *Die Nabatäer,* München, 1970 • G. R. H. Wright, *PEQ,* 1970, 111–15 • P. J. Parr, *Near Eastern Archaeology in the Twentieth Century,* New York, 1970, 348–81 • K. Schmitt-Korte, *ADAJ* 14 (1971), 47–60 • A. Negev, *RB* 79 (1972), 381–89 • P. C. Hammond, *PEQ,* 1973, 27–49 • G. R. H. Wright, *PEQ,* 1973, 83–90 • A. Negev, *RB* 80 (1973), 364–83 • P. C. Hammond, *The Nabataeans — Their History, Culture, and Archaeology,* Göthenburg, 1973 • A. Negev, *The Nabataean Potter's Workshop at Oboda,* Bonn, 1974 • P. C. Hammond, *The Excavations of the Main Theater at Petra 1961–1962,* London, 1975 • A. Negev, *RB* 83 (1976).

POLEG, TEL

IDENTIFICATION. Tel Poleg is a mound in the Sharon Plain on the banks of Naḥal Poleg (el-Faliq River) near an ancient man-made breach in the *kurkar* ridge, about 6 kilometers (3.5 miles) south of Netanya. The mound was discovered in 1954 in the course of development works, during which it was largely destroyed, parts of it being preserved only on the east, north, and west sides.

EXCAVATIONS

In 1959, R. Gophna, Perhiya Beck, and J. Naveh carried out trial soundings at the site on behalf of the Department of Antiquities. On the east side — the summit of the mound — the east end of a fortified structure was discovered built of brick on bedrock. The remains included a section of a wall (23 meters long, 2.7 meters thick) with parts of small rooms built against it. The finds on the floors of the rooms date to the Middle Bronze Age II-A and correspond to finds in strata F–G at Tell Beit Mirsim and strata XIV–XIII at Megiddo.

In the debris of the building were pits full of ashes and pottery from the Iron Age II-A–B.

In the summer of 1962 and spring of 1964, excavations were carried out by R. Gophna on the west side of the mound, which forms a kind of wide terrace. He discovered the remains of a fortress from the Middle Bronze Age II-A, built of brick on bedrock. Overlying it were the remains of large settlements from the Iron Age II-A–B and the Persian period. Of the fortress was cleared the west wall (100 meters long, 5 meters thick, and preserved in some sections to a height of 3 meters), a large tower (15 by 8.5 meters) in the southwestern corner, a rampart of *kurkar* built against the wall to a height of 2.5 meters, and the foundations of the right side of what seems to be a gateway (25 meters long) in the northwest corner of the fortress. The entrance through this gateway into the fortress was probably of the indirect type.

On the basis of the pottery found inside the walls of the fortress and in a damaged tomb within the walls, the fortress can be dated to the Middle Bronze Age II-A. The pottery is similar to that uncovered in 1959 in the fortified structure on the summit of the mound, but the almost total destruction of the mound makes it impossible to determine the relationship between the two structures. It appears likely that the ancient breach in the *kurkar* ridge north of the mound was originally a fosse for the defense of the northern flank of the Middle Bronze Age fortress.

Tel Poleg was the first site excavated in the basin of Naḥal Poleg, which was found to contain remains of settlements from the Canaanite and Israelite periods. This discovery strengthens the assumption that already at that time there was a road along the Sharon coast. The Canaanite fortress at Tel Poleg was erected to protect this road and formed a link in the chain of settlements in the southern part of the Sharon Plain in the Middle Bronze Age II, like Tell Jerishe and Tel Rosh ha-'Ayin. The Iron Age settlement at Tel Poleg is part of the occupation in this region, remains of which have also been cleared at Tell Qasile, Tell Kudadi, and near Tell Makmish.　　　　R. GOPHNA

BIBLIOGRAPHY

R. Gophna, *EI* 11 (1973), 111–19 (Hebrew).

General plan of the mound and excavated areas.

Plan of Area C: 1. Gate. 2. Western wall. 3. Tower. 4. Rampart. 5. Border of kurkar *quarry.*

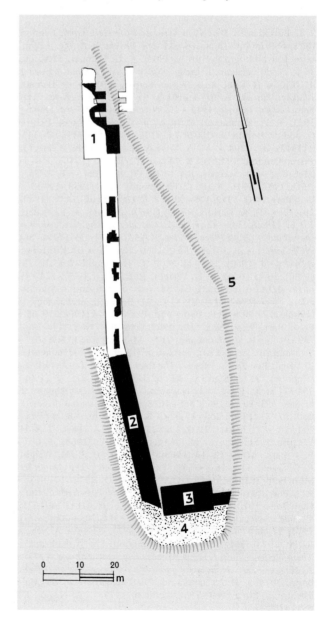

EL-QAFZE CAVE

IDENTIFICATION AND EXCAVATIONS. The el-Qafze Cave lies in a dolomite rock on the western slope of the Qedumim Mountain, about 2 kilometers (1.2 miles) south of Nazareth. The cave consists of a chamber 27 meters long and about 20 meters wide. A passage opening in its north wall is almost wholly covered with earth. In the ceiling of the cave are several natural vaults, one of which forms a chimney rising about 30 meters and opening onto the slope of the mountain. The cave was discovered in 1932 by two monks from Nazareth, who collected a number of flint tools bearing Paleolithic characteristics. These implements were brought to R. Neuville, who in 1933–35, together with M. Stekelis, conducted excavations there on behalf of the Paris Institute for the Paleontology of Man.

The following strata were discovered (from top to bottom):

Stratum A. Thickness 2.75 meters. Remains of a Byzantine monastery, as well as contemporary pottery and a human frontal bone (Homo I).

Stratum B. Thickness .1–1 meter. Brown clay. Pottery from the Early Bronze Age I–III.

Stratum C. Thickness .4–1 meter. Brown clay mixed with small angular stones containing the remains of a fireplace, animal bones, and a human frontal bone (Homo II). An assemblage of flint implements from Upper Paleolithic, stage III (?).

Stratum D. Thickness .6–.85 meter. Brown clay with stone debris and small angular stones; remains of a fireplace and an assemblage of implements from the Paleolithic, stage II.

Stratum E. Thickness .75 meter. Brown clay without small stones. The flint industry belongs to Upper Paleolithic, stage I.

Stratum F. Thickness .1 meter. A thin layer of yellowish-brown clay. Mousterian industry. All the tools are covered with white patina.

Stratum H. Thickness .4–.7 meter. Brown clay mixed with a few stones. Remains of fireplaces and an assemblage of Upper Levallois implements.

Stratum I. Thickness .25–.6 meter. Light-brown clay mixed with large stones. Remains of fireplaces and Middle Levallois implements.

Stratum J. Thickness .3–1 meter. Light-brown clay mixed with stone debris. Remains of fireplaces and Lower Levallois implements.

Stratum K. Thickness .4 meter. Light-brown clay containing much sand and a few small stones. Lower Levallois.

Stratum L. Thickness .5–.8 meter. Blackish-brown clay, mixed with small stones. Remains of fireplaces; skeletons of the early Palestinian man (Homo III, IV, V, VI, VII), but the excavators succeeded in unearthing skulls only.

Mousterian scrapers.

Stratum M. Bedrock.

In 1936, the British blew up the cave, and since then the site has been considered dangerous.

In all the inhabited strata, petrified animal bones were found. The animal and human remains are undergoing examination in Paris, and their study is not yet complete. The report of the excavations, including that of the material culture, has been completed by M. Stekelis in Jerusalem, and will be published after the conclusion of the paleological and anthropological studies. M. STEKELIS

BIBLIOGRAPHY

R. Neuville, *Le Paléolithique et le Mésolithique du Désert de Judée,* Paris, 1951, 179–84. •
From 1965 to 1975 excavations were conducted in the cave under the direction of B. Vandermeersch of the University of Paris. For the preliminary reports, see: B. Vandermeersch, *C. R. Académie des Sciences* 262 (1966), 1434–36; 268 (1969), 2562–65; idem, *RB* 74 (1967), 60–63; idem, *Bull. Soc. Prehis. Fr.* 66 (1969), 157–58 • B. Vandermeersch and A. Ronen, *Quaternaria* 16 (1972), 189–202 • B. Vandermeersch, in: *The Origin of Homo Sapiens,* ed. F. Bordes, Proceedings of the Paris Symposium, 2–5 September 1969, Paris, 1972, 49–54.

Above: Neanderthal skull. Below: View of the cave.

QASILE, TELL

IDENTIFICATION. Tell Qasile lies within the borders of Tel Aviv on the north bank of the Yarkon River, at a distance of about 150 meters from the river and about 1.75 kilometers east of its estuary. The economic life of the settlement on the site was based to a great extent on the river. Its waters were used for irrigation, allowing the development of a diversified agriculture and it is very likely that in various periods the settlement served as an inland port, and ships sailed upstream through the estuary of the Yarkon River and anchored near the mound. This is also borne out by the discovery there of imported pottery. The role of this settlement as an inland port is also reflected in the biblical account of the shipment of cedar trees sent for the building of the temples in the days of Solomon (II Chronicles 2:16) and of Zerubbabel (Ezra 3:7). Floats of trees were sent up the Yarkon and unloaded at one of the settlements on its banks, probably Tell Kudadi (q.v.) or Tell Qasile.

EXCAVATIONS

Three consecutive seasons of excavations were conducted at Tell Qasile from 1948 to 1950 on behalf of the Israel Exploration Society, under the direction of B. Mazar and with the participation of Trude Dothan, I. Dunayevsky, and J. Kaplan. The excavations were concentrated in the southern part of the mound over an area of about 1,200 square meters, and in 1949 and 1950 excavations on a smaller scale were also conducted on the northwest slope of the mound. The boundaries of the mound were traced, and its area was established as 150 meters long from north to south and 100 to 110 meters wide from east to west. The overall area of the ancient settlement was thus some 15 to 16 dunams. The buildings situated on the boundaries of the settlement on the south and west slopes of the mound were destroyed by erosion. Scanty remains have survived of the fortifications dating from the end of the twelfth to the beginning of the tenth century B.C. (strata XI–X; see below). The fortifications of the later strata have all been washed away by erosion.

Large sections of the southern part of the mound were cleared down to virgin soil and twelve main strata were distinguished. They range in date from the Iron Age I-B to the Arab period:

I   Arab period, including the Mamelukes
II   Byzantine period (fourth–sixth centuries A.D.)
III Late Roman period (third–fourth centuries A.D.)
IV   Herodian period (first century A.D.)
V   Hellenistic period (third–second centuries B.C.)
VI   Persian period (fifth–fourth centuries B.C.)
VII Iron Age II-C (eighth century B.C. to 732 B.C.)
VIII Iron Age II-B (ninth century B.C.)
IX$_1$
IX$_2$ Iron Age II-A (tenth century B.C.)
X   Iron Age I-B (pre-Israelite period at Tell Qasile — second half of the eleventh and beginning of the tenth century B.C.)
XI
XII Iron Age I-B (Philistine period, second half of the twelfth and first half of the eleventh century B.C.)

With the exception of a few sherds from a short-lived settlement in the Middle Bronze Age I, the earliest remains on the mound date from the beginning of the Iron Age.

Philistine Period (Strata XII–XI)

STRATUM XII. The buildings of this stratum were constructed on the *kurkar* rock and few remains of them have survived. The best preserved building was found in the southern sector of the excavations. It was built of mud brick and consisted of two adjoining structures, the length of their common front measuring 12 meters. Depressions and pits cut into the *kurkar* in this stratum were encountered all over the excavations. In the center of the area were remains of brick walls. In the area of the fortifications, a pavement of large stone slabs running beneath the brick wall of stratum XI and continuing westward is attributed to stratum XII. It appears that the inhabited area of stratum XII was more extensive here than that of strata XI–X. The pavement was destroyed at its western end by erosion. It probably reached up to the city wall which was also washed down the slope. The architectural remains in stratum XII appear to belong to large buildings which were razed when the city was destroyed by a conflagration and by building activities in later periods, especially in stratum X, where the foundations of the structures penetrated almost down to the natural *kurkar* rock.

STRATUM XI was completely cleared in the southern part of the mound where a large building, built mostly of *kurkar* stones, was found. The plan of

Above: General view of the southern part of the mound.
Below both pages, left to right: Plan of the southern residential
quarter, stratum X; Building L, stratum VIII;
Building G, stratum VI.

the structure was not fully traced. East of it was a large square, and nearby were two clay crucibles containing remains of smelted copper. In the northern sector of the mound the buildings of this stratum were destroyed down to their foundations when the buildings of stratum X were erected. The nature of the ruins indicates that the settlement was destroyed by an earthquake.

The fortifications on the west include a massive brick wall (about 5 meters thick) of stratum XI. No architectural continuity was noted between strata XII and XI. The latter was laid out on a different plan and a new wall was added.

It was possible to distinguish clearly between dif-ferent strata of Iron Age I (strata XII–X) at Tell Qasile, and separate and well-defined pottery assemblages could be established in each of these strata. Changes and developments can be traced in the ordinary local pottery, in which the Canaanite pottery tradition continues, as well as in the Philistine ware.

The Philistine pottery of stratum XII (which includes the main types: bowls, craters, jugs with strainer spouts, and stirrup vases) contains several distinctive features which date it to the early phase of its appearance in Israel: thick white slip, bichrome decoration on some of the vessels with narrow, close-set lines, similar to the Mycenaean

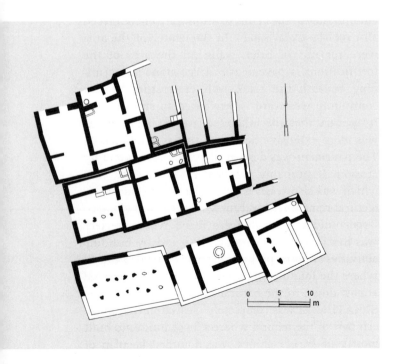

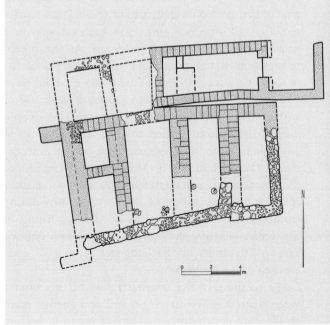

"close style," and the bird motif limited here to stratum XII, one example only having been found in stratum XI. The ceramic assemblage of stratum XI is similar to that of stratum XII, although a change is discernible in the Philistine pottery, where there is a deterioration in the ornamentation and monochrome decorations become more frequent.

Other finds in this stratum include bronze arrowheads, a bone graver, spindle whorls, flint sickle blades, and numerous loom weights and various stone objects, such as grindstones and mortars. Iron objects were not found in strata XII and XI. The ceramic finds of these strata parallel those of Megiddo VII-A–VI-B, Tell Beit Mirsim B-3, and Beth-Shemesh III.

STRATUM X. Since buildings of this stratum were encountered throughout the excavated area, it was possible to establish both the plans of the individual buildings and of an entire quarter. The houses of this stratum were built on an almost uniform plan, consisting of a square court situated in one corner and two adjoining long and narrow rooms meeting at an angle. This plan may possibly be the archetype of the four-room house, widespread in the Iron Age II. Some of the houses had a narrow paved strip along the outer wall of the court and a row of pillars bounding it on the inner side, indicating that the court was roofed. Of special

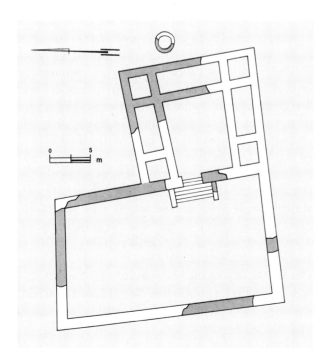

interest is a house in the northwest corner of the excavation. It contained a large court with two wide doorways opening onto the street. Some of the rooms of the buildings were used as storerooms and others, in which numerous finds were made, served as dwelling rooms and workshops. The buildings in the north part of the excavated area formed a complete residential quarter. They were surrounded on three sides by streets and comprised two rows of attached houses accessible only from the street.

To the south of this quarter, part of a second block of buildings was cleared, which differed from the first. The western building, consisting of a large room with two column bases along its length, was not an ordinary dwelling house but was probably used for industrial purposes, like the building in stratum XI.

These quarters were planned anew in stratum X and only in a very few places (in the southern area) is there a continuity between the buildings of strata XI and X. The city was destroyed by a conflagration, and a great many finds were uncovered in the ruins, especially in the storerooms, which shed light on the rich material culture of this stratum.

The city wall of stratum XI (see above) was reconstructed by the inhabitants of the city of stratum X and continued in use until the final destruction of this city.

A large amount of pottery and other objects were discovered in the buildings of the stratum, mostly in the storerooms. The change in the character of the settlement can also be seen in the material culture. New forms and styles are added to the pottery repertoire and Phoenician-type pottery and Egyptian imported ware appear here for the first time. The most striking change, however, occurs in the forms and decoration of the Philistine pottery. The white slip and bichrome ornamentation disappear and are now replaced by a red slip, usually with irregular burnish, and brown painted decoration. Some of the Philistine types of vessels vanish, and new types appear, which were created through a fusion of Philistine and Canaanite elements and new traits which become common in Israelite pottery. The blending of these three elements is especially evident in a group of craters. The Philistine elements are represented in the horizontal handles and the degenerated spiral pat-

*This page, below: Scaraboid seal, stratum VIII.
Bottom: Ostracon inscribed: "For the king one thousand
and one hundred (log of) oil ... Ḥiyahu".
Opposite page: Hebrew seal: "'Ashanyahu, servant of
the king" 6th or beginning of the 5th century* B.C.

tern, the local tradition is seen in the shape of the craters and in some of the decorations, and the new feature is the burnished red slip. Parallels to the ceramic finds of stratum X are found in stratum IV at Tell Abu Hawam, stratum VI-A at Megiddo, and at Tell Jerishe. The crater described above has been found so far only in Megiddo and Tell Jerishe.

In stratum X iron objects, such as knives and the blade of a sword, appear for the first time together with various bronze implements. Among the finds is a conical seal engraved with figure of an animal and above it the figure of a man with outstretched hands.

The Period of the United Monarchy (Strata IX$_2$–IX$_1$)

STRATUM IX$_2$. On the ruins of the city of stratum X arose the Israelite settlement (stratum IX$_2$). The changes in the organization of the new city are evident mainly in the fortifications. It appears that the strong brick wall of the Philistine city (strata X–XI) went out of use with the destruction of stratum X. In the area of the fortifications was discovered a row of attached buildings of the Israelite period, the outer face of which, toward the slope, was destroyed by erosion. The city wall probably stood to the west of these buildings and was also washed away. Also in the center of the mound major changes took place in the transition from stratum X to stratum IX$_2$. The northern row of buildings in the block of houses in stratum X appears to have been totally razed, and in the open area several silos were dug. The southern row of buildings of this block, however, continued to exist also in stratum IX$_2$, with only the interior of the buildings undergoing alterations. The major change was the addition of a wall dividing the court and thus creating the type of dwelling known as the four-room house. Another innovation was the change of direction of the row of houses—the entrance was now from the north, from the area of the silos. It is not known whether buildings also stood to the south of the quarter and were destroyed by erosion, or whether there was a reduction in the area of the city.

STRATUM IX$_1$. In the eastern part of the excavated area was found a public building (14 by 12 meters) that was erected in stratum IX$_1$. Its construction was the main innovation in this stratum. In the northeast part of the building was an entrance hall containing the lower part of a flight of stairs leading to an upper story. South of the entrance hall was a row of four long narrow rooms, one of which was divided into two parts. These rooms were probably accessible from the upper story through openings in the ceiling. Evidently a public building, this structure indicates that the site was an administrative center in this period. The dwelling houses of stratum IX_2 continued in use in IX_1 with nearly no changes. The walls dividing the courts in stratum IX_2 were, however, replaced by rows of columns.

This stratum was poor in ceramic and small finds. In addition to the local pottery, which generally had a red slip and irregular burnish, there is also Cypriot ware of the Cypriot-Phoenician types white-painted I–II and black-on-red I–II. The pottery for the most part parallels that of stratum IV-B–IV-A at Megiddo, stratum III at Tell Abu Hawam, stratum II-A at Beth-Shemesh, and stratum B at Tell Beit Mirsim. Some bronze and iron implements were also found in this stratum.

The Period of the Israelite Kingdom (Strata VIII–VII)

STRATUM VIII. The public building continued in use also in stratum VIII. The block of buildings continued to exist as well, undergoing a certain change of plan with the disappearance of the rows of columns of stratum IX_1.

STRATUM VII. In this stratum the continuity which was noted between the buildings of strata X–VIII is no longer apparent. The large public buildings of stratum VIII ceases to exist and is replaced by ordinary houses. Few building remains can be attributed to stratum VII, most of them having been destroyed by building activity in the Persian period (stratum VI). In strata VIII–VII, as in strata IX_2–IX_1, no remains of city walls were discovered, but it can be assumed that a city wall did exist and was washed down the slope by erosion.

The Israelite town was probably destroyed in 732 B.C. when Tiglath-Pileser III invaded the Israelite kingdom and razed numerous towns. This destruction brought the settlement at Tell Qasile to an end, and the site was not again occupied until the Persian period.

In the pottery found in strata VIII–VII the red slip with regular burnish is predominant. The bowls and deep bowls show wheel-made concentric bur-

nishing for the first time. Some bowls of Samarian ware were also found, in both ivory and red. Cooking pots of the shallow type occur as well as those with narrow grooved mouths from which two handles extend to the shoulder. One large jar resembles Cypriot-Phoenician ware in both shape and workmanship. It has a slip in various shades of red and is well burnished. The front of the jar is decorated with the drawing of a galloping horse.

Other finds include an Astarte figurine of the Pillar type, two scarab seals, stone weights, and copper and iron implements.

The pottery of strata VIII–VII belongs on the whole to ninth and eighth century B.C. types common in the Israelite kingdom.

The Hebrew Inscriptions. Before the beginning of the excavations two ostraca were found on the surface of the mound. The pottery type and the paleographic excavations date them to the late stage of the Iron Age.

OSTRACON No. 1. The inscription is deeply carved on the inside of the ring base of a vessel with reddish slip. The script is the cursive Hebrew common in Israel and Judah in the eighth century B.C. The ostracon is damaged only on the edges. It reads: "For the king, one thousand and one hundred [log of] oil . . . Ḥiyahu."

This was apparently a receipt or a record of a quantity of oil sent by an official, whose name was Ḥiyahu, through the port of Tell Qasile. The liquid measure is not mentioned in the inscription but

the "log" was probably intended.

OSTRACON No. 2. The inscription is carved on the sherd of a large vessel, with points separating the words. It reads: "Gold of Ophir to Beth-Horon... thirty shekels."

The term "gold of Ophir" in the Bible refers to gold of a special, superior quality, named after its country of origin, Ophir. The quantity of gold is given in the second line in the single letter shin which is an abbreviation of the word "shekel." Three parallel horizontal lines represent the number of shekels (thirty), following the accepted system of writing numerals in Phoenician inscriptions. This was evidently an official document certifying the dispatch of a consignment of thirty shekels (half a talent) of gold of Ophir to Beth Horon.

The Persian Period (Stratum VI). Building remains of stratum VI are scattered over the entire western part of the excavated area, all of them belonging to a large public building. To construct this building, a large area was leveled, and all building remains of the last Israelite stratum (VII) were torn down.

Although most of the building was demolished when later buildings were erected, it was possible to reconstruct its plan on general lines. It was a square building with a court surrounded by rooms on three of its sides. On the west side was a large rectangular court. The difference in floor levels between the court and the building indicates that a staircase connected the two. East of the building was a leveled square with a circular silo and north of it a ditch containing a considerable quantity of objects and pottery of the Persian period.

The pottery of stratum VI includes characteristic types of the Persian period: jars with flat angular shoulders or with high basket handles, and heavy pots with ribbed bodies and flat or ring bases. A small quantity of Attic pottery of the fifth–fourth centuries B.C. was found, including a fragment showing a dancer in the black-figure technique. A Hebrew seal, found prior to the excavations, may also belong to this period. It is in the shape of a flat limestone plaque, and bears the carving of a human figure and along the edges the Hebrew inscription: "'Ashanyahu, servant of the King."

The Hellenistic Period (Stratum V). The few remains from this stratum found scattered over the mound do not form an identifiable pattern. It was also difficult to establish the connection between this stratum and the following stratum IV.

The Herodian Period (Stratum IV). The remains of a large building have survived from this stratum in the eastern part of the excavations. The plan of the building is difficult to establish. Its foundations penetrated to a considerable depth, pointing to a very large and massive structure. The foundations are of unhewn stones and only in one section has a single course, built of well-dressed ashlars, survived above the foundations. Both in plan and construction technique this building resembles Herodian buildings at Samaria. The same date is also indicated by the pottery found on the surviving floors of the building. Fragments of *terra sigillata* ware were uncovered, one of which bears the potter's mark X A P I C from the time of Augustus.

Late Roman Period (Stratum III, third–fourth centuries A.D.**).** To this stratum belongs a large building, which was probably a market. It extendered over the whole of the eastern part of the excavations. The part of the market unearthed consists of three long narrow rooms, a wide hall containing two rows of columns to the west, and a section of a similar hall on the east side. The market was probably entered from the west, from a street running along its western facade. East of this street was a row of buildings from the same period. Rooms and courts were excavated, but it proved impossible to attribute them to clearly defined buildings. The large building can be compared with a nearly contemporary structure discovered in Tiberias. A pottery kiln, found in the southern end of the mound, may also belong to this stratum.

From stratum II (Byzantine period) and stratum I (Arab period) only a few remains scattered over the whole area were preserved.

TRUDE DOTHAN – I. DUNAYEVSKY

BIBLIOGRAPHY

B. Maisler (Mazar), *IEJ* 1 (1950–51), 16–76; 125–40; 194–218; idem, *JNES* 10 (1951), 265–67; idem, *EI* 1 (1951), 45–71 (Hebrew) • J. Kaplan *BIES* 22 (1957), 97 (Hebrew).

The excavations at Tell Qasile were resumed in 1971 and continued until 1974, under the direction of A. Mazar. They were sponsored by the Israel Exploration Society, the Institute of Archaeology of the Hebrew University, and the Museum Haaretz, Tel Aviv – Jaffa. In the last two seasons, a new area measuring 850 square meters, area C, was opened in the northeast sector of the site. In this area was discovered the cultic center of the city during the Iron Age.

Area C.

STRATUM XII. This level was represented by two subphases in the test pits and sections dug beneath strata XI and X. Of the earliest Iron Age settlement on the site (stratum XII-b, twelfth century B.C.), only meager patches of floors and walls were found. Above these poor remains was constructed the first of a series of temple buildings (stratum XII-a, building 319). The external dimensions of the temple were 6.4 by 6.6 meters. Its brick walls, which lacked stone foundations, varied in thickness from .5 to 1 meter. The entrance of the building was in the east wall where a large stone slab served as a threshold. The temple consisted of a single room with plastered brick benches along the walls and a beaten lime floor. A raised platform, also of plastered brick, with a frontal projection which probably originally contained steps, was located at the west end of the room. Although the platform was preserved only to a height of .5 meter, it had undoubtedly been higher during its existence. It is possible that the area along the rear of the temple served as a storeroom, as in the later temples of strata XI and X. In a layer of brick debris on the floor was found a group of pottery vessels, including a unique Philistine jug with a convex-shaped body, its upper section in the shape of a flask and decorated with a stylized lotus motif and geometric patterns.

A spacious open courtyard stretched east of the temple up to the north and east edges of the excavations. Its lime floor was repaired several times. Between the floors were alternate layers of gray and black ashes which suggest that organic material had been gathered together in the courtyard area and set on fire. The ashes contained sherds and numerous animal bones as well as several unusual objects: an anthropomorphic juglet, a scarab engraved with a chariot scene, and an ivory knife handle with remains of the iron blade still held in place by bronze rivets. On the north side of the courtyard was a long narrow room belonging to the temple complex.

South of the temple and the courtyard, a wall, 25 meters long, bisected the excavation from east to west. It enclosed a series of buildings that continued southward. The wall was repaired during strata XI – IX, a fact that implies an architectural continuity from stratum XII onward.

STRATUM XI. Building 200 represents the stratum XI temple erected directly above that of stratum XII. The walls of the new building closely follow the lines of those of the earlier temple, with the exception of the north and east sides where the building was enlarged. It now measured 7.75 by 8.5 meters. The walls, approximately 1 meter in width, were constructed of *kurkar* stones. The entrance, 1.4 meters wide, was located near the north end of the east wall. Like the earlier temple, this one also consisted of a single room surrounded by brick benches, but it differed in its interior arrangement. In the southwest corner of the room, two brick walls, each consisting of two courses only, were built at right angles to one another, enclosing a space 1.5 by 2.8 meters. It is not certain whether these walls reached a full height and formed a proper room, or whether they were foundations of a raised platform which served as a holy of holies, a suggestion favored by the excavator. Inside the corner space created by the partitions a rich assemblage of cult vessels was discovered, including an anthropomorphic mask, an ivory bird-shaped cosmetic bowl, a seashell that served as a horn, several clay figurines, numerous beads, and pottery vessels that included a group of small votive bowls. In the temple area itself, a bronze dagger and arrowhead were found together with Philistine vessels. It is possible that the corner space may have been used as a hidden storeroom beneath the brick-built platform.

There was evidence that the floor of the courtyard east of the temple had been repaired and raised three times. On the north side of the court an interesting assemblage was discovered in a depository pit (favissa), dug through the accumulations of stratum XII down to bedrock and sealed by the stratum X floor. The assemblage included an anthropomorphic vessel of a female figure whose breasts served as spouts, a pottery rhyton in the shape of a lion's head, decorated with Philistine motifs, and a rich collection of pottery including a horn-shaped vessel and decorated bell-shaped bowls. On the north side of the court were two rooms which belonged to the temple complex. Beyond them was a street running to the west.

Below: General plan of the mound after the 1974 season.
Opposite page: Schematic plan of the temples.
A, building 319, stratum XII. B, building 200,
stratum XI. C, building 131, stratum X. D, building 300,
strata XI-X.

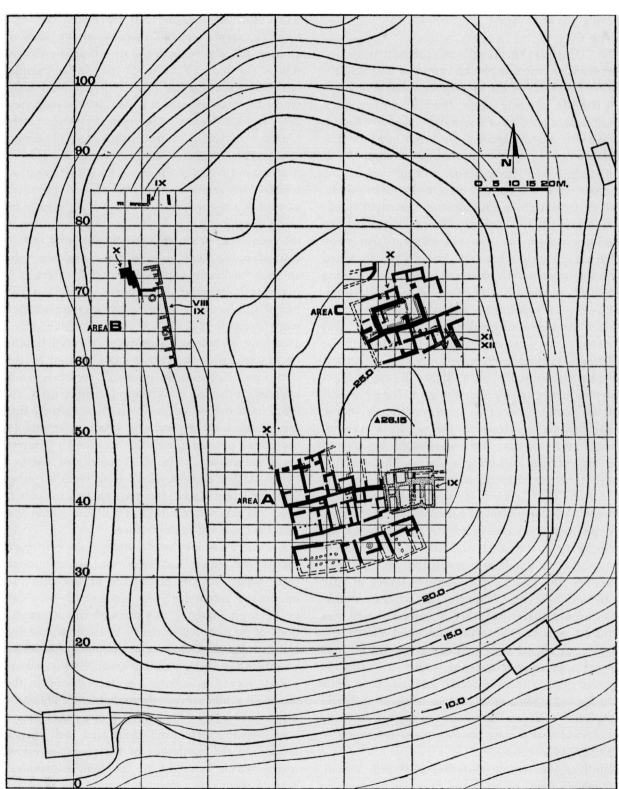

A miniature shrine (building 300) was attached to the west wall of the temple. It was first built in stratum XI and continued to exist unchanged during stratum X. The shrine consisted of a single brick-built room (3.5 by 5.6 meters) with an entrance at the east end of the north wall and plastered benches along the walls. In the southwest corner the benches extended up to a raised platform formed by two steps. Thus the shrine is a "bent axis" building like the stratum X temple (see below). Next to the raised platform were three fenestrated cylindrical cult stands decorated with geometric designs, and near them lay two bowls with projections on their bases. The decorated head and wings of a duck were attached to one of the bowls. A similar bowl was found in a porch in front of the shrine.

South of the temple were the remains of a large building which was apparently founded in stratum XII and continued to exist with a number of alterations in stratum XI and finally went out of use in stratum X.

From the abundance of finds made in stratum XI, several aspects in the development of the pottery could be noted. The white slip common in stratum XII disappeared, and in stratum XI a red slip is found on a large number of the vessels. Hand burnishing is rare. Many of the vessels are decorated with Philistine motifs, including the distinctive bird design.

STRATUM X. The temple of stratum X (building 131) was based on the previous temple, although it was enlarged on the east and measured 8 by 14.5 meters. The north, west, and south walls of stratum XI continued in use but the east wall was canceled and now served as the foundation for a bench. A new antechamber was added on the east side of the temple. The entrance, 2.9 meters wide, was situated in the north wall of the antechamber. There were two rows of benches along its walls. An opening in the west wall of the room led to the cella whose internal measurements were 5.65 by 7.2 meters. An artificial fill raised the floor .6 meter above that of the earlier temple. Two round stone column bases were set into the fill on the long east–west axis. They served as supports for columns of cedar wood, as was shown by the analysis of charred wood remains found next to the bases. Around the walls were tiered benches similar to those in the antechamber. On the west side of the cella was a brick partition forming a long, narrow cell. A brick platform, raised .9 meter above the floor, was built against the east face of the partition. The benches along the north wall of the cella extended up to the platform, while on the south it was reached by two plastered steps, one of which was built around the western column (the circular imprint of the wooden column was preserved in the step). The walls, benches, and floor of the temple were all coated with a thick, light-brown plaster. The building is of the bent-axis type, and it was impossible to look directly into the cella from the outside.

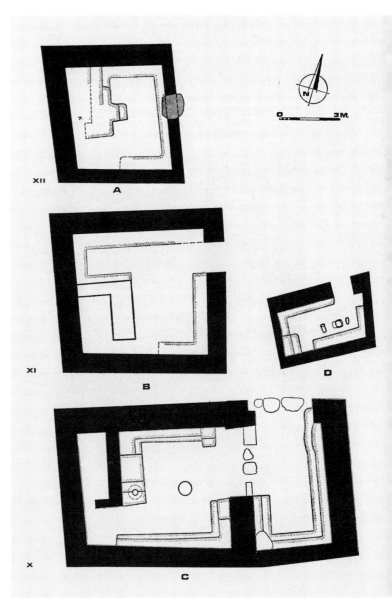

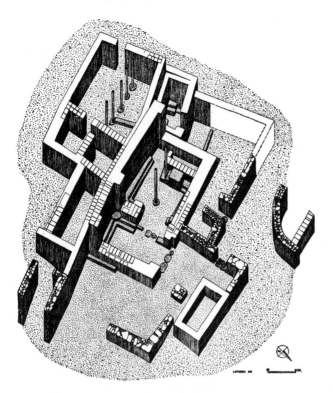

The temple was destroyed by a conflagration and a large number of objects were discovered on its floor. Among the cult artifacts were the following: a pottery plaque in the form of an architectural facade in Egyptian style, with either two goddesses or a god and goddess, depicted in a frontal stance; a cylindrical cult stand with two lionesses attached to the rim; a cylindrical cult stand decorated with human figures walking to the side; a bowl decorated with the head and wings of a bird; a large conical jar decorated with floral designs and a bird; a bowl decorated with heads of bulls; pomegranate-shaped vessels, etc. The pottery in the temple included types typical of stratum X, including Phoenician bichrome ware. In the rear cell of the temple were found stirrup jars and bell-shaped bowls decorated with Philistine geometric motifs. Two metal objects were also discovered in the temple: a bronze double axe and an iron bracelet.

To the north and east of the temple was a large courtyard enclosed by strong stone walls with a

Both pages, counterclockwise from above:
Area C. Axonometric view of stratum X, looking
southwest; General view of the temple, stratum X,
looking west; General view of stratum XII temple,
looking northwest. Visible above it are the stone walls
of strata XI-X temples; General view of miniature
shrine 300, looking west.

rectangular room built of brick on the north side. A square stone foundation, 1.2 by 2 meters, apparently the base of a sacrificial altar, was discovered in the courtyard.

Another courtyard lay northwest and west of the temple. It was entered from the street on the north through a well-built entrance. In the east side of the court was a stone-built service room which contained various installations and pottery vessels. In the south the court incorporates the miniature temple (300), which was erected during the previous level and continued unchanged also in stratum X.

South of the temple complex was a row of buildings bordered by the east–west wall of stratum XII, mentioned above. One of the houses (building 225), which was completely cleared, measured 8.5 by 13.5 meters and included two square rooms on the east and a courtyard divided by a row of columns into roofed and open areas. This building was also destroyed by fire, and on its floor lay scores of vessels including numerous storage jars, Egyptian

Both pages, left to right: Bird-shaped cult bowl, stratum X; Anthropomorphic vessel, stratum XI; Cult stands with bowls, from miniature shrine 300 — strata XI–X; Decorated cult vessel, stratum X.

imported vessels, and some richly decorated Philistine ware. South of the building was a street running east-west.

The line of the walls and streets in area C run parallel to each other, and their orientation is similar to that of area A, indicating that the Philistine city was well planned with parallel streets intersecting one another at right angles.

STRATA IX–VII. Above the thick destruction level of the Philistine temple of stratum X, the excavators found a section of a lime floor which they attributed to stratum IX. In this stratum, the north wall of the temple was rebuilt with bricks and the east wall continued unaltered. The other walls, however, were so badly damaged in later periods that it was impossible to trace their plan in strata IX–VIII. In the courtyard a new lime floor was laid during stratum IX, sealing the square foundation of the stratum X altar, which was apparently replaced by a round stone installation constructed slightly to the east. The rooms south of the temple were also reconstructed and their floors raised. In a later phase, probably in stratum VIII the east wall of the temple was rebuilt of massive stones, and the north wall was strengthened by a row of large stones. New walls were constructed north of the temple. The finds from this level are scanty, as it lay directly below the surface and was considerably damaged by erosion and later disturbances. However, it is clear that during strata IX–VIII the temple continued to be in use. A revised study of the pottery shows that stratum VIII dates to the late tenth century B.C. After its destruction, probably during the campaign of Shishak to Palestine, the site was abandoned for a long time.

No architectural remains in area C could be attributed to stratum VII but typical eighth–seventh century B.C. pottery was found in eroded layers of earth above the temple ruins. Two cuttings in the west side of the mound contained pottery typical of the end of the Iron Age, and it is possible that they represent the remains of a short-lived settlement on the mound at the end of the seventh century B.C. The stratigraphy and dating of stratum VII in area A seems to require further revision.

STRATUM VI. Several pits from the Persian period in area C contained potsherds, including the handle of an amphora bearing a stamped impression with the Hebrew letters 'nb. In the northernmost edge of the mound was discovered a square shaft,

2 meters wide and 12 meters deep. The bottom of the shaft is 1.8 meters above sea level, and residue showed that it had been used as a water shaft. Pottery of the Persian period was found inside the shaft together with fragments of human skeletons. The shaft apparently served for irrigation during the Persian period, and went out of use and was blocked up at the end of that period, during the conquest of Alexander the Great.

STRATA V–I. A pit, dug into the Iron Age levels in area C, was attributed to the Herodian period (stratum IV). Otherwise, there are no remains of strata V and IV in this area. Two strata of the Byzantine period were uncovered in the western part of the area. Stratum II$_2$ consists of several walls and a plastered pool. Stratum II$_1$ contained a public bathhouse. The caldarium consisted of a main room with two side chambers. The main room terminated in an apse at its east end. The entire complex was heated by the hypocaust, which contained rows of arched brick columns. The bathhouse was destroyed at the end of the Byzantine period. A silver coin, the latest datable find from this period, indicates that the destruction of the Byzantine settlement was connected with the Persi-

an invasion of A.D. 614. A round well built of dressed *kurkar* stones found in the center of area C contained glazed sherds of the Middle Ages.

SUMMARY

The Tell Qasile temenos, which at its peak included two courtyards, an altar, a central temple, and a secondary miniature temple, is of the greatest importance for the light it sheds on the Philistine cult during the twelfth–eleventh centuries B.C.

The discovery of the temple suggests a possible connection between the temple and the ostracon found at Tell Qasile, mentioning the name "Beth-Horon," which can be understood as denoting the temple of the god Horon. However, there is a gap between the earliest possible date of the ostracon and the date of the last temple, that of stratum VIII (late tenth century B.C.).

A. MAZAR

BIBLIOGRAPHY

A. Mazar, *Qadmoniot* 6 (1973), 20–23 (Hebrew): *idem, BA* 36 (1973), 42–48: *idem, Annual of the Museum Haaretz* 15–16 (1974), 38–47 (Hebrew): *idem, IEJ* 23 (1973), 65–71: 25 (1975), 77–88.

EL-QÔM, KHIRBET

IDENTIFICATION. Khirbet el-Qôm is located in the southern Judean hills about 9 kilometers (6 miles) north/northeast of Tell Beit Mirsim, on the Wadi es-Saffar, which runs from Lachish up into the hills toward Hebron. Long ago identified by F. M. Abel with Saphir of Micah 1:11, it was not definitely recognized as an Iron Age site until 1967, when salvage operations were carried out by W. G. Dever on behalf of the Hebrew Union College in Jerusalem. These excavations recovered a considerable amount of Iron Age pottery and other material from scores of robbed tombs. The tombs were typical bench tombs of the Iron Age.

Inscriptions. Two of the Iron Age tombs were of particular interest. In tomb I were found two inscriptions, one of which was cut into the sidewall near the entrance to the rear chamber:

> l'wpy . bn
> ntnyhw
> (h)ḥdr . hzh
> "Belonging to 'Ophai, the son of
> Nethanyahu [is]
> this tomb-chamber."

The second inscription was written in paint above the doorway to the rear chamber:

> l'w (ph) b(t) ntnyhw
> "Belonging to 'Ophah, the daughter [or Uzza the son] of Nethanyahu."

Both these inscriptions can be dated on paleographic grounds to the late eighth century B.C.

Tomb II produced a single four-line inscription, badly defaced. Here is a tentative reading:

> (1)'ryhw . hkšb . ktbh
> brk . 'ryhw . lyhwh
> wm'rr . yd l'šr t(hhws) 'lh
> l'nyhw
> "Belonging to 'Uriyahu. Be careful of his inscription!
> Blessed be 'Uriyahu by Yahweh.
> And cursed shall be the hand of whoever
> [defaces it!]
> [Written by 'Oniyahu.]"

This inscription, also eighth century B.C. in date, appears to be slightly earlier than the first two.

Additional epigraphic material has been acquired and traced with some assurance to Khirbet el-Qôm. This material consisted of eleven inscribed stone weights, including most of the known varieties: a Ziph royal stamped jar handle; an inscribed bowl reading '*l* ("El"); and a water decanter with the name *yḥml* ("Yaḥmol"), scratched around the upper shoulder.

EXCAVATIONS.

In the spring of 1971, a brief season of excavation was conducted by J. S. Holladay, Jr., on behalf of the Hebrew Union College and the Canada Council. It was established that the first occupation of the site began in the Early Bronze Age II and continued into the Early Bronze Age IV–Middle Bronze Age I. Much additional evidence for the Iron Age came to light, including a roughly hewn cyclopean city wall and a three-entryway gate. Crude house remains, courtyards, and cisterns of the Iron Age were also found. The site was evidently reoccupied in the late tenth century B.C., and it continued to grow and prosper until it was destroyed in the Babylonian campaigns in the early sixth century B.C.

A glimpse of the later occupation was provided by the discovery of eight ostraca on the floor of a late third-century B.C. house just inside the city wall in the southern quarter. Most of the ostraca were economic documents in Aramaic. One contained an Aramaic/Greek bilingual text. These ostraca are of considerable importance for the dating of the Aramaic script in this little-known period.

The latest substantial occupation of the area is apparently represented by a number of loculi tombs in the vicinity, undoubtedly of the Herodian period.

W. G. DEVER

BIBLIOGRAPHY

W. G. Dever, *HUCA*, 40–41 (1969–70), 139–204 • D. Barag, *IEJ* 20 (1970), 216–18 • J. S. Holladay, *ibid.* 21 (1971), 175–77 • W. G. Dever, *Qadmoniot*, 4 (1971), 90–92 (Hebrew).

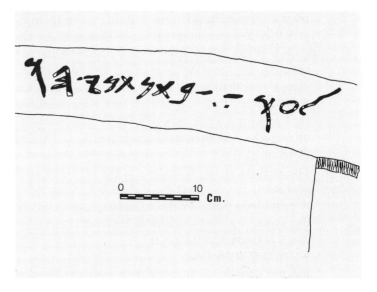

Both pages, counterclockwise from left, top:
Chamber 3 of tomb I, seen from the central chamber.
Hole at top left the former location of inscription I.
Note inscription 2 above doorway; Tomb II,
chambers 3 and 4. At right, repository, below chamber 3;
Tomb I. Detail of two head niches on benches in the
northwest corner of chamber 1; Tomb I. Inscription 2:
"Belonging to 'O..., the daughter of Nethanyahu.";
Inscription 3, from tomb II; Inscription 3, from tomb II.

QUMRAN, KHIRBET-'EIN FESHKHA

The archaeological investigations at Qumran and 'Ein-Feshkha are closely connected with the discovery of the Dead Sea Scrolls. The first manuscripts were found by chance in 1947 by Bedouin shepherds in a cave (number 1) situated near the northwestern shore of the Dead Sea. The cave was excavated in 1949 by a joint expedition of the Jordan Department of Antiquities, the Palestine Archaeological Museum, and l'Ecole Archéologique Française of Jerusalem. The site of Khirbet Qumran, approximately 1 kilometer (.6 mile) south of the cave and slightly farther west of the Dead Sea, was excavated under the same auspices in five successive campaigns, from 1951 to 1956. The last campaign surveyed the region situated between Qumran and the source of 'Ein Feshkha, 3 kilometers to the south. Near this source a building complex was excavated in 1958. A second cave containing scrolls, discovered by Bedouin in 1952, prompted the above institutions, together with the American School of Oriental Research in Jerusalem, to explore the entire cliff face dominating Khirbet Qumran. It was during this campaign that cave 3 containing manuscripts and the Copper Scroll was found. In 1952, Bedouin opened a fourth cave in the marl terrace. When the joint expedition subsequently cleared this cave, it found a fifth cave on the same terrace. Cave 6, the source of scroll fragments purchased from Bedouin, was then located at the entrance to Wadi Qumran. In the course of the 1955 expedition at Khirbet Qumran, caves 7–10 were discovered at the edge of the plateau overlooking Wadi Qumran, south of Khirbet Qumran. Cave 11, which had been searched by Bedouin in 1956, was cleared by archaeologists during the last season of excavations at Khirbet Qumran.

The present article is limited to the archaeological aspects of the discoveries. It does not touch upon the problems posed by the manuscripts themselves, but shows the close connection between the archaeological finds and the texts.

KHIRBET QUMRAN

Khirbet Qumran is situated on a spur of the marl terrace, bounded on the south by Wadi Qumran and on the north and west by ravines. During the five campaigns of excavation, a building complex, extending over 80 meters from east to west and 100 meters from north to south, was completely cleared. Several periods of occupation were distinguished clearly:

The Iron Age. The earliest settlement dates from the Israelite period. Several walls, re-used in later phases, belonged to a rectangular building, in front of which was a courtyard with a large round cistern. Its plan resembles those of Israelite fortresses of the Judean desert and the Negev. The pottery associated with these structures ranges from the eighth century to the beginning of the sixth century B.C. This date is confirmed by a royal *lamelekh* seal impression and by an ostracon with several early Hebrew characters, which are attributed to a period shortly before the Babylonian Exile. The settlement was destroyed during the fall of the Kingdom of Judah. It is probably to be identified with *Ir ha-Melaḥ* ("City of Salt"), one of the six cities of Judea listed in Joshua 15 : 61–62 as situated in the wilderness.

PHASE I-a. After several centuries of abandonment, Qumran was settled once again. At this time the remnants of the Israelite buildings were re-used for the most part with some additions being made. Two new cisterns were dug near the large round one. The date of the founding of this new settlement is difficult to fix. The scant pottery uncovered is hardly distinguished from that of the following period, nor were any coins found. Since the buildings of phase I-b were apparently constructed in the time of John Hyrcanus (134–104 B.C.), phase I-a — which was of short duration — may possibly have begun under John Hyrcanus himself or, more likely, during the reign of one of his immediate predecessors, his father Simeon (142–134 B.C.) or his uncle Jonathan (152-142 B.C.).

PHASE I-b. In this period, the buildings were further enlarged and took on their more or less final form. They consisted of a main building with a massive tower, a central courtyard, and rooms for communal use, a large assembly hall (which also served as a refectory) to the south, and an adjacent pantry where more than a thousand vessels were found — small jars, jugs, dishes, plates, and bowls. In the southeast was a potter's workshop with a basin for washing the clay, a storage pit, a place for a potter's wheel, and two kilns. Another building, situated to the west, consisted of a courtyard surrounded by storerooms. Between the two buildings were three cisterns from phase I-a and workshops. Other cisterns and two baths were dug nearby. To the north of this complex was a large, walled courtyard and to the south an esplanade that extended to Wadi Qumran. Around the buildings the excavators found animal bones, mostly of sheep and goats, but also of cows and calves, deposited beneath large potsherds or occasionally in covered cooking pots. These were evidently the remains of ritual meals — a rite so far known as

Caves in the marl terrace.

unique to Qumran.

The pottery of this phase dates to the end of the Hellenistic period. The coins permit a more precise dating for its beginning. It is certain that the buildings were occupied during the reign of Alexander Jannaeus (103–76 B.C.), and they may possibly have been constructed earlier under John Hyrcanus. The end of this phase is marked by two catastrophes — an earthquake that damaged two cisterns, the tower of the main building, the pantry of the assembly hall, and a corner of the second building, and a conflagration that left a thick layer of ash in the open areas near the buildings. It is possible

that the earthquake affected buildings already burned and in ruins, but this is not supported by any positive evidence. It seems more likely that the earthquake damaged the occupied buildings, which then caught on fire from burning hearths. This is the same earthquake mentioned by Josephus *(Antiquities* XV, 121 ff.; *War* I, 370–80) as having occurred in 31 B.C., a date corroborated by the coins found in this level.

The site was abandoned at the end of phase I-b. The buildings were not repaired immediately, nor was the water system restored to a usable con-dition. Sediment soon spread over the ash layer. Repairs made in phase II were discovered above the silt as well as on virgin soil.

PHASE II. The site was deserted for a brief period and was resettled by the same community which had abandoned it. The general plan and function of the main buildings remained unchanged, and evidence was found that the unique ritual meals

Below: Air view of the main building. Opposite page: Plan of the settlement in phase 1b. 1. Entrance of the aqueduct. 2–3. Reservoires. 4. Tower. 5. Room with benches along the walls. 6. Scriptorium. 7. Kitchen. 8. Assembly hall and refectory. 9. Pantry. 10. Potter's workshop. 11. kilns. 12. Cattle pen.

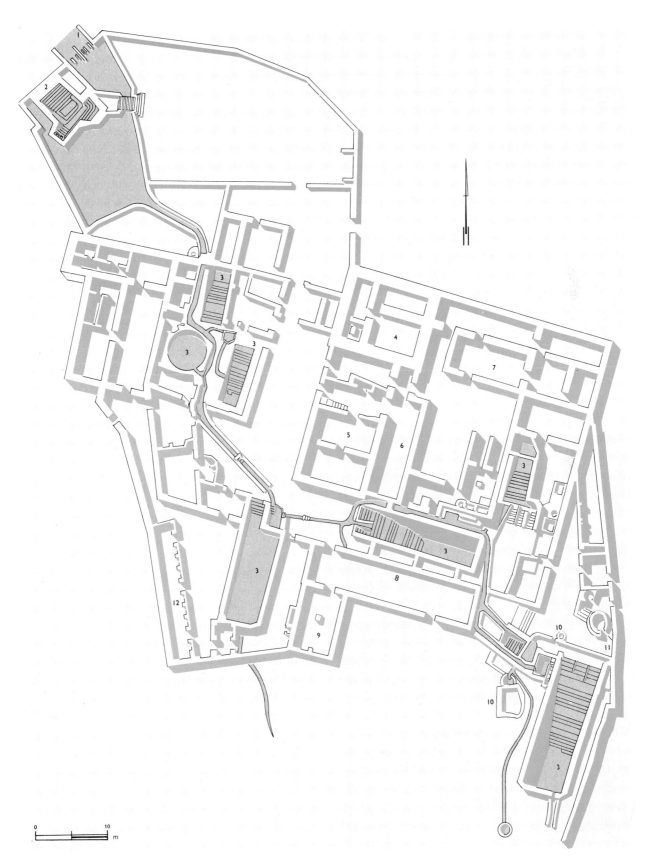

mentioned above continued to be practiced. Most of the rooms had evidently been cleared of debris, for the rubble was found outside the buildings. Some of the rooms and two of the cisterns went out of use. The most severely damaged structures were strengthened. The new constructions of this period departed from the previous plan only in minor details. Phase II, the last major period of occupation, provides much instructive information on the function of the buildings. A large room with five fireplaces was apparently the kitchen. The potter's workshop continued in use. Two other workshops between the main buildings are of indeterminate nature. Nearby was a flour mill and a baking oven. In one of the rooms of the main building were found the remains of three tables, one long and two shorter ones made of plastered mud brick. Also found were a low bench along one of the walls and two inkwells, recovered from the debris. All the evidence suggests that this room may well have been the writing room (scriptorium) in which the scribes and copyists worked.

A great quantity of pottery was found in phase II. Aside from certain special forms which originated in phase I-b and continued in the following phase as a result of the deep-rooted tradition of the local workshop, the pottery is virtually identical with the pottery dating from the first century A.D. found in the Jewish tombs in Jerusalem and in the excavations at Herodian Jericho. The beginning and end of this phase can be fixed by the coins and the historical sources. Following the earthquake of 31 B.C., the buildings remained unoccupied until the end of Herod's reign. Settlement was resumed under Herod Archelaus, probably between the years 4 and 1 B.C. The termination of this phase can be dated even more precisely. Khirbet Qumran was destroyed during the Jewish War in June of the year A.D. 68 when, according to Josephus, the Roman army occupied Jericho and Vespasian visited the Dead Sea. The coins discovered confirm this proposed history of the site. The latest coins of phase II are four Jewish coins of the Year Three of the Jewish War (in contrast to sixty-eight coins of the Year Two). The Year Three, according to the era in which the coins were struck, began in March–April, A.D. 68, a date verified by the coins discovered in the following stratum. The earliest are Roman coins of Caesarea and Dora minted in A.D. 67–68, the same year in which the units that occupied Jericho and destroyed Qumran were stationed at Caesarea.

PHASE III. The above-mentioned coins were not lost during the attack on Qumran, for they were found not in the destruction layer but in the level above, that of the Roman military garrison stationed on the site. This garrison was responsible for the radical changes found in phase III. Only a part of the ruins was restored to use. Some small rooms were built haphazardly over the leveled rubble. Only one of the numerous cisterns was utilized, and the canal system was greatly simplified. The public buildings and the workshops were in ruins and a single baking oven had been constructed on the rubble. The pottery, which is scanty, is similar in form to contemporary ware encountered at other first-century A.D. sites. The ceramic types characteristic of Qumran are now absent. The coins are less numerous, and the latest, which undoubtedly belong to this occupation, date from the year A.D. 72–73. It seems that the garrison at Qumran

Below: Steps of reservoir cracked in the earthquake of 31 A.D.; Opposite page: Assembly hall which also served as the refectory.

was withdrawn immediately after the fall of Masada in A.D. 73.

The Bar-Kokhba War. The abandoned buildings served as hiding places or centers of resistance by Bar Kokhba's insurgents during the Second Jewish Revolt in 132–135. The rebels constructed no new buildings, but they left behind a number of their coins. They represent the final episode in the history of Khirbet Qumran.

The most important periods in the history of Qumran are phases I-b and II, during which the settlement reached its greatest extent. The plan of the settlement, which was practically unchanged throughout the two periods, had two interesting aspects: the elaborate water supply system and the communal buildings. The rainwater collected in Wadi Qumran was conveyed to the settlement through an aqueduct, which supplied eight cisterns in phase I-b and seven cisterns in phase II. A large settling basin was constructed at the point where the aqueduct entered the walls and smaller basins were dug before each cistern or group of cisterns. There were two baths, one near the entrance on the northwest, and the other on the southeast. This system was designed to fill the needs of a large community living in an arid region. However, the care taken in constructing these installations may suggest that they were intended for the

ceremony of ritual immersion. The communal buildings held an important position at Qumran. They include a large kitchen, a large refectory, several assembly halls, storerooms, and workshops. There were few rooms, on the other hand, which might have served as actual living quarters. An extensive cemetery comprising some 1,100 graves was uncovered to the west of the ruins. These are individual graves, dug in rows and oriented on a north–south axis. All the graves excavated in the main part of the cemetery are of men. In an extension to the east, where the graves are placed haphazardly, women and children were also buried. The large number of interments in the cemetery is altogether out of proportion to the small amount of living quarters and the length of time the site was occupied. It was therefore concluded that Khirbet Qumran was the center of a sect of which most of its members lived dispersed throughout the area.

The Qumran Area. The cliffs dominating Khirbet Qumran are honeycombed with many natural caves. The survey in 1952 revealed twenty-six caves or crevices containing pottery identical with that of Qumran. Among these are the caves, numbers 1, 2, 3, and 6, containing scrolls to which number 11 was added in 1956. These caves were used by the people of Qumran during the phases I-b and II. Some were suitable for living quarters but many

served only as storerooms, or as hiding places for those who lived in nearby tents or huts. In fact, one of these crevices was found to contain a tent pole. The caves in the marl terrace on the other hand, are not natural and had been dug out to form dwellings. Two small cemeteries, in which men, women, and children were buried, were discovered north and south of the Qumran Plateau.

The number of people who lived in or near the caves and who assembled in the buildings of Khirbet Qumran during the village's most populous period probably reached some two hundred. These people earned their livelihood from various occupations, as is indicated by the workshops, by raising flocks and by growing a number of crops suitable for the arid soil of this region. An ancient road connecting Qumran and the el-Buqei'a Plain runs above the cliff, along a plateau where various cereals were grown. Between Khirbet Qumran and 'Ein Feshkha, 3 kilometers to the south, the littoral plain was irrigated by means of small springs, where even today the slightly saline water of the region facilitates the growth of reeds and scrub. Date palms were also cultivated, as is shown by the palm trees, fronds, dried dated, and pits found in the ruins and in the caves. The salt and asphalt of the Dead Sea probably provided additional occupations for the local inhabitants.

The natural resources of the region were exploited as early as the Iron Age. Remains of a building similar to one found under the ruins of Khirbet Qumran is visible south of Wadi Qumran. The building may date to the ninth century B.C. After

a very brief occupation it was abandoned when the occupants moved to the Qumran Plateau, which boasted a more favorable climate and a better defensive position. The wall bounding the irrigated and cultivated area seems to date from the same period. Near this wall, which continued to be used by the religious community of Qumran, was discovered a square structure, containing pottery contemporary with that of Khirbet Qumran. This structure was evidently a watchtower or a building where agricultural works were carried out within the protective confines of the wall. It is very likely that this ancient wall extended to 'Ein Feshkha where a wall, though differently constructed, was built along the course of the first wall.

'EIN FESHKHA

An important settlement lay immediately to the north of the large spring at 'Ein Feshkha. It contained a large rectangular building with a central courtyard surrounded by rooms and was flanked on the south by an enclosure wall with a shed and on the north by a courtyard containing cisterns. The rooms on the west were used for living quarters or administrative purposes, and the remainder of the building was occupied by storerooms. This building was clearly not a private residence, and was suited to the needs of a religious community. As at Khirbet Qumran, here, too, mainly public buildings are found, while the members of the sect dwelled in the surroundings.

The excavators distinguished three occupational phases, whose dates can be determined by the pottery and coins.

Of the first phase little evidence has remained, but the pottery is identical to that of phase I-b at Qumran, a date which is also confirmed by coins which range from the time of Alexander Jannaeus down to Matthias Antigonus. The second phase is undoubtedly contemporary with phase II at Qumran. The pottery is identical, and the coins range in date from the reign of Herod Archelaus until the second year of the First Jewish War. The temporary abandonment of the settlement between phases I and II and the widespread destruction which marks the end of phase II demonstrate even more clearly that Feshkha and Khirbet Qumran existed at the same time. Phase III was more difficult to date. Only a small portion of the ruins had been reoccupied. Although it can be assumed that, as at Qumran, a Roman garrison was stationed at Feshkha, this is not confirmed by the numismatic evidence. Unlike Qumran no Roman coins between the years A.D. 67/68 and 72/73 are found, and there were many coins from the time of Agrippa II and one coin of Domitian. It seems then that Feshkha remained abandoned for some time after its destruction in A.D. 68, and toward the end of the first century A.D., a small settlement existed on the site. Another parallel in the history of the two sites appears somewhat later when, as several coins of the Bar-Kokhba Revolt indicate, a band of insurgents passed through Feshkha or remained there for some time. To the south of the building is a cattle pen, which was enlarged in phase II. Along its north wall a shed was constructed, one side of which provided shelter in Byzantine times for the gardener of the monastery at Khirbet Mird (9 kilometers [5.5 miles] to the west), as is related by John Moschus (*Pratum spirituale,* 158).

In phase II, another enclosure was built on the north side of the building. In its eastern half is a system of canals and reservoirs which are clearly not cisterns, although their function is unknown. According to one theory, these were ponds for breeding fish. Another more plausible theory is that they were vats of a tannery. Such an installation, indeed, requires large quantities of water. While there are positive grounds for this hypothesis, nevertheless, its plan does not entirely correspond to that of known Roman tanneries, and

Opposite page, left: Bowls in situ in the pantry.
Right: Tables in the Scriptorium, *reconstructed.*
This page: Pottery vessels of the first century A.D.

the analysis of samples extracted from the vats revealed no trace of tannin, essential for processing the hides.

In any case, the connection between Feshkha and Qumran is certain. Feshkha was the less important settlement, based on agriculture and perhaps industry, and served the main community at Qumran.

SUMMARY

The area was inhabited several times, commencing with the Israelite buildings of the City of Salt to the Byzantine hermitage at 'Ein Feshkha. The most important occupation extended from the second half of the second century B.C. down to the year A.D. 68, and it left its traces in the caves of the cliffs and the marl terrace, in the buildings at Qumran and Feshkha. The people who dwelled in the caves and in the huts near the cliffs assembled at Qumran to engage in their communal activities. They worked in the workshops of Qumran or on the farm at Feshkha, and after their death they were buried in one of the two cemeteries. This was a highly organized sect, as is indicated by the careful planning of the buildings, the water system, the numerous communal facilities, and the orderly arrangement of the graves in the large cemetery. The special method of burial, the large assembly hall that also served as a collective dining room, and the remains of meals that were so meticulously interred, all indicate that this community had a religious character and practiced its own peculiar rites and ceremonies. The scrolls discovered at Qumran confirm these conclusions and furnish ad-

This page, top to bottom: Entrance to cave 11; Workshop and kiln (locus 101); 'Ein-Feshkha. Cisterns and channels in the northern enclosure.

ditional information. The archaeological evidence proves that the scrolls belonged to the religious community that occupied the caves and the buildings at Qumran. These scrolls represent the remains of their library, which contained works describing the organization of the community and the laws that governed its members.

The archaeological discoveries are thus interpreted in the context of a living community. Some of the scrolls contain allusions to the history of this sect, which had detached itself from the official Judaism of Jerusalem in order to lead a separate existence in the desert, absorbed in prayer and labor while awaiting the Messiah. The interpretation of these historical references has been the subject of much debate. The archaeological discoveries cannot be expected to provide a decisive answer. They merely lend credence to the hypothesis that a community flourished on the shore of the Dead Sea from the second half of the second century B.C. until A.D. 68, and that the events described in the manuscripts occurred at Qumran during this period.

The religious affiliation of the community has also been the subject of controversy. Most scholars, however, consider the community to have been in some way connected with the Essenes. This is not contradicted by the archaeological evidence, which indeed provides corroboration. Pliny relates that the Essenes lived in isolation among palm trees in a region west of the Dead Sea — at a safe distance from its pestilential salt water. To the south is the region of En-Gedi. There is only one site which corresponds to this description between En-Gedi and the northern end of the Dead Sea: the Qumran plateau. There is only one region where palm trees can grow in quantity and where it is certain they did grow in ancient times: the region between Khirbet Qumran and Feshkha. The Essenes of Pliny, then, were the religious community of Qumran-Feshkha.

R. DE VAUX

BIBLIOGRAPHY

R. de Vaux, *RB* (1949), 234–37, 586–609: 60 (1953), 83–106, 540–61; 61 (1954), 206–36; 63 (1956), 533–77: 66 (1959), 225–55 • J. T. Milik, *Ten Years of Discovery in the Wilderness of Judaea*, London, 1959 • S. Schulz, *ZDPV* 75 (1960), 50–72 • H. Bardtke, *TLZ* 85 (1960), 263–74 • J. B. Pool–R. Reed, *PEQ*, 1961, 114–23 • R. de Vaux, *L'archéologie et les manuscrits de la Mer Morte*, London, 1961: idem, *Archaeology and the Dead Sea Scrolls* (The Schweich Lectures of the British Academy), London, 1973 • P. Bar-Adon, *EI* 10 (1971), 72–89 (Hebrew).

RABBATH-AMMON

IDENTIFICATION AND HISTORY. Rabbath-Ammon is identified with present-day Amman by the similarity in name and the topographical and archaeological evidence. The city is not mentioned in historical sources predating the Bible, but the archaeological finds indicate that it was settled as early as the Middle Bronze Age. A Late Bronze Age temple was discovered there.

Rabbath-Ammon is first mentioned in the Bible in the accounts of the Israelite conquest, in the story of the bedstead of King Og of Bashan (Deuteronomy 3:11), in the topographical description of Aroer (Joshua 13:25), and especially in the description of its conquest in the days of King David. Joab, David's army commander, captured only the "royal city" and the "city of waters," and the rest of the city was taken by David (II Samuel 12:26–31, I Chronicles 20:1–3).

Rabbath-Ammon apparently freed itself from Judah's suzerainty following the split of the Judean Kingdom and became once more the capital of the re-established Ammonite state. Aside from various prophecies (Amos, Jeremiah), there are few references to Rabbath-Ammon until the mention of its destruction at the hands of the *bnei Qedem* at the beginning of the sixth century B.C. (Ezekiel 25:5). During the Persian period it was under the rule of the Tobiads.

Ptolemy II changed the city's name to Philadelphia and made it into a Hellenistic city. The name took root slowly, for Zenon (third century B.C.) and Polybius (second century B.C.) still use the old name of Ραββαθαμμάνα.

In 218 B.C. Antiochus III conquered Rabbath-Ammon by penetrating through the water works of the upper city. These are the installations which were uncovered by the Italian archaeological expedition.

During the decline of the Seleucid state, Rabbath-Ammon was ruled by the tyrants Zenon Cotylas and his son Theodorus, and it successfully withstood the siege of Alexander Jannaeus. Pompey annexed the city to the Decapolis (63 B.C.). At the end of the Second Temple period, Rabbath-Ammon was engaged in border disputes with the Jews in Jewish Transjordan (Paraea). In the year A.D. 66, the city of Rabbath-Ammon fought against the Zealots.

From the time of Trajan, Rabbath-Ammon was included in the province of Arabia (A.D. 106). When the new route from Elath to Damascus was built, the city stood on the crossroads of this road and astride the routes to the desert and to Gerasa, and it consequently became a large and rich city. It declined slightly from its greatness during the Byzantine period. Following the Arab conquest in A.D. 635, it was again given its Semitic name, Amman, and became the capital of the Balqa district. In the Crusader period, it was ruled by a Transjordanian prince called Ahamant.

During the Mameluke period, Rabbath-Ammon was deserted, and it was resettled in 1876 by a group of Circassians on the initiative of Sultan Abdul-Hamid. In 1921, Rabbath-Ammon became the capital of the Emirate of Transjordan, and it is today the capital of the Kingdom of Jordan.

In the center of the site is the acropolis, which stands on three terraces. At its foot, in the water-rich Amman Valley, stood the Roman city. Today, the modern city of Amman is located there. There are ancient cemeteries in the surrounding mountains across the valley, especially to the south.

EXCAVATIONS

In 1927, an Italian expedition, led by G. Guidi, conducted excavations at the site. These were later directed by R. Bartoccini in the years 1929–33. The results of the excavations were published in a very fragmented manner. The rest of the discover-

City coin of Philadelphia-Rabbath-Ammon.

Qumran.   Cemetery in the foreground and main building in the center. Air view from the east.

ies (principally tombs and a number of houses) were revealed as a result of the widespread building activities in Amman from 1945 on. G. L. Harding examined the Late Bronze Age temple after it was discovered in 1955, and J. B. Hennesy excavated it in 1966.

The Finds. Middle Bronze Age objects were discovered in tombs on Jebel Qal'ah and near the top of the acropolis. The Italian excavators attributed the walls of the upper terrace of the acropolis to the end of the Middle Bronze Age (about the sixteenth century B.C.).

In 1955, during the expansion of the Amman airport, a small temple was discovered. It is almost square in plan (15 square meters) and its outer walls (2 meters thick) were made of unhewn stone, and their foundations were erected inside leveled ditches. Foundation offerings and remains of fowls and animals, which were sacrificed during the construction, were revealed beneath the walls. About forty gold utensils, beads, cylinder seals, and scarabs were found in the fill layers. These, too, were probably brought as offerings.

Besides local pottery, much imported ware was also found — Cypriot and Mycenaean (Late Mycenaean II–III). Many fragments of Egyptian stone vessels and of bone and ivory objects were also found. Hennesy detected three stages of construction and use, and in his opinion the temple was founded at the end of the fourteenth century B.C. and abandoned during the following century.

The site contains a large number of objects from the Iron Age, especially from the eighth and seventh centuries B.C. Building remains from this period are apparently concentrated on the upper terrace of the citadel. Some were uncovered by the Italians.

A great many interesting finds were discovered within the confines of the city. Of chief importance is the building inscription discovered in the citadel, and the fragment of another found in the area of the theater, both dating from the ninth century B.C. These are the only known monumental Ammonite inscriptions. Another inscription discovered recently at Tell Siran in the outskirts of the city is incised on a bronze bottle. It is a dedicatory inscription of Amminadab son of Ḥiṣalel son of Amminadab, King of the Ammonites, and dates from the seventh century B.C. Mention should also be made of several seals of royal Ammonite offi-

cials. Among them are Adonipelet, servant of Amminadab, Adoninur servant of Amminadab, Aliah maidservant of Ḥananel and 'Anmwt maidservant of Dblbs. Other short inscriptions were found incised on a group of stone statues which apparently represent Ammonite rulers or gods. Similar statues have been recently uncovered by chance in the city suburbs.

A group of seven tombs were excavated by G. L. Harding, and another tomb was examined by R. Dajani. All the graves are situated within the confines of the city and are of the type common in Israel and Transjordan at the end of the Iron Age, namely, shaft tombs which contain burial chambers surrounded by benches. They date from the seventh and the beginning of the sixth centuries B.C. The tombs contained, inter alia, pottery of the type known as Ammonite ware.

In surveys conducted by N. Glueck and others, it was established that on the western side of the city and at a slight distance from it, there existed a line of fortifications consisting of eighteen or nineteen round towers. Glueck attributed them to the Ammonite period, and their Ammonite origin was confirmed in excavations at Rujm el-Malfuf and Khirbet el-Hajar, carried out by R. Boraas and H. Thompson respectively.

In the foundations of the Roman sanctuary from the time of Hadrian (on the middle terrace of the upper city), the Italians exposed a rock which had been shaped to a point on its east side. A channel was cut into the rock face, and to the south was built a flight of steps. On the north side is a kind of small cave. In Bartoccini's opinion, the rock was an altar to Milcom, the god of the Ammonites, which existed in the days of King David and later.

Hellenistic remains include the wall of the acropolis, constructed of polygonal blocks in dry construction, a subterranean reservoir at the north end of the acropolis, connected to the interior of the citadel, and two reliefs (a frontal Osiris, and Bastet in profile) dating from the fourth–third centuries B.C., found in secondary use in the Roman agora.

The majority of the remains on the site date from the Roman era. Nabataean remains are few, despite the fact that Rabbath-Ammon was located on the border of the Nabataean Kingdom. In 1946, Harding published his report of a Nabataean tomb, made up of two subterranean rooms, which had been filled with earth and rocks in an earlier period. The

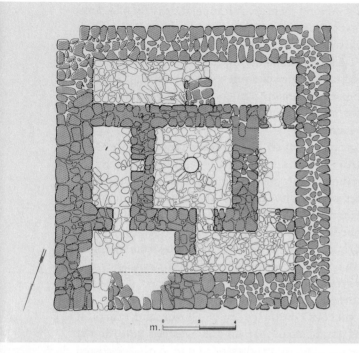

Nabataeans dug a narrow corridor through this debris. The tomb contained Late Hellenistic lamps, a Herodian lamp, egg-shaped phials, Eastern *terra sigillata,* glass bottles, and two, almost whole, painted Nabataean bowls.

Most of the extant ancient buildings in Rabbath-Ammon belong to the Antonine period, which was the city's most prosperous era. These include the nymphaeum, odeum, and theater in Naḥal Ammon, the propylaea and steps of the acropolis, the sanctuary of Zeus, built on the second terrace of the acropolis above the Ammonite altar, another sanctuary on the summit of the acropolis, and the agora, a plaza surrounded by a double colonnade, which possesses a magnificent entrance and posts for guards. The agora (53 by 38 meters from east to west, approximately 5,000 square meters in area) is enclosed by a wall with a bench one meter above the surrounding area. The double colonnade stands

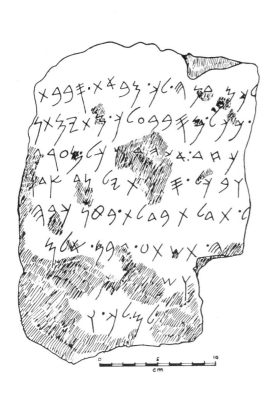

Both pages, counterclockwise from top left:
Plan of the LBA temple; Air view of the LBA temple;
Nabataean bowls, first half of the 1st century A.D.;
Stone statue of Ammonite god or king, dating to the
Iron Age; Facsimile of the Amman citadel inscription.

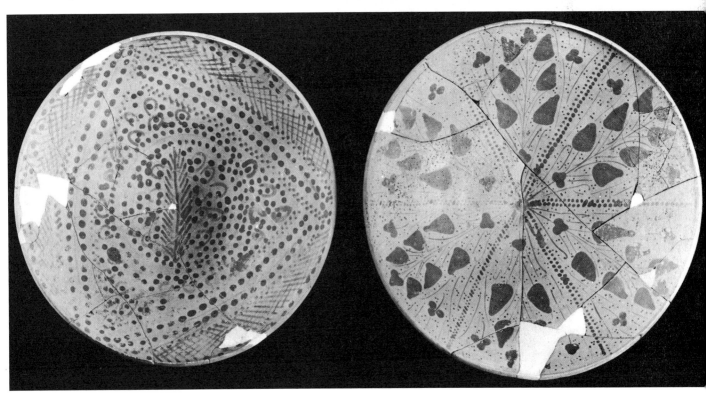

on a double stylobate, and has niches (3 meters wide) in the interior. On the eastern side of the agora were storehouses and white mosaic floors. At the facade, beyond the entrance, was a wide portico.

A large family tomb built inside a cave also belongs to the Roman period (published by Harding in 1950). Three small coffins and eight graves hewn in the floor were found in the cave chamber. Its rich finds include hundreds of pottery vessels, some fifty glass vessels, twenty-six gold earrings, silver articles (including coins), and many bronze objects. Most of the coins (among them also a coin of Agrippa I) are from the middle of the third century A.D.

Another Roman tomb was discovered (published in 1950), and also contained a wealth of objects. Judging from the coins found in it, the tomb should be attributed to the second century A.D.

At the entrance to the second terrace stands an ancient Arab building lavishly decorated in a style similar to that of Khirbet el-Mafjar. Houses of the same period were also discovered in the excavations in the acropolis (published in 1951): two large houses with courtyards and liwans. Some of the upper rooms were built on arches. The finds include incense burners of bronze, bone inlays, iron tools, and coins of the early Arab period and the Byzantine-Arab transition period.

M. AVI-YONAH — E. STERN

Below: Roman theater. Opposite page, top: Icarus — Part of a sculpture portraying Icarus and Daedalus — Hellenistic style. Bottom: Acropolis. Roman Temple.

BIBLIOGRAPHY

Survey: C. R. Conder, *Survey of Eastern Palestine* 1, London, 1889, 19 • Brünnow-Domaszewski, *Die Provincia Arabia*, 208–31 • L. Harding, *The Antiquities of Jordan*, London, 1959, 61–70.

Italian Excavations: G. Guidi, *Bolletino dell'Assoziazione internazionale per gli Studi Mediterrani* 1 (1930), [3], 15 ff. • R. Bartoccini, *ibid.* 3 (1933), [2], 16 ff.; 4 (1933–34), 4–5, 10 ff.; *idem, Bolletino d'Arte*, 1934, 275–85; *idem,* Atti del IV Congresso nazionale di studi romani, 1938, 1–8; *idem, Bollettino del R. Istituto di Archaeologia e storia dell'Arte* 9 (1941), 3–5.

Finds: G. L. Harding, *QDAP* 11 (1944), 67 ff.; 105–06 • E. Henschel–Simon, *ibid.*, 75–80 • G. L. Harding, *ibid.* 12 (1946), 37–40; 14 (1950), 81–94; *idem, ADAJ* 1 (1951), 7–16, 30–33 • R. D. Barnett, *ibid.*, 34–36 • Y. Aharoni, *IEJ* 1 (1950–51), 219–22 • Y. Yellin-Kallai, *ibid.* 3 (1953), 123–26 • G. L. Harding, *ADAJ* 3 (1956), 80; 4–5 (1960), 114 • W. A. Ward, *ibid.*, 8–9 (1964), 47–55 • G. R. H. Wright, *ZAW* 78 (1966), 351–57 • J. B. Hennesy, *ibid.*, 357–59; *idem, PEQ*, 1966, 155–62 • R. W. Dajani, *ADAJ* 11 (1966), 41–47; 12–13 (1967–68), 65–67 • S. H. Horn, *BASOR* 193 (1969), 2–13 • F. M. Cross Jr., *ibid.*, 13–19 • W. F. Albright, *ibid.* 198 (1970), 38–40 • R. S. Borras, *ADAJ* 16 (1971), 31–45 • M. M. Ibrahim, *ibid.*, 91–97 • H. O. Thompson, *AJBA* 2 (1973), 23–30, 31–38 • H. O. Thompson–F. Zayadine, *BASOR* 212 (1973), 5–11 • F. M. Cross Jr., *ibid.*, 12–15 • H. O. Thompson–F. Zayadine, *BA* 37 (1974), 13–18 • V. Hankey, *Levant* 6 (1974), 131–78.

RABAH, WADI

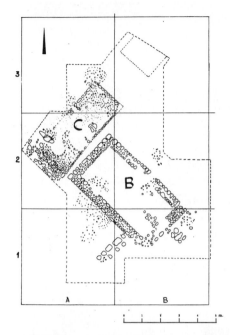

IDENTIFICATION. The ancient site is situated on the south bank of Wadi Rabbah, one of the tributaries of the Yarkon, about 1 kilometer east of Tel Rosh ha-'Ayin. Two Chalcolithic levels and mixed remains of the two Neolithic phases, Jericho IX and the Yarmukian, were identified there. At Tel Rosh ha-'Ayin itself, no remains earlier than the Early Bronze Age were found, and thus Wadi Rabah is the most ancient site in the area. It was abandoned at the end of the Chalcolithic period, and occupation was resumed during the Early Bronze Age on virgin soil close to the springs nearby, forming the first settlement at Rosh ha'Ayin.

EXCAVATIONS

In November, 1952, J. Kaplan conducted excavations at Wadi Rabah on behalf of the Israel Exploration Society. The first occupation of the site, stratum I, was found to belong to the Ghassulian phase of the Chalcolithic, and stratum II to an earlier phase, which had already been noted in 1950–51 in Kaplan's excavations in ha-Bashan Street in Tel Aviv (q.v.) and in 1955 at Tuleilat Batashi.

The pottery of stratum II is very similar in form to that of Jericho VIII: carinated bowls, bow-rim jars, and pithoi with flat thickened tops and small narrow ledge handles. However, there is a greater amount of slipped and decorated ware at Wadi Rabah than at Jericho VIII. Jars and not only bowls are red-burnished, and black burnish unknown in Jericho VIII also appears. Incised decoration is also frequent: herringbone pattern, chevrons, and parallel lines (sometimes on both faces of the vessel), roller impressions in geometric patterns and combing in broad bands.

The conclusion that the Wadi Rabah finds antedate those of Jericho VIII is illustrated by the fact that most of the pottery is burnished, whereas at Jericho VIII burnishing appears only on bowls, and at Tuleilat Ghassul none at all is found. In all these three phases of the Chalcolithic Age, the pottery shows a continuous evolution.

If we compare some of the pottery of these three phases with Halafian ware as a whole and particularly the Halafian ware and its imitations occuring in strata XVI–XIX at Mersin, Cilicia, a correlation can be found between the Middle Chalco-

Above, top: Room B and Wall C. Bottom: Foundations of building B, stratum II (Wadi Rabah culture).

lithic of Mersin and the Chalcolithic of Palestine. Since, however, certain shapes and ornamentation characteristic of the Wadi Rabah ware were encountered only in stratum XIX at Mersin, Wadi Rabah can be placed in the same horizon as that stratum, i.e., the beginning of the Middle Chalcolothic period in Syro-Cilicia (as it appeared at Mersin). The Chalcolithic phase of Wadi Rabah has since been discovered in many other parts of Israel.

J. KAPLAN

BIBLIOGRAPHY

J. Kaplan, *Chalcolithic and Neolithic Settlements in Tel Aviv and Its Surroundings,* Tel Aviv, (1948) (Stencil, Hebrew); *idem, IEJ* 8 (1958), 149–60; *idem, EI* 5 (1958), 9–24 (Hebrew, with English summary); *idem, BASOR* 159 (1960), 32–36; 194 (1969), 2–39.

RABUD, KHIRBET

IDENTIFICATION. Khirbet Rabud is a mound of about 60 dunams situated on the summit of a rocky hill surrounded on three sides by the bed of the Hebron River (map reference 15150933). It is the only large mound with Late Bronze Age remains in the mountainous area south of Hebron. Its water sources (apart from cisterns) were two wells about 3 kilometers north of the site: Bir 'Alaqa el Foqani and Bir 'Alaqa el Taḥta (upper and lower wells of 'Alaqa). The upper part of the mound was denuded down to bedrock but remains were preserved near the walls on the slopes.

The identification of the site with Debir = Kirjath-Sepher was first proposed by K. Galling and additional proof for this identification was provided by the excavations: 1. Biblical Debir was located south of Hebron in a district which included Anab, Socoh, and Eshtemoa (Joshua 15:49), all of which lay in a five-kilometer radius from Khirbet Rabud. 2. There is complete agreement between the archaeological finds and the biblical account of the history of Debir as an important Canaanite city (Joshua 11:21, etc.), Levitical city (I Chronicles 6:43), and an administrative center in Judah which is not mentioned after the First Temple period. 3. The story of Achsah daughter of Caleb (Joshua 15:15–19, Judges 1:11–15) became intelligible when considered in the context of the water-supply system at Rabud, which at the end of summer was dependent solely on the nearby upper and lower wells. 4. No remains of any other Canaanite city have been found in the mountainous area south of Hebron.

EXCAVATIONS

Two short seasons of excavations were conducted at the site in 1968 and 1969, sponsored by the Archaeological Department of Tel Aviv University and the American Institute for Holy Land Studies in Jerusalem. They were directed by M. Kochavi. Two trenches (A and B) were opened on the west side of the mound, and a number of burial caves were investigated in the Ush e-Ṣaqra cemetery on the east flank.

The first settlement on the mound dates from the Early Bronze Age I. Sherds of this period were found in both trenches. Some of the tombs were also in use in this period. Middle Bronze Age I

sherds were also found in trench A and in one of the tombs. The first walled city dates from the Late Bronze Age II-A (fourteenth century B.C.). Four strata of this period were revealed in trench A and were attributed to the fourteenth and thirteenth centuries B.C. The small wall, which enclosed an area of about 60 dunams, continued to be employed in all the strata. In this period burial in the Ush e-Ṣaqra caves was at its height. The finds in the tombs include a rich collection of imported Cypriot and Mycenaean ware together with local pottery.

Iron Age strata were encountered in both trenches. In trench A a stratum from the period of the Israelite settlement (twelfth century B.C.) lay directly above the last Late Bronze Age level. A rock-cut cistern as well as a number of tombs were attributed to the tenth century B.C.

A massive wall (W1) was erected in the ninth century B.C. (stratum III-B). It was revealed in both trenches, and about 900 meters of its course could be traced on the surface of the mound. The wall was some 4 meters thick and enclosed an area of 50 dunams. It was constructed in unequal sections (4–20 meters long), and the joints between the sections project about .5 meter from the line of the wall. The gate was probably erected on the northeast side where the village, which bears the name of the mound, now stands. The destruction level (stratum II-B), which was distinguished in all the rooms adjoining the wall, should be attributed to Sennacherib's campaign in 701 B.C. In this stratum, a great amount of pottery was found including vessels with *lamelekh* stamps and a seal inscribed "Shalom son of Aḥa."

The wall was rebuilt in the seventh century B.C. and it was widened in places to 7 meters (strata I-B, II-A). An unwalled settlement was also established in this period on a lower terrace northeast of the mound. Khirbet Rabud and the unwalled settlement were completely razed with the destruction of the First Temple. Only a few buildings, not surrounded by a wall, could be attributed to the period of the return from Babylonian Exile (stratum I-A). A Roman watchtower on the summit of the mound is the latest remnant of the ancient occupation of the site.   M. KOCHAVI

BIBLIOGRAPHY
K. Galling, *ZDPV* 70 (1954), 135–41 • H. Donner, *ZDPV* 81 (1965), 24–25 • M. Kochavi, in: *Excavations and Studies*, ed., Y. Aharoni, Tel Aviv, 1973, 49–75 (Hebrew): idem, *Tel Aviv* 1 (1974), 1–32.

ER-RAM

IDENTIFICATION. A Nabataean temple about 40 kilometers (24.5 miles) east of Aqabah (map reference 190887). The ancient name of the place is preserved in the Arabic name Jebel Ramm. In Nabataean inscriptions uncovered in the ruins of the temple and in the small shrine of Allat, near the spring of 'Ein esh-Shellaleh at the foot of the mountain, the name of the place appears as "Iram" (ארם).

The shrine of Allat near the spring of 'Ein esh-Shellaleh was first discovered by G. Horsfield in 1931. About a year later, the site was surveyed by R. Savignac, who found many Nabataean and Greek graffiti. During a survey of Jebel Ramm in the same year (1932) the remains of a temple were discovered. In 1934, the site was excavated under the direction of Horsfield and Savignac on behalf of the Ecole biblique et archaéologique française and the Jordan Department of Antiquities. In 1959, new excavations were undertaken by Diana Kirkbride, on behalf of the British School of Archaeology in Jerusalem in conjunction with the Jordan Department of Antiquities.

HISTORY

The history of the site is not recorded in any source and is known only from the epigraphic material found there. The dating is based on two Nabataean inscriptions found at the site, one in the ruins of the temple and the other at the spring of 'Ein esh-Shellaleh. The first inscription contains a fragment of a date: "And this is written on the day/ . . . of Ab in the year 40 and . . . ," from which we may infer one of two alternatives: 1. this refers to the forty-first or forty-fifth regnal year of Aretas IV, the only Nabataean king to rule more than forty years; the date of the inscription is then A.D. 31 or 36; 2. that the date is given according to the era of the Provincia Arabia, which would make it the year A.D. 147 or 151. The excavators found no mention of Aretas IV's surname (Philodemos) in the inscription, and hence they were more inclined to accept the second date. The other Nabataean inscription, found in the ruins of the shrine of Allat at 'Ein esh-Shellaleh, has been quite definitely assigned to the reign of Rabel II (A.D. 70–106). Since the king's two wives are mentioned, it is assumed that the inscription belongs to the later years of his reign. A third inscription, carved on the base of an altar in the ruins of the temple, is a Roman inscription which appears to mention the name of

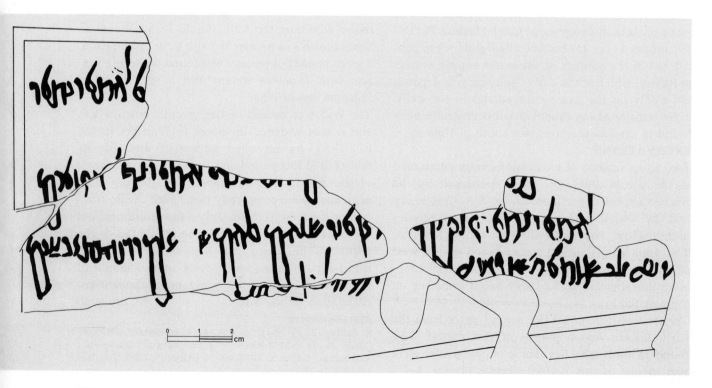

the Emperor Caracalla (A.D. 211–217), and belongs
not to the temple itself but to a later period.

It is difficult to accept the opinion of the excavators
that the temple was built in the first half of the
second century A.D. All the Nabataean temples in
Hauran (such as the temple of Seeia), in Transjordan (the ruins of et-Tannur, q.v.), and in the
Negev (Eboda, q.v.) were built on the same plan
about the end of the days of Obodas II or during
the reign of Aretas IV, the great period of Nabataean prosperity. It seems therefore that the temple at
er-Ram, which was erected near the main Nabataean caravan route leading from Arabia to Transjordan, was also built in the days of Aretas IV, and
the date in the inscriptions found in the temple is
to be interpreted accordingly. This view is corroborated by the typical Nabataean pottery found
in the temple area, which at Eboda was assigned
to the first half of the first century A.D.

In the days of Rabel II, the water from three or
four of the eleven springs near 'Ein esh-Shellaleh
was brought through canals to a large reservoir.
Excavations at Nabataean Eboda (q.v.) have also
yielded information on the water installations constructed in the reign of Rabel II. A Nabataean military camp was also apparently built in that period
near 'Ein esh-Shellaleh.

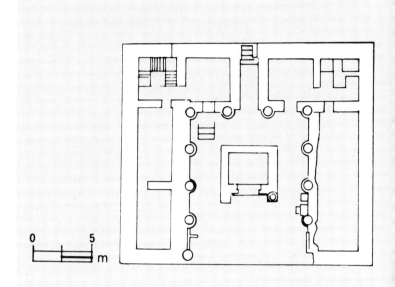

*Opposite page: Nabataean inscription. This page,
below: Altar with latin inscription. Right: Nabataean
temple, top; Kirkbride's reconstruction; Bottom:
Horsfield's and Savignac's reconstruction.*

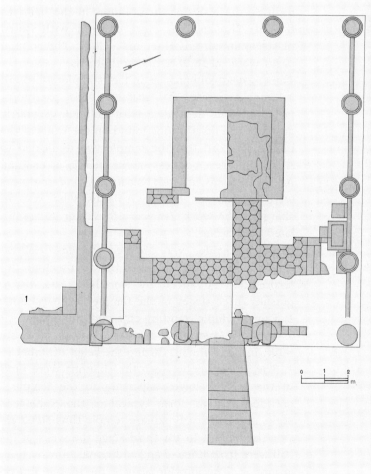

EXCAVATIONS

The main section of the temple consists of a hall (13 by 11 meters) which is entered from the east. The hall contains engaged columns, five on the north and south sides and four on the west side. Other rooms were built along the walls of the hall. In the center of the hall stood a small shrine (external measurements 4.94 by 4.1 meters) with stone-faced wooden beams set in the foundations to protect the building from earthquakes. The floor of the shrine was elevated .6 meter above the floor of the hall. The entrance of the temple, which also faced east, was flanked by antas with engaged pillars. The walls of the shrine were built of ashlar, and their typically Nabataean oblique dressing served to strengthen the plaster. A molded frieze probably decorated the upper part of the walls of the shrine.

The columns supporting the walls of the hall are well cut. On the drums of the two columns that are still standing in position were two mason's marks, which consist of two Nabataean letters indicating the order of the columns in the hall (see Eboda). The columns were covered with fluted plaster painted red, blue, and yellow. The column bases were made of torus-scotia-torus.

The engaged columns are in fact completely round columns separated by coarsely built partitions, plastered and decorated with colored geometric designs. The inscriptions found on the walls of the building record that the temple was dedicated to Allat, the great goddess of the people of er-Ram. All the artisans, masons, plasterers, and sculptors were Nabataeans except Anianus who was in charge of the work. He was a Syrian or an assimilated Nabataean.

Diana Kirkbride, who directed the new excavations in the temple, disputes the architectonic interpretation advanced by Horsfield. She distinguishes three stages in the temple's construction: 1. a small temple standing on a podium, which was a tetrastyle, peripteral prostyle. It was probably built, in her opinion, during the reign of Rabel II. 2. The partitions between the columns were built in the second stage, imparting to the temple a pseudo-peripteral form typical of the Nabataean style, and the nearly square temple thus stood inside the hall. 3. In the third stage the walls of the hall were strengthened and additional annexes built around it. The interior plan of the temple underwent no modifications at this stage.

It was correctly pointed out by the excavator that this is the only example of a Nabataean peripteral temple erected before the year A.D. 106, and from the inscription in 'Ein esh-Shellaleh she inferred that the temple was built in the reign of Rabel II.

SUMMARY

The general plan of the temple of er-Ram does not differ essentially from that of the other Nabataean temples erected toward the close of the reign of Obadas III and especially those built in the days of Aretas IV. The distinctive feature of this plan is a courtyard surrounded by porticoes on three sides, and the *theatron* of the temples in Seeia, where the shrine stands inside a hall. At er-Ram a shrine was first erected within porticoes, without a *theatron*, or else the porticoes took the place of the *theatron*, and in the second stage, partitions were built between the columns of the porticoes, thus converting them into a closed hall.

The temple at er-Ram is evidently to be assigned to the period of the reign of Aretas IV, while the water installations, and perhaps also the military camp near 'Ein esh-Shellaleh, are to be assigned to the reign of Rabel II. A. NEGEV

BIBLIOGRAPHY

R. Savignac, *RB* 41 (1932), 581–97; 42 (1933), 405–22; 43 (1934), 572–78 • R. Savignac and G. Horsfield, *RB* 44 (1935), 245–48. Diana Kirkbride, *RB* 67 (1960), 65–92.

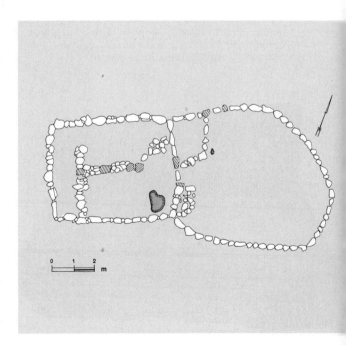

RAMAT MATRED

IDENTIFICATION. Ramat Matred (Matrada), situated about 7 kilometers (4 miles) southwest of Eboda in the Negev, contains a settlement from the Iron Age. The settlement was discovered during a survey, which was part of a study of ancient agriculture in the Negev carried out on behalf of the Hebrew University under the direction of M. Evenari. Along the valleys where the soil is suitable for farming, some twenty-five houses were found dispersed over a distance of about 1.5 kilometers, forming two clusters of seven to ten houses each. In addition to the houses and their courtyards, corrals, cisterns, and remains of terraces were also found in the valleys. In one of the clusters — settlement 108 — the plan was drawn of the adjoining cultivated area covering about 50 dunams and enclosed by a fence.

EXCAVATIONS

In 1959, excavations were carried out at the site under the direction of Y. Aharoni. Three houses were unearthed, each of them comprising two or three rooms. In front of the houses were large courtyards with silos and paved areas used for household tasks. Although the walls are built simply and of local stone, the houses are similar in plan to other buildings from the Israelite period.

Characteristic features of these houses are the stone pillars built in some of the walls and on both sides of the entrances. A burned layer on the floors of the rooms attested to a sudden and total destruction of the settlement. All the pottery discovered belongs to approximately the tenth century B.C. Two types can be distinguished: 1. wheelmade pottery common in that period in the country, some with a red-burnished slip; 2. coarse, handmade ware, very poorly fired. The latter type includes open cooking pots with flat bases, some of them with small lug handles. This type of pottery is known only from the Negev — as for example, from excavations at Tell Kheleifeh (Ezion-Geber) — and it was probably made for the local population by nomadic potters who used the most primitive methods.

A systematic archaeological survey was conducted at Ramat Matred and the close vicinity, and resulted in the discovery of twenty-seven sites from Middle Bronze Age I, eighteen sites from the Iron Age (six of which belong to Ramat Matred), and five from the Nabataean and the Byzantine periods. Along Nahal Avdat and Nahal La'anah, east and south of Ramat Matred, a line of four forts from the Israelite period were discovered on the road between Eboda and Beer Hafir. They belong to the network of strongholds standing along the route to Kadesh-Barnea, the biblical "way of the *atharim*" (Numbers 21:1). Settlement 108 lies about 3–4 kilometers from the nearest fort (142) on this line.

The agricultural settlement at Ramat Matred is to be dated to the tenth century B.C. It was apparently established near the Israelite caravan route in the time of the United Monarchy. After a brief period of prosperity it was completely destroyed at the end of the tenth century, probably by the armies of the Egyptian Pharaoh Shishak who included in the list of the towns conquered and destroyed by him many settlements and forts (חגרים) in the Negev.

Y. AHARONI

BIBLIOGRAPHY

Y. Aharoni, M. Evenari, L. Shanan, N. H. Tadmor, *IEJ* 10 (1960), 23–36, 97–111 • Y. Aharoni, *Qoves Sefer Eilat*, Jerusalem, 1963, 63–65 (Hebrew).

Opposite page: Ramat Matred. A building from the Israelite period. This page: Handmade pot of the type known as Negev ware; ca. 10th century B.C.

RAMAT RAḤEL

HISTORY OF THE SITE. The mound of Ramat Raḥel is situated on a prominent hill (818 meters above sea level) almost midway between the Old City of Jerusalem and Bethlehem. The site is occupied today by Kibbutz Ramat Raḥel. The ancient name of the site has not been preserved, but about 400 meters west of the mound is the well of Bir Qadismu, which preserves the name of the Byzantine church Kathisma (Κάθισμα).

In the course of the excavations carried out on the mound, it was established that the first settlement was founded in the ninth or eighth century B.C. when a royal stronghold was constructed surrounded by gardens and farmhouses. This was followed by a fortress with a magnificent palace in its center, erected by one of the later kings of Judah. The many seal impressions stamped *Yehud* (Judah) found on the site indicate that it was an administrative center during the Persian period. At the end of the Second Temple period, an ordinary settlement containing a large number of workshops occupied the site, which shared the fate of Jerusalem when that city was destroyed. The Tenth Roman Legion was later stationed there. According to various sources from the Byzantine period, the Kathisma Church and a monastery were built on the site. A poorly constructed Arab settlement that occupied the area in the eighth century A.D. terminates the history of the site.

IDENTIFICATION

The excavations did not confirm B. Mazar's proposal to identify the site with Netophah, since according to the Bible that city existed in the days of David (II Samuel 23:28 and *passim*), and no remains of so early a period were uncovered there. The results of the excavations prompted Y. Aharoni to suggest that the site is to be identified with Beth-Haccerem, an assumption shared by most scholars. Beth-Haccerem is first mentioned in a roster of Judean cities of the Bethlehem district which cannot be earlier than the ninth century B.C. (addition of the Septuagint to Joshua 15:29a, Καρεμ). In the time of Jeremiah, fire signals to warn Jerusalem were sent up from Beth-Haccerem (Jeremiah 6:1). In the days of Nehemiah, Beth-Haccerem was a district center (Nehemiah 3:14). From the Mishnah *(Middot* 3, 4) and from the Judean Desert Scrolls (Genesis Apocryphon XXII, 14, Copper Scroll X, 5), it is learned that Beth-Haccerem and the Valley of Beth-Haccerem were very close to Jerusalem. All these sources are consistent with the conclusions arrived at from the excavations, and it can be assumed that the ancient royal citadel was built on the site of the king's vineyards, hence the name Beth-Haccerem *(cerem* means "vineyard"). The later citadel and the palace, which was described by Jeremiah (22:13–19), were probably built by Jehoiakim, son of Josiah (609–598 B.C.). The window balustrades found in the excavations (see below, stratum V-A) are apparently those mentioned by Jeremiah in the above-named passage.

The church and the monastery that were built on the site in the Byzantine period are known by the name of Kathisma, called after the name of the sacred well *(Bir Qadismu)* where, according to Christian tradition, Mary, mother of Jesus, rested on her way to Bethlehem.

EXCAVATIONS

In 1931, a burial cave dating from the end of the Second Temple period was discovered south of the mound. It was excavated by B. Mazar (Maisler) and M. Stekelis on behalf of the Palestine Exploration Society. Excavations on the mound itself were undertaken in the summer of 1954 under the direction of Y. Aharoni, on behalf of the Department of Antiquities and the Israel Exploration Society. Five seasons of campaigns were conducted on the site. In 1959, the Hebrew University in conjunction with the above-named institutions sponsored the excavations, and in the following three years they were under the joint sponsorship of the three Israel

institutions and the University of Rome. M. Kocha-vi also assisted in the publication of the results together with L. Y. Rahmani and Antonia Ciasca, G. Garbini, and M. Testini of the University of Rome.

STRATIGRAPHY OF THE SITE

After five seasons of excavations the following main occupational levels were distinguished :

I. Early Arab period, seventh to eighth centuries A.D.

II-A. Late Byzantine period, sixth to seventh centuries A.D.

II-B. Middle Byzantine period, fifth to sixth centuries A.D.

III. Late Roman and Early Byzantine period, third to fourth centuries A.D.

IV-A. Herodian period, first century B.C. to first century A.D.

IV-B. Persian-Hellenistic period, fifth to third centuries B.C.

V-A. End of Iron Age, about 608–597 (587 ?) B.C.

V-B. Iron Age II-C, eighth to seventh centuries B.C.

Stratum V-B—The Early Citadel. Only a few remains were uncovered in this stratum since it had been almost completely destroyed during construction work carried out by the builders of stratum V-A. Near the southeast edge of the mound the excavators uncovered a section of a casemate wall which probably belongs to this stratum. One of its walls, which has been preserved above floor level, is built of ashlar masonry, like the inner wall of the later casemate wall (see below, stratum V-A), from which it can be inferred that the early casemate wall had also belonged to a royal citadel. On the northern slope of the mound, the excavators discovered a quarry which supplied the building stones and which was covered by the wall of stratum V-A. The early citadel was not large since less than 50 meters north of the casemate wall was an agricultural terrace, and the area was evidently planted with gardens or vineyards. At a distance of 100 meters north of the casemate wall were the remains of a house, evidently a private dwelling that had been built at the foot of the royal citadel and destroyed and filled with stones when the wall of stratum V-A was erected. Two seal impressions were found in this house bearing the inscription "[Belonging] to Shebna [the son of] Shaḥar." The same seal impression is known from Tell en-Naṣbeh and Lachish.

Most of the finds made in this stratum came from

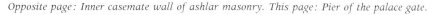

Opposite page: Inner casemate wall of ashlar masonry. This page: Pier of the palace gate.

General plan of the Iron Age citadel, strata VA-VB.

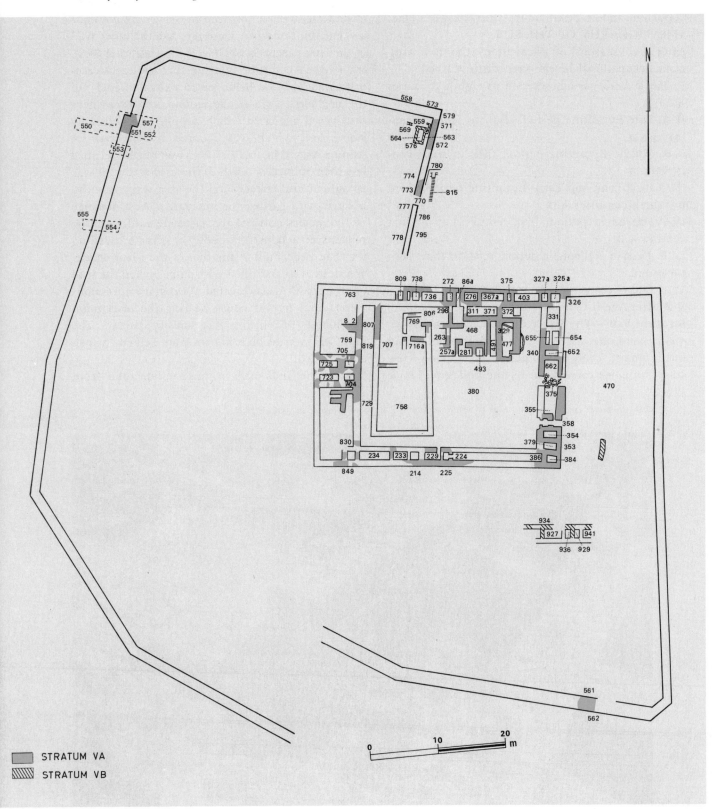

STRATUM VA
STRATUM VB

the fill used to level the ground in constructing stratum V-A. The pottery was of the eighth and seventh centuries B.C. One hundred forty-five jar handles with the royal *(lamelekh)* stamp were found, most of them of the two-winged type (class C) and some of the four-winged type (classes A and B). More than half came from the rubble fill of stratum V-B, and it appears that they belonged to this stratum and in all probability went out of use before its end. Seal impressions were also found with names, some identical with stamps discovered at other Judean mounds, such as Tell en-Naṣbeh, Beth-Shemesh, and Lachish. One handle bore two impressions side by side, one *lamelekh*/Hebron with the two-winged symbol and the other a private seal **לנרא/שבנא** "[belonging] to Nera [son of] Shebna." This is the first instance that the impressions of royal and "private" seals were found stamped on the same handle. A Hebrew ostracon was also found bearing two names, **אחיהו, חסדיהו** (Aḥiyahu, Ḥasdiyahu).

Stratum V-A. Near the end of the Iron Age, there arose on the site a new royal citadel whose construction must have required a large measure of technical skill and effort. Not only were the fortress and its buildings constructed on a completely new plan, with an inner and outer citadel, but all the former buildings seem to have been razed to the ground and the terrain of the hill was considerably changed.

THE OUTER CITADEL was surrounded by a massive wall (3–4 meters thick), at least partly built with salients and recesses. Although only short sections of the outer wall were uncovered, it was possible to reconstruct its course without difficulty, following the topography of the site. The north and south walls of the outer citadel were approximately 165 meters long, and those running east and west 186 meters long, enclosing an area of about 20 dunams. Near the northwest corner of the wall was uncovered a section built in the middle of the slope, supporting a layer of artificial fill 2–3 meters high. The ancient quarry of stratum V-B (see above) was uncovered beneath this fill which also contained sherds similar to those found in the other fills of stratum V-A as well as many royal seal impressions. This fill seems to have served to level the area of the outer citadel. The homogeneous composition of these fills indicate that the outer wall must have been built at the same time as the inner fortress. Several trial pits made in the area of the outer citadel failed to reveal any building remains of the Iron Age (except for the scanty remains of stratum V-B). Hence, it appears that either the construction of the citadel was for the most part not completed, or that its leveled areas were used mainly for the muster of troops and chariotry.

The outer wall did not encircle the inner citadel on all sides. It made a right-angle turn and reached the inner citadel in the middle of its northern wall. This section of the outer wall was built of dressed stone laid in headers and probably one of the gates leading to the outer citadel stood here. Most probably an additional gate stood in the south, because the terrain reveals there a similar depression in the contour of the slope. Two gates must then have led to the level area on the west side of the outer citadel, which was somewhat lower than the rest of the area. The inner citadel was reached by ascending to an upper terrace encircling the western, southern, and eastern inner wall.

Proto-Aeolic capital.

Window balustrade of the palace.

THE INNER CITADEL is not large (about 75 by 50 meters), but its excellent construction leaves no doubt that it was the royal palace. This citadel is surrounded by a casemate wall similar in shape and size to other such walls of the Iron Age. In the north and south, its total thickness was 5.2 meters, comprising the outer wall, 1.6 meters, the inner wall, 1.1 meters, plus a 2.5 meter space between them. These dimensions apply to the foundations. The upper parts of the walls are thinner, at least in several of the sections. A well-preserved 50-meter-long section of the northern wall displays an upper course laid in headers (about 1.1 meters long) through the depth of the wall.

The rooms of the wall were for the most part unfilled and seem to have served mainly as storerooms. In the north wall, it was difficult to determine their original purpose, since most of them had been re-used in stratum IV-A. It is nevertheless clear that in their original form they were used as living quarters. In the middle of the southern wall, however, a complete section has been preserved. Here was found the threshold of a doorway, which led from the courtyard to one of the rooms of the wall, from which narrower doorways, also provided with thresholds, opened on rooms east of it. The walls and floors of these rooms were coated with a thick smooth plaster, which seems to indicate they were used as storerooms. Door sockets in the thresholds prove that the doors were barred from without.

THE GATE was in the center of the east wall. The total thickness of the wall at this point was 7 meters, and the outer wall near the gate was more than 2 meters thick. The straight double gateway was closed by two doors in a line with the two casemate walls. Above floor level, only the southern wall of the outer entrance has been preserved. It is built of large ashlars carefully fitted together. The passage between the two openings of the gate is paved with large massive stone flags which bear signs of a great conflagration. A narrower gate situated farther south apparently served for daily needs.

The gate leads into a wide inner court in the southeast quadrangle of the inner citadel. Beneath a heap of debris from the adjacent buildings, the court was found to be paved with a layer of leveled and well-packed limestone.

THE BUILDINGS OF THE CITADEL ran along the northern and western sides of the inner courtyard. The northern buildings, which abutted the casemate wall, apparently served for storage and domestic needs. In its center was an open court with rooms on all sides and two long storerooms in the east. One of the northern rooms of the building served as a passageway to a postern in the casemate wall. This was an underground corridor, which was covered with long dressed stone blocks, three of which were found in situ. The inner doorway of the passage, with a rounded stone lintel, is well preserved. Only a narrow and low opening gives access to the outside. The postern is opposite the outer gate, in the same section of the casemate wall that also serves as an outer wall, and thus it led directly from the inner citadel to the outside. In the area of the outer gate was discovered an opening to a tunnel hewn out of rock, which was perhaps connected with the postern gate.

The main buildings stood in the western part of the inner citadel. The construction of later buildings caused great damage to the structures in this area, and it was impossible to determine their inner plan. The western section of the casemate wall is about 14 meters broad and evidently served as a part of the palace.

The few wall fragments preserved above floor level show that the finest building techniques of the period were employed in the construction of the buildings and walls. In addition to the excellent workmanship of the gate described above, another well-built construction is the inner wall of the southern defenses, which was built of smooth ashlars laid in two headers and a stretcher. This wall closely resembles the inner wall of Samaria. On the floor of the inner court were found three complete Proto-Aeolic capitals as well as fragments of additional capitals. Another complete capital was found re-used in the crypt of a columbarium in stratum IV-A. In all were found the remains of at least six Proto-Aeolic capitals used to decorate the gates of the citadel and the buildings. This is the first time that such capitals have been discovered in Judea. They are similar in style to the capitals found at Samaria and to the one found by N. Glueck at Medheiba' in Transjordan. A fragment of a smaller Proto-Aeolic capital decorated on both sides was found on the slope of the mound.

Aside from the capitals, the excavators uncovered other fragments of decorative architectural ele-

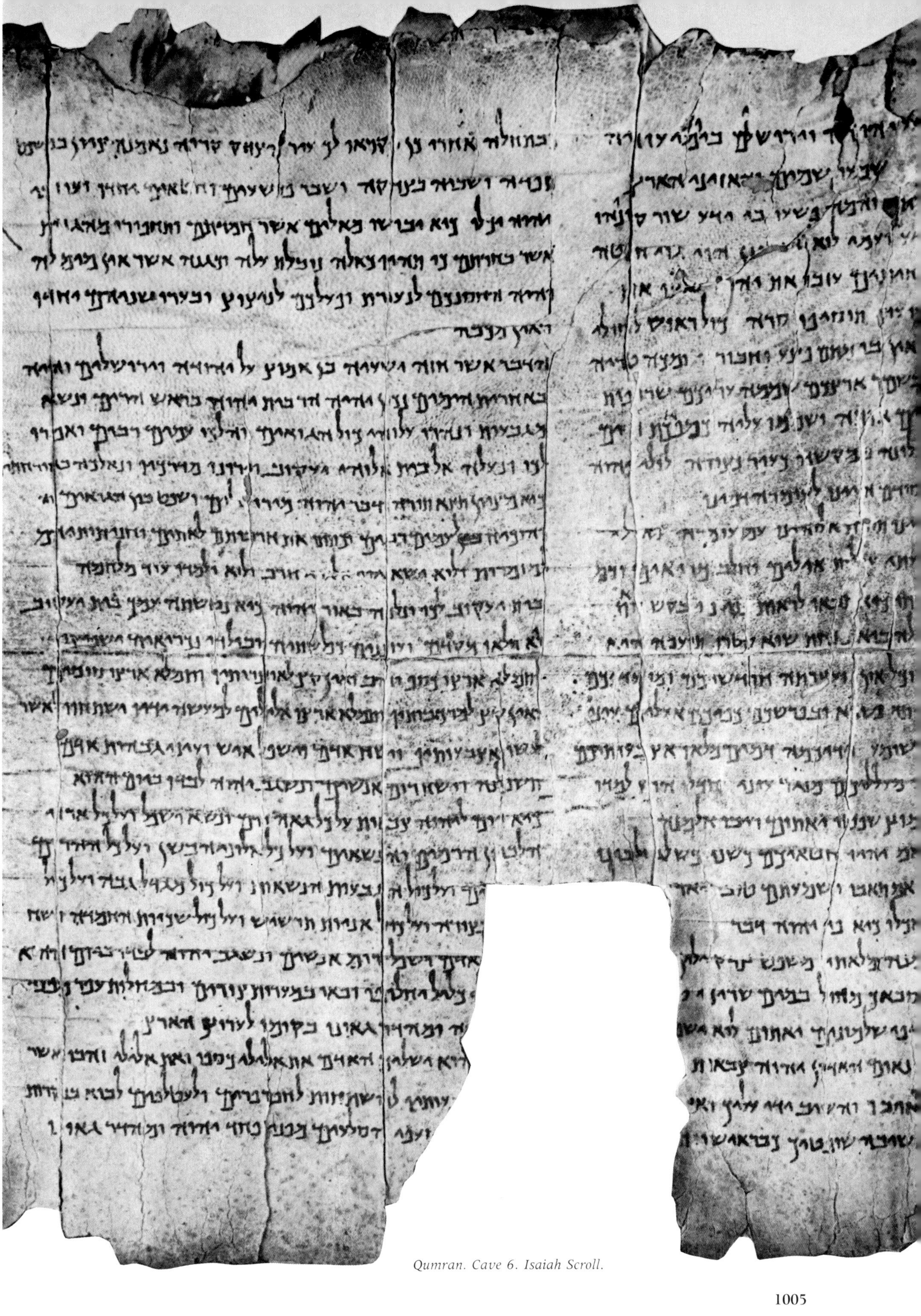

Qumran. Cave 6. Isaiah Scroll.

ments: a stone carved with two triangles several stones cut in pyramidal shape, probably used as crenellations on top of the city wall or the roofs; window balustrades consisting of a row of colonettes decorated with palmettes topped by capitals joined to one another in the Proto-Aeolic style. During the excavations of B. Mazar and M. Stekelis in the burial cave, a stone was found on the surface of the mound that bore on both faces a similar decoration of colonettes and linked capitals. A comparison with the motif of "the woman at the window"—common in ivory inlays—definitely established that these are the decorated window balustrades that adorned the facade of the palace. The colonettes and the capitals are of limestone and bear clear marks of red paint. At the top are grooves for inserting the beam which appears to have been made of wood. These windows may well be those of the house of Jehoiakim described by Jeremiah: "And cutteth him out windows; and it is ceiled with cedar, and painted with vermilion" (Jeremiah 22:14). These fragments of window frames were found in the heap of debris in the northwest corner of the citadel, and it can be as-

sumed that they adorned the upper story of the western facade of the western building to be seen by whoever ascended from the outer citadel.

The finds in the various rooms were meager, since most of the rooms had been destroyed below the floor level when the Byzantine buildings were erected. By far the richest find was uncovered in the eastern room of the northern building, where no Byzantine structure had been constructed. In it was found a heap of about two hundred pieces of pottery, mostly burnished bowls. Goblets of Assyrian Palace Ware were found here for the first time in Israel, as well as sherds of a jar painted black and red and depicting a king seated on a throne. Among the various seal-impressions found in stratum V-A, is one bearing the inscription לאליקם נער יוכן ("To Elijaqim steward of Yochin [Jehoiachin]"), which is identical with those found at Tell Beit Mirsim and Beth-Shemesh. W. F. Albright ascribed this stamp to an official of King Jehoiachin, the son of Jehoiakim. Stratum V-A may thus be attributed to the time of the reign of this king. It was probably destroyed with the destruction of the First Temple.

Stratum IV-B—Persian-Hellenistic Citadel. The main finds in this stratum are the many stamped jar-handles of the Persian period. Because of the fragmentary state of the buildings of this period, it is difficult to determine their plan. The area of

the inner citadel of stratum V-A remained in ruins and was not rebuilt in stratum IV-B. Most of the seals were found in refuse pits dug into the rubble. A number of strong walls of stratum IV-B were uncovered farther south, but since no floors were preserved their date cannot be established.

Several stamps found were identical with stamps from other mounds in Judea: Yehud stamps with the letters יהד; יה; יהד and an additional symbol (which previously was read העיר = ''the city''); ירשלם (Jerusalem); an F-shaped symbol; representations of animals, mostly lions; and rosettes. Among the stamps first found in Ramat Raḥel are examples with יהוד written *in pleno*, יה/וד written in two lines, יהוד/חננה similar to the stamp יהוד/אוריו found in Jericho, מצה in reverse (mirror-writing), etc.

Of special interest are stamps which bear the word פחוא, evidently an Israelite-Aramaic form of the word הפחה (district governor), which recently has been discovered on a Judean coin of the fourth century B.C. A number of seals are inscribed only יהוד/פחוא but some also contain a proper name יהוד/יהועזר/פחוא (four examples) and לאחזי/פחוא (five examples). Yehoezer and Aḥzai were probably two governors of the Persian province of Judea whose names had been previously unknown. F. M. Cross, on the other hand, suggested that the word be read פחרא (''potter'').

The exact date of the stamps cannot be determined since they were found in dump pits and fills whose contents are mixed. The pottery found with them, however, belongs for the most part to the late stage of the Persian period and the beginning of the Hellenistic period, and it is likely that most of the stamps date from the fourth century B.C.

Among the 270 seal impressions found, twenty-three bear the stamps ירשלם, twenty-one יהד, two bear the F symbol, sixty-nine יה, forty-nine יהד , twenty-eight יהוד, ten יה/וד in two lines, fifteen are פחוא stamps, forty-five bear images of animals, four of rosettes, and four miscellaneous.

Stratum IV-A — Herodian Settlement. In the area of the inner citadel of stratum V-A, a number of structures were uncovered — particularly small rooms — as well as various kinds of workshops and cisterns. On the floors vessels were found dating from the end of the Second Temple period. These installations were scattered throughout the area of the earlier citadel. Not only were ancient stones used in their construction, but here and there rooms of stratum V-A had also been reconstructed, especially in the sector of the northern casemate wall, which was evidently partly preserved. It seems that an ordinary settlement of the poorer classes was established here for the first time in the history of the site. It can thus be concluded that the citadel was no longer in existence, having been destroyed and abandoned in the Hellenistic period. There are

Opposite page, left: Sherd of jar with drawing of king seated on throne — Assyrian style. Below, both pages left to right: Jar handle with two stamps: Lamelekh/Hebron and ''(belonging to) Nera (son of) Shebna'' — 7th century B.C.; Jar handle stamped: Yehud/Yehoezer/governor'' — ca. 5th century B.C.; Jar handle with stamp: ''(belonging to) Ahzai (governor)'' ca. 5th century B.C.

no further references to a district of Beth-Haccerem in the Herodian period.

Most of the burial caves uncovered on the slopes of the hill, containing ossuaries, pottery, and glass from the end of the Second Temple period, probably belonged to this settlement. On a fragment of an ossuary was the inscription שמע[ון בר אלעזר] and on the lid of an ossuary a Greek inscription which reads: "Of Marilla [and] of the small children."

A columbarium cave was uncovered next to one of the burial caves, and in its center lay an early Proto-Aeolic capital which now served as an altar. One of the volutes of the capital was hollowed out in the form of a bowl.

One of the burial caves that was found blocked with the original closing stone contained, besides

Remains of the Roman and Byzantine periods. 1. Roman villa. 2. Byzantine storehouses. 3. Roman-Byzantine bathhouses. 4. The Kathisma Church.

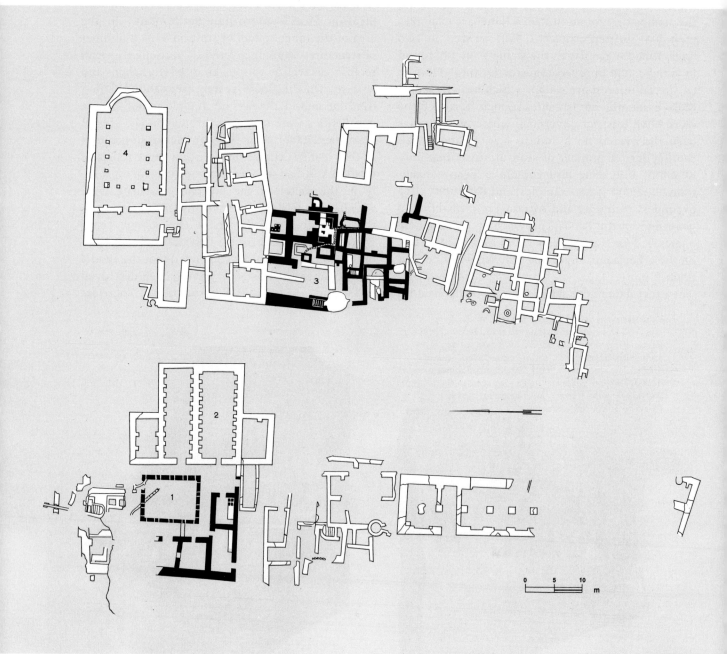

plain ossuaries and glass vessels, a number of lamps of the third century A.D. The form of the grave is typical of the Jewish burial caves in the vicinity of Jerusalem. This may perhaps be taken as proof of the existence of a Jewish community in Jerusalem or its environs in this late period.

Stratum III — Buildings of the Tenth Roman Legion. After the destruction of the Second Temple, the site was abandoned for about two hundred years, until the second half of the third century A.D., when buildings were erected by the Tenth Roman Legion which was stationed in Jerusalem from the reign of Titus to that of Diocletian. In the northern section of the western buildings of stratum V-A was built a typical Roman villa, the courtyard with a peristyle and surrounded by rooms. North of this villa were temporary structures of which only earth-filled foundations remained. A number of burial caves on the rocky slope north of the Roman villa were converted into plastered cisterns during this period.

Above the inner gate of stratum V-A a bathhouse was uncovered, consisting of a row of rooms with mosaic floors, pools of various shapes, and a hypocaust, all connected by a network of clay pipes and stone channels. The columns of the hypocaust and the floor were made of tiles, which bore the stamp of the Tenth Roman Legion.

All the Roman buildings continued to be used in the Byzantine period after undergoing repairs, and consequently no floors of the period of their original use have been preserved.

Stratum II — The Kathisma Church and Monastery. In the Byzantine period in about the year A.D. 450, there arose on the site a church and a monastery, which were erected by a wealthy matron of Jerusalem. These buildings are known from various sources as the Church of Kathisma (Κάθισμα). The church, which occupied the northeast corner of the inner citadel of stratum V-A, was built in the form of a basilica with an additional row of columns on the west side and adjoining it on the west was an annex which appears to have been the narthex. The mosaic floor with geometric designs is preserved only in the south and west sections of the church.

East of the church were the rooms of the monastery — a long, paved vestibule and rows of rooms arranged around an additional vestibule. West of the church was a large pool, and to its west were

two large halls which arose on the foundations of the northern building of stratum V-A. The bathhouse and the villa, as stated above, continued in use in this stratum as well, and south of these were many other rooms and buildings, some of them workshops and service rooms.

Two building layers are clearly evident in many of the structures, and this stratum was consequently subdivided into stages II-A and II-B. Most of the vessels found on the floors belong to the later stage (II-A). An Arab name from the end of the seventh century A.D. was incised on one of the jars, suggesting that the stratum existed until that time.

Stratum I. Poorly built structures of the Early Arab period were uncovered in this stratum, and with this the history of the settlement on the site comes to an end.

SUMMARY

The importance of the excavations conducted at Ramat Rahel lies chiefly in strata V-A—IV-B, that is, in the particularly rich finds from the end of the Iron Age and the Persian period. The first palace of a Judean king to be systematically investigated was found here, and here too was one of the most complete royal citadels thus far unearthed. This palace is also one of the most instructive examples of Israelite-Phoenician architecture, and its discovery considerably enriches our knowledge in this field. The many seal impressions of the Persian period are an important epigraphic addition to our scant knowledge of the period of the Return from the Babylonian Exile.

Y. AHARONI

BIBLIOGRAPHY

R. von Reiss, *ZDPV* 12 (1889), 19 ff. • A. S. Schneider, *JPOS* 14 (1934), 230 ff. • B. Maisler (Mazar) and M. Stekelis, *Mazie Jubilee Volume* (1934–35), 4–40 (Hebrew) • M. Cohen, *BJPES* 13 (1947), 83–86 (Hebrew) • L. Kadman, *BIES* 20 (1956), 47–48 (Hebrew) • Y. Aharoni, *IEJ* 6 (1956), 102–11, 137–55 • L. Y. Rahmani and U. Ben Horin, *ibid.*, 155–57 • Y. Aharoni, *BA* 24 (1961), 98–118; *idem, Excavations at Ramat Rahel, Seasons 1959 and 1960*, Rome, 1962 (with contributions by Antonia Ciasca, G. Garbini, L. Y. Rahmani, P. Testini); *idem, Excavations at Ramat Rahel, Seasons 1961 and 1962*, Rome, 1964 (with contributions by Antonia Ciasca, M. Kochavi, P. Matthiae, L. Y. Rahmani, P. Testini).

Discussions: F. M. Cross, Jr., *EI* 9 (1969), 20–27 • E. Stern, *BASOR* 202 (1971), 6–16 • Y. Yadin, in : *Eretz Shomron, The Thirtieth Archaeological Convention of the Israel Exploration Society*, Jerusalem, 1973, 52–66 (Hebrew) • N. Avigad, *Qedem* 4 (1976).

RAMLA

HISTORY. Ramla was founded during the years A.D. 705–715 by the Umayyad Caliph Suleiman bin 'Abd el-Malik. As its name attests *(ramel* — "sand") the town was built on sand dunes, about 4 kilometers (2.5 miles) south of Lod. To promote its growth, the Caliph Suleiman erected his own palace there on a site called the House of Dyers, as well as a splendid mosque which was completed by his successors. He also had part of the population of nearby Lod move to the new town. Ramla was made the capital of the newly created province "Filistin" (which included the regions of Judah and Samaria), and it became the most important economic center of the country in the Early Arab period. Ramla boasts many ancient buildings from the Early Arab, Crusader, and Mameluke periods, among them the White Mosque.

EXCAVATIONS AT THE WHITE MOSQUE

Excavations at the mosque were conducted by J. Kaplan in 1949 on behalf of the Ministry of Religious Affairs and the Department of Antiquities. The excavations attempted to ascertain which buildings, both aboveground and subterranean, belonged to the original mosque enclosure. It was revealed that the mosque enclosure was built in the form of a quadrangle (93 by 84 meters), with its walls oriented to the four cardinal points. It included the following structures: 1. the mosque itself; 2. two porticoes along the east and west walls of the quadrangle; 3. the north wall; 4. the minaret; 5. a building in the center of the area; 6. three subterranean cisterns.

The mosque was of the broad-house type, and was divided into two parts by a central row of pillars. The facade was pierced by thirteen openings. In the center of the rear wall was the mihrab. The roof was cross-vaulted and flat on the top. The excavations disclosed that the right half of the mosque deviates some 6 degrees north of the traditional east–west orientation. Of the west portico, only the foundations have survived. Of the east portico, a structure has remained that includes the main entrance. The north wall of the enclosure is divided in two by the minaret, which stands on the foundations of the wall. In the east part of the wall is a pointed arch, and a wide mosaic pavement extends along its west side. An Arabic inscription over the entrance to the minaret states that it was built by the Sultan Muhammad ibn Qalaun in the year A.D. 1318.

Of the building in the center of the enclosure only the foundations remain. This was possibly the building which held the basins for ablutions. The three subterranean cisterns were uniformly constructed of pillars topped by arches that supported barrel-shaped vaults. The southern and western cisterns were supplied by an underground water duct fed by a spring (probably from the vicinity of Gezer), and the eastern cistern received the run-off rainwater collected from the mosaic floor near the north wall. Also found in the excavations were two inscriptions that mention repairs made to the mosque. The first inscription relates that Sultan Baybars built a dome over the minaret and added a door to the mosque. The second inscription

The Minaret.

states that in A.D. 1408 Saif ad-din Baighut az-Zahiri had the walls of the southern cistern coated with plaster.

SUMMARY

Both the writings of the Arab geographers and the evidence uncovered in the excavations indicate that the building complex of the mosque was constructed in three main stages. The first stage may be dated to the period of the Umayyads, when the enclosure was erected in its original form. Of the earliest buildings there remain only the left side of the mosque oriented east–west, the east wall with the portico, the north wall (aside from the minaret), and the three subterranean cisterns. To the second phase during the time of Saladin is attributed the construction of the right side of the mosque, the western enclosure wall, and the central ablutions building. The third phase included the minaret, the portico east of the minaret, and

Inscription stating that the minaret was erected by Muhammad ibn Qalaun in 1318.

Ruins of the White Mosque.

The White Mosque enclosure.

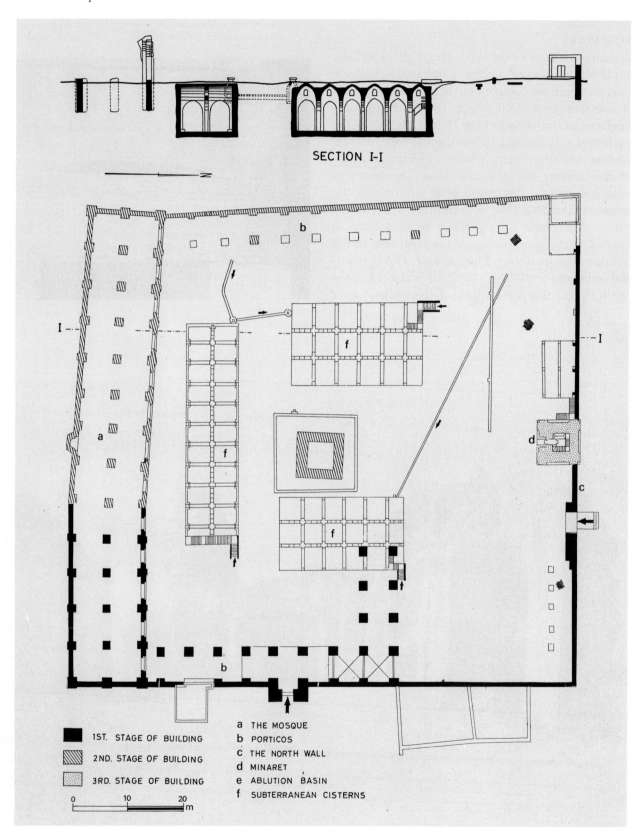

SECTION I-I

■ 1ST. STAGE OF BUILDING	a	THE MOSQUE
▨ 2ND. STAGE OF BUILDING	b	PORTICOS
⬚ 3RD. STAGE OF BUILDING	c	THE NORTH WALL
	d	MINARET
	e	ABLUTION BASIN
	f	SUBTERRANEAN CISTERNS

0   10   20
m

two halls attached to the east wall, outside the area of the mosque enclosure.   J. KAPLAN

OTHER EXCAVATIONS

Of the various excavations carried out in different areas of Ramla during the last decade, the major undertaking was conducted in October, 1965, by M. Rosen-Ayalon and A. Eitan. This excavation was concentrated in an area in the southwest part of the town. Several trial soundings on a smaller scale were dug simultaneously to complete the general picture. A large amount of finds — mainly of pottery, but also of glass, stone, and metal — was discovered immediately beneath the surface. The material was of a homogenous character and could be ascribed to the eighth or beginning of the ninth century A.D. Although this would point to a relatively brief period, four levels of settlement were distinguished, the lowest resting directly on virgin soil.

Slightly southwest of this area, no traces of occupation were found, but a trench to the north of the excavation revealed similar finds. This area must therefore have been the southwest limit of

Below: Mold for neck of jar and clay neck made from mold.
Bottom: Pottery lamps — Early Arab period.

the town in the Umayyad period. Several trial trenches, dug around the White Mosque and farther to the east, revealed that the border of the early settlement of the town continues eastward, where only early finds were uncovered, while toward the center later finds, up to the thirteenth-fourteenth centuries, were found above the early levels.

Found together with the large amount of complete objects and sherds were a number of installations, water channels, and ovens. There were also numerous wasters and molds, all pointing to the pos-

Right: Pottery horse — Early Arab period.
Below: Section of Muslim mosaic floor.

sibility of a potter's workshop having been located in the vicinity.

Although the pottery was for the most part non-glazed, limited quantities only being glazed, it presents a wide range of shapes, techniques, and decoration, and is of exceptional value for the history of Islamic pottery in Israel, especially for its early period.

A salvage excavation was carried out north of this area by A. Druks, followed by another undertaken by M. Broshi. In both cases, the pottery finds were very similar to those of the first excavation, corroborating the assumption that Ramla must have been an important center of pottery manufacturing during the early centuries of Muslim rule (A. Druks also found some Iron Age sherds, which are puzzling in this area).

An extraordinary discovery was made in 1973 in the southeast part of the town, in the courtyard of one of the private houses of the old quarter. Here a mosaic pavement, the first found in Ramla, was excavated by M. Broshi. The mosaic comprises three "carpets," two of them made up of various geometric patterns framing assorted floral, abstract, or geometric motifs. The one exception is the tiny unidentifiable animal in one of the medallions. Though thoroughly consistent with many of the pre-Islamic traditional mosaic decorations, they do not resemble any known Byzantine pattern. The third mosaic is the most conclusive and explicitly stamps the whole ensemble with its Islamic character. This is an inscription in early Kufic script, the only one known in Islamic floor mosaics. It consists mainly of a Koranic quotation, inscribed within an arch supported by two columns. This mosaic find suggests that a kind of private chapel was located in one of the early Islamic buildings of Ramla, its date also probably somewhere during the eighth century.   MIRIAM ROSEN-AYALON

BIBLIOGRAPHY

Conder-Kitchener, SWP 2, 271–73 • Clermont-Ganneau, ARP 1, 25 • L. A. Mayer, J. Pinkerfeld, H. Z. Hirschberg, Some Principal Muslim Religious Buildings in Israel, Jerusalem, 1950, 25–27 • J. Kaplan, 'Atiqot 2 (1959), 106–15 • L. A. Mayer, ibid., 116–17 (English Series) • Z. Vilnai, Ramla, Present and Past, Ramleh, 1961 (Hebrew) • M. Rosen-Ayalon and A. Eitan, IEJ 16 (1966), 148–50; idem, Qadmoniot 1 (1968), 138–40; idem, Ramla Excavations, Jerusalem, 1969 • M. Rosen-Ayalon, IEJ 26 (1976), 104–19.

ER-RAS, TELL (Mount Gerizim)

As a result of the discovery in 1962 of fragments of fifteen massive Aswan granite columns, strewn around the northern base of Mount Gerizim, an investigation was launched to determine the reason for the presence of such columns in that locality. The fragments were of such number, magnitude, and technical sophistication as to suggest that somewhere in the vicinity of Mount Gerizim a well-built structure of monumental proportions had once stood.

A clue to the use of the columns was found on a number of coins minted in the second and third centuries A.D. at Neapolis (modern Nablus). Several of these coins issued during the reigns of Antoninus Pius (A.D. 138–161) and Elagabalus (A.D. 218–222), among others, depict on their reverse a mountain with two peaks, each surmounted by a building. The larger and more detailed building, on the peak to the left, is a Greek-style temple with peripteral columniation. In front of the tetra-style facade of the temple, a stairway descends to the foot of the mountain and intersects a colonnaded street running along the mountain base. Buildings are shown on either side of the stairway, and a roadway winds up the valley between the two mountain peaks.

On the assumption that the designer of the dies for these coins was attempting to depict an existing temple and mountain near Neapolis rather than imaginary ones, an effort was made to determine the perspective from which the die cutter would have viewed the mountain. A photograph taken in a southeasterly direction from the center of modern Nablus showed a mountain profile that matched the one depicted on the reverse of the coins of the Neapolis mint. The valley between the two mountain peaks with the winding roadway appears clearly on both coin and photograph. The peak to the left of the two peaks of Mount Gerizim, which appeared on the photograph and which had the same profile as the peak to the left on the Neapolis coins, was the northernmost peak of Mount Gerizim on top of which is located Tell er-Ras. On the basis of this evidence, it was assumed that in the second and third centuries a

Above: Coin of the Neapolis mint — Antoninus Pius.
Below: General view of the mound, looking northeast.

Greek-style temple stood at Tell er-Ras on the northern extension of Mount Gerizim, which looms directly above the remains of ancient Shechem to the east and also above modern Nablus to the west.

The only recorded archaeological effort at Tell er-Ras was by C. W. Wilson in 1866 on behalf of the Survey of Western Palestine. Thereafter, the mound did not attract archaeological notice. In 1930, an expedition under A. M. Schneider of Göttingen dug on the higher central peak of Mount Gerizim but apparently did not concern itself with Tell er-Ras.

In A.D. 333, the Bordeaux Pilgrim, while making a journey to Jerusalem, passed by Mount Gerizim and noted that a stairway of three hundred steps ascended to the summit of the mountain. Epiphanius (A.D. 315–403), however, writing later in the same century, wrote that there were "more than 1,500" steps leading up the side of Mount Gerizim. Procopius of Gaza (died about A.D. 538) confirms Epiphanius' statement. Marinus of Neapolis (fl. about A.D. 440) wrote that there was a temple to the Most High Zeus on Mount Gerizim above Neapolis, which had been built by the Emperor Hadrian (A.D. 117–138).

EXCAVATIONS

An exploratory examination of Tell er-Ras was undertaken by R. J. Bull of Drew University in the summer of 1964. The excavation began as part of the joint expedition to Tell Balatah directed by G. E. Wright, both of which were sponsored by the American Schools of Oriental Research. A trench was dug across part of the top of the small mound, 120 meters by 80 meters, and on the first day of excavation part of a large structure was discovered amid heavy stone fall and off-cuttings. At the end of three weeks of digging, something of the nature of at least one structure at Tell er-Ras was known. This structure, called building A, was 21.48 meters long on its north–south axis by 14.16 meters wide on its east–west axis. On three sides (east, west, and south) were exposed the remains of a three-stepped *krepis* made of .38 meter high semi-hewn limestone blocks set in lime mortar. Only one drafted facing stone of the *krepis* was found intact. The *krepis,* originally sheathed in white marble, rested on a three-course podium also formed of roughhewn blocks set in cement. Only a small amount of Roman and Byzantine pottery was re-

covered from the probe trenches, but great quantities of polished marble and granite facing fragments were found. Sixty large architectural fragments were also recovered, including some badly battered Corinthian capital remains and pieces of large column bases.

A major campaign of excavation at Tell er-Ras was launched in the summer of 1966, during which building A was defined as the foundation of a temple oriented 14 degrees east of north, with a *pronaos* 8.24 meters wide and 3.3 meters long and a *naos* 8.24 meters wide and 10.12 meters long. Many architectural fragments were recovered, and the temple was dated to the second century A.D. by ceramic, architectural, and coin evidence. The builders had elevated the temple by constructing it on a platform. To accomplish this, a rectilinear configuration with 2-meter-thick walls was built, 64.91 meters long on the north–south axis by 44.21 meters wide on the east–west axis and was then filled with 8 to 10 meters of coursed rubble and cement and some earth. Previously existing structures and walls within the rectilinear perimeter were incorporated as they stood within the fill that made up the platform. The congruence of literary, numismatic, and archaeological evidence led the excavator to conclude that building A at Tell er-Ras was the Temple of Zeus built by the Emperor Hadrian.

Six plaster-lined interconnected vaulted cisterns were built sometime in the third century contiguous to the northern wall of the temple platform. Three cisterns were on each side of a monumental staircase that led from a green-marble-covered approach road up to the temple platform. The staircase itself and the approach road were both at the head of the long series of steps, which led up the side of the mountain from the city below. All the vaultings of the cisterns had collapsed at approximately the same time, probably due to an earthquake. In each cistern, great quantities of off-cuttings, architectural fragments, building stones, and voussoirs sealed in a 17 centimeter black silt layer. One hundred and eighty-three datable coins, all from the fourth century or earlier, and a great quantity of pottery and artifacts were recovered from the silt. More than 80 percent of the coins were from the first half of the fourth century, and 80 percent of the remainder were from the time of Julian II (A.D. 360–363) or before. The coins suggest that the collapse of the vaults probably occurred during the reign of Julian as a result of the earthquake of A.D. 362.

Two inscriptions were found, one carved on a fragment of a limestone column, the other punched in a flat piece of copper. The column fragment (.25 meter in diameter) was inscribed with the letters ΔII ΟΛΥΜ[Π ΙΩ] and was found in the stone fall of cistern 2. In the silt layer of the same cistern, a piece of flat copper (56 by 37 millimeters) had been punched with a series of small holes to form an inscription which read Διὶ Ὀλυμπίῳ . εὔπλοεις καὶ ἀμύντωρ.

Since the Neapolis coins had indicated the location of the Zeus Temple on Mount Gerizim, a survey was undertaken to locate the steps depicted on the coins and mentioned in the literary sources. Sixty-five steps were found cut into the bedrock outcroppings of the mountain. All of the steps located lay on a line which ran from the northern end of a

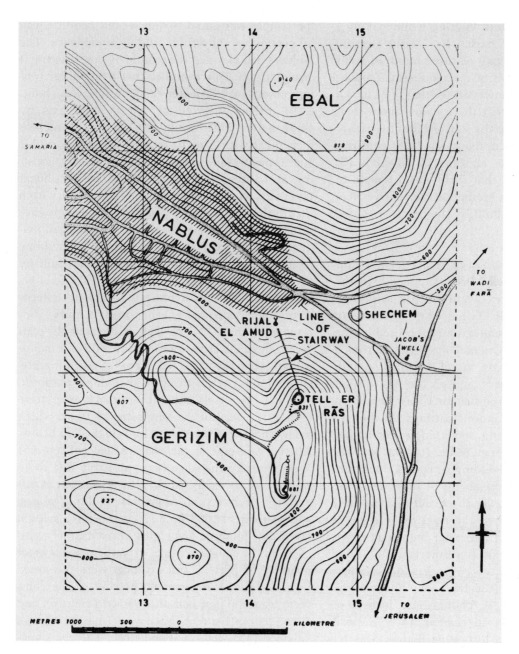

Plan of Tell er-Ras, showing line of stairway. Opposite page: Air view of the mound.

short green-marble-surfaced roadway in front of the temple on top of Tell er-Ras to the small mosque Rijal el 'Amud at the foot of the northwest slopes of Mount Gerizim. Based on the average height of the risers, the number of steps between the elevation above sea level of Rijal el 'Amud and the elevation above sea level of the temple was calculated as approximately 1,500, which is also the number of steps mentioned both by Epiphanius and Procopius of Gaza.

Near the top of the steps and on the slopes of the mountain about 100 meters due north of the Zeus Temple, foundations of buildings were found on both sides of the stairway. One building had originally contained at least four rooms. The largest room examined contained an eight-color mosaic floor with a complex geometric design. The sides of the building and the border of the mosaic within it paralleled the line of the stairway. Considering the size of the tesserae and the technique of construction, the mosaic floor was dated to the fifth century A.D.

The east-west probe trench cut in 1964 across the top of the mound disclosed that beneath the *krepis* of the Zeus Temple and the three-course platform on which it rested was a structure composed of at least three courses of unhewn stone laid without cement. The excavations in 1966 sought to determine the nature and date of the lower structure, called building B, which lay sealed under the cement and hewn stone of the Zeus Temple. Trenches perpendicular to building A and building B were dug on the east, west, north, and south sides of the mound. Excavation was with sledge, chisel, and pick, since on all four sides of building B there were 8 to 10 meters of coursed rubble and cement laid against it. Within this massive fill no architectural fragments or numismatic evidence were

found, and the only pottery retrieved was occasional sherds of Roman vessels. In three trenches, bedrock was reached at about 819 meters, and in all three of them, building B was found to be composed of between sixteen and eighteen courses of unhewn stone and rose to a minimum height of 8.7 meters above bedrock. The stones used in building B were of local limestone, about 1.2 meters long, 1 meter wide, and .5 meter thick. The building B remains were approximately the same height above bedrock on all four sides, but on the west side, at 6.77 meters above bedrock, there was an offset of 1.95 meters. This offset or revetment appears to be the same width and the same height along the entire length of the western side of building B. The revetment abuts the rest of building B and is of the same material and built in the same manner as the rest of the structure. The building's dimensions, including the western revetment, were

Opposite page: View of the mound, looking west. Remains of Zeus temple (building A). This page, left: Ten-meter high eastern face of building B. Below: Tell er-Ras — sketch plan.

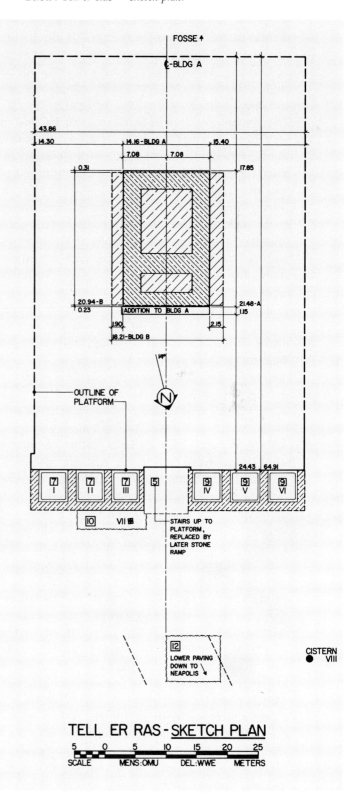

TELL ER RAS - SKETCH PLAN

established as 20.93 meters on the north–south axis and 20.14 meters on the east–west axis.

The interiors of the *naos* and of the podium of the Zeus Temple and of the center of building B were probed to determine whether or not they had internal structuring. None was found. In the podium of the Zeus Temple, however, the unhewn stones of building B were preserved twenty-one courses high, three courses higher than the highest course preserved at the sides of the structure.

The remains of building B can perhaps best be visualized as a half cube 20 by 20 by 10 meters, some 4,000 cubic meters of unhewn stone set in a square-shaped foundation trench cut into the bedrock of the mountain top.

During the excavation of building B, it became apparent that in order to stabilize the building as a foundation for the Zeus Temple, the Roman engineers had ringed the building with a girdle of stone and cement which was in places 10 meters high and 8 meters thick.

In the summer of 1968, work centered on completing the excavation of the cisterns and the examination of structures related to building B. The investigation of the northern of the perimeter of walls that formed the platform on which the Zeus Temple stood revealed that to the south of, and contiguous to, the 2-meter-wide hewn stone Roman wall was another wall, 1.4 meters wide and 4.9 meters high, built without cement of unhewn stone and founded on bedrock. Although the southern wall of the complex of walls which surrounded building B could not be excavated in 1968, in the opinion of the excavator, building B was constructed in the center of a courtyard of walls and on a center line which was the north–south axis of building B and the mid-point of the gateway in the east–west wall north of building B.

At the close of the 1968 season, it was discovered that part of the northeast corner of the perimeter wall around building B was not founded on bedrock but in earth. The foundation trench in which that part of the wall ran produced a modest amount of pottery, the latest of which was from the Hellenistic period and dated to the third century B.C., a date which was attributed to the construction of the walls around building B. Since building B was similarly built in the center of the courtyard of walls, and like the walls also founded on bedrock, it too was judged to be a third-century B.C. construction.

No steps or approach to building B were found in the trenches dug on the east, south, or west of the building. A probe dug midway between the gate and the northern face of building B yielded no evidence of steps or rampway which could be related to the structure.

A search for literary evidence which would help in the identification of building B raised, among other problems, the question of the location of the Samaritan Temple. The traditional location of the temple is a flat exposed area of limestone near the summit of the highest peak of Mount Gerizim, but it contains at present no datable remains. In 1930, an archaeological expedition under the direction of A. M. Schneider examined the high peak of Mount Gerizim, but found no evidence of the Samaritan Temple there.

While difficulty surrounds the date of the founding of the Samaritan Temple on Mount Gerizim, and the literature of its continuing history is confused, there is good literary evidence for its existence. Josephus gives an account of Sanballat's efforts and success in gaining permission from Darius III (336–330 B.C.) to build a temple on Mount Gerizim modeled after the temple in Jerusalem *(Antiquities* XI, 257). From the year 167/166 B.C., if Josephus is correct, it was known as the temple of Zeus Hellenios *(ibid.* XII, 261, 264), and in II Maccabees 6 : 2, it is called the temple of Zeus Xenios. Finally Josephus speaks of the destruction of the Samaritan Temple in 128 B.C. by John Hyrcanus two hundred years after its founding *(ibid.* XIII, 254–57).

The existence of a monumental structure from the Hellenistic period, built immediately above ancient Shechem, the former chief city of the Samaritans, in addition to literary evidence that the Samaritan Temple was situated on Mount Gerizim until its destruction in 128 B.C. by John Hyrcanus led the excavator of Tell er-Ras to conclude that building B and its related walls were part of the Samaritan Temple and that the half cube of unhewn stones was probably the remains of the Samaritan altar of sacrifice.

R. J. BULL

BIBLIOGRAPHY

C. W. Wilson, *PEF*, 1873, 69 • Hill, *BMC*, XXXVIII and Plates V, VI, VII, XXXIX • A. M. Schneider, *ZDPV* 68 (1951), 209–34 • R. J. Bull, *AJA* 71 (1967), 387–93 • R. J. Bull and E. F. Campbell, *BASOR* 190 (1968), 4–19 • R. J. Bull, *PEQ*, 102 (1970), 108–11.

ROSH HA-NIQRA, TEL

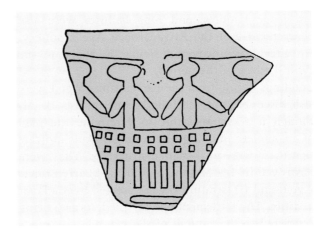

IDENTIFICATION. A small mound on the lowest terrace of the Rosh ha-Niqra ridge, on the lands of Kibbutz Rosh ha-Niqra, about 1 kilometer from the sea and 1.5 kilometers from the Israel–Lebanon border (map reference 161276). In Arabic, the site is called Khirbet el-Musheyrife or et-Taba'iq.

The mound has clearly defined boundaries on three sides. On the west and south its slopes are quite steep but not very high, and to the east the mound is bounded by a small valley. On the north, however, the ground rises gradually toward the nearby mountain, and the boundary on this side is indistinguishable.

The proposal of W. M. Thomson and E. Renan to identify el-Musheyrife with Misrephoth-Maim (Joshua 11:8, 13:6) is generally accepted. In the list of settlements drawn up in 1251 by the knight Jean d'Ibelin, the name of the site appears in the form La Meserefe. The name probably indicates that salt was obtained there from seawater by evaporation in ponds (thus, Y. Ben-Zvi), but it is also possible to vocalize the second part of the name so as to read *mi-yam* — "of the sea" or "western," which would be a simple geographical definition (thus, M. Noth and Y. Yadin).

In a survey conducted at Tel Rosh ha-Niqra, pottery was found from the Early Bronze and Late Bronze Ages as well as a small number of sherds from the Iron Age. At the foot of the mound, pottery was uncovered from the Roman, Byzantine, and Arab periods. At Minet el-Musheyrife, situated on the shore, Roman and Byzantine pottery was found in abundance. This was probably the site of the port and perhaps also of the salt ponds.

EXCAVATIONS

In 1951–52 two seasons of excavations were conducted on the mound on behalf of the Department of Antiquities. Three areas on the eastern side of the mound were investigated: area I on the lower part of the mound to the southeast and areas II and III on the summit of the mound, near the east end.

In area I, buildings were uncovered from the Early Bronze Age I — the earliest occupation on the mound. The inhabitants of this first settlement used the large rock surfaces as floors and enlarged them by adding cobbled terraces. The walls, erected on the rock and on the floors, were built of courses of stone in their lower part and of mud brick in the upper part. The main finds were coarse storage vessels in the form of hole-mouth jars with broad, flat bases, covered with a red slip and decorated with thumb-indented bands. Decorated lug hand-

Above: Cylinder seal impression — EBA. Below: Decorated bone handle — EBA.

les, ledge handles, and loop handles were also characteristic of the Early Bronze Age I pottery. An adze was uncovered similar in shape to the typical adzes of the period.

Buildings dating from the Early Bronze Age I were also discovered at the foundations of area II. Although it was impossible to determine the plan of a complete building, the rounded walls indicate that these were oval-shaped structures. They were destroyed by fire and the buildings of Early Bronze Age II and III (stratum I) were erected over a layer of ashes. The settlement was fortified, its area being restricted to the summit of the mound.

In area II, a section of the defenses of the settlement was cleared. A fortified gateway was apparently placed between walls enclosing it on the north and the south. Other walls protected the eastern access, forming a kind of forward entrance. The main building is a square (8 by 8 meters) possibly representing the tower of the gateway. It is divided by an inner partition wall. The outer walls on the north and south are 3 meters thick, and the eastern wall is 2 meters thick; the entrance of the gate, paved with stone slabs, some reaching 1 meter in length, in 2.4 meters wide, and that of the forward entrance is 2 meters wide.

The pottery finds attest that the eastern fortifications of the mound were erected in Early Bronze Age II–III. Some sherds of Khirbet Kerak ware were found on the summit of the mound. After the destruction of the fortifications, this area was abandoned and never reoccupied.

In 1950, a rock-hewn tomb of the Roman period was cleared south of the mound. It is rectangular in plan (.45 by .6 by 1.8 meters) and was covered with several stone slabs. The tomb contained three skeletons, fragments of three glass vessels and a glass bowl.

In 1953, a grave was accidentally discovered on the slopes of the mountain, northwest of the lands of the kibbutz, to the east of the highway leading to Lebanon in an area of abandoned quarries. The grave consisted of a pit dug in the ground, containing a large number of bones and pottery from the end of Early Bronze Age.   MIRIAM TADMOR

BIBLIOGRAPHY

M. Prausnitz, 'Atiqot 1 (1955), 139 • Miriam Tadmor and M. Prausnitz, 'Atiqot 2 (1959), 72–88 • Aharoni, LB, 21, 48, 90, 171 • Miriam Tadmor, EI 11 (1973), 286–89 (Hebrew).

ES-ṢAFI, TELL

IDENTIFICATION. Tell eṣ-Ṣafi is located at the place where the Wadi Elah enters the Shephelah, on its south bank (map reference 13591237). The mound, 232 meters above sea level and about 100 meters above the valley bed, dominates the road leading through Wadi Elah into the mountains, which passes along the foot of Azekah. It also guards the main north–south route of the Shephelah running through the plain, at the foot of the mound to the west, toward Gezer. On the north and east the mound slopes steeply, revealing white limestone cliffs, while to the south, it is connected by a saddle to the range behind it, and its slope is gradual. The summit of the mount is crescent shaped, and has a moderate slope to the south. Here the acropolis was located.

The identification of the site is disputed. J. L. Porter in 1887 was the first to identify it as Gath, and this was accepted by many scholars — including F. J. Bliss, the excavator of the mound. Another suggestion, also widely accepted at the time, located there the biblical city of Livnah. This suggestion was based (aside from various biblical and other sources) on the Arabic name "Tell eṣ-Ṣafi," meaning "the White Mound," and on the French Crusader name Blanche Garde ("White Citadel"). The persistence of the word "white" was taken as a connection with the biblical name Livnah, which also means "white." It was suggested that these three interrelated names had their origin in the white cliffs, which are visible from afar. Two main sources from the Byzantine period, however, contradict this assumption. Eusebius states that in his day there was a village named Λοβανά in the vicinity of Eleutheropolis (Beth Govrin) (Onomasticon 120, 25). On the Medeba map, on the other hand, there is a place called Σαφιθά, which is identified with Tell eṣ-Ṣafi. The mound therefore was already then known by the name it bears today, and a settlement called Labana was situated at that time near Beth-Govrin. White cliffs are also found on the slopes of other mounds in the vicinity. In the light of these facts, Z. Kallai returned to the early suggestion of C. W. M. Van de Velde and V. Guérin to search for a place in the vicinity with a name like Mizpeh, which could have undergone

Below: General plan. 1. Weli. 2. Weli. 3. City wall.
4. Ruins of modern village. 5. Cemetery.
Right: Limestone head in cypriot style — Persian period.

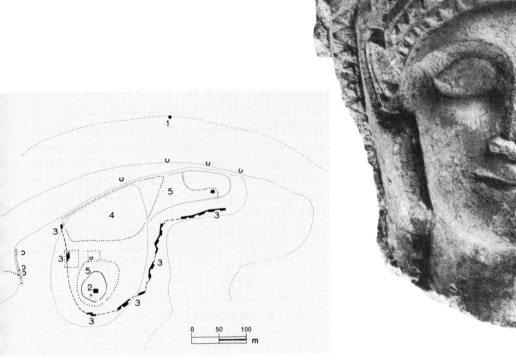

a change to Σαφιϑά . W. F. Albright suggested that Tell eṣ-Ṣafi should be equated with biblical Makkedah (Joshua 10 : 10, etc.). There have been other suggestions as well, but current archaeological research tends to prefer the original proposal to identify it with Gath.

INVESTIGATION OF THE SITE

In 1899, excavations were conducted on the mound, sponsored by the British Palestine Exploration Fund, under the direction of Bliss with the assistance of R. A. S. Macalister. The expedition originally intended to excavate mainly at Tell eṣ-Ṣafi. However, the license granted by the Ottoman authorities permitted them to excavate a ten-square-kilometer area, and the expedition thus also excavated the nearby mounds of Tell Zakariyeh, Tell Judeideh, and Tell Sandahanna. Tell eṣ-Ṣafi was excavated for two seasons in 1899. The results of the excavations were published in a comprehensive report in 1902. The account of the excavation was written by Bliss, and the summary of the findings was compiled by Bliss and Macalister.

When the excavators arrived at the mound, they realized that the sites suitable for excavation were very limited. In the south part of the summit, the natural place for the acropolis, there was a holy *maqam*, and around it extended a cemetery which it was also impossible to excavate. To the north, in the main part of the mound, stood houses of the Arab village and behind them on the east, another cemetery stretched over the remainder of the summit. The excavations therefore were confined to small separated sections, which can be included within five main areas: area A, a narrow strip across the width of the summit between the *maqam* and the village; area B, a second section in the same place, east of area A, toward the center of the mound; area C, the city wall — traced on the south and west slopes; area D, the east side of the mound; area E, the remains of the Crusader fortress in the southern cemetery.

Area A. Three soundings were made in a continuous line from east to west. The average depth of the deposit found was 10 meters. Another six soundings were sunk farther to the west. The depth of the deposit was found to decrease toward the center of the mound, where it was only 4 meters. In all these soundings, three main assemblages of pottery were discovered and designated by the excavators as 1. Early Pre-Israelite period, 2. Late Pre-Israelite and Jewish periods, and 3. Arab period.

Area B. In this area, which is closer to the center of the mound, eleven adjoining soundings were made. The stratigraphy here was disturbed, and the pottery was mixed. In one of the soundings, a child burial in a jar was found.

Area C. Sections of the wall were visible above surface level. Other sections were exposed in the excavations. The maximum thickness of the wall was 4 meters. The lower courses were built of roughly squared stones, with a fill of smaller stones between them. In one place, a course of bricks was also preserved, and many fallen bricks were found near the wall, leading the excavators to conclude that the upper part of the wall was built of bricks. Towers 10–11.3 meters long projected from the wall to a distance of .6 meter. The spaces between

Philistine jug with strainer spout.

them measured 9.3 to 11.6 meters. The foundation stones of the towers were laid in straight courses, only the corners built of ashlar masonry. In several places, the face of the wall was plastered with mud and coated with another layer of white plaster — a substance made up of white powdery limestone mixed with straw and water. The wall had the form of a crescent, parallel to the ridge of the mound. Judging by the depth of the wall foundations in the deposit, the excavators attributed it to Rehoboam (928–911 B.C.), and they found confirmation in II Chronicles 11:8 (as was mentioned above they equated the mound with Gath).

Area D. A sounding — about .2 by 27 meters — was made on the east side of the mound. The average depth of the deposit was 8.5 meters. The excavators distinguished four strata of settlement: 1. The lowest stratum contained remains of stone or brick buildings and pottery of the early Pre-Israelite period. 2. Above stratum I was uncovered a group of rooms with walls of rough stones bound with mortar. The pottery of this stratum was Late Pre-Israelite, with the addition of Mycenaean sherds. In this layer was found a building with three stone pillars. The excavators interpreted them as a row of *massebahs,* and considered the building a temple (see below). 3. Above these two strata, several walls were discovered similar in building technique to that of stratum 2. It was thus difficult for the excavators to distinguish between the buildings of these two strata. This stratum contained pottery from the "Jewish" period. Several vessels bore *lamelekh* stamps. There was also early Greek pottery which the excavators dated to 770–550 B.C., Greek black- and red-figured ware (500–350 B.C.), and isolated sherds of "Seleucid" pottery. 4. Near the surface were uncovered some large rooms, their walls containing a number of stones in Crusader style. The pottery was local Arab ware.

Area E. Since actual excavations could not be conducted here because of the *maqam,* Bliss and Macalister attempted to trace the remains of the Crusader fortress Blanche Garde, which were visible on the surface. The fortress was built on the south, elevated sector of the mound, in A.D. 1140. It was one of a series of fortresses on the southwest border of the Kingdom of Jerusalem, one of whose functions was to encircle Ashkelon, held by the Arabs until 1153. In 1191, the fortress was destroyed by Saladin. The first to examine these ruins was M. Rey, who visited the site before the erection of the *maqam,* and was therefore able to draw a general plan of the fortress. According to his description, the fortress was square (each side 60 meters long), and in two of its corners there were remains of towers. In 1875, when C. R. Conder visited the site, the *maqam* had already been built on top of the fortress, and Condor found only "cuttings in the rock which were very difficult to trace." Bliss and Macalister noted the upper part of a wall built of Crusader-style masonry, near the east wall of the *maqam.* In their opinion, this was a remnant of one of the towers discovered by Rey, whereas the second tower was totally destroyed during the construction of the *maqam.* Additional remains of the fortress, including a gate, were discovered in area B.

The main finds of the excavations at Tell eṣ-Ṣafi were discovered not in the stratigraphic excavation but in an old rubbish dump in the middle of area C, on the southern flank of the mound. Among the finds were sherds from the early Pre-Israelite period, Egyptian beads and ornaments of various periods, part of an Egyptian stele, pottery from the "Jewish" period bearing personal names, *lamelekh* and other stamps, five fragments of an Assyrian limestone stele, early Greek sherds and black- and red-figured ware, fragments of about forty pottery masks, about thirty pottery and stone figurines from the Greek period (see below), and a number of coins — two Ptolemaic, one Roman, one Arab, and two silver Crusader coins.

On the basis of the results of the excavation and of the finds in the dump, the excavators were of the opinion that Tell eṣ-Ṣafi was first settled in the seventeenth century B.C., and was abandoned in the Seleucid period not to be resettled until Crusader times. Albright examined the pottery published in Bliss and Macalister's report, and revised the dating thus:

PERIOD	BLISS–MACALISTER	ALBRIGHT
Early Pre-Israelite	?–1500 B.C.	3000–1800 B.C.
Late Pre-Israelite	1500–800 B.C.	1800–1000 B.C.
Jewish	800–300 B.C.	1000–587 B.C.
Seleucidan	300– B.C.	400–100 B.C.

As to the dates of the later periods, Albright is in agreement with the excavators. According to Albright the first settlement of Tell eṣ-Ṣafi was a great deal earlier than the excavators had assumed, and its founding is ascribed to the beginning of the Early Bronze Age. Albright's revisions are confirmed by potsherds collected by R. Amiran and Y. Aharoni during a survey on the mound in 1955. They attributed the many sherds gathered on the west, south, and east slopes of the mound to all phases of the Bronze and Iron Ages, as well as later periods — the Roman period and the Middle Ages. The bulk of the sherds are from the Iron Age, especially the Iron Age II.

Albright claimed that the building considered a temple by Bliss and Macalister (area D, stratum 2) was in reality a typical pillar building of the four-room type from the Iron Age, apparently dating from between 1000 and 800 B.C. Similar buildings have been found in almost all the sites containing strata from this period.

The city wall was dated by the excavators to the time of Rehoboam. H. Thiersch attempted to raise the date because of the similarity between the construction of the towers and Assyrian fortifications. C. Watzinger dated it even later, to the Neo-Babylonian period. However, until additional data become available, A. G. Barrois's statement is apparently correct that its exact date within the Iron Age cannot be fixed.

Among the finds are many Philistine pottery vessels, *lamelekh* stamps, Hebrew stamps with personal names, *Neṣef* and shekel weights from the end of the First Temple period, and a group of figurines from the Persian period (fifth to fourth centuries B.C.). Similar figurines have been found recently in the temple of the same period at Makmish (q.v.), and at nearby Tel Ṣippor (q.v.).

E. STERN

BIBLIOGRAPHY

M. Rey, *Etudes sur les monuments de l'architecte militaire des Croisés en Syrie et dans l'isle de Chypre,* Paris, 1877, 173–75 • Bliss-Macalister, *Excavations, passim* • W. F. Mueller, *OLZ* 3 (1900), 105 • W. F. Albright, *AASOR* 2–3 (1921–22), 12–17; *idem, BASOR* 15 (1924), 9 • I. Benzinger, *Hebräische Archaeologie* 3, Leipzig, 1927, *passim* • A. G. Barrois, *Manuel d'archéologie biblique* 1, Paris, 1939, 142–43 • W. F. Albright, *Archaeology and the Religion of Israel²,* Baltimore, 1953, 65–66, 193 • F. M. Cross–G. E. Wright, *JBL* 75 (1956), 217–18 • W. F. Albright, *The Archaeology of Palestine,* London, 1960, 30–31 • R. Giveon, *JEA* 51 (1965), 202–04 • Aharoni, *LB,* index • Z. Kallai, *Enc. Miqr.* 4, 421–23 (Hebrew) • N. Na'aman, *BASOR* 214 (1974), 25–38.

TELL ES-SA'IDIYEH

IDENTIFICATION. Tell es-Sa'idiyeh, situated on the south bank of the Wadi Kufrinjeh 1.8 kilometers east of the Jordan, about halfway between the Dead Sea and Tiberias, was tentatively proposed by W. F. Albright in 1926 as the location of Zaphon ("northward"), largely on the basis of Judges 12 : 1. In 1943, N. Glueck suggested the identification of Zarthan on the grounds of biblical references such as Joshua 3 : 16 and I Kings 7 : 46. The excavations at Tell es-Sa'idiyeh have not as yet produced evidence in support of either of these proposals or for another alternative.

A surface survey of pottery was made by Glueck in 1942, and in 1953 soundings were carried out at the site by H. de Contenson. In the winter of 1964, the University Museum of the University of Pennsylvania undertook a major excavation on the highest part of the mound under the direction of J. B. Pritchard. The initial campaign was followed by two ten-week seasons during the winters of 1965 and 1966 and by a six-week campaign in 1967 with J. E. Huesman acting as the field director.

EXCAVATIONS

The results of each of the four major areas of excavations are described below.

1. **The low bench to the west (el-Gharbi),** built up by the debris of occupation in the Early Bronze Age, was used as a cemetery during the transitional period between the Late Bronze Age and the Iron Age I. In 1964 and 1965, forty-five graves of this period were excavated. The most elaborate of these burials was tomb 101, which contained within its mud-brick walls a single skeleton accompanied by a bronze wine set (laver, bowl, strainer, and juglet), a bronze tripod, storage jars, 571 beads of gold and carnelian, two electrum pendants with chain for suspension around the neck, two electrum toggle pins, five ivory cosmetic containers, a bronze caldron, a bronze lamp, and other vessels. In two other tombs, 102 and 117, skeletal material was wrapped in cloth and covered with bitumen. Tomb 102 also contained a bronze sword, a scarab, a piece of ivory, two bronze bowls, and a bronze jug with handle riveted to the body. The remainder

of the graves in the cemetery were poorer in contents. The ceramic and other evidence points to the last half of the thirteenth through the first half of the twelfth centuries as the span over which the cemetery was in use.

2. **North side of the mound.** On this side of the mound was found a stairway leading from the summit to a water source at the base. In addition to the ninety-five steps actually preserved, there were originally some forty-five more that had been destroyed by the erosion of the upper course. The 2.25-meter-space between the stone-built walls of the stairway is divided by a mud-brick wall along its entire length, which provided support for the roof camouflaging this means of access to the spring at the foot of the mound from inside the city. Although the date for the construction and use of this civil-defense installation has not yet been determined with certainty, it should probably be placed toward the end of the Iron Age I.

3. **Excavations in the northwest side of the mound (esh-Sharqi).** By the end of the 1967 season, four main levels of occupation had been distinguished in the excavated area of 1,375 square meters in the northwest side of the mound. These are summarized in the order of their settlement.

LEVEL IV was established on the remains of an occupation that had been destroyed by fire. It contained ten houses built of mud brick laid on stone foundations. The settlement was surrounded by a city wall, about 3.5 meters thick, also built of mud brick on a shallow stone foundation. Among the structures is a three-room house with an altar or table, covered with white plaster, in which were two shallow basins, one containing the well-known tripod incense burner imbedded in ash and charcoal.

LEVEL III was built according to the same orientation as level IV and consisted of houses and streets erected on the remains of the previous level.

In LEVEL II, twelve houses of identical plan and nearly the same size were constructed as a single unit of multiple houses. Six dwellings opened onto one street and six onto another parallel street. The houses, measuring on the average 4.83 by 8.37 meters, consisted of a large front room or court with

Opposite page: The mound, seen from the north. This page, right top: Wine set of bronze found in tomb 101 of the cemetery. Bottom: Tomb 101 of the cemetery.

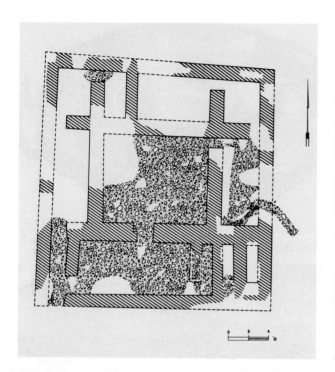

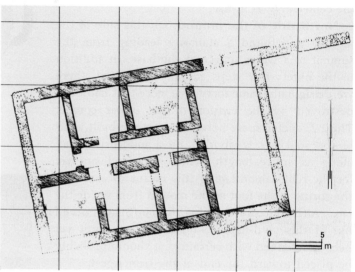

Both pages, counterclockwise from left: Plan of the Persian palace on the acropolis; Plan of the Hellenistic fortress on the Acropolis; Walls of the Hellenistic fortress on the Acropolis; Plan of the block of dwellings found in level 2; Stairway leading up the north side of the mound; Limestone censer burner with inscription.

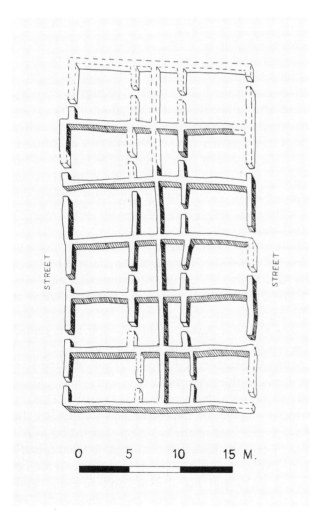

STREET

STREET

0   5   10   15 M.

a row of mud-brick columns to support the roof, and a smaller room at the back. A paving of rounded stones usually covered half of the larger room. The preliminary study of the pottery indicates that the houses of this level should be dated to the middle of the eighth century B.C.

LEVEL I consisted of a smoothed surface into which were cut ninety-seven circular pits and two rectangular bins lined with mud brick. The appearance of two-row barley and wheat in the crevices of one of the bins suggests that the entire area was a threshing floor in the latest period of occupation.

4. **Sounding on the "acropolis."** Three layers of occupation extending from the Roman through the Persian periods have thus far been encountered on the highest part of the mound, the "acropolis," but the stratigraphic sequence there has not yet been correlated with that of the Iron Age layers described above.

Acropolis level 3 contained a palatial building, 21.95 by 22.05 meters. It consisted of seven rooms built around a paved courtyard with a drain and a tower at the southeast corner. A carbon-14 test obtained from a charred roof beam of the palace gave a date of 343 ± 52 B.C. A limestone incense burner decorated with geometric designs, a horse and a human figure bore the inscription *lzkwr*, "Belonging to Zakkur."

Over the level of this palace was built a Hellenistic structure, 21.2 by 13.3 meters. Its mud-brick walls were separated from a stone foundation by a layer of reeds laid crosswise to the length of the wall. The fortresslike building had been roofed with sycamore beams covered with a surface of mud spread over reeds.

The latest occupation of the acropolis was represented by a Roman building, a watchtower or fortress, and two plastered water reservoirs.

J. B. PRITCHARD

BIBLIOGRAPHY

W. F. Albright, *AASOR* 6 (1926), 45–47 • N. Glueck, *ibid.*, 25–28 (1951), 290–95 • H. de Contenson, *ADAJ* 4–5 (1960), 49–56 • J. B. Pritchard, *ILN*, March 28, 1964, 487–90; July 2, 1966, 25–27; *idem*, *Expedition: the Bulletin of the University Museum of the University of Pennsylvania* 6 (1964), 2–9; 7 (1965), 26–33; 10 (1968), 26–29; *idem*, *ADAJ* 8–9 (1964), 95–98; *idem*, *BA* 28 (1965), 10–17, 126–28; *idem*, *Archaeology* 18 (1965), 292–94; 19 (1966), 298–99; *idem*, *RB* 72 (1965), 257–62; 73 (1966), 574–76; *idem*, in: *Ugaritica* 6, Paris, 1969, 427–34; *idem* in: W. Ward (ed.), *The Role of the Phoenicians in the Interaction of Mediterranean Civilization*, Beirut, 1968, 99–112.

SAMARIA

HISTORY OF THE CITY. Samaria, the capital of the kingdom of Israel and center of the region of Samaria, bears the name of the hill of Samaria on which Omri, King of Israel, built his city. The site is identified with the village of Sebastia. The place was renamed Sebaste by Herod when he rebuilt the city. The town lay on a high hill (430 meters above sea level) towering over its surroundings. It was situated at a crossroads near the main highway running northward from Shechem, in a fertile agricultural region. It was probably due to these topographic and strategic advantages that the site was chosen as the capital of the Kingdom of Israel, even though it lacked an adequate water supply.

The Bible records the foundation of Samaria as follows: "In the thirty and first year of Asa king of Judah began Omri to reign over Israel, twelve years: six years reigned he in Tirzah. And he bought the hill Samaria of Shemer for two talents of silver, and built on the hill and called the name of the city which he built, after the name of Shemer, the owner of the hill, Samaria" (I Kings 16:23–24). Even after the fall of the Kingdom of Israel the Assyrians called it "the house of Khomry" after Omri, the founder of the dynasty and of Samaria. Omri succeeded in strengthening the kingdom, but because of his failures in his wars with Aram, he was forced to cede to the king of Aram "streets" in Samaria for merchants to set up their bazaars (I Kings 20:34).

Ahab, Omri's son, reigned from 871 to 852 B.C. Toward the end of his reign Samaria was besieged by Ben-Hadad II, King of Aram, and his allies (I Kings 20:1). Ahab struck back at Ben-Hadad at the gates of Samaria, and later, following the decisive battle at Aphek *(ibid.* 26–30), he obtained the return to Israel of the cities previously captured by the Aramaeans, and he also acquired trade concessions in the markets of Damascus *(ibid.* 34). In the battle with the Assyrians at Qarqar (853 B.C.), Ahab occupied an important position among the twelve members of the coalition. According to Assyrian sources, his army consisted of 2,000 cavalry and 10,000 foot soldiers. In the last year of his reign, Ahab and his ally the Judean King Jehoshaphat, waged war with the Aramaeans to re-

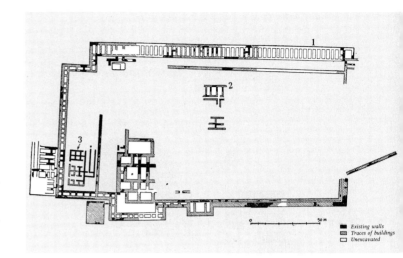

Right: Palace of the kings of Israel. 1. Casemate wall.
2. "Ivory house" 3. "Ostraca house".
Below: Plan of the site: 1. Roman city wall.
2. West gate. 3. Hellenistic wall and tower. 4. Roman
shrine. 5. Colonnaded street. 6. Shops. 7. Theater.
8. Temple of Kore. 9. Hellenistic round towers.
10. Israelite inner wall. 11. Summit temple, forecourt.
12. Summit temple. 13. Israelite casemate wall
14. Lower Israelite wall. 15. Church. 16. Roman shrine.
17. Basilica. 18. Forum. 19. Paved street. 20. Roman
conduit. 21. Israelite tombs. 22. Hippodrome.
23. Church and mosque. 24. Israelite building fragment.
25. "Ivory house". 26. Gate (?).

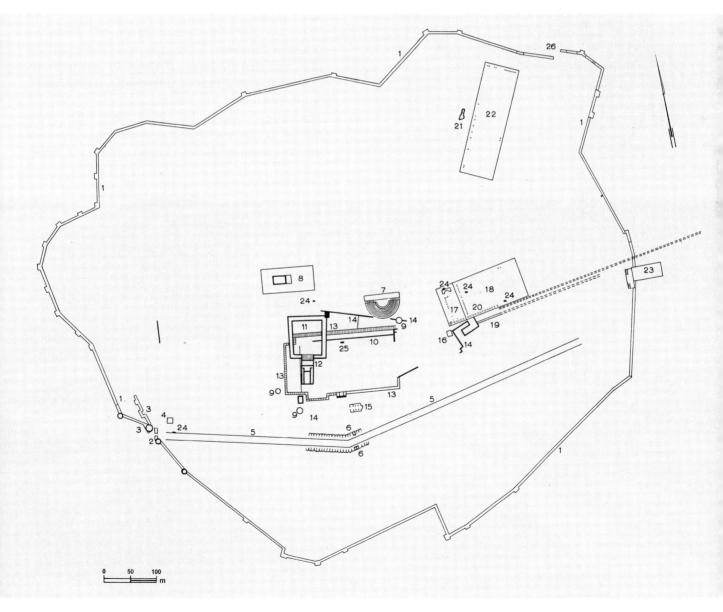

Below: West gates. Bottom: Israelite city wall.

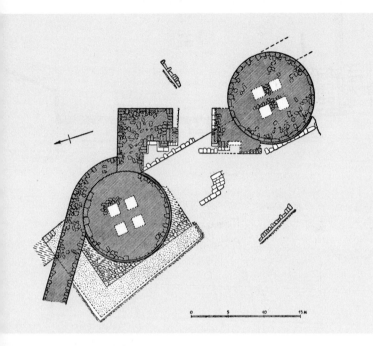

capture Ramoth-Gilead for Israel. Before setting out to battle, the two kings sat on the threshing floor at the entrance of the gate of Samaria and asked the prophets to inquire of God what lay before them *(ibid.* 22:1–10). In the battle of Ramoth-Gilead Ahab was fatally wounded. His body was brought to Samaria and his chariot was washed of his blood in the pool of Samaria *(ibid.* 22:33–38). With the marriage of Ahab and Jezebel, the daughter of Ethbaal, King of Tyre, the alliance with Phoenicia was consolidated, and Tyre's cultural influence on Israel increased. For his wife Ahab built in Samaria a sanctuary to Baal and Astarte *(ibid.* 16:32–33; II Kings 10:21) and a temple in the city of Jezreel, thus arousing the wrath of the prophets of Israel and especially of Elijah. The statement in the Bible "Now the rest of the acts of Ahab, and all that he did, and the ivory house which he made, and all the cities that he built" (I Kings 22:39) indicates that Ahab was a man of unbounded energy and a zealous builder.

The reign of Joram the son of Ahab witnessed a decline in the political and economic position of the Kingdom of Israel. Samaria was put under

heavy siege by the Aramaean King, Ben-Hadad, and famine spread through the city (II Kings 6 : 24–30). The Bible relates in connection with this great famine, that the "gate of Samaria" served as the marketplace for food (ibid. 7 : 1). When Joram renewed the war against Aram for Ramoth-Gilead, Jehu, the commander of his army, who had been anointed king by the prophet Elisha, revolted against Joram. Jehu annihilated Ahab's family and put an end to the cult of Baal in Samaria. He paid tribute to the Assyrians (841 B.C.). His submission is related on the Black Obelisk of Shalmaneser III. On the obelisk Jehu is referred to as the "Son of Omri," i.e., king over the land of the House of Omri (= Israel). Jehu lost large tracts east of the Jordan. In the days of the great Israelite King, Jeroboam II (784–748 B.C.), Samaria reached the zenith of its prosperity and expansion. Jeroboam conquered Damascus, extending the borders of his kingdom from the entrance of Hamath to the sea of the 'Arabah (II Kings 14 : 23–29). In the days of Samaria's greatness, there emerged a powerful aristocracy which pursued a life of luxury. Instances of injustice appeared, causing the prophet Amos to protest strongly against the luxuries in the palaces and "ivory houses" in Samaria and against the pomp of the cult at Bethel (Amos 3 : 9–15 ; 4 : 4).

The death of Jeroboam II was followed by the beginning of the decline and disintegration of the Kingdom of Israel. Large territories were split away from the country during the military expeditions of Tiglath-Pileser III in the years 743 and 738 B.C. Menahem, King of Israel, had to pay heavy tribute to the Assyrians (783 B.C.). Pekah and Hoshea attempted to revolt against the Assyrians, but Shalmaneser V marched against Samaria and held it under siege for three years (II Kings 17 : 5–6 ; 18 : 9–10). In 721 B.C. Sargon II conquered the city and part of its inhabitants were deported to remote districts of the Assyrian Empire.

Samaria became the center of the province of the same name and the seat of the Assyrian, Babylonian, and the Persian governors. The Assyrian kings settled colonists there from various countries (II Kings 17 : 24) who mixed with the local Israelite population, thus causing an increasing cultural and religious amalgamation. During a period of Assyrian weakness, Josiah, King of Judah (II Kings 23 : 8), raided the towns of Samaria and destroyed the High Places set up by the kings of Israel. This event encouraged those in Samaria who had remained faithful to the Lord, and many of them went on pilgrimage to Jerusalem after its conquest by Nebuchadnezzar (Jeremiah 41 : 5). Nevertheless, in the course of time there arose a Samaritan community which broke away from the people of Israel. Sanballat the Horonite, the Persian governor of Samaria, stood at the head of the opposition to the building of the city wall in Jerusalem in the time of Nehemiah.

When the Persian Empire fell to Alexander the Great, Samaria too was conquered (332 B.C.), and thousands of Macedonian soldiers were settled there. Samaria became a Greek city, differing from an ethnic, cultural, and religious point of view from the provincial cities of the Samaritans, whose religious center was Mount Gerizim. During the reigns of the Hellenistic kings, Samaria experienced a number of wars and conquests, but no destruction so complete as that inflicted upon it by John Hyrcanus in 108 B.C. According to Josephus, Hyrcanus razed the city to the ground and sold its inhabitants into slavery.

In the time of Pompey (63 B.C.), Samaria was annexed to the Roman province of Syria, and under Gabinius (57 B.C.) the city revived. In 30 B.C., the Emperor Augustus granted it to Herod, who rebuilt it, adorned it with buildings, and named it Sebaste in honor of Augustus (in Greek Sebastos = Augustus) (Antiquities XV, 246). Herod too settled foreign soldiers there, and again the complexion of the population of the city changed. During the First Jewish War in A.D. 66–70, the city was once more destroyed. Septimius Severus granted it the status of a Roman colony with all the inherent privileges (A.D. 200). When Christianity became dominant, the city had already begun to decline, although in the fourth century A.D. Sebaste became the seat of a bishop. A popular tradition locating there the tomb of John the Baptist lent the site a certain importance in the eyes of the Christians, who built churches there. After the Arab conquest, various travelers described the many extant ruins.

HISTORY OF EXCAVATIONS

Two archaeological expeditions excavated at Samaria. From 1908 to 1910 an expedition of Harvard University excavated there, first on a small scale, under the direction of G. Schumacher, and later more extensively under the direction of G. A. Reisner and C. S. Fisher. This expedition unearthed

the western part of the fortress of the Israelite kings (the acropolis) from the time of the dynasties of Omri and Jehu, including the casemate walls, the royal residence, and the storehouse within its precincts. Especially noteworthy finds are the ostraca (see below). Also uncovered were the ruins of the Hellenistic fortifications of the acropolis, the Roman city wall, and the west gate, houses, the temple of Augustus, the forum, the basilica, and remains of the stadium.

The second expedition worked at the site during the years 1931–1935 under the sponsorship of five institutions: Harvard University, the Palestine Exploration Fund, the British Academy, the British School of Archaeology in Jerusalem, and the Hebrew University. The director of the excavations was J. W. Crowfoot, with E. L. Sukenik as assistant field director. K. Lake represented Harvard University. Kathleen Kenyon and Grace M. Crowfoot also participated in the expedition, assuming a major role in the publication of the excavation report, as well as N. Avigad and the architect J. Pinkerfeld. The Joint Expedition extended the area previously excavated by clearing the fortress of the Israelite kings. The finds from the royal quarter included a collection of ivory carvings. A burial cave and a cult place (?) from the Israelite period were also uncovered. Smaller projects included the exploration of the Hellenistic fort, the colonnaded street, the forum, and the stadium. Also discovered were the remains of a temple dedicated to Kore, a theater, Roman tombs, and a church, and the water system of the Roman city was investigated.

The excavators met with considerable difficulty in distinguishing between the various strata, since the town had been destroyed several times and was always rebuilt in stone and the foundations of the buildings were laid on bedrock. The builders dismantled the previous structures, reused their stones, and deepened the foundations down to bedrock. Foundations of buildings of different periods were therefore frequently found not superimposed but side by side. Foundation trenches that penetrated through several strata of construction disturbed the stratigraphy and the deposits. The conditions on the site forced the excavators to dig according to the strip system, that is, the earth removed from every excavated strip had to be dumped into the previously excavated strip, a system with numerous disadvantages.

RESULT OF THE EXCAVATIONS

The Israelite Period to the Assyrian Conquest.
Samaria was found to consist of an upper city (acropolis), the royal quarter situated on the summit of the hill, and a lower city extending over the slopes and along the foot of the hill. Very little of the lower city was excavated, only scattered building remains were cleared, attesting that the Israelite city stretched from the Roman gate in the west to the middle of the forum in the east, over a distance of about 800 meters. In Crowfoot's opinion, the area of the walled city did not exceed 75 dunams, and the more distant remains belonged to buildings standing outside the walls. Kathleen Kenyon, on the other hand, claimed that the Israelite town was equal in size to that of the Roman city.

The Acropolis. The royal quarter was enclosed by

Opposite page, top left: Samaria ostracon No. 21: "In the tenth year. To Shamaryau from Tetel. A jar of fine oil". Top right: Fragment of monumental Hebrew inscription... asher..... Bottom: Section of Israelite inner wall. This page: Samaria ostracon No. 1. From the excavations of the joint expedition. The letters are incised.

walls, and two main systems of fortifications were distinguished. The first wall, which the excavators called the inner wall, encompassed an area on the summit of the hill measuring 178 meters from east to west and about 89 meters from north to south. The wall was 1.6 meters thick and built of fine ashlar masonry laid in headers and stretchers carefully fitted together. Inside the walled-up area were discovered remains of various buildings, one of which built against the south wall to the west consisted of a central courtyard surrounded by rooms (27 by 24 meters). This building is considered to be part of the palace of the Israelite kings. North of

This page: Fragment of cuneiform inscription, apparently from the time of Sargon II.
Opposite page: Ivories.

the northern wall on a lower level, the so-called lower terrace, were discovered the remains of another long wall (called the lower wall), but its continuation is unknown.

The inner wall, the earliest wall of the city, was attributed by the Joint Expedition to Omri. Since the wall was not particularly strong and was probably incapable of defending the royal quarter, a new and much stronger fortification system was built. The summit plateau was enlarged to the north by 16.5 meters and to the west by about 30 meters and surrounded by a casemate wall, a double wall divided into rooms by partitions. Only part of this wall was preserved, but the rock-cut foundation trenches have survived so that the course of the wall could be traced. These trenches have also survived in the other structures. The total thickness of the northern casemate wall was 10 meters (the outer wall was about 1.8 meters thick, the inner wall about 1 meter, and the space between them about 7 meters), and the crosswalls inside the double wall formed long and narrow rooms. The western casemate wall was thinner (5 meters), and the casemates were smaller. The west part of the south wall was also of the casemate type, but in its continuation toward the east, it was built as single wall again the earlier inner wall, which was erected on the rock terrace. Together the two walls formed a thick and massive defense. The south wall contains several salients and recesses, and near its west end was built a solid square block (16 by 12 meters), which was probably a tower. In the opinion of some archaeologists, it may have defended the gate that stood there. In the space between the western casemate wall and the earlier inner wall stood a storehouse (25 by 18 meters), the so-called Ostraca house where the inscribed potsherds were found (see below). A pool (10 by 5 meters) was built against the casemate wall in the northwest corner of the area of the royal quarter. It has been suggested that this may have been the pool in which Ahab's chariot was washed when his body was brought from the battle at Ramoth-Gilead. At a distance of about 17 meters from the southeast corner, the wall makes a sharp turn to the northeast and continues in this direction for about 40 meters. This oblique turn was probably due to the topography of the site, but it is also possible that the area of the royal quarter was entered from this side, i.e., from the east. Nearby

were found three proto-Aeolic capitals which may have been set at the entrance to the forecourt of the royal quarter.

About 150 meters east of the corner of the wall, near the south side of the Roman basilica, remains of considerable Israelite building were discovered. These remains were part of the fortifications of the city, and probably included a gate. The walls and the foundation trenches form a kind of meander. Only three courses of the main wall (31.5 meters long) running west-east have survived. The stones were dressed with marginal drafts. At a distance of 4 meters from the wall were discovered the foundations of a rectangular structure (36 by 21 meters), which the excavators interpreted as a tower. The narrow passage between the wall and the tower probably led to the city gate. This east gate stands on the level of the middle terrace, and it is not clear how it was connected with the city walls.

Building Technique. The Israelite masonry at Samaria is renowned for its outstanding quality. The foundation stones were laid in rock-cut trenches or on rock-cut steps and set as headers only, whereas the walls were built of courses of headers and stretchers or of two headers alternating with one stretcher. The stones of the lower courses, which are not visible, are dressed with marginal drafts on two or three sides, an irregular boss remaining in the center. The dressing of the stones was done on the spot during construction, in order to assure careful fitting of the stones and the courses. The upper, visible courses were dressed smooth. All the ashlars were set dry, i.e., without mortar, and with outstanding precision. The interior of the walls was also constructed of large regular stones, which considerably increased the stability of the structures. The superstructures of the city walls and of the other walls were probably of brick. It is assumed that the Israelites learned this outstanding masonary work from the Phoenicians.

Stratigraphy. The first expedition distinguished three Israelite building phases: the palace from the time of Omri, the casemate wall and the storehouse from the reign of Ahab, and the buildings west of the casemate wall from the days of Jeroboam II. The Joint Expedition dug a stratigraphic section across the royal quarter. Early Bronze Age I pottery was found on the rock but the site was not resettled until the Israelite period. Kathleen Kenyon distinguished eight pre-Hellenistic building and ceramic periods, six of them belonging to the period of time between the foundation of the city in 876 B.C. and its conquest in 721 B.C. This division is based on both architectural and ceramic considerations, and the building periods I–VI coincide with the ceramic periods I–VI as shown here below:

PERIOD I — Omri: construction of the inner wall and the palace;

PERIOD II — Ahab: construction of the casemate wall and probably also of the east gate;

PERIOD III — Jehu and others: repair of the casemate wall, rebuilding of earlier structures, erection of new buildings;

PERIOD IV — Time of Jeroboam II and others: repair of the casemate wall, alterations in existing buildings and construction of new ones, probably also of the storehouse;

PERIOD V-VI — Changes and repairs: burned layer attributed to the conquest of Samaria in 721 B.C.

The proposals for the first two periods — decisive for establishing the chronology of the pottery — have been questioned, at Samaria. The disagreement is rooted in the different approaches to archaeological methodology. The pottery of period I was found in the fills of the structures of period I, according to Kathleen Kenyon's terminology, and she attributes this pottery to the construction period of the buildings, claiming that it was brought by the builders in the time of Omri. For the same reason she ascribes the pottery of period II — which is very similar to the earlier pottery — to building period II.

These conclusions are disputed, however, by W. F. Albright, Y. Aharoni, R. Amiran, and G. E. Wright, who maintain that pottery of periods I–II found in the fills of structures I–II predates these buildings, and on the grounds of a typological comparison with pottery from other excavations, they date it earlier, to the tenth and beginning of the ninth century B.C. The pottery attests to the fact that a small settlement existed on the site prior to the foundation of the city of Samaria. Kathleen Kenyon also did not overlook this problem. Although she noted the discovery of two walls covered by floors of buildings from period I, when discussing the pottery she states that there was no trace of occupation from the beginning of the Early Bronze Age until the time of Omri. This controversy has not yet been resolved from the methodological standpoint, and the stratigraphic problem will be clarified only with further excavation.

This writer, for the time being, shares the view of those who claim that pottery periods I–II precede building periods I–II and that the pottery of period III — which is richer and more varied than the preceding ones — parallels building periods I–II. Wright has also suggested a correction in the chronology of the walls. In his opinion Omri, who resided in Samaria six years only, could not have succeeded in building the first wall and the palace in such a short time. It is difficult as well to assume, according to Wright, that Ahab could have erected so extensive a fortification such as the casemate wall during the twenty-two years of his reign. Wright therefore considers that Omri only began the construction of the first wall and that Ahab completed it, whereas Jehu, the founder of the next dynasty, built the casemate wall.

Wright's contentions are not acceptable to the present writer. It is highly improbable that Omri should have established his residence in a city that was not

Hellenistic round tower.

walled and in which there were no dwelling quarters suitable for a king. He in all probability began the fortifications of the hill and the building of his palace while still living in his previous capital, Tirzah, and he transferred his capital to Samaria only after the site had been prepared, that is, after the main buildings had been wholly or nearly finished. He could certainly have completed erecting the inner wall, which is a single wall only 1.6 meters thick. The building of the casemate wall, on the other hand — for which the summit of the hill had to be widened by an artificial fill — was indeed a major undertaking requiring a great deal of time, considerable means, and the vision of a great builder. But in the twenty-two years of Ahab's reign, it was certainly possible to complete it, and in fact the work was finished in an even shorter time, since during Ahab's reign Samaria withstood the siege of the Aramaeans only by virtue of its strong fortifications. (It should be noted that this discussion refers only to the fortifications of the acropolis: in times of emergency the acropolis could also shelter the inhabitants of the lower city, of whose walls almost nothing is known.) Ahab — who married Jezebel, the daughter of the king of Tyre — certainly received ample assistance from the Phoenicians for this extensive construction work. During his reign, prosperity prevailed in the Kingdom of Israel, and the Bible relates that Ahab was a builder of cities and palaces. Archaeological finds from sites other than Samaria also attest that Ahab was a great builder. He erected strong fortifications at Hazor and at Megiddo. At the latter site he probably also built the large stables, an assumption borne out by an Assyrian source recording the considerable number of war chariots that stood at Ahab's disposal. It cannot therefore be conceived that in his own capital, Samaria, he would have sufficed with merely completing the construction of the unpretentious "inner wall" begun by his father.

For these reasons it is difficult to attribute the construction of the casemate wall to Jehu. Even though Jehu founded a new dynasty, put an end to the cult of Baal, and won the confidence of the prophets, his reign does not seem to have been propitious for such a large building project as this. During his reign the Kingdom of Israel suffered political defeats and lost extensive territories. Jehu was the first Israelite king to pay heavy tribute to the Assyrians. Commercial relations with Tyre were broken off with the killing of Jezebel, and it is hardly likely that the Phoenicians would nevertheless have supplied him with aid for the erection of fortifications. Furthermore, the Bible does not attribute any building activity to Jehu.

Those archaeologists, therefore, seem to be correct who have ascribed the erection of the casemate wall to Ahab and only its repairs to Jehu and his successors. The following chronological table summarizes the different views of the construction of the walls and the correlation between the building and ceramic periods at Samaria, up to its conquest in 722 B.C.

The Samaria Ostraca. In the 1910 excavations, sixty-three potsherds with Hebrew inscriptions in black ink were discovered in the northern storerooms of the so-called Ostraca house. Several other illegible ostraca were also found. These sherds were records of shipments of oil and wine sent by various settlements in the district of Samaria to the royal household as taxes in kind. These very short inscriptions are of considerable value for the light they shed on the language, script, personal names, taxation system, and organization of the kingdom of Israel and of the topography of the territory of the tribe of Manasseh. Two frequently repeated formulas in the ostraca are "In the ninth year, from Yaṣit, to Aḥinoam, a jar of old wine" and "In the tenth year, from Ḥaṣerot, to Gaddiyau, a jar of fine oil." In some of the inscriptions the year is indicated by numerical signs. These inscriptions have been generally interpreted as meaning that in a certain year of the king's reign, a shipment was dispatched from a certain locality (for example, Yaṣit, Ḥaṣerot) to the court official in charge of taxes (for example, Aḥinoam, Gaddiyau). Y. Yadin rejects this theory. He claims that the lamed prefixed to the personal name is the possessive lamed, and therefore this name represents the sender and not the tax collector. It should be noted that many of the names are formed with the suffix *yau (yw)*.

	KENYON		WRIGHT		AVIGAD	
	Building	Pottery	Building	Pottery	Building	Pottery
Early Bronze Age	—	+	—	+	—	+
Property of the Shemer family: tenth century — beginning of ninth century	—	—	—	1–2	0	1–2
Omri (882–871 B.C.)	I	1	I		I	
Ahab (871–852 B.C.)	II	2		3	II	3
Jehu (842–814 B.C.)	III	3	II		III	
Jeroboam II (784–748 B.C.)	IV	4	III	4	IV	4
748–721 B.C.	V–VI	5–6	IV–VI	5–6	V–VI	5–6

0 — Remains of walls beneath building period I.

This page, below: City coin of Sebaste-Samaria — 2nd century A.D. *Bottom: Temple of Augustus. Corner tower of forecourt. Opposite page: Herodian temple.*

The component *ba'al* appears frequently.

The various suggestions for dating the ostraca are based on paleographic and ceramic evidence and also on several numerals appearing in the inscriptions and interpreted as 15 or 17(?). The ostraca were consequently attributed to kings who reigned for at least fifteen or seventeen years. G. A. Reisner dated them to the reign of Ahab (871–852 B.C.), B. Mazar to Jehoahaz (814–800 B.C.), Albright and others to Jeroboam II (according to their reckoning 786–746 B.C.). Yadin, on the other hand, interprets the sign as representing the numeral 9 and attributes the ostraca to the time of Menahem, who reigned ten years. In the ninth year of his reign (738 B.C.) he paid tribute to Pul, King of Assyria (II Kings 15:19–20), and for this purpose he imposed a special tax on his subjects in the ninth and tenth years of his reign. The sherds of the vessels on which the inscriptions were written belong to Samaria's stratum IV or V, that is, to the eighth century B.C.

In addition to this collection of ostraca, some scattered sherds bearing short incised inscriptions in Hebrew, mostly names, were discovered in various sites in the excavations. A fragment of a stone slab was found on which the word *asher* (''which,'' ''who'') was carved in large letters, attesting that as in the neighboring lands, stelae with monumental inscriptions were erected in Israel as well.

The Ivories. The group of ivory objects found in Samaria is the most important collection of miniature art from the Iron Age discovered in Israel. The first ivories were found during the excavations of the Harvard Expedition on the floor of the Ahab courtyard north of the Ostraca house. The largest of these was found together with a fragment of an alabaster jar on which was incised the name of the Egyptian King Osorkon II (914–874 B.C.). This find is of importance for dating the ivories.

The Joint Expedition discovered in various spots in the royal quarter a great number of ivory plaques and hundreds of ivory fragments, most of them difficult to assign to a definite stratum.

The largest concentration of ivories was found in the rubbish deposit of the building (Ivory house) near the inner wall in the north. Since this debris had been accumulated from various conflagration layers and was probably moved from place to place, it was impossible to ascribe it with certainty to definite building phases.

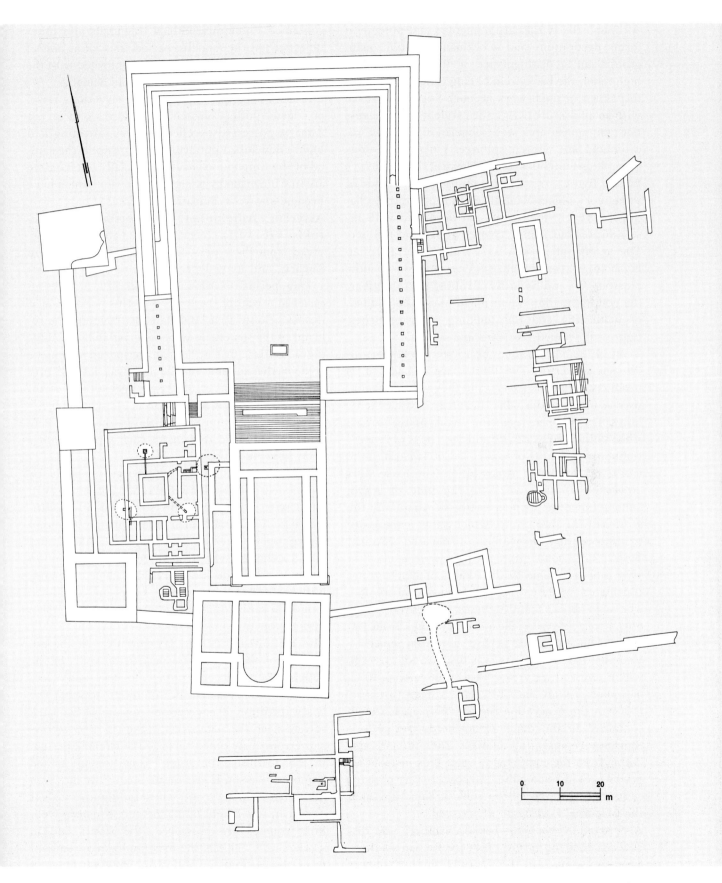

Although the ivories are numerous and diverse in form, decoration, and workmanship, two main groups can be distinguished: 1. Plaques carved in high relief, the background being generally worked in pierced or open work (à jour). Syrian influence with an admixture of Egyptian style is recognizable both in motifs and style. Figures frequently represented are winged sphinxes (cherubim), lions grapplings with bulls, the "woman at the window," human figures, etc. To this group are to be added some ivory objects sculptured in the round, 2. Plaques carved in low relief, and decorated with insets of precious stones, colored glass, gold foil, etc. The motifs are taken as a rule from Egyptian mythology: the infant Horus seated on a lotus blossom, Isis and Nephthys flanking the *djed* pillar, the god Ra holding the image of Maat, the goddess of truth, the god Hah holding palm branches, figures of winged creatures and others.

Many of the ivory plaques bear letters in Hebrew—Phoenician script. The ivories are considered as products of Phoenician art, and they were probably used as inlays in the palace furniture of the Israelite kings. The Bible mentions the "ivory house" which Ahab built (I Kings 22:39) and the "beds of ivory," symbolizing the life of luxury led in Samaria in the words of reproof of Amos (6:4). The excavators attributed all the ivories to the time of Ahab. Others, however, tend to ascribe to Ahab only the ivories of the first group, which show a similarity to ninth-century ivory objects discovered at Aralan Tash. The second group, which is very close in style and technique to the ivories of Nimrud, are considered to date from the eighth century B.C. The ivory objects found at these two sites were probably booty taken by the Assyrian kings from Damascus, Phoenicia, and perhaps also from Samaria.

Various. East of the city was discovered a trench, which covered an area of 30 by 26 meters. It is 4–6 meters wide and 2–5 meters deep (listed as E 207 in the excavation report). This great trench contained an abundance of potsherds and pottery figurines representing humans and animals and dating from the eight century B.C. This installation probably had some cultic purpose. It was perhaps connected with one of the cults in Samaria which the prophets so strongly denounced.

A network of rock-cut burial chambers was discovered north of the city, near the Roman stadium. Deep pits sunk into the floors of these chambers contained numerous pottery fragments and other objects from the Israelite period, as well as animal bones. These pits were probably connected with the cult of the dead, widely practiced in Samaria.

The most common finds in the excavations were, of course, pottery vessels of all forms and styles. Samaria possessed excellent pottery, attesting to a highly developed pottery craftmanship in the capital of the Kingdom of Israel. Especially outstanding are fine burnished vessels with red slip, which have become known as Samarian ware.

Assyrian, Babylonian, and Persian Rule (Periods VII–VIII). Very few remains have survived from these periods. Sargon did not destroy Samaria, and its walls continued to be in use over a long period of time. The Harvard Expedition ascribed a wall of the fortress to this period, but it in fact belongs to a later date (see below). The remains of the structures were removed in later building activities. In the Persian period an extensive area of the summit of the hill was leveled and covered with a layer of brown agricultural earth, which was perhaps brought from elsewhere for the planting of a garden around the palace of the Persian governor. No remains of such a palace, however, have survived.

Among the small finds—also scanty—should be mentioned pottery showing Syrian influence (VII) and Greek pottery from the sixth and fifth centuries B.C. A fragment of a stele with an Assyrian inscription is attributed to Sargon II. Also found was a cylinder seal with an Assyrian inscription and a letter to the local governor named Avi-aḥi, written in Babylonian on a tablet in cuneiform letters. Several Aramaean ostraca from the Persian period were also uncovered.

The Hellenistic Period (Period IX). At the beginning of the Hellenistic period the walls of the Israelite acropolis continued in use and were strengthened by a number of round towers. The first expedition discovered the remains of two such towers near the southwest corner of the fortress and erroneously dated them to the Israelite period. In the northeast the Joint Expedition unearthed another tower built astride the lower Israelite wall (diameter 13 meters, and still standing in excellent condition to a height of 8.5 meters). Nineteen well-built courses are preserved, the stones laid in headers only. This is the most impressive remnant from the Hellenistic period to have survived in

Israel (end of the fourth century B.C.). Remains of the city wall, dating from the same period, were discovered near the western Roman gate where the gate of the Hellenistic city had probably also stood.

In the Late Hellenistic period, in approximately the second century B.C., the upper city was defended by a very strong fort wall, the thickness of which reached 4.2 meters at its base. In its general lines it was built along the course of the wall of the Israelite acropolis, encompassing an area of about 230 by 120 meters, and strengthened by square towers. The Harvard Expedition dated it erroneously to the neo-Babylonian period. This fort wall was probably destroyed by John Hyrcanus, together with the whole city in 108 B.C.

The Roman Period. During this period the city reached the peak of its greatness and splendor. Its gates and towers, the very impressive colonnaded street, the magnificent temples, theater, stadium, and forum — all lent it the aspect of a Roman city.

The tower-strengthened city wall surrounded an irregular area of about 640 dunams. The diameter of the city from east to west was one kilometer and slightly less from north to south. Only sections of the city wall are still extant, its stones were removed and used for the construction of the neighboring town of Shechem. The city gate was situated in the west, and defended by two round towers (diameter of both 14 meters, preserved to a height of 8–11 meters), standing on square foundations of the Hellenistic period. The towers are attributed to the time of Herod, and the wall of the gate between them is dated to the reign of Septimus Severus (end of the second or beginning of the third century A.D.). To the same period is also to be ascribed

Tomb 220 — end of second, beginning of third century A.D.

the colonnaded street, which started near the west gate, continued eastward and perhaps terminated near the east gate. Some six hundred columns were erected along the street over a distance of 800 meters. Two of the columns still bear Corinthian capitals. Trial soundings were carried out by the Joint Expedition in one section of the street. The width of the roadway was 12.5 meters (in its eastern part the street narrowed somewhat) and on both sides stood monolithic columns, 5.5 meters high (including the capitals), supporting a roofed portico along which were built shops. This was a bazaar street.

On the summit of the hill in the western sector above the Israelite fortress were found the remains of a residential quarter from the time of Gabinius. The plan of the Roman city was found to consist of regularly laid streets and dwelling houses with a central courtyard (atrium) surrounded by porches and rooms. Above the remains of these houses, on a height overlooking the entire city and with a view of the sea, Herod erected a temple in honor of the Emperor Augustus. This Augusteum consisted of the temple building proper (35 by 24 meters) and a large forecourt, both of which were oriented on a single south–north axis. For the construction of the wide forecourt, a platform (83 by 72 meters) was erected, the fill of which was retained by subterranean corridors built around it. The retaining wall on the northern slope, which was initially 15 meters high (up to the level of the forecourt), is still extant to a height of 7 meters. A wide staircase led from the forecourt to the temple, which stood on a base rising 4.4 meters above the level of the forecourt. The foundations of the building were laid on bedrock at a depth of 9 meters. The few ashlars from the walls still remaining are dressed with typical Herodian margins. The temple, which was entered through a porch, was divided into a wide nave and two very narrow aisles. During the reign of Septimus Severus (second century) the Augusteum was rebuilt according to its original plan, but was slightly lengthened. The wide stairs visible today and the altar standing in front of them date from this period. Near the altar was found the torso of a huge statue, probably of the Emperor Augustus.

North of the Augusteum stood the temple dedicated to the goddess Kore (36 by 15.5 meters) in a temenos (84 by 45 meters), which may have been surrounded by columns. Of the temple building, only the deep foundations were discovered. They were laid on bedrock and built of courses of alternate headers and stretchers. In the fill of the building were found architectural remains of an earlier temple, dating from the third century B.C. and dedicated mainly to the cult of the goddess Isis, as is attested by a Greek dedicatory inscription to Serapis-Isis. To this temple are attributed two sculptured stones with reliefs of caps wreathed with laurel and crowned with a star, the symbol of the Dioscuri. The temple was probably destroyed by John Hyrcanus. In the Roman period, the temple of Kore was erected on this site, as is attested by the octagonal altar with an engraved dedicatory inscription to Kore.

Also connected with the cult of Kore was the stadium (230 by 60 meters), situated in the northeast sector of the city. Some of its columns were visible. The stadium was only partly excavated. Two building periods were distinguished, the first from the time of Herod. The stadium was enclosed by four porticoes with Doric columns and walls coated with colored plaster. At about the end of the second century, the stadium was rebuilt, this time in Corinthian style. In a cistern in the area of the stadium were found a statue of Kore and a Greek inscription dedicated to the goddess. An altar was uncovered bearing an inscription to the Lady Kore by the high priest.

At the foot of the northeast end of the acropolis were the remains of a theater, of which small sections were cleared: a section of the foundations of the stage and some architectural details of its facade, a section of the paving of the orchestra, parts of the first four rows of seats and of the gangway in the middle of the auditorium. The auditorium had two blocks of seats. The lower block of seats containing fourteen rows was divided by six flights of steps into seven groups. The external diameter of the theater was about 65 meters. The facade of the stage was decorated with niches alternately rounded and rectangular. The theater is dated to the first quarter of the third century A.D.

In the plain between the hill of the acropolis and the village of Sebastia, which is today the threshing floor of the village, lay the forum (128 by 72.5 meters). The walls of the forum in some places reached bedrock at a depth of 4–6 meters, and supported an artificial fill. The forum was enclosed on all its sides by roofed porticoes, of which mainly the west portico is still extant. Of its twenty-four columns, seven are still standing in situ, and of the others, only the bases resting on a stylobate have survived. In the middle of the west wall is a door leading to the basilica adjoining the forum.

The basilica was also not completely excavated. All details of its plan, however, were ascertained. Its length from north to south is 68 meters, its width 32.6 meters. The northern portico of the forum continues along the northern side of the basilica. Three rows of columns in the form of an inverted U divide the basilica into a nave and aisles. Some of the columns are still standing in situ while only the bases of others are preserved. The 6-meter-high columns are monolithic; two of them are topped by Corinthian capitals. At the northern end of the nave was built a bema with a semicircular niche and four benches. The forum and the basilica probably filled the function of the agora of Sebaste. Most of the remains visible today are of the second century A.D., but various other remains point to an earlier period of construction, perhaps to the time of Herod or Gabinius.

Beneath the southern end of the forum and of the basilica runs an aqueduct which carried water to the Roman city from springs on the hills east of the city, near the villages of Nakurah and Jinsiniah. The water supply of the inhabitants of the Israelite city, however, was limited to rainwater which was collected in cisterns.

The Tombs. In the southeast corner of the village of Sebastia a Roman mausoleum was uncovered. Its excavation was begun by the Harvard Expedition and was completed in 1937 by the Department of Antiquities of the Mandatory Government. The square structure (5.5 by 5.5 meters) is built of hewn stones, and its walls are decorated on the outside with pilasters. The tomb consists of one chamber (3.3 by 3.3 meters) with arched niches on three of its walls. Two of the niches held stone sarcophagi. Five other sarcophagi lay on the floor of the chamber. The chamber is domed (5 meters above the floor) with spherical pendentives — one of the earliest constructions of this kind. At the entrance to the tomb there is a stone door turning on hinges. Along the facade of the building was a portico consisting of two rows of four columns each. Two decorated sarcophagi stood here. One of them is outstanding in its rich reliefs of columns, garlands,

masks, and human figures. Near the sarcophagi were found five stone busts. The mausoleum is dated to the second and beginning of the third century A.D.

East of the city, outside the walls, were discovered several rock-cut tombs. One of them (tomb E 220) consists of a court with two main sepulchral chambers. The court (12.15 by 7.95 meters) was cut out of rock, its walls being faced with dressed stones and decorated with pilasters. The two entrances had stone doors turning on their hinges. The two sepulchral chambers (4 by 5 meters each) are lined with ashlar masonry, and loculi are cut into their walls. In some of the loculi stood sarcophagi with gable-shaped lids. Another sarcophagus stood in the court. The tombs contained numerous objects, including glass vessels, jewelry, pottery lamps, etc. The tomb was probably built in the second century A.D. and remained in use also in the third century.

Small Finds. The numismatic evidence at Samaria reflects the history of the town and its economy. Most of the coins are Ptolemaic in the third century B.C. and Seleucid in the second century B.C. At the end of the century, city coins, especially those of Acre, also appear. Jewish coins are found from the time of the Hasmonaeans and of Herod, and in the first century A.D. coins of the Procurators are frequent. In Sebaste itself coins were minted during the reigns of the emperors Domitian, Commodus, Septimus Severus, Caracalla, and Elagabalus, but these coins are not numerous. Byzantine, Arab, and Crusader coins were also found.

The imported pottery — black-glazed ware, Megarian bowls, and stamped handles of Rhodian jars — is evidence of commercial relations with foreign countries in the Hellenistic period. During the Roman period much *terra sigillata* ware was imported. The pagan character of the city of Sebaste is quickly apparent from the statues of Hercules, Dionysus, Apollo, and Kore.

The Late Periods. From the Byzantine period only a few remains have survived, scattered over the lower city and none on the summit of the hill. Among the ruins of the Latin cathedral dedicated to John the Baptist (twelfth century), situated within the village, were found five column capitals from the fifth century A.D. South of the hill, the Joint Expedition cleared a monastery from the Middle Ages in which, according to tradition, the head of John the Baptist was hidden. The church of this monastery includes remains of a previous basilican church with an apse. N. AVIGAD

BIBLIOGRAPHY

Excavation reports: G. A. Reisner, C. S. Fisher, and D. G. Lyon, *Harvard Excavations at Samaria (1908–1910)* 1–2, Cambridge, Mass., 1924 • J. W. Crowfoot and G. M. Crowfoot, *Early Ivories from Samaria,* London, 1938 • J. W. Crowfoot, K. M. Kenyon, and E. L. Sukenik, *The Buildings at Samaria,* London, 1942 • E. L. Sukenik, *Qedem* 2, (1945), 42–47, 59–65 (Hebrew) • J. W. Crowfoot, G. M. Crowfoot, and K. M. Kenyon, *The Objects from Samaria,* London, 1957.
Studies and chronology (see also under ostraca below): W. F. Albright, *BASOR* 150 (1958), 21–25 • G. E. Wright, *ibid.* 155 (1959) 13–29 • K. M. Kenyon, *BIAL* 4 (1964), 143–56. Y. Aharoni and Ruth Amiran, *IEJ* 8 (1958) 171–84.
The Samaria Ostraca: W. F. Albright, *JPOS* 5 (1925), 38 ff: 11 (1931), 24 ff • D. Diringer, *Le inscrizioni antico-ebraiche palestinesi,* Florence, 1934, 21–68 (with bibliography) • B. Maisler (Mazar) *JPOS* 12 (1948), 117–33 • S. Moscati, *Epigrafia ebraica antica,* Rome, 1951, 27–37 • R. Giveon, *BIES* 22 (1958), 55–61 (Hebrew) • Y. Yadin, *IEJ* 9 (1959), 184–87; *idem, Scripta Hierosolymitana* 8 (1960), 1–17 • F. M. Cross, *BASOR* 163 (1961), 12–14 • A. F. Rainey, *IEJ* 12 (1962), 62–63 • Y. Yadin, *ibid.,* 64–66 • Y. Aharoni, *ibid.,* 67–69; *idem, LB,* 315–17; *idem, BASOR* 184 (1966), 13–19 • A. F. Rainey, *PEQ,* 1967, 32–41 • Y. Yadin, *IEJ* 18 (1968), 50–51.
Guides to Samaria: R. W. Hamilton, *Guide to Samaria-Sebaste,* Jerusalem, 1944 • A. Parrot, *Samarie, capitale du Royaume d'Israel,* Neuchâtel, 1955.
Late Samaria: L. H. Vincent, *RB* 45 (1936), 221–32 • J. W. Crowfoot, *Churches at Bosra and Samaria-Sebaste,* London, 1937 • R. W. Hamilton, *QDAP* 8 (1938), 64–71.

During the years 1965–67, small-scale excavations were conducted at Samaria under the sponsorship of the Jordan Department of Antiquities, and directed by F. Zayadin. These investigations were concentrated mainly in the area of the theater, the colonnaded street, the west gate, and the temple of Augustus. An Iron Age tomb was also uncovered.

In 1968, the western sector of the mound was briefly examined by J. B. Hennessy, who exposed several strata of the Hellenistic and Roman periods. Two important chance discoveries are connected with Samaria. One is a hoard of papyri and seals found in the Shinjeh Cave (q.v.) in Wadi Daliyeh. These were the property of fugitives who had fled from Samaria in the fourth century B.C. The other find, fragments of a throne of bronze, probably belonged to the governor of Samaria in the Persian period. EDITOR

BIBLIOGRAPHY

F. Zayadin, *ADAJ* 12–13 (1967–68), 77–80 • J. B. Hennessy, *Levant* 2 (1970), 1–21 • Miriam Tadmor, *IEJ* 24 (1974), 37–43.

SEFUNIM CAVES

IDENTIFICATION. The two Sefunim caves, an eastern cave and a western cave (called Irāq el-Barud in Arabic), are situated in Wadi 'Ein Abu-Hadid, the northern tributary of Naḥal Mitla (Wadi Misilya), about 1.3 kilometers east of the Haifa–Tel-Aviv highway, near Megadim (map reference 14832381). They were discovered in 1904 by E. Graf von Mülinen.

EXCAVATIONS

The west cave is situated on the left bank of the valley and consists of two chambers: the first (20 by 30 meters) is light and ventilated, whereas the inner chamber (20 by 25 meters) is dark. In 1941, a sounding was carried out by M. Stekelis at the entrance of the cave, near the east wall. The stratigraphy is as follows (from top to bottom):

A-1. 0–.1 meter: fairly hard gray earth; Tahunian.

A-2. .1–.3 meter: brown clay mixed with rubble; Kebaran flint implements.

B. .3–.6 meter: soft brown clay with rubble; broken bones and Upper Paleolithic flint implements.

C. .6–1.1 meters: compact brown clay mixed with a few small stones; flakes bearing signs of fire and burned bones: Middle Aurignacian.

D. 1.1–1.2 meters: the excavations ceased at this level.

Three lithic industries were distinguished in the excavation:

1. IN LAYER A-1, which contained only a small amount of material, were found three adzes, one pick, flakes without retouch (12), and cores (4). The industry was called Tahunian by Stekelis.

2. LAYER A-2 was defined as Kebaran (see Kebara Cave). It contained 230 tools: an outstanding group of microliths, which accounts for one third (31.8 percent) of the industry; typical Kebaran bladelets; various blunted back bladelets; micro-Chatelperron and micro-Gravette bladelets.

Scrapers represent 28.3 percent of the industry. Most are of the bulb-end type, but a few are made of flakes or of blades (5.8 percent). The majority of the blades (26.1 percent) are retouched. Four quadrangular sickle blades with Heluan type retouch were found. They appear to be intrusive and therefore are not reliable for dating the layer to the "advanced Kebaran" period as Stekelis did, later correcting himself.

Burins account for 13.5 percent of the industry; they are mainly angle-burins, bec-de-flûte, flat, and nose burins.

3. IN LAYER B, the proportion of Chatelperron points (made of blades) is higher than that found so far in any other Palestinian site: 24.6 percent of a total of 175 tools. They are 4–7 centimeters long with oblique retouch and very similar to Western European Chatelperron specimens. Other blades are truncated and retouched (22.8 percent), and there is also a small group of retouched bladelets (5.7 percent).

Scrapers (20 percent) are made of flakes for the most part or of blades. Their ends are convex. Burins (24 percent) include angle-burins, bec-de-flûte, flat or nose scrapers, or burins on truncature.

4. LAYER C yielded 145 tools in which two new elements are noteworthy: (a) Among the scrapers (31.7 percent) there is a higher proportion of carinated scrapers and core-scrapers (19.1 percent); (b) The appearance of Font-Yves points made on small blades (12 percent).

Retouched blades are predominant (46 percent). Burins (11.5 percent) are atypical for the most part.

This industry and the fifty-one tools from layer D (where excavation was discontinued) are to be attributed to the Middle Aurignacian, as defined by Dorothy Garrod.

SUMMARY

Stekelis correlated layer A-1 with the Tahunian culture and layer A-2 with layer C at Kebara. He was reluctant to place layer A-2 in the "advanced Kebaran" phase because of possibly intrusive sickle blades. Layers B, C, and D were correlated with strata D-I–D-II at Mugharet el-Wad and the industry related to the Middle Aurignacian.   O. BAR-YOSEF

BIBLIOGRAPHY

E. Graf von Mülinen, *ZDPV* 31 (1908), 81–82. M. Stekelis, *BASOR* 86 (1942), 2–14; idem, *Bulletin of the Research Council of Israel* 109, 1–2 (1961), 302–20.

SEPPHORIS

HISTORY AND IDENTIFICATION OF THE SITE.
Sepphoris (Ṣippori) was a Jewish town in Lower Galilee, about 5 kilometers (3 miles) northwest of Nazareth. It is first mentioned in connection with the beginning of the reign of Alexander Jannaeus (Josephus, *Antiquities* XIII, 338), but the existence of an earlier settlement is indicated by the discovery of a burial pit containing funerary equipment (re-used) dating from the Iron Age II and also by the name of the site (Ṣipporim, Ṣippori). In the Hasmonaean period, Sepphoris was probably the administrative center of the whole of Galilee. After the Roman conquest, Gabinus established there one of his administrative councils (synedria) *(Antiquities* XIV, 91; *War* I, 170). Sepphoris submitted to Herod who attacked it during a snowstorm *(Antiquities* XIV, 413; *War* I, 304). After Herod's death the Romans conquered the city during the "war of Varus" and sold its inhabitants into slavery *(Antiquities* XVII, 289; *War* I, 68). With the partition of Herod's kingdom, Sepphoris was granted to his son Antipas, who resided there until he founded Tiberias and made it his capital. During the First Roman War, the inhabitants of Sepphoris sided with Vespasian, surrendered their city to him *(War* III, 30–34), and struck coins in his honor as the "Establisher of Peace" (εἰρηνοποιὸς). After the destruction of the Temple, the priestly family of Jadaiah settled in Sepphoris. During the reign of

City coin from the time of Trajan (A.D. 98–117).

*Below: Plan of the site. 1. Theater. 2. Fort.
3. Basilica. Bottom: Theater (reconstruction).*

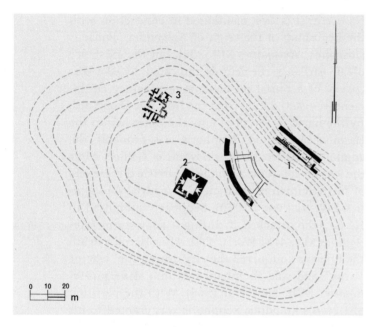

Hadrian the "ancient government" of Sepphoris, i.e., the Jewish local city government, was abolished, a gentile administration was appointed, and probably at the same time the name of the city was changed to Diocaesarea (Διοκαισαρεία — meaning the city of Zeus and of the emperor). However, after Rabbi Judah ha-Nasi and the Sanhedrin established their seat there for seventeen years until the rabbi's death *(Tanḥuma* 2, 215), the local government in the city was once more turned over to a Jewish town council. Sepphoris was the seat of the Sanhedrin until its transfer to Tiberias in the days of Rabbi Judah, its second president, but it remained a Jewish town even during the Christian-Byzantine rule. During the reign of Emperor Constantine, a certain Comes Josephus the Apostate tried in vain to erect a church there. During the reign of Constantius II, the Jewish revolt against Gallus Casear began in Sepphoris (A.D. 351). The Roman troops garrisoned in the city were disarmed, and the rule of the Jewish leader Patricius was established. The Roman commander Ursicinus marched on Sepphoris and succeeded in crushing the revolt. Sepphoris, however, continued to be a

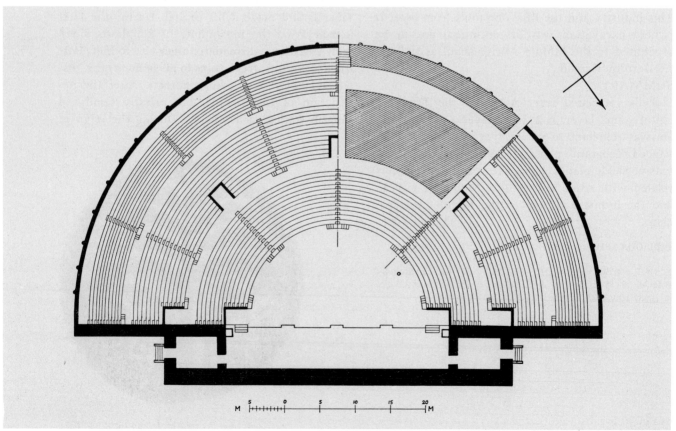

Jewish city in the fifth century and later. From the fifth century a Christian bishop resided there. In Crusader times Sepphoris (Le Sephorie) was a city and fortress in the principality of Galilee. In the eighteenth century the governor of Galilee, Zahir al-'Amr, fortified it anew. There is no doubt that ancient Sepphoris is to be identified with the Arab village of Ṣaffuriye, the present-day settlement of Ṣippori.

EXCAVATIONS

Part of a mosaic floor of a synagogue containing an inscription (see below) was accidentally discovered in Sepphoris in 1909. Fifty years later an inscription describing the renovation of a church by the bishop Marcellinus (about A.D. 518) was found, also by chance. Systematic excavations on the site were carried out by a University of Michigan expedition under the direction of L. Waterman, assisted by S. Yeivin, N. E. Menasseh, and C. S. Fisher, from July to September, 1931. The results were published in 1937. The excavations were concentrated mainly on the summit of the hill on which the settlement lies, near the fort with Crusader foundations, built partly of Roman sarcophagi and re-used Roman ashlars. Two trenches were dug, one (S-I) on the northeast side, and the other (S-II) in the northwest corner of the acropolis.

In the first trench was discovered a Roman theater, dug into and built on the slope of the hill. It had a diameter of about 37 meters and contained 4,000–5,000 seats, arranged in three tiers, consisting of thirteen, thirteen and eleven rows (from the bottom to the top). A wall decorated with engaged columns ran around the *cavea*. Two doors were found, which formed the entrances leading into the interior of the theater. The exits *(vomitoria,* each 2.2 meters wide) had cylindrical vaults. The seats were built of stone slabs set on rock-cut steps. The orchestra was also cut into the rock and was paved with stone slabs. Beneath it were laid lead drainpipes, the outlet of which was an open channel passing beneath the stage. The stage (31 by 6 meters) had a wooden floor, and at its two ends were steps leading down to the orchestra. The back wall was adorned with rich architectural decorations. In the front wall of the stage, grooves were cut to receive the beams supporting the wooden planks of the floor. Beneath the stage were the dressing rooms for the actors. The excavators assume that the stage also included a side room at either end which could be entered from the outside. There were no doors in the back wall of the stage, and the surface of the hill and foundations of the theater form a 4-meter-steep slope. The excavators therefore assume that behind the stage itself there was no colonnade approach. In a trench dug down to bedrock northeast of the theater was found an oil press.

The second trench struck upon a building which the excavators labeled the Christian basilica. In this building the remains of two periods were identified. The upper layer contained six fragments of columns with Ionic capitals. The excavators were able to assign each column to its base, and the columns were found to form two rows. In the southeastern corner was a mosaic floor with a black band around an L-shaped white mosaic. In a nearby room was another mosaic floor with a geometric pattern. Five centimeters beneath the mosaic floor a plastered concrete floor (2 centimeters thick) lay directly on bedrock. In the opinion of the excavators this was the baptistry with a rock-cut square apse next to it. To the north were discovered the foundations of rock-cut walls running parallel to the apse.

The excavators also explored the aqueduct of the city, which was partly built on a masonry substructure (1.1 meters high and 1.2 meters wide) and partly cut in the rock as a tunnel (3.5 meters wide and 6.5 meters high). A 100-meter-long section of it was exposed. At a distance of 1 kilometer southeast of the village was a reservoir (22 by 16 meters). The finds included a Rhodian handle and fragments of Arretine ware. In the cellar of the "basilica" were found various objects from the Byzantine period: hairpins, kohl sticks, spoons, knife handles, and a needle, all made of bone; glass bangles and a glass weight; a mortar and a shallow basalt basin on three legs, and a carved ivory (?) plaque representing an athlete. In the theater a bone hairpin and a fragment of a gold chain were found, as well as four Seleucid coins, eight coins of Alexander Jannaeus, two of John Hyrcanus (probably John Hyrcanus II), three of the Herodian Dynasty, one coin of Bar-Kokhba, coins of the cities of Ashkelon, Tyre, Sidon, Dora, one coin of a Roman procurator, 177 of Roman emperors, ten Byzantine, and three Arab coins.

INTERPRETATION OF THE FINDS

Waterman and Manasseh believed that in the second trench they had discovered an early Christian church, which had originally been dug in the rock, beneath ground level, for fear of persecution by the Romans, but it seems more plausible to define this building as a Roman villa, the rock-cut square "apse" merely being a room, while the "baptistry" was probably a cellar entered by steps. From the floor around the columns, it can be deduced that a colonnade surrounded the open courtyard. No Christian signs or symbols were found on the floors or among the finds, which is further evidence that this building was not used for cultic purposes.

In the list of coins published in the excavation report, several corrections should be noted: Number D 20 is a coin of Bar-Kokhba, the inscription should be read "Shim'on" (Simeon) and not "Shomron" (Samaria) as stated there. Number E 24 is not a coin of Palmyra but of Tyre. E 35 is a coin of Archelaus, E 33 of Dora, and G 41 of the Roman procurator Felix.

Tombs. In the years 1930–31, the Institute of Archaeology of the Hebrew University conducted excavations under the direction of E. L. Sukenik, bringing to light several burial caves in the surroundings of Sepphoris. The tombs are both rock cut and built and contain loculi. In one of the graves an inscription was written on the plaster of the walls: "This is the tomb of Rabbi Yudan, the son of . . son of . . ." This tomb consists of two chambers connected by a narrow passage. The first room is square-shaped with thirteen rock-cut loculi. In the southern wall of the passage, eight loculi were cut in two rows, one above the other. The second room is round and has fourteen loculi.

Another tomb, situated northwest of the village, is known as the Tomb of Jacob's Daughters. This is a

Crusader church.

SHA'AR HA-GOLAN

Fort.

built monumental tomb (12 by 9.25 meters, thickness of walls 1.8–4.4 meters) containing a vaulted chamber (5.5 by 3.5 meters) of dressed stone. In the north wall, opposite the entrance, is a recess with a vault reaching a height of 2.7 meters. In the west and east walls, ten loculi were cut, five in each wall. The foundations of the building are rock cut. It also had a second story. The tomb is attributed to the second or third century A.D.

The Synagogue. In the section of the mosaic floor uncovered north of the Crusader church was preserved a white border with another inscribed black border and a row of diamonds. The field of the mosaic contained a circle (diameter .6 meter) interlaced with a square. The circle and the square are laid in rainbow lines. Inside the circle is a damaged inscription of four lines, in black on white, which was published in 1909. It reads: "Remembered be for good Rabbi Yudan, the son of Tanhum the son of . . .who gave . . ."

M. AVI-YONAH

BIBLIOGRAPHY

E. L. Sukenik, *Tarbiz* 3 (1932), 107–09 (Hebrew) • S. Klein, *Sefer ha-Yishuv* 1, 130–42 (with bibliography) (Hebrew) • L. Waterman. N. E. Manasseh, S. Yeivin, C. S. Bunnel, *Preliminary Report of the University of Michigan Excavations at Sepphoris,* Ann Arbor, 1937 • M. Avi-Yonah, *IEJ* 11 (1961), 184–87 • N. Avigad, *EI* 11 (1973), 41–44 (Hebrew).
The Synagogue: C. Clermont-Ganneau, *CRAIBL* (1909), 677–83 • M. Avi-Yonah, *QDAP* 3 (1934), 40 • J. B. Frey, *Corpus Inscriptionum Iudaicarum* 2, Rome, 1952, 173–76 (includes bibliography).

IDENTIFICATION. Sha'ar Hagolan is a Neolithic site, situated near Kibbutz Sha'ar ha-Golan in the Jordan Valley. It was discovered in 1943, and was surveyed, explored, and excavated by M. Stekelis from that date until the end of 1952. The early homogeneous Neolithic culture uncovered there forms a new complex of the Neolithic cultures in the Near East, which was given the name "Yarmukian" after the River Yarmuk, on the bank of which it came to light. It was subsequently discovered that this culture spread over an area which includes the entire Jordan Valley, where such remains have been found at Khirbet Sodah, Tel 'Ali (q.v.), and Horvat Minha (q.v.).

EXCAVATIONS

Excavations were conducted at Sha'ar ha-Golan in 1949–52. The following strata were distinguished (from top to bottom):

STRATUM I. 0–.6 meter. Black marshy earth, containing rolled basalt boulders and pottery from the transition period between the Early Bronze and Middle Bronze Ages.

STRATUM II. .6–.8 meter. Gray earth, mixed with basalt pebbles, flints, and small stones. Some scattered inclusions of dark yellow clay were also found.

STRATUM III. .8–.9 meter. Thin gravel layer; sterile.

STRATUM IV. 9–1.2 meters. Light-brown clay layer, the upper part sandy and mixed with fine gravel and the lower part clean; sterile.

STRATUM V. 1.2–1.6 meters. Occupation layer with signs of a conflagration; Neolithic flint implements.

STRATUM VI. 1.6–2 meters. Dark-brown clay, mixed with sand; Neolithic occupation remains.

STRATUM VII. 2–2.4 meters. Loose river pebbles of basalt and flint, with limestone, sandy clay, and fine gravel. Thickness of the exposed part of the stratum was .4 meter. Lower part covered by alluvial deposits.

During the excavations, two huts were discovered half dug into the soil with roofing made of organic matter resting on wooden posts. In one of the huts was a two-level hearth, above which was erected a cone-shaped cairn built of three courses of large basalt stones, with a fill of clay soil between them (diameter at the base 2 meters, height about .6 meter). Inside was a human burial, with a skeleton laid on its back with legs slightly flexed. Around and beneath the skeleton were various types of flint implements, fragments of animal bones, incised river pebbles, an incised rib bone, and a broken figurine. The second hut (6 square meters) contained a workshop for flint implements and art objects. In it was uncovered the raw material for flint tools (nodules and cores) and for the production of art objects (river pebbles of soft and hard limestone and basalt) as well as finished and unfinished flint tools in various stages of production, waste material, fragments of pottery, and of art objects. This workshop is unique in the entire Near East. Its contents throw light on the techniques used by the inhabitants of the site and by other Neolithic societies in the region which produced similar implements. In general, it can be stated that the Yarmukian (and the Neolithic) carried on the same traditional techniques developed in the Paleolithic society, with the addition of a new and important element: the polishing of the finished implement (as found on the working edge of some of the axes, adzes, knives). The Yarmukian improved production techniques also by the use of cores with inclined striking platforms forming an angle of 45 degrees with the axis of the core (it was now possible to chip blades and bladelets in the desired length and breadth). A further improvement was denticulation of the implements from both directions of the edge — from the outside toward the inside and vice versa — which was obtained by a more meticulous spacing of the teeth of the denticulation.

The complex of implements was enlarged by a number of new types, such as axes, arrowheads, spearheads, denticulated sickle blades, grinding tools, and querns. During the five seasons of excavations at Sha'ar ha-Golan, a total of 2,300 flint tools was collected, and included adzes, picks, hoes, chisels, knives, made of thick flakes or of flint nodules or cores and chipped on both faces. The complex of the flint implements comprises the following: tools with polished working edge (7.44 percent of the total); awls (32.85 percent) made of small thin flakes, all of them with sharp retouched points; blades (5.6 percent) retouched on one or both sides or on the bulbar face, their form is symmetrical and the edges are parallel, and some of them show retouch made by pressure on both faces; burins (2.27 percent) are angled, oblique and truncated; arrowheads and spearheads (1.16 percent) including wingless ones and some with very fine pressure retouch; denticulated sickle or saw blades (14.35 percent) with one retouched edge and sometimes with two); a few are rectangular in shape, others are triangular. Of particular interest is a composite tool, about 23 centimeters in length and made of four rectangular blades, fixed one next to the other in a haft (not preserved), while a fifth, triangular blade, served as the tip of the tool. Scrapers on flakes and blades represent 2.18 percent and include end scrapers and double end scrapers, side scrapers and rounded scrapers. The last group is characterized by a fine retouch. Push planes and scrapers are made of cores (23.08 percent), their working edge shows a very fine nibbled retouch. Borers (.47 percent) have a strong, retouched point. A small quantity of stone implements (thirty-six items) was also collected, among them large and small bowls, and grinding stones. On one of the bowl fragments appears a herringbone pattern in relief.

Among the few bone implements found are fragments of needles and of a sickle haft, the latter made of a jawbone after the teeth had been removed, an axe handle made of an antler, and fragments of points with polished ends.

Ever since the discovery of the site, thousands of objects of flint, stone, and bone, potsherds and art objects, belonging to the same types discovered in the excavations, have been picked up on the ground and at the bottom of fish ponds of Kibbutz Sha'ar ha-Golan, while many are still scattered in the surroundings.

Potsherds were collected (both during and outside excavations) of jars, pots, bowls, and others. The pottery is handmade, of local coarse clay, fired in an open hearth and therefore porous and very brittle. Most of the ware is covered with a red slip and decorated with various geometric motifs — among which are herringbone patterns. The decorations were incised on the vessels with a chisel or a pointed stick — after application of the red slip but before firing — so that it generally appeared as the natural color of the clay. During the excavations and the survey, a large number of figurines were found which form a unique and remarkable col-

Sera'. Area A. View on the silo of stratum V and the fort of stratum VI.

Schematic figurine of a woman. Right: Head of a woman.

lection. Most of them are made from river pebbles, and a smaller number of local clay mixed with quartz grits or chaff. They are painted with red mineral pigment and represent in very schematic style human, mostly female, figures and male and female genitalia.

SUMMARY

The excavations and the survey in the lands of Kibbutz Sha'ar ha-Golan have shown that a Pottery-Neolithic settlement had existed on an ancient terrace of the Yarmuk, which was based on a combination of agriculture, fishing, and hunting. Raw material for its tool industry (flint, basalt, river pebbles, and clay) was available in abundance and in excellent quality on the banks of the Yarmuk and at its mouth. The tools and art objects were produced in the settlement itself (in the workshop) for local needs only. It seems that the inhabitants practiced spinning too (stone spindle whorls were found in the survey). Round huts, half dug into the ground, roofed with organic matter and each provided with a hearth served as dwellings. The inhabitants buried their dead inside their dwellings, as was customary in Middle Paleolithic times (burial within the caves). This custom provides evidence for the existence of strong family ties and of the

belief in a link between the living and the dead. They also apparently practiced secondary burial either in a hiding place or beneath the floor. The numerous figurines point to the existence of a developed fertility cult of man, the earth, and plants. This cult gives expression to the material-utilitarian concern of the Yarmukian culture in increasing the yield of their field crops and in economic prosperity. The art objects (aside from the decorations on the pottery and stone vessels) show a strong inclination for the plastic arts, and attest to the aesthetic sense, imagination, and creative ability of the artists.

The stratigraphy of the site indicates that the settlement, situated on an ancient river terrace, was brought to an end by an overflow of the Yarmuk that forced its inhabitants to abandon the site.

Stekelis dates the site of Sha'ar ha-Golan to the Neolithic coeval with the Pottery-Neolithic A of Kathleen Kenyon's excavations at Jericho (J. Garstang's stratum IX) and with the Early Neolithic in M. Dunand's excavations at Byblos.   M. STEKELIS

BIBLIOGRAPHY

M. Stekelis, *The Yarmukian Culture of the Neolithic Period*, Jerusalem, 1972.

ESH-SHARI'A TELL (Tel Sera')

IDENTIFICATION. Tell esh-Shari'a is situated in the northwestern Negev midway between Gaza and Beersheba and some 20 kilometers (12.5 miles) northwest of the latter (map reference 119088). The mound lies on a low natural hill overlooking the north bank of Naḥal Gerar (Wadi esh-Shari'a), a tributary of the dominant feature of the northern Negev—the Besor River (Wadi Ghazzeh).

The identification of Tell esh-Shari'a with one of the biblical cities in the northwestern Negev has long been disputed by scholars. It has been identified with Hormah (W. F. Albright), Gerar (A. Alt), and Philistine Gath (G. E. Wright). Other scholars, however, following Y. Press, prefer an identification with Ziklag (B. Mazar, Y. Aharoni, Z. Kalai), which seems to be supported by historical and geographical data as well as by the archaeological evidence. Ziklag is mentioned in Joshua 15:31 as a city of Judah and in I Chronicles 4:30 as a city in the territory of Simeon. Biblical sources refer to Ziklag as a town in the "country of the Philistines" (I Samuel 27:6–7) or the "south of the Cherethites" (I Samuel 30). In Saul's time it was under the political patronage of Philistine Gath and was given to David by Achish, the king of Gath, as a refuge during his flight from Saul (I Samuel 27:6). Thereafter Ziklag became crown property and served as David's headquarters until he went to Hebron to become king over Israel. Ziklag is last listed among the Judean cities during the period of the return from Babylonian Exile (Nehemiah 11:28).

The mound is shaped in the form of a horseshoe with very steep slopes on all but the western side. Naḥal Gerar meanders around the mound, and several springs yield fresh water all year round.

The area of the ancient city on the summit is approximately 16 dunams and is 168 meters above sea level. Judging from the *kurkar* outcrops at the base of the mound, the accumulation of habitational debris may reach 10–12 meters. Quarrying operations during the construction of the Turkish railroad nearby formed a wide, deep crater on the western slope. Surface explorations on the mound and in the strata exposed by the Turkish crater indicate that the site was inhabited from the Middle Bronze Age to the Persian period (seventeenth to fourth centuries B.C.). A fragmentary mosaic floor on the summit suggests that the mound was occupied by a large Byzantine building, perhaps a church or monastery. Chalcolithic and Early Bronze Age potsherds collected at the site, especially on the lower eastern slope, indicate a limited occupation during that period. On the south bank of Naḥal Gerar and on the plain opposite the mound a large area of some two dunams is scattered with Roman and Byzantine remains, including a well-preserved bathhouse and plastered water reservoirs. During the Roman period, the town apparently moved down to the plain on the south bank of Naḥal Gerar, and the summit of the mound was occupied by public buildings.

EXCAVATIONS

Five seasons of excavations have been carried out so far at Shari'a from 1972 to 1976 under the direction of E. D. Oren with E. Netzer as field architect and sponsored by the Archaeological Division of the Ben Gurion University of the Negev, with the assistance of the Hebrew University, Jerusalem, and the Israel Exploration Society.

In the first season (1972), two areas were excavated in the southern part of the mound, in order to obtain a stratigraphical cross section of the occupation levels and to study the unusually steep slope to the east: area A in the southeastern corner of the mound and the steep slope to the east, and area B in the southwestern corner and the west slope, as well as in the Turkish crater. In the second season (1973), area C was opened on the western slope near the path ascending to the summit of the mound, and area R on the southern bank of Naḥal Gerar, opposite the mound. The northern edge of the mound and the northeastern slope were excavated in the third season (1974, area D), while in the fourth season a step trench (area A-I) was dug down to bedrock in the southern slope.

STRATIGRAPHY

After five seasons of excavations at Tell esh-Shari'a a tentative chronology was established.

The entire summit of the mound was occupied by a Muslim cemetery, of which over 150 stone-lined and other individual graves have been found so far. The graves disturbed the upper occupational levels of the mound down to the Iron Age buildings of stratum VII. Some poorly preserved floors and installations of the early Islamic and Mameluke periods (stratum I) were noted in area D.

To the Byzantine Period (stratum II), fourth–sixth centuries A.D., belong the remains of a large stone structure, probably a church or monastery, situated in the center of the mound where a fragmentary mosaic floor was discovered by chance in the early 1950's. To the north of this, in area D, a drainage system was excavated with plastered, stone-lined channels leading to a plastered pool, which contained dozens of ribbed Byzantine water jars. This installation cut through and completely destroyed the western wing of the Iron Age III citadel of stratum VI. In area R, on the southern

STRATUM	PERIOD AND LOCATION
	Muslim cemetery (over the entire summit)
I	Early Islamic and Mameluke periods (area D)
II	Byzantine period, fourth–sixth centuries A.D. (areas D, R)
III	Roman period, first century A.D. (areas A, B, D, R)
IV	Hellenistic period, second–first centuries B.C. (area D)
V	Persian period, fifth–fourth centuries B.C. (areas A, B, C, D)
VI_{1-5}	Iron Age III (II-C), seventh–sixth centuries B.C. (areas A, B, D)
VII_{1-5}	Iron Age II (II-A), tenth–ninth centuries B.C. (areas (A, B, D)
VIII_{1-5}	Iron Age I (I-B), eleventh century B.C. (areas A, B)
IX_{1-3}	Late Bronze Age III (II-B) — Iron Age I, Early twelfth century B.C. (area A)
X	Late Bronze Age III (II-B), thirteenth century B.C. (area A)
XI	Late Bronze Age II (II-A), fourteenth century B.C. (areas A, A-I, B)
XII	Late Bronze Age I, sixteenth–fifteenth centuries B.C. (areas A, A-I, B)
—	Middle Bronze Age III (II-C), seventeenth century B.C. (areas A-I, B)
—	Middle Bronze Age I, twenty-second–twentieth centuries B.C., sherds on surface
—	Chalcolithic and Early Bronze Age, sherds on surface

bank of Naḥal Gerar, a well-preserved bathhouse was partly excavated. It consisted of a hypocaust with red brick arched niches and clay pipes built in the walls, as well as a system of stone-lined channels for drainage around the bath. The pottery from this complex included late Roman Red Slip ware, providing a fifth–sixth centuries A.D. date for the latest use of the bath.

Roman Period. Just below the surface in area D the remains of a sizeable Roman villa (stratum III) were partly excavated in the 1974 and 1975 seasons. The structure was largely destroyed by the Muslim graves and Byzantine drainage system and only the stone foundations and sections of the floor remained. The floors were covered with many fragments of painted wall plaster decorated with geometric and floral designs in white, yellow, red, blue, green, and black. Similar colorful frescoes of the Herodian period are known from the Jewish Quarter in Jerusalem, Herodium, Masada, and Jericho. The debris of the villa also yielded many examples of Aretine pottery, Nabataean and pseudo-Nabataean sherds, "Herodian" oil lamps, and measuring cups of white limestone. A large tower in the northeastern corner of the mound also belongs to this period. Its stone foundations were erected on a massive stone platform which cut into the buildings of stratum VI.

Persian Period (stratum V), fifth–fourth centuries B.C., is represented, as at other sites in the northern Negev, by numerous grain-storage pits. In area A was uncovered a well-preserved brick-lined silo, some 5 meters in diameter, of the same type found at Tell Jemmeh. The brick floor of the silo was still covered with a thick layer of organic matter, perhaps the remains of grain or cereals. The silo and storage pits yielded a large collection of domestic pottery and glazed Attic ware including a red-figured lecythos, bone spatulae, bronze fibulae, Aramaic ostraca, and a finely worked limestone incense altar which was decorated on two sides with incised Proto-Aeolic capitals topped with lotus leaves.

Iron Age III (stratum VI), seventh–sixth centuries B.C., is the last fortified city at Shari'a. A large structure was excavated in area A with long rooms and thick walls, apparently part of the citadel which guarded the southwestern approach of the city. Several storage pits nearby, one very large (7 meters in diameter and 3 meters deep), cut through the earlier strata down to the Late Bronze Age structures. The pits yielded many spiral-burnished bowls, pillar figurines of the Egyptian type, and two Hebrew ostraca. One of the ostraca mentions the place name עצם, perhaps the same city listed in the territory of Simeon (Joshua 19:3). Another citadel, which guarded the northern and northeastern approaches to the city, was explored in area D on the northern edge of the mound. Its mud-brick walls are preserved to a height of 2 meters. The structure was rectangular in plan, consisting of long (14 meters) narrow basement halls enclosed by an unusually thick wall (4 meters wide) and a massive platform of bricks some 10 meters to the south. The citadel was connected to the defense system of the city on the east by casemate rooms, which were completely destroyed by the building of the platform for the Roman tower in the northeastern corner of the mound. The citadel was found buried under heaps of burned bricks and charred beams, testifying to the wholesale destruction by fire that turned the brick

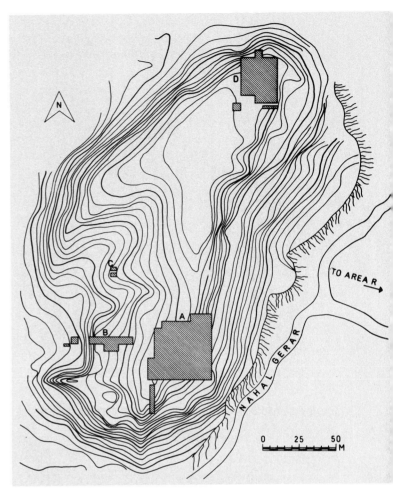

Right: General plan of the site and excavated areas.
Below: Air view of the site. Area A and LBA Residency in the foreground.

Below: Area A. "Residency" of strata X–IX — 13th–12th centuries B.C. *Bottom: Part of the Residency of the 13th century* B.C.

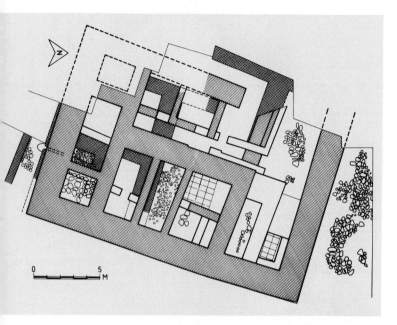

walls red and resulted in the collapse of the upper stories. A socketed, crescent-shaped bronze standard and a bronze bell were found on the brick-lined floor of the northern basement. Similar standards are occasionally depicted on chariots in Assyrian reliefs. Lying nearby was a heavy iron chain about 1 meter long, ending in a pitchfork-like instrument of four prongs. The purpose of this object has not yet been determined, though it may well have belonged to a chariot or battering ram. A well-preserved socketed bronze spearhead was discovered on the floor of a narrow central basement hall, which served in all likelihood as a staircase leading to the upper stories. It was some 65 centimeters long and was complete with rings on both ends of the socket. Similar spears are also represented on Assyrian reliefs as well as on orthostats from north Syria. Discovered among the burned bricks in the southern hall was a faience statuette of the Egyptian goddess Sekhmet, as well as a long Aramaic ostracon containing at least five lines of writing. A group of intact vessels was found in a room adjacent to the east wall of the citadel and under the burned bricks, including a jug incised on its shoulder with the word לירמ. The ceramic evidence, especially fragments of Assyrian Palace ware, *mortaria,* basket-handled jars, and Greek wine amphorae, suggests that the citadel was destroyed in the late seventh or early sixth century B.C., perhaps during one of the Babylonian military campaigns to southern Palestine, or by an Egyptian military expedition of the Saitic Dynasty. This date is substantiated by the finds from a series of large pits which cut into the floors of the citadel and were sealed by another building erected over the citadel. The pits and the later building yielded an identical pottery assemblage, including a Corinthian aryballos of late seventh century B.C. date. The repertoire of stratum VI as a whole is closely paralleled in the late seventh–early sixth century B.C. deposits at Meṣad Ḥashavyahu, En-Gedi, and Tell Jemmeh in Palestine and Naukratis and Daphnae in the Egyptian Delta.

Iron Age II (stratum VII), tenth-ninth centuries B.C. The most intensive building activity of the Iron Age at Shari'a can be noted in stratum VII, which is represented by four to five phases of rebuilding, and an accumulation of debris some 3 meters thick. The sun dried, mud-brick walls of this stratum are preserved to a considerable height usually on *kurkar* foundations, and the bricks are of consistently high quality and uniform size. The latest phase (in the early ninth century B.C.) came to an abrupt end, apparently as a result of an earthquake. Stores of intact vessels were found scattered on the floors together with considerable heaps of fallen bricks, as well as high walls, which had collapsed onto the floors in their entirety.

The architecture of stratum VII, especially in area A, is represented by well-planned public and private structures. One such building, uncovered in the southeastern corner of the mound, consists of long narrow halls surrounded by a massive wall. The bricks were laid in two rows, in a fashion somewhat similar to the header-and-stretcher technique characteristic of Israelite architecture. The floors were of beaten earth with a pebbled surface. The plan and contents of this building suggest that it served as a public storehouse. The best

planned and preserved structures are the two four-room houses in area A. Of these, building 149 measures 13 by 11 meters, and its walls have survived to a height of some 2 meters. Remains of white plaster are still visible on the walls. The building consists of a rectangular courtyard (6 by 8 meters) surrounded by narrow rooms on its southern and eastern sides, and very thick walls on the northern and western sides. The entrance was from the north. The courtyard is divided into two by a row of seven pillars, of which only the large stones are preserved. The west wing of the courtyard, which was apparently covered by a roof, was paved with large pebbles and crushed chalk, while the floor of the eastern wing was made of crushed bricks. A brick bench ran along the east wall. This wing must have served for cooking for it contained clay *tabuns* full of ash, small depressions sunk into the floor and lined with sea-

"Four room" house, on the right. Thirteenth century B.C. *structures, on the left.*

shells, as well as cooking pots still resting on ashes. Around these installations were many complete or restorable storage jars, cooking pots, hand-burnished bowls and jugs, footed chalices, a "foot-bath", painted "Ashdod" sherds and a sizeable heap of unbaked clay balls that were used as jar stoppers or clay heaters. Scattered among the vessels were stone grinders and pounders as well as pottery palettes and ivory kohl sticks for mixing cosmetics. Two small rooms on the east were almost without finds and served in all likelihood as staircases to the second story of the house. That building 149 had a second story is evident both from the accumulation of fallen bricks with complete vessels on top of them in the area of the courtyard, and by the unusually thick walls on the courtyard's northern and western sides. A wall that collapsed in an earthquake fell intact into the long hall bordering the courtyard on the south.

Iron Age I (stratum VIII). Excavation immediately below the four-room houses in area A indicated that its architectural antecedents are to be sought in the Iron Age I (eleventh century B.C.) At least three phases of structures were observed, of which the latest followed the plan of the four-room houses. The architectural continuity is emphasized by the walls, which are built directly upon the earlier walls, the location of the installations in the courtyards, the succession of pebbled floors and rows of stone bases for pillars, as well as the paved floors at the entrance to the building. A similar continuity is seen in the area to the south of building 149, which was used for dumping throughout the Iron Age I–II. The discovery of quantities of Philistine pottery on the earliest floors of these buildings suggest that the four-room house originally belonged to the Philistine architectural tradition and was later adopted by the Israelites. The early occurrence of this house plan in the eleventh century B.C. is well attested at a number of sites, including the northern Negev. On the eastern slope the foundations of the tenth century B.C. houses were sunk into a thick layer of ash, which belonged to a series of large storage pits of the eleventh century B.C. The pottery repertoire of stratum VIII includes typical late Philistine sherds such as decorated bowls with horizontally tilted handles, "beer jugs" with strainers, pilgrim flasks, and stirrup vases alongside hand-burnished pottery as well as "Ashdod" pottery painted with black and white bands on a red background. It should be pointed out that so far no remains, architectural or otherwise, of the early Iron Age I have been encountered. The pits and earliest phases of stratum VIII buldings were founded directly on the debris of the Late Bronze Age strata. It must be concluded, therefore, that area A remained unoccupied during the later half of the twelfth century B.C. and that the foundation of the Philistine settlement cannot be earlier than the eleventh century B.C.

Late Bronze Age (strata IX–XII). Of the Late Bronze Age settlements only the last two strata, X and IX of the thirteenth century B.C. and early twelfth century respectively, have been excavated on a large scale in area A. The earlier strata are recorded in a number of probe trenches, in a step trench in the southern slope and in the Turkish crater.

A large and well-preserved structure was uncovered immediately below the surface of the steep eastern slope and under the Iron Age I deposits on the crest of the mound, and is assigned to stratum IX, from the early twelfth century B.C. Three structural phases were distinguished in this building, which is over 25 meters long with massive walls enclosing a series of small rooms and corridors. Although its eastern wall was almost completely eroded, its *kurkar* foundation indicated that it was at least 2 meters wide. The mud-brick walls are preserved in some places to a height of 2 meters. Some of the rooms had well paved mud-brick floors.

The presence of burned beams and a considerable accumulation of broken bricks and pottery on top of the beams testifies to a thorough destruction by fire, which turned the bricks red and resulted in the collapse of the second story. In every room excavated, there was an astonishing profusion of pottery vessels intermixed with charcoal and animal bones. A large proportion of this collection belongs to a type of plain bowl with string-cut base, which is well known in Egyptian contexts of the New Kingdom period, and is most common in the third structure of the Fosse Temple at Lachish. As at Lachish, here too a large number of the bowls were crudely made. Many of them had cracked in the kiln. Carinated bowls and jugs decorated with the palm tree-and-ibex motif and pilgrim flasks

Opposite page: Mycenaean vessels, from area A, 14th–13th centuries B.C. Below: Egyptian scarab, Nineteenth Dynasty.

were also found. Among the pottery forms to which a special ceremonial use may be attributed were tubular stands pierced with holes and many cup-and-saucer bowls. Egyptian imports are represented by drop-shaped vases and high-necked cups, faience and alabaster vases, and faience heart-shaped and palmette-shaped beads which belonged to a necklace similar to one found in the Fosse Temple at Lachish. A group of bronze objects was found on the floor of one room, including a socketed staff, finishing in a loop in the form of the Egyptian scepter. Another room yielded lumps of blue and yellow pigments, decorated ivory objects, and a group of scarabs and seals of Nineteenth Dynasty types. Perhaps the most intriguing find of all was a group of eleven bowls and ostraca inscribed with texts in the Egyptian hieratic script of the New Kingdom period, one of the bowls mention "Year 22", apparently of Ramses III. These texts deal with taxes paid to the local temple or fortress by the citizens of the Canaanite city at Shari'a. This is the first time that such records have been found in Palestine. They shed considerable light on the tax system in Canaan under

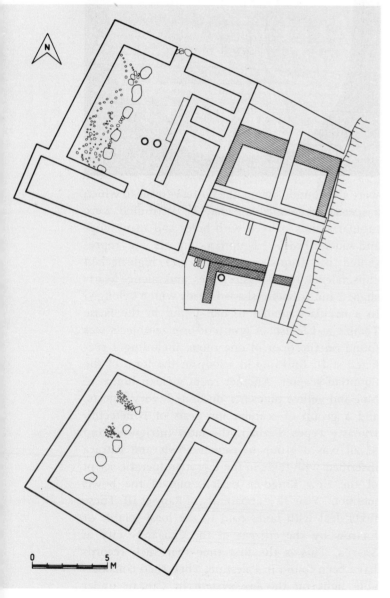

Egyptian rule. Two circular refuse pits were excavated outside the southern enclosure wall. These contained animal bones and some beautifully decorated Egyptian faience vessels such as a bowl painted with lotus flowers, a pilgrim flask, a vase modeled after the Mycenaean stirrup vase, a glass cup with yellow bands as well as a number of Nineteenth Dynasty scarabs. The contents of this structure are very similar to that of the Fosse Temple at Lachish, especially of the latest temple. Judging by the thick walls and the arrangement of rooms on the eastern wing, it seems likely that this structure served as a fortress, or perhaps the residence of the local governor. The charred beams found here were identified as the precious cedar of Lebanon, and its presence at Shari'a is additional proof of the importance of this structure. It is similar in plan and size to the Nineteenth Dynasty Egyptian Residency at nearby Tel Sharuḥen, making it likely that the former also served as the fortified residence of the local (Egyptian?) governor. At the same time, the contents of the hieratic inscriptions, the collection of animal bones and cult vessels from both rooms and refuse pits, and the close parallels to the Lachish temples, all suggest that the fortified complex at Shari'a also included some sort of a sanctuary. The structure was destroyed by fire toward the middle of the twelfth century B.C., perhaps by an early wave of the Sea Peoples, and the area remained deserted until the eleventh century B.C.

Below the brick floors of the structure just described, there came to light the remains of an earlier building (from stratum X), which was distinguished by its stone-paved floors and brick walls built on stone foundations, as well as a nicely plastered stone drain. The floors of this structure yielded Mycenaean vases, including a fragment of a Mycenaean charioteer vase, stirrup vases, Cypriot imports, and bronze toggle pins. Stratum X is assigned to the late thirteenth century B.C.

In the 1975–76 seasons, the excavations south of the Residency partly revealed the remains of a large structure with very thick walls. A plastered bench was built against the northern wall, and on a small platform nearby were preserved remains of painted plaster. The three successive floors in this building were packed with a great many complete pottery vessels intermixed with charcoal and animal bones. The upper floor contained a collection of alabaster vases, a tall tubular stand, pottery vessels in the shape of pomegranates, and ivory inlays. The second floor produced a tubular stand decorated with palm trees and ibexes while the third floor included many decorated vessels, a Mycenaean kylix, Cypriot juglets, and a bone plaque incised with sun rays. Nearby was a *favissa* containing Egyptian and Mycenaean objects. This building was also destroyed by fire toward the middle of the twelfth century B.C.

The remains of the Late Bronze and Middle Bronze Ages down to virgin soil were partly explored in the step trench in the southern slope as well as in the probe squares in the Turkish crater. The evidence indicates that the Canaanite settlement at Shari'a was established sometime in the seventeenth century B.C.

ENVIRONMENTAL STUDY OF THE TELL ESH-SHARI'A REGION

The Ben Gurion University expedition conducted an environmental study of the Naḥal Gerar region in the vicinity of Shari'a. In August, 1974, the

Opposite page, top: Pottery in situ in Israelite "four room" house, 10th century B.C. Bottom: Area A. Plan of stratum VII buildings, 10th–9th centuries B.C. Below: Israelite "four room" house, 10th century B.C.

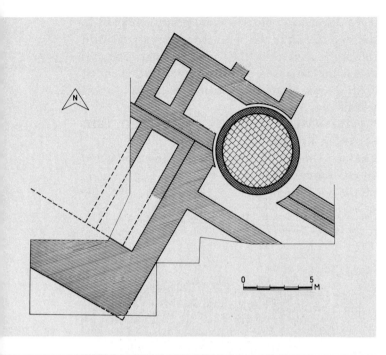

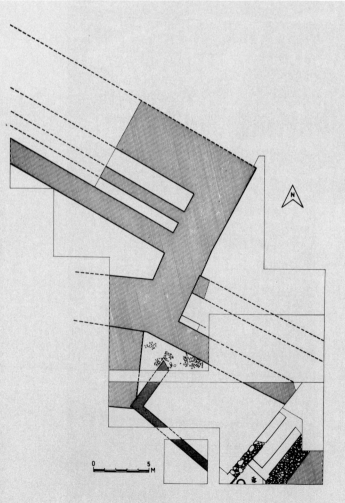

expedition, under the direction of E. D. Oren and A. Mazar, excavated Tel Maaravim, which was probably a daughter settlement of the Canaanite and Philistine city of Shari'a. Tel Maaravim is a small site (2–3 dunams) on the northern bank of Naḥal Gerar and about 1.5 kilometers east of Shari'a. Four phases of occupation were distinguished. PHASE 4 was represented by a very thick layer of ash. The pottery from this deposit indicates that the Canaanite settlement was founded in the Late Bronze Age II.

PHASE 3 is distinguished by the remains of a domestic structure, which was preserved to a height of 1 meter above its floor level. The building comprised a courtyard, partly paved with stone slabs, with small rooms around it. There were almost no finds on the floors, indicating that the building had been deserted. The few potsherds found among the fallen bricks, including a bowl decorated on the inside with the palm tree-and-ibex motif, belong to the thirteenth century B.C.

PHASE 2. The architectural remains of this phase suffered badly from erosion and from the penetration of Arab graves. The ceramic repertoire included painted late Philistine ware and hand-burnished pottery of the eleventh century B.C.

PHASE 1. To this phase are assigned many stone-lined Arab graves.

The excavations at Tel Maaravim, albeit limited in scale, furnish a clear picture of the history of a daughter settlement of the Canaanite and Philistine city at Shari'a. It is interesting to note that at Tel Maaravim, as at Shari'a, no evidence has been found so far for an early Philistine settlement of the twelfth century B.C.   E. D. OREN

BIBLIOGRAPHY

Identification: Alt, *KSch.* 3, 429–50 • W. F. Albright, *BASOR* 14 (1925), 6 • J. Press, *Encyclopaedia of Eretz Israel*, 4, Jerusalem, 1955, 806–07 (Hebrew) • Aharoni, *LB*, index • G. E. Wright, *BA* 29 (1966), 28 ff. • Z. Kallai, *The Tribes of Israel*, Jerusalem, 1967, 300 (Hebrew) • B. Mazar, *Cities and Districts in Eretz Israel*, Jerusalem, 1975, 114, note 12 (Hebrew).
Excavation reports: E. D. Oren, *IEJ* 22 (1972), 167–69; 23 (1973), 251–54; 24 (1974), 264–66, 267–70; *idem. RB* 80 (1973), 401–05; *Qadmoniot* 6 (1973), 53–57 (Hebrew).

*Opposite page, top: Area A. Plan of stratum VI
citadel and stratum V silo. Bottom: Area D.
Plan of the stratum VI citadel. This page, below left:
Area D. Corinthian vase, late 7th century* B.C.
*Right: Bronze Assyrian standard and bell, stratum VI.
Bottom: Pillar figurines, 7th century* B.C.

SHAALBIM

IDENTIFICATION. Shaalbim, a city of the tribe of Dan (Joshua 19:42), from which the original Amorite inhabitants were not ejected by the children of Israel, was a tributary of the House of Joseph (Judges 1:35). Eliahba the Shaalbonite was one of David's "mighty men" (II Samuel 23:32, I Chronicles 11:33). In the days of Solomon; it was one of the cities that provided food for the king and his household (I Kings 4:9). Jerome mentions the place by the name of Selbi. The site is identified with the Arab village Salbit in the northwest part of the Valley of Aijalon about 3 kilometers north of Emmaus.

EXCAVATIONS

A fragment of a mosaic pavement bearing a Samaritan inscription was found in the village shortly after it had been occupied by the Israeli forces in the summer of 1948. The following summer E. L. Sukenik and N. Avigad excavated the site on behalf of the Hebrew University. In the course of these excavations, they uncovered the foundations of a rectangular building (8.05 by 15.4 meters)

Below: Inscription from the synagogue: "The Lord shall reign for ever and ever"
(Samaritan version of Exodus 15:18). Bottom: Fragment of synagogue
mosaic pavement. Upper and lower levels.

whose facade was oriented to the northeast in the direction of Mount Gerizim, the holy mountain of the Samaritans. Column bases were nowhere encountered, but there seems to be no doubt that the building was of the basilica type (divided into a nave and two aisles) but without an apse. The excavators assumed that in the southern part of the building (not excavated) there had been a colonnade or a kind of narthex. Remains of additional rooms were uncovered north and west of the building. In the center of the white mosaic floor was a rectangular panel decorated with geometric patterns (6 by 3.2 meters) and a circular medallion (1.45 meters in diameter) in the center. The southern part of this medallion has been preserved. It is adorned with two seven-branched menorahs flanking a stepped design of a mountain, symbolizing, in the opinion of the excavators, Mount Gerizim. Two fragmentary lines of a Greek inscription appear above the menorahs. The northern corner of the rectangle contains the Samaritan version of the verse: "The Lord shall reign for ever and ever" (Exodus 15:18). Smaller fragments of three lines of another Samaritan inscription appear in the southern part of the rectangle. The floor was made of black and red tesserae, and 15–28 centimeters above it were found three sections of a later mosaic floor adorned with geometric and floral designs.

Judging from the plan and orientation of the building, the Samaritan inscriptions and the menorah decorations, it can be concluded with a fair degree of certainty that these remains belong to an ancient Samaritan synagogue. Another Samaritan synagogue has been uncovered at Beth-Shean.

Sukenik attributed the construction of the synagogue to the fourth century A.D., during the flourishing period of the Samaritan settlement in the days of Baba Rabba. From the style of the floor, however, it appears more likely that the synagogue was built in the fifth century. The building was probably destroyed during one of the Samaritan revolts against Byzantine rule (A.D. 484 or 529), and the later floor was laid when the building was restored after the revolt had been crushed.

D. BARAG

BIBLIOGRAPHY

For the site: Abel, *GP* 2, 438. For the Synagogue: E. L. Sukenik, *Bulletin of the L. M. Rabinowitz Fund* 1 (1949), 15–30, Pls. 14–16 • M. N. Tod, *ibid.* 2 (1951), 27 f., Pl. 12 • Goodenough, *Jewish Symbols* 1, 262–63.

SHARON PLAIN

SURVEYS. An extensive archaeological survey of the Sharon Plain — the Coastal Plain between the Yarkon in the south and the Carmel range in the north — is still underway. Since in antiquity the region was marshy and forested with oak trees, it was assumed that up to the Roman period it was only sparsely settled. This opinion was supported by Egyptian documents from the New Kingdom period, where, as a rule, only the settlements situated along the Via Maris and its branches are mentioned.

During partial archaeological surveys of the Sharon, carried out by B. Mazar, R. Gophna, and M. Kochavi, mounds dating from the Bronze and Iron Ages were discovered also in the western part of the plain, mainly in the river basins. Excavations in the Sharon revealed, for the most part, tombs, farms, and agricultural installations from the Roman and the Byzantine periods (with the exception of Tel Mevorakh, Caesarea, Tel Poleg, and Tel Zeror, *qq.v.*).

The survey and excavations, as well as chance finds made in the basin of the lower course of Naḥal Alexander (Emeq Ḥefer), have yielded information on the history of this region during the Bronze and the Iron Ages, and on the Sharon as a whole. The settlers of the Early Bronze Age I-A, like those of the Neolithic and Chalcolithic periods, whose remains have survived in this region (see Ḥederah), established their settlements on the fringe of the marshes. The remains of two large settlements were discovered and investigated in areas of former marshland, between Mishmar ha-Sharon, Ma'abarot, and 'En ha-Ḥoresh. It appears, however, that already in the Early Bronze Age II these villages were abandoned, and settlement in the Sharon plain was concentrated in the hills bordering the eastern parts of the plain. A hoard of thirty-seven copper tools and weapons discovered in 1962 at nearby Kefar Monash probably came from one of these settlements. The tools include axes, adzes, chisles, a saw, etc. Most of the weapons are spearheads and daggers. In 1967, a rare crescentic copper axhead was discovered, 200 meters north of the hill where the hoard had been found.

The remains of a large settlement of seminomads

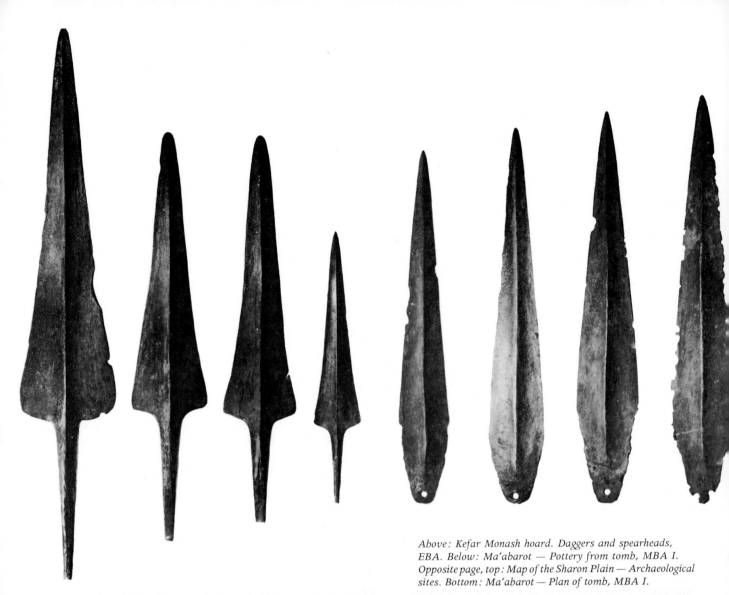

*Above: Kefar Monash hoard. Daggers and spearheads,
EBA. Below: Ma'abarot — Pottery from tomb, MBA I.
Opposite page, top: Map of the Sharon Plain — Archaeological
sites. Bottom: Ma'abarot — Plan of tomb, MBA I.*

from the Middle Bronze Age I were also found near the marsh — not far from a village of the Early Bronze Age I-A.

Farther west, on the *kurkar* hill of Kibbutz Ma'abarot, a cemetery of that period was excavated by R. Gophna in 1966–1967, on behalf of the Department of Antiquities. Twelve shaft tombs were investigated. The pottery assemblage is typical of the ceramic ware found in the northern part of the country. Among the weapons found in the tombs the most noteworthy is a fenestrated ax of bronze.

Finds discovered on the surface of Tel Ḥefer (Tell Ibshar, map reference 141198), attest to the fact that in the Middle Bronze Age II and Late Bronze Age this site was the center of occupation of the area.

A small mound near Moshav Burgata contained remains which may furnish evidence for Israelite settlement in the Sharon during the Iron Age I. A great number of the potsherds discovered on this mound are also typical of the settlements of this period uncovered east of the Sharon, in the hills of Manasseh and Ephraim (see Bethel, Dothan, Shiloh).

Trial excavations were conducted in 1960 on a mound on the coast near Mikhmoret (Minet Abu-Zaburah) on behalf of Leeds University under the direction of B. Isserlin. The remains of a harbor settlement from the Persian and Hellenistic periods were cleared. The settlement was founded at the end of the Iron Age, but a site from the Late Bronze Age II-A-B discovered nearby suggests that a port had existed there as early as the Late Bronze Age.

In the southern Sharon, remains of additional settlements from the Bronze and Iron ages were discovered and partly cleared at Tell Poleg (q.v.) in the basin of Naḥal Poleg, near Tel Makmish (q.v.), and at Kefar Shemaryahu. At the last site, excavated by J. Kaplan in 1962 on behalf of the Department of Antiquities, remains of a temple from the Middle Bronze Age II were uncovered and also remains from Iron Age II-B–C.

Extensive cemeteries, mainly from the Roman and Byzantine periods, were partly excavated on the *kurkar* ridges stretching along the Sharon plain. They attest to the widespread occupation of the Sharon during those periods.

Burial caves have occasionally been found in Ne-

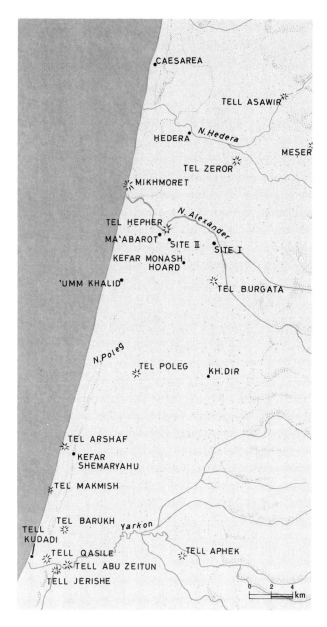

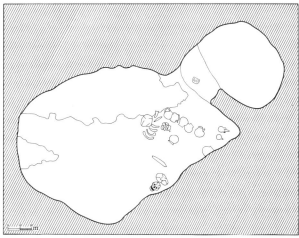

tanya. They apparently belong to a large settlement from the Roman and Byzantine periods, the remains of which were covered by the Arab village Umm Khalid (excavations by J. Ory and F. Berger). In Kefar Shemaryahu part of the Roman cemetery of Apollonia was exposed, and the first cave was excavated in 1940 by E. L. Sukenik on behalf of the Hebrew University. Additional burial caves were cleared in 1962 by F. Berger on behalf of the Department of Antiquities.

Near Ḥederah (q.v.) two built graves from the Roman III period were excavated in 1932 by E. L. Sukenik on behalf of the Hebrew University. In 1951–52, J. Kaplan, on behalf of the Department of Antiquities and Tel Aviv Municipality, cleared a cemetery near Tel Barukh from the Roman and the Byzantine periods. It was a Samaritan cemetery in the opinion of the excavator. Near the Herzliya Pituaḥ Quarter, a burial cave from the third century A.D. was investigated in 1952 by J. Ory on behalf of the Department of Antiquities.

Farms and agricultural installations from the Roman and Byzantine periods have been excavated in the region: a Byzantine farm near Sha'ar Ḥefer (F. Berger, 1951, Department of Antiquities); a Byzantine winepress at Yanuv (F. Berger, 1961, Department of Antiquities); remains of winepresses and an oil press at Apollonia (I. Ben-Dor and P. P. Kahanah, 1950, Department of Antiquities).

Remains of a farm of the Arab period were excavated at Khirbet Dir Isfin (Y. Naveh and F. Berger, 1959, Department of Antiquities).   R. GOPHNA

BIBLIOGRAPHY

B. Maisler, *ZDPV* 58 (1935), 82 ff. • R. Gophna, *Ancient Settlements in Emeq Ḥefer* (Guide Book for the Regional Museum Emeq Ḥefer), 1962 (Hebrew) • J. Karmon, *BIES* 23 (1959), 111–33 (Hebrew); *idem, PEQ*, 1961, 43–60 • R. Gophna and M. Kochavi, *IEJ* 16 (1966), 143–44. R. Gophna, *Archaeological Survey of Emeq Ḥefer*, 1970 (Hebrew) • *idem, The Settlement of the Coastal Plain of Eretz Israel during the Early Bronze Age* (unpublished dissertation), 1974 (Hebrew). • L. Y. Rahmani, *IEJ* 24 (1974), 124–27 • Sh. Dar, *Ancient Settlements in 'Emeq Ḥefer*, Ma'abarot, 1977 (Hebrew). **Excavations:** Apollonia, *'Alon* 3 (1951), 41–43 (Hebrew) • Herzliya, *'Alon* 5–6 (1957), 36–37 (Hebrew) • Ḥederah, Roman tombs, *QDAP* 2 (1932), 185 • Kefar Monash, R. Hestrin and M. Tadmor, *IEJ* 13 (1963), 265–88 • R. Gophna, *IEJ* 18 (1968), 47–49 • A. Ben-Tor, *IEJ* 21 (1971), 201–06 • T. F. Watkins, *PEQ*, 1975, 53–63 • Kefar Shemaryahu, *QDAP* 10 (1940), 195–96 • Mikhmoret, J.B.S. Issrelin, *Annual of Leeds University Oriental Society* 2 (1961), 1–5 • Ma'abarot, R. Gophna, *Qadmoniot* 2 (1969), 50–51 (Hebrew); *idem, IEJ* 19 (1969), 174–77; Netanya, *QDAP* 8 (1938), 175; 10 (1940), 204, *'Alon* 1 (1946) 5 (Hebrew) • Sha'ar Ḥefer, *'Alon* 4 (1953), 6 (Hebrew).

SHARUHEN, TEL

IDENTIFICATION AND HISTORY. Tel Sharuhen (South Tell el-Far'a, not to be confused with Tell el-Far'a, North) was the site of one of the most important cities of the Negev in antiquity. It is located approximately 24 kilometers (15 miles) south of Gaza and 30 kilometers (18.5 miles) west of Beersheba (map reference 1000076).

W. F. Albright's suggestion to identify the site with the Sharuhen mentioned in descriptions of Egyptian military expeditions and in the Bible has been accepted by most scholars. W. M. F. Petrie erroneously identified the site with biblical Beth-Pelet (Joshua 15:27) on the grounds of unsound etymological assumptions.

Sharuhen is mentioned in three Egyptian sources. Ahmose's account of the Hyksos' expulsion relates that the Egyptians laid siege to Sharuhen for three years. Sharuhen appears again in the description of Thutmose III's first campaign where it is stated: "The garrison which was there was in the town of Sharuhen, while from Iursa to the outer ends of the earth had become rebellious against his majesty." It is last mentioned in the description of Pharaoh Shishak's campaign. All these sources clearly indicate that Sharuhen was situated not far from the Via Maris.

In the Bible Sharuhen is mentioned only in Joshua 19:6. In the parallel verse Joshua 15:32, the name Shilhim appears instead of Sharuhen. In Shishak's roster the name is also written SRHM = SLHYIM (number 125). In the Septuagint the name "Sharuhen" does not appear. The town's name is translated as "their fields."

The mound lies on a natural hill, about 100 meters above sea level, near the Besor River (Wadi Shellaleh). It is about 66 dunams in area and contains an accumulation of approximately 14 meters of occupational debris.

EXCAVATIONS

W. M. F. Petrie conducted excavations at the site in 1928 and 1929 on behalf of the British School of Archaeology in Egypt. The first volume of his report was published in 1930 and dealt with the excavations conducted on the north end of the mound and in several cemeteries. The second volume (written by E. MacDonald, J. L. Starkey, and

G. L. Harding) appeared in 1932 and contained the reports of the excavations of the early sites at the foot of the mound and additional cemeteries as well as excavations at the south end of the mound and the extension of the excavation on the north side. The two seasons of excavation at Sharuhen brought to light a nearly continuous occupation from the Middle Bronze Age II-B to Roman times. The latest remains are trenches from World War I, which criss-cross the surface of the site.

Middle Bronze Age II-B. The first settlement on the mound was established by the Hyksos. Its characteristic feature is the glacis topped by a wall. The east side of the mound is defended by a steep slope descending to the Besor River, while on the north and south sides the natural slopes run down to the tributaries of the Besor. The slopes were smoothed on the top to prevent ascent by the enemy. The west side, having no natural protection, was fortified by a fosse 24 meters wide at the top, whose outer bank descends 8 meters at a 40-degree angle. The trench was 1.2 meters wide and 2.5 meters deep. The glacis sloped 18 meters at a 33-degree angle from its top to the upper edge of the fosse. The glacis, made of beaten earth, was leveled off at the top to form a foundation for the wall. At the top of the natural slope on the north end of the mound was thrown a rampart which stood 6 meters above the hill and was 5 meters wide. In three places within the rampart excavations revealed a wall, consisting of an earth fill sandwiched between two brick walls (the inner 1.5 meters thick, and the outer .6 meter thick).

THE GATE. At the top of a ravine on the northwest corner of the mound, Petrie uncovered what he described as a threshold of large stones. Since this was the easiest approach to the mound, he believed that the stones represented the remains of the city gate. However, the remains were too scanty for such a conclusion, especially when at the south end of the mound were found the well-preserved remains of a fine gate built of mud brick on leveled earth with an underbedding of sand (like the rampart in the northeast corner on the top of the slope). The passageway (18 by 3.5 meters) of the gate, which was flanked by two towers, contained three pairs of piers (each 2 meters wide), which divided it into two broad rooms, entered through three narrow passages. The floor of these rooms stood 2 meters above the level of the central entranceway. Of the towers flanking the gate, only the northwestern one has survived. It contained four small chambers. A stone-paved threshold and two sandstone steps led from the gate into the city. The construction of the wall on the gate side and its juncture with the gate are not explained in the excavation report, but according to the plan, about a third of the tower projects from the line of the wall. Petrie mentions another section of wall belonging to this gate, which was uncovered in the trench on the west side of the mound.

The ceramic finds indicate that the gate was in use during both the Middle Bronze Age II and the Late Bronze Age, and indeed two separate stages of construction were distinguished: the first of brick, and the second of clay piled on top of the earlier foundations.

Similar gates, also connected with Hyksos fortifications, are found at sites dating from the same period, such as Beth-Shemesh, Gezer, Hazor, Megiddo, Shechem, and Tell Beit Mirsim (qq.v.). As at Sharuhen, at most of these sites the gate was also built in the Middle Bronze Age II and continued in use during the Late Bronze Age. Gates of this type have also been excavated in Syria, and they seem to have originated in the north, perhaps in Anatolia.

THE HYKSOS BUILDINGS. The second season's digging at the north end of the mound brought to light architectural remains dating from the Middle Bronze Age. Here, as in the section of the southern gate, the area was first leveled with a layer of earth on which the building foundations were laid. The remains were not clear, and the plan of the structure was not established. Directly above the Hyksos walls was a building with a paved courtyard and rooms on three sides (the fourth side was not excavated). In two rooms west of the courtyard were found ovens. The building, which was destroyed by fire, most probably dates to the Late Bronze Age II.

Late Bronze Age, THE RESIDENCY. This large building (25 by 22 meters) in the north section of the mound is by far the finest structure uncovered in the excavations. Its foundations are of brick, in places set upon a single stone course, and lie directly on the Hyksos rampart in the north. The structure is made up of rooms on all four sides of a central courtyards. The bedroom has a raised platform set in a recess, serving apparently as a couch or bed. Adjoining the bedroom is a bathroom containing a plastered water tank raised about 1 meter above the floor and reached by a flight of plastered steps. In a storeroom of the building were found remains of forty-five store jars, some of which were sealed with conical clay stoppers stamped with the figure of a god riding a lion. Adjoining the Residency to the west stood a smaller building (19 by 22 meters), which probably housed the domestic offices and services.

The Residency was entered through a large paved courtyard, from which a flight of steps led to the building itself. The pavement of the courtyard shows traces of a path leading to the gate. Remains of steps leading either to the roof or to a second story were found in a small room in the southwest of the building.

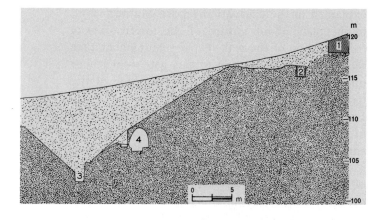

Below: Cross section of Hyksos glacis and fosse. 1. IA I Wall. 2. LBA wall. 3. Fosse. 4. Tomb 902, LBA I. Bottom: Plan of the mound and cemeteries.

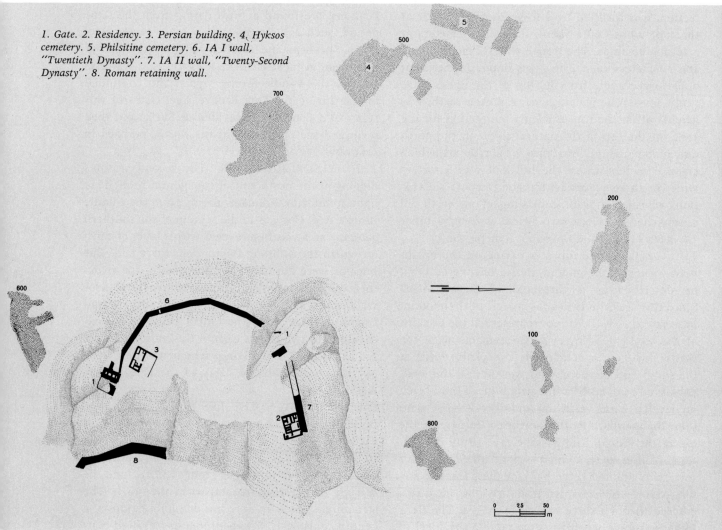

1. Gate. 2. Residency. 3. Persian building. 4. Hyksos cemetery. 5. Philsitine cemetery. 6. IA I wall, "Twentieth Dynasty". 7. IA II wall, "Twenty-Second Dynasty". 8. Roman retaining wall.

The Residency was built at the end of the Late Bronze Age and apparently remained in existence until the eleventh century B.C., when it was destroyed by fire. It underwent at least two stages of construction on the same foundations, but the dates of these stages cannot be determined. The general plan is surprisingly similar to buildings of the Nineteenth Dynasty in Egypt.

Of special interest are two finds, apparently dating to the beginning of the building's existence (end of the thirteenth century). The first is the fragment found in the courtyard of a jar inscribed with a cartouche of Seti II (end of the Nineteenth Dynasty). The other is a small charred wooden box found in one of the rooms. It was decorated with ivory inlays on which were carved a hunt in the swamps and the figure of the ruler, his servants, and dancing girls. The scenes themselves are clearly Egyptian, but the workmanship is Canaanite. Mycenaean motifs are also present.

If the wall shown in one of the plans of the excavation report does indeed belong to the Twentieth Dynasty, as the excavator suggests, then Sharuhen is the only city known to have been fortified during the Iron Age I.

The Iron Age. The next level of occupation is found mainly to the south of the Residency. Petrie also noted traces of later construction in the Residency itself. The inhabitants of level X apparently added walls and floors to the ruins of the Residency (which were still standing at that time to a considerable height) and re-occupied it. To the south, however, they erected new buildings.

According to the plan, level X is divided into two phases. Various architectural remains can be discerned, but they are not sufficient to give a clear picture of the buildings in this level. The finds date this level to the Iron Age II-A.

The next level, V-W, consists of a number of different phases. As Petrie himself states, it is quite difficult to arrive at a clear plan of any of the buildings. The only clear section is KV-VE, a paved courtyard about 2 meters wide in which the bottom sections of four pillars were found. It is very similar to the courtyard of the typical Israelite house, partially covered by a low roof supported on pillars. The roofed half of the courtyard housed the domestic animals, while the various household tasks were carried out in the other half. No trace has survived of any rooms around the courtyard.

Below: Residency. Bottom: South gate.

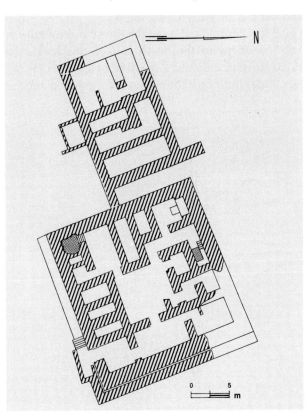

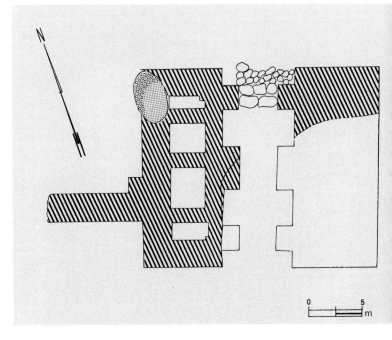

Most of the walls in this level were built of brick on stone foundations. The excavators uncovered several sections of paved floor (probably of courtyards) and a large number of ovens.

Level T-U seems to have been a phase of considerably more activity, but it too is quite fragmentary and cannot be fully understood.

Level R-S contains some of the finest architecture at Tel Sharuhen. In the north end of this level, the excavators uncovered a massive brick wall (5 meters wide) built on a foundation of a single course of stone set deep into a layer of ash. Facing it was a brick retaining wall 2 meters thick, whose foundations were somewhat higher than those of the first wall. Nearby stood a building (23 by 10 meters) erected on a brick foundation, set in a layer of clean sand. The building consisted of a long courtyard enclosed by rooms on the north, south, and west sides. Various other sections of buildings also attest to intensive building activity in this level. It is difficult to determine the dates of the last two levels. The ceramic find is mixed and also includes

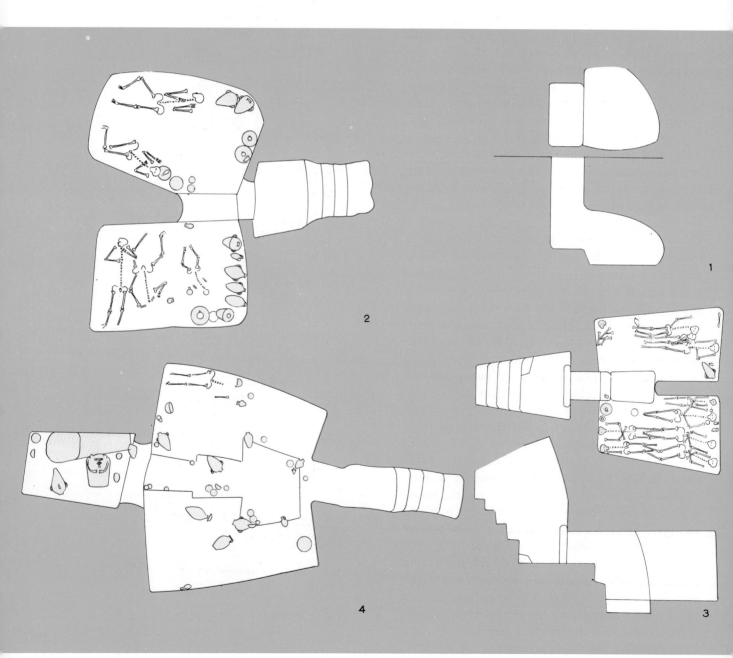

Opposite page: Typical tombs. 1. Tomb 1026, MBA I-II. 2. Tomb 550,
MBA II. 3. Tomb 960, LBA II. 4. Tomb 552, Philistine. Below: Lid and side
of ivory box showing a hunt in swamps and a ruler and his servants, ca 1300 B.C.

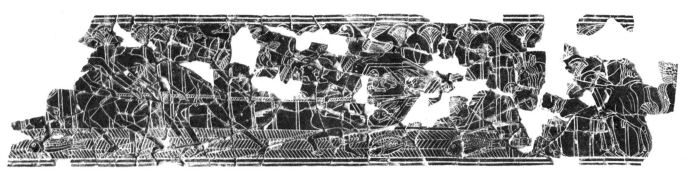

pottery from the Persian period. Petrie ascribed level R-S to Pharaoh Shishak who, in his opinion, rebuilt the cities in the south of Palestine after having conquered them. None of the cemeteries at Sharuhen contained burials dating to the period from the middle of the ninth to the seventh centuries B.C. — a fact which may indicate a gap in the settlement of the mound in that period. It is there-fore possible that "Shishak's level," the last of the Iron Age settlements, actually dates to the end of Iron Age II (seventh–sixth centuries B.C.) and was established and fortified by one of the later Judean kings during one of the periods of southward expansion.

The architectural remains above the gates in the southern part of the mound are too fragmentary to form a clear picture. In the north, the Persian remains are very meager, and in the south only one structure recognizable as a house was found. It was square, with a large courtyard and rooms along the south side probably built around another interior courtyard.

The Roman Period. A clear plan was obtained of the Roman settlement. At the north end of the mound stood a fortified structure (20 by 15 meters) with stone foundations. It consisted of a courtyard with rooms on three sides. To the west of this structure were two thick, well-built, parallel walls (perhaps the remnants of a gate) and a large hall with two columns covered with white stucco. On the floor of the hall were found three hoards of coins dating from the first century A.D. In the center of the mound, not far below the surface, were exposed the stone foundations of Roman

Below: Aramaic ostracon, ca. 400 B.C. Bottom: Silver bowl and ladle, Persian period.

houses, and in the southern part of the mound were remains of long, parallel halls, similar to Roman army barracks or storehouses.

On the east side, at the foot of the mound, stood a retaining wall approximately 100 meters long and 10 meters thick. The wall was constructed of carefully laid courses of sandstone bound with small stones and mortar. At the time of the excavations, the wall stood 3 meters above ground level, but it was not fully excavated. Petrie records the discovery of some sherds of Roman pottery in the wall.

No remains later than the first century A.D. were discovered in the excavations, except for a stamped, Byzantine clay stopper which was picked up on the surface of the mound.

THE CEMETERIES

A large part of both seasons of excavations was devoted to the numerous cemeteries around the mound. More than 350 tombs, lying mostly to the north, south, and west, were excavated. Unfortunately Petrie's descriptions of the tombs are rather brief and sometimes incomplete.

Middle Bronze Age II Burials. Tombs of the Middle Bronze Age II were found in cemeteries 500, 700, and 1000. Cemetery 1000 contained rectangular shaft graves with one or two burial chambers, occasionally separated by a high step. In cemetery 500 two other types of tombs were discovered. One consisted of a long narrow stepped passageway leading from the north toward two oval burial chambers communicating by a very large opening. The second type also had a stepped passageway leading down to two rectangular-shaped burial chambers. The threshold at the entrance to the chambers was raised and extended inward to form a high step between them. Between the two burial chambers, a partition wall built as a continuation of the high step supported the ceiling.

Late Bronze Age Burials. Burials of the Late Bronze Age were found in cemeteries 100, 500, 600, and 900. The most interesting of these are the tombs of cemetery 900, which had been dug into the slope of the glacis which had gone out of use. In contrast to the previous period, tomb construction had improved greatly. The entrance was now a stepped passageway leading from the west to the entrance and continuing to a pit in the center of the tomb. Around this pit, along the walls of the tomb, ran a wide ledge. The burial chambers were either square or round, and some tombs contained two chambers. Tomb 960 was the only one which had not been plundered, and it had also been left structurally intact. In it ten skeletons were laid full length on their backs, with their heads against the chamber walls. In tomb 902 were found nine skeletons, and at the head of one of them several Mycenaean vessels had been placed. Cemetery 900 was very rich in finds, which included pottery decorated with animal motifs characteristic of Late Bronze Age ceramics. This cemetery dates from the thirteenth to the middle of the twelfth century B.C., i.e., prior to the beginning of the Philistine settlement.

Iron Age I Burials. Burials dating to the Iron Age I were found in most of the cemeteries excavated, and provide confirmation of the stratigraphic evidence, namely, that a rich and densely populated settlement flourished here in this period.

Of special importance are four tombs, which together with a fifth smaller one Petrie designated as the "graves of the five lords of the Philistines." These tombs consist of a passageway of six or seven stairs leading down into a nearly square chamber. The stairs continue in the chamber proper to a rectangular depression cut in the center of the floor. In two of the tombs, 542 and 552, this rectangular depression extends beyond the wall opposite the entrance and leads into another small chamber cut along the central axis of the tomb. The dead, it seems, were laid both in the central depression and on the ledges around it, but with no particular orientation. These tombs contained very rich finds, including an especially large quantity of Philistine pottery.

Worthy of special note are two cigar-shaped anthropoid clay coffins from tombs 552 and 562. The human faces depicted on the lids have a short beard, and the arms emerge from behind the ears and join beneath the beard. Similar coffins are known from Beth-Shean and Lachish, from Sahab in Transjordan and from Egypt.

The Philistine tombs date from the twelfth to the eleventh centuries B.C., and according to both Petrie and Albright their sequence was 542, 552, 532, 562.

Cemetery 100 also belongs to the Iron Age I (and to the end of the Late Bronze Age). Its tombs are small and carelessly made, and most of them were plundered in antiquity.

Iron Age II Burials. Cemetery 200 belongs to this period, with most of its tombs dating to the tenth and beginning of the ninth century B.C. The tombs were cut deep into the ground and lined with stone. They were usually covered with large stone slabs on which stood vessels which were apparently brought as offerings to the dead after the tomb had been sealed. Most of these tombs contained rich finds, including a large quantity of jewelry including armlets, rings, and necklaces. Tomb 201 apparently served as a family burial place, and despite its small size (3.8 by 1.2 by 1.7 meters), at least 116 adults were buried in it.

Burials in pottery vessels were also discovered in cemetery 200. The jars, similar in shape to Phoenician vessels, lay near the surface. The jars were closed with inverted bowls or piles of stones. Inside were found charred bones and small offering bowls.

The rich finds in this cemetery included a Hebrew seal on which were carved a griffon wearing the double crown of Egypt and the Hebrew inscription LḤYM (tomb 228).

As was mentioned above, no burials were found dating from the period between the ninth and seventh centuries B.C., perhaps indicating a gap in the settlement of the site.

Burials from the Persian period were discovered in cemeteries 100, 600, and 800. Tomb 650 consisted of a large burial chamber with a bricked-up entrance and a forecourt. This tomb yielded a metal frame of a couch with the metal corners and tie rods connecting the legs, a silver fluted bowl with an omphalos bottom, kohl vials, and a silver dipper with a handle shaped like a girl swimming. On one of the metal frame corners of the couch were several Hebrew letters. This grave is dated to the fifth or fourth century B.C.

A great quantity of metal objects were uncovered in the cemeteries at Sharuhen. These include iron weapons, which make their first appearance in graves of the Iron Age I. Four different types of metal bowls were discovered in the cemeteries. Two are characteristic of the Iron Age and two of the Persian period. Metal strainers were also found, as well as spoons with handles terminating in duck's heads.

An ostracon inscribed in Aramaic and dating to approximately 300 B.C. was picked up on the surface of the mound.   YAEL YISRAELI

BIBLIOGRAPHY

Identification: Aharoni, *LB*, index • W. F. Albright, *BASOR* 33 (1929), 7 • Abel, *GP* 2, 451 • A. Kempinski, *IEJ* 24 (1974), 145–152.
Excavations: W. M. F. Petrie, *Beth Pelet* 1, London, 1930 • J. G. Duncan (with contributions by J. L. Starkey and F. Petrie), *Corpus of Palestinian Pottery*, London, 1930 • E. Macdonald, J. L. Starkey, and L. Harding, *Beth Pelet* 2, London, 1932 • J. H. Iliffe, *QDAP* 4 (1935), 182–86.
Aramaic Ostracon: A. Cowley, *JRAS* 1925, 111–12 • J. Naveh, in: *Bible and Jewish History, Festschrift J. Liver*, Tel-Aviv, 1972, 184–86 (Hebrew).

Hazerim by Sharuhen

IDENTIFICATION AND SURVEY. Six Iron Age settlements were examined in the vicinity of Tel Sharuhen by R. Gophna during a survey and soundings conducted in 1960–1963 in the region of the Besor River (Wadi Shellaleh–Wadi Ghazzeh) on behalf of the Israel Department of Antiquities.

These settlements contained remains of huts, grain pits, millstones, ovens, and pottery. All the sites, which ranged in size from 2 to 10 dunams, revealed little occupational debris and meager archaeological finds. The ceramic group was homogeneous throughout. The evidence indicates that these settlements existed for a very short time only. Five of the six sites can be dated to the Iron Age II-A. The sixth, the largest of the group, was settled during the Iron Age II-C.

It is possible that these sites are the biblical *hazerim* that existed at various times during the Iron Age in the vicinity of the large settlement at Tel Sharuhen. Their connection with Sharuhen seems obvious because of their proximity to that site (1.5 to 6 kilometers) and from the fact that the mound was visible from all of them. Moreover, the pottery found in each of them is identical with that discovered by Petrie's expedition in the excavations at Tel Sharuhen. The pottery of the five *hazerim* dating to the Iron Age II-A was found at Tel Sharuhen in strata X, V, and W. The ceramic find of the sixth *hazer*, dating to the Iron Age II-C, has its counterpart, apparently, in strata R-S at Sharuhen.   R. GOPHNA

BIBLIOGRAPHY

R. Gophna, *Yediot* 27 (1963), 173–80; 28 (1964), 236–47; idem, *'Atiqot* 3 (1966), 44–51; 6 (1970), 25–30 (all Hebrew).

SHECHEM

IDENTIFICATION. Shechem was one of the important cities of the north-central Palestinian hill country during the second and first millennia B.C. References in the Bible indicate that the ancient site was located near the border of the tribal areas of Ephraim and Manasseh (Joshua 17 : 7), and in the vicinity of Mount Gerizim (Judges 9 : 7). Josephus states that it was situated between Ebal and Gerizim (Antiquities IV, 305). Eusebius in his Onomasticon places it in the suburbs of Neapolis by Jacob's Well. The Bordeaux Pilgrim (A.D. 333) gives the same location. This tradition is also followed by the Medeba map in the mid-sixth century A.D., which places the site by the traditional tomb of Joseph between Jacob's Well and Sychar. These references fit precisely the locations of the modern village of Balatah and its tomb of Joseph, with Jacob's Well a slight distance to the southeast and the village of 'Askar, identified with Sychar, to the northeast of the lower slope of the Ebal.

Jerome appears to reject this tradition and to identify Shechem with Neapolis (modern Nablus), a "new city" founded within the Ebal-Gerizim pass by Vespasian in A.D. 72, and to regard Sychar as a mistake for Sichem. While the latter has been debated, the assumption that Neapolis–Nablus was a rebuilding on the site of ancient Shechem was generally followed into modern times. Thus E. Robinson rejects the views of Eusebius and the Bordeaux Pilgrim for those of Jerome.

In 1903, the German scholar H. Thiersch, during a horseback tour of Palestine, encamped at Balatah and in his diary for June 26 described his discovery of a hill of ruins directly north of the village, in which a section of a cyclopean wall lay exposed for 8 meters and traceable for 30 meters. He concluded: "Though the hill at first seems unimportant and not very striking, yet its extent is considerable and its situation remarkable. It controls the plain of Askar and at the same time blocks the pass. These two together are not true of modern Nablus. From this the situation of old Shechem is fixed with certainty and the earlier supposition [Nablus] is refuted . . . Here in any case the investigation must begin."

The excavations of E. Sellin in 1912 have confirmed this location of Shechem at Tell Balatah.

The mound lies at the eastern opening of the Nablus pass, about 2.5 kilometers (1.5 miles) from the center of the city and 66 kilometers (41 miles) north of Jerusalem. Its southern slopes are covered by the modern village, but the area within the walls of the ancient city may be calculated as between 40 and 50 dunams. At their highest the ruins rise approximately 21 meters above the 500 meter contour which passes through the village and along the eastern foot of the mound. Near the mound is a copious spring.

Balatah, lying near the crossroad, is in a pivotal position, all roads in north central Palestine having to pass by it. The plain stretching east and south furnished the economic basis for the development of a great city-state in the second millennium B.C. Its nearest rivals were Jerusalem and Gezer to the south, and Megiddo to the north.

EXCAVATIONS

In 1908, a hoard of fine bronze weapons from Balatah was purchased by F. W. Freiherr von Bissing, and subsequently housed in the Museum Lunsingh Scheurleer, The Hague. This find led the biblical scholar E. Sellin to choose the Balatah hill for excavation, and during the fall of 1913 and the

General plan. 1. German excavations. 2. North gate. 3. East gate. 4. Temple. 5. Temenos 6. Modern Village.

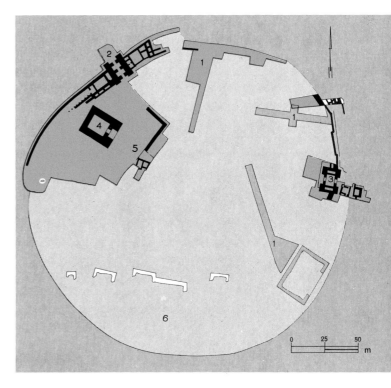

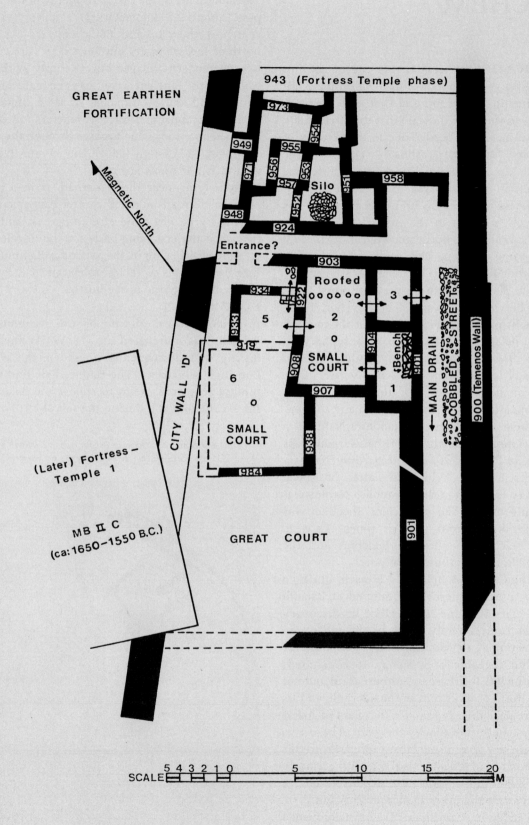

GREAT EARTHEN
FORTIFICATION

943 (Fortress Temple phase)

973

949   955   954

971   956

957   953   Silo   951   958

952

948

924

Entrance?

903

934   Roofed   3

922

933   5   2   904

Bench

919   SMALL   901
COURT

908   1

907

6   938

SMALL
COURT

984

Magnetic North

CITY WALL 'D'

MAIN DRAIN

COBBLED STREET

900 (Temenos Wall)

(Later) Fortress –
Temple 1

MB II C
(ca: 1650–1550 B.C.)

GREAT   COURT

901

SCALE   5 4 3 2 1 0   5   10   15   20
M

spring of 1914, he was able to spend some eight weeks in preliminary work under Austrian auspices before the outbreak of World War I. The western wall was followed in a northeasterly direction for some 75 meters, when a large gate was encountered with flanking towers and three entryways, which he cleared. He also dug a north–south trench, 52 meters in length. Sellin distinguished four levels of occupation, which he identified as Greek, Jewish (or Samaritan), Israelite, and Canaanite.

Four additional campaigns were undertaken during the spring and summer of 1926 and 1927, under German and Dutch auspices with financial assistance from the United States. Both sides of the northwest gate were excavated, and structures adjoining the outer wall at this point were unearthed. Sellin interpreted these structures as the palace of the city. Above the "palace" on the south was built a double or casemate wall running above and parallel to the outer cyclopean wall and connecting with the inner tower of the gate. Farther south a great building was unearthed with very thick walls and with a courtyard, in front in which were found the base of an altar and a large *massebah*. Podiums for smaller stones stood in place on both sides of the entrance. Sellin rightly interpreted this great building as a temple, evidently the temple of El-berit mentioned in Chapter 9 of the book of Judges, though this interpretation was not accepted by many scholars, including his assistant, G. Welter. An extensive and deeper probing below the temple was carried out directly to the east and south of the structure.

On the mound's east side was uncovered a different type of city wall, with offsets and insets, and a two-entry gate (the East Gate) set in it. Two additional trenches were dug east–west and southeast–northwest. Their stratification was found to be the same as that of the prewar excavations. Sellin dated the cyclopean wall and the temple to the early part of the Late Bronze Age, and attributed the eastern offset-inset wall and the repairs to the western casemate to the latter part of the same age. The trench at the southeast was particularly rich in objects of the Canaanite period. Among them were two cuneiform tablets, one of which

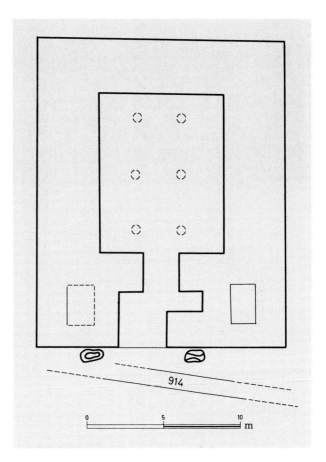

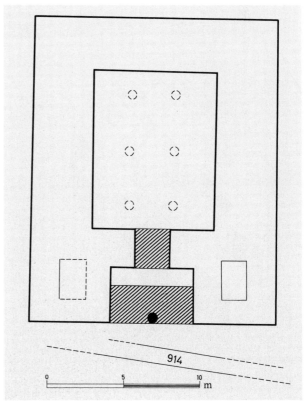

Opposite page: Plan of temenos 4. This page, top: Plan of temple 1b. Bottom: Plan of fortress-temple 1a.

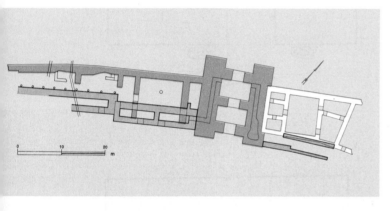

Above: Cylinder seal in Middle Assyrian style, ca. 1200 B.C. Below: North gate and wall A. Bottom: East gate (reconstruction).

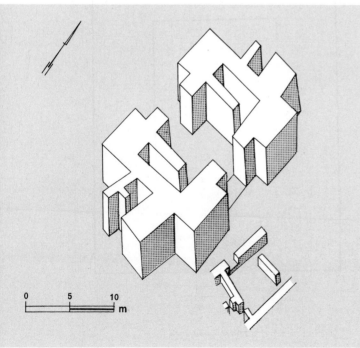

Sellin claimed was from a Middle Bronze Age house.

At this point Sellin was removed from the excavations and was replaced by his assistant Welter. Except for digging several sections, preparing fine plans, and unearthing a Middle Bronze Age II villa (which he considered a temple) on the slopes of Mount Gerizim, Welter did very little actual work at the site. For failure to publish his results, he in turn was removed in 1932 and Sellin reinstated. H. Steckeweh was engaged as archaeologist, but was able to carry out only some surface exploration in September, 1934. For a variety of reasons no further work was done by the expedition, and most of Sellin's records, his completed excavation report, and many small objects, including the cuneiform tablets, were destroyed during the bombing of Berlin in the fall of 1943.

In 1956, Drew University and the McCormick Theological Seminary, together with the American Schools of Oriental Research, began work at the site under the archaeological direction of G. E. Wright. Five seasons of excavation were projected through 1964, in the course of which the architectural features were reexamined, and the stratigraphy of the site was studied and dated with more precision than had been possible hitherto. The more important of these results will be utilized in the historical sketch below.

Early History

The excellent spring at Balatah seems always to have attracted settlers to the area. The earliest evidence of occupation on the mound itself, however, is an extensive settlement from the Chalcolithic period above bedrock on the western side below the temples (the Drew-McCormick Expedition's fields V and VI), and also above bedrock in field IX near the houses of the Arab village. As at Tell el-Far'a (North), here too no building remains but only traces of a campsite were found from that period. No other evidence of an early extensive occupation, other than occasional sherds in later fills, were encountered before the nineteenth–eighteenth centuries B.C.

Shechem in the Canaanite Period. In field VI, immediately above and within the Chalcolithic deposit, there were major leveling and filling operations in the area to prepare it for some public function in Middle Bronze Age II-A (about 1850–1750 B.C.). The area at that time was not within the known city fortifications. During the first phase of Middle Bronze Age II-B (about 1750–1650 B.C.) the first city wall (named wall D) was erected around the area. With its construction the drainage flow was changed from a northwesterly to a southerly direction. This area of public buildings was then separated from the city by a heavy wall (wall 900), about 2.3 meters thick, which remained in use at least as late as the sixteenth century B.C. Between wall D and wall 900, a succession of four different courtyard buildings were erected during the period, with a cobbled street and drain bordering them along wall 900. While the interior arrangement of the rooms varied during the four phases, the large outer court and smaller inner court remained constant features. Architecturally, no parallels for these structures have been found (but see below). Because they are public buildings, separated from

Below: Cross section of the mound between city wall A and wall 900, the eastern limit of the temenos. Bottom: East gate and steps leading down to city.

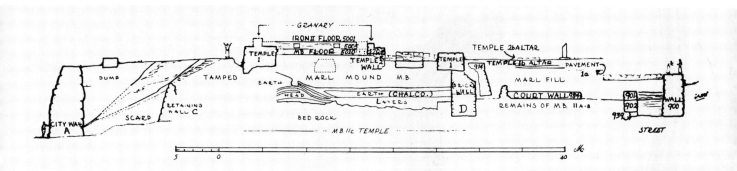

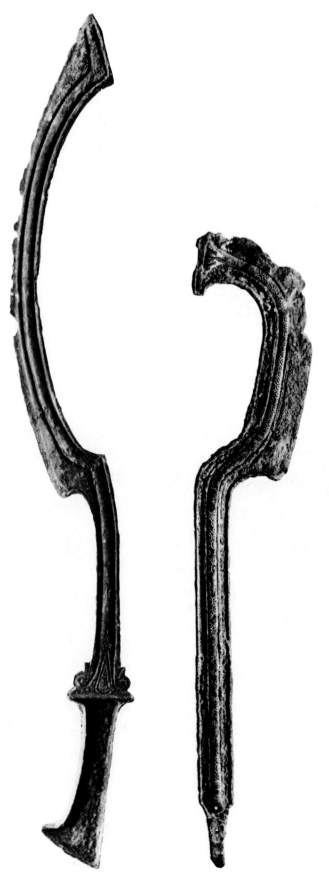

the rest of the city by a stout wall, the writer has suggested that they represent a courtyard temple, the rites of worship taking place within the courts while the rooms housed the local priests. Temples of this type are known from the Late Bronze Age in Beth-Shean IX and in Anatolia. During the second phase of the courtyard temple, dating from the latter part of the eighteenth century, wall D was used as an inner retaining wall for a large earthen embankment with a 5-meter high battered wall (wall C) erected against the outer slope to protect it against attack. It has been traced around the northern and western sides of the mound, and the outer towers of the East Gate were found to be based on the C stone revetment. The height of this eastern fortification was at least 10 meters and probably much more, while its width was about 27 to 30 meters at its base. Wall D, about 2.5–2.85 meters wide (six cubits), was the stone socket for a free-standing brick superstructure. It is thus comparable to other Middle Bronze Age II-A or early B fortifications found at Tell Beit Mirsim, Jericho, and Megiddo. The C embankment with battered wall at its base is Hyksos in conception and execution.

The earliest references to the city in Egyptian sources and in the traditions of the Hebrew patriarchs apparently allude to the smaller city of Middle Bronze Age II-A, the main part of which did not extend as far to the north and west as the installations just described. The first datable reference to the city in the form *skmm* appears to have been in the Egyptian Execration texts (nineteenth century B.C.). Another early reference is contained in the Khu-Sebek inscription on a stele from Abydos dated to the reign of Senusert III (1878–1843 B.C.). Speaking of an Asiatic campaign, it states: "his majesty reached a foreign country of which the name was *skmm* . . . Then *skmm* fell, together with the wretched Retenu." This suggests a city-state of some importance during the second half of the Twelfth Dynasty.

Israel's patriarchal traditions preserve the memory of Shechem as the place in Canaan most closely associated with the family of Jacob (cf. Genesis 37: 12). At its sacred shrine *(maqom)* and "oak of Moreh", both Abraham and Jacob worshipped (Genesis 12:6, 35:4), and on the land which Jacob purchased from the *bene-Ḥamor,* the city's inhabitants, an altar was erected and Joseph was buried (Genesis 33:18–20, Joshua 24:32). While a covenant was made with the inhabitants of the city which allowed intermarriage, there also persists the memory of a bloody destruction of the city by Simeon and Levi (Genesis 34, 49 : 5—7). It is not improbable that both the traditions of shrine and worship played an important role in Israel's later national life.

During the first part of the "Hyksos" period, the city was extended westward, and the compound of the courtyard temple was included within new fortifications. The fortification system was rebuilt on a much larger scale during the latter part of the Middle Bronze Age (II-C, 1650-1550 B.C.). Approximately 9 meters west of the first battered fortification (wall C), the free-standing cyclopean wall A was erected (about 10 meters high, over 4 meters wide at the base, with the external face slightly battered). The top of the C embankment was pulled down against wall A during its construction, so that the end result was a battered wall against an artificial earthen slope. More fill, mainly of occupational debris, was thrown over the courtyard temple area as far as the top of the latter's enclosure wall (wall 900) in order to create a courtyard for the massive fortress-temple *(migdal)*.

This temple measured (externally) 26.3 meters by 21.2 meters, with walls 5.1 to 5.3 meters thick and was oriented 28 degrees south of east. As was first suggested by R. B. Y. Scott, this means that the building was meant to be 50 by 40 by 10 of the long, or sacred, cubits of Ezekiel, the first Palestinian building to demonstrate so early a use of the long cubit. Only the heavy stone foundations of the walls are preserved. They were surfaced with pebbles, which were then plastered over as a base for the brick superstructure. Only a small corner of the latter was recovered. The front of the temple was dominated by two towers flanking an entrance hall, 7 meters wide by 5 meters deep, in which there was a single stone column. This hall led into the cella, 13.5 meters by 11 meters, by a short passage, 3.25 by 3.25 meters. The building dates from the end of the Middle Bronze Age, as is evidenced by the recovery of pottery from that age in the fill between two plastered floors, both of which belonged to this period. In the rebuilding of the second phase, the column was removed from the entrance which was narrowed, and sockets for *massebahs* were installed on each side of it. In the court to the east was found the base of a

Opposite page: *Swords, MBA II-A. This page, above: Seal inscribed "(belonging to) mbn", ca. 600 B.C. Below: Dagger and fenestrated axhead, MBA II-A.*

large altar belonging to this phase.

The Northwest Gate set in wall A is also constructed of massive masonry. Its three entries are typical of the Syro-Palestinian city gates of the period between the eighteenth and thirteenth centuries B.C. The East Gate, however, is much wider, with two entryways between large protruding orthostats. It is set in wall B, an offset-inset wall about 3.25–3.75 meters wide (i.e., 8 cubits), the stone foundation of which is preserved, though its brick superstructure was deliberately pulled down so that the bricks fell inward rather than down the slope. Wall A was found deep within debris, 11 meters east of the East Gate. It was covered over in the Early Hellenistic period. As on the western side of the mound, here too, wall A appears to have been erected along the outer edge of the C embankment, while wall B on the northern and eastern sides was built above the embankment, the slope between the two being filled and plastered as a glacis. The street that emerged from the East Gate turned southward along the top of the plastered glacis.

This enormous effort to create an impregnable mound at Shechem during the "Hyksos" period indicates that during the seventeenth–sixteenth centuries Shechem must have governed a city-state covering nearly the entire hill country from Megiddo in the north to Gezer in the south, its nearest rivals in size and strength. Yet during the sixteenth century B.C. (before the advent of the Late Bronze Age bichrome ware), the eastern and northern areas of the mound were destroyed in two violent conflagrations, and during the second the brick top of wall B was pulled down within the city. These destructions must surely be related to the Egyptian conquest of Palestine, and it is not unreasonable to credit the first to Pharaoh Ahmose I (about 1570–1546 B.C.) at the end of his reign, and the second to Amenhotep I (about 1546–1526 B.C.) in the early years of his reign.

Judging from the extreme rarity of bichrome ware at Shechem, it is doubtful that the city recovered its vigor before the second half of the fifteenth century B.C. During the Amarna period, it again controlled the hill country between Jerusalem and Gezer to the south and the Esdraelon Plain to the north. Toward the end of the reign of Pharaoh Amenhotep III (about 1417–1379 B.C.), Shechem was ruled by a king named Lab'ayu, who was universally hated by his contemporary city-state kings. This deep animosity may testify to Lab'ayu's political and military vigor and his virtual independence from Egypt, in fact if not de jure. He was killed by troops of the king of Megiddo, but his sons carried on in like manner (cf. Amarna Letters, Kundtzon edition, Numbers 242–46, 25–54).

The traditions of the Hebrew conquest of Canaan preserve no memory of a conquest of Shechem, the territory of which was claimed by the Joseph tribes (Joshua 16–17). On the contrary, it is the site of a covenant ceremony which inaugurates Israel's tribal league in Palestine (cf. Deuteronomy 11:29–31; 27; Joshua 8:35; 24). These passages, including Joshua 24:26 ("And Joshua . . . took a great stone, and set it up there under an oak, that was by the sanctuary of the Lord"), have suggested to some scholars that in the early days of Israel a yearly covenant-renewal ceremony was held there, and Genesis 35:1–7 has been interpreted as suggesting an annual pilgrimage from Shechem to Bethel. It is in connection with the abortive attempt to establish kingship in Israel under Abimelech that the most detailed information on the city is provided (Judges 9). Here again we read of the "oak of the pillar" where Abimelech was crowned (surely associated with that mentioned in Joshua 24:26), of the "house of Millo" (9:6, 20), of the "tower" (migdal-shekhem — 9:46–47), and of the temple of the Lord of the Covenant ("Baal-berith," 9:4, "the god Berith," 9:46). While this temple was often assumed to have been Canaanite, it is difficult to dissociate it from the miqdash, oak, and standing stone mentioned in Joshua 24:26. In any event, neither temple nor city was destroyed by Joshua. Instead, a covenant was concluded, and the territory of the city-state entered Israel's tribal league without conquest.

In the Late Bronze Age, the defenses of the city were rebuilt, and large rectangular bricks replaced the square ones of the Middle Bronze Age II. In a major repair of the East Gate, new guardrooms were added. The temple was rebuilt, but with a smaller cella and a 5-degree shift in axis to 33 degrees south of east. The base of a stone altar, 2.2 by 1.65 meters, was found in the court and dated to the second phase of the Late Bronze Age. Near it, and aligned with the Late Bronze Age temple, was a carefully smoothed large stone pillar, .42 meter thick, 1.48 meters wide, with the top broken off

Left: City coin of Neapolis, 3rd century A.D.
*Below: Hoard of silver tetradrachmas belonging
to Ptolemy I-V, 3rd to 2nd centuries* B.C.

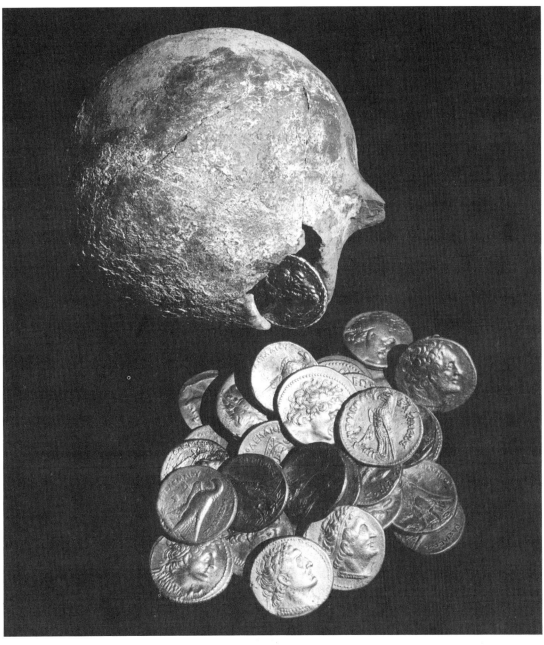

diagonally but still 1.45 meters high. It was found lying over a large stone base in situ with a socket into which the *massebah* fit. Stratigraphically this stone must belong to the period of Temple 2, rather than to the earlier Middle Bronze Age temple. It is not unreasonable to assume that the tradition of the "great stone" said to have been erected "in the sanctuary of the Lord" (Joshua 24:26, cf. Judges 9:6) is to be associated with this *massebah* and that the temple was erected over a traditional patriarchal sacred place. A continuation of this cultic tradition seems to be present in three very different types of biblical literature: the patriarchal narratives, Joshua 24 and Judges 9, which refer to a sacred place, tree, and covenant. The name of the deity mentioned there, El-Berit, may well go back to patriarchal and Amorite times. At any rate it can no longer be simply assumed to be "Canaanite" of the Late Bronze Age type. The central cultic object was apparently a sacred stone, which in the second millennium appears to have been used, not only as a memorial for important ancestors, but also as a witness to an experience of theophany or covenant.

The Bronze Age city with its temple was violently destroyed, and a correlation with the Abimelech story of Judges 9 seems proper.

Shechem in the First Millennium B.C. The rebuilding of Shechem seems to have been a very lengthy process, which was accelerated only during

SUMMARY OF THE BRONZE AGE DISCOVERIES AND CHRONOLOGY

PHASE	DATE (APPROX.)	WALL NO.	
Temenos 1	1800–1750 B.C.	968	Massive fill and leveling of the area. First structures outside known fortifications.
Temenos 2	1750–1725 B.C.	939	Simple courtyard temple and streets 9–7 enclosed between city wall D and temenos wall 900.
Temenos 3	1725–1700 B.C.	902	Casemate-courtyard temple and street 6. Wall C and the great, 30-meter wide, earthen embankment between C and D. Major destruction.
Temenos 4	1700–1675 B.C.	901	Pillar-courtyard temple and streets 5–4. Wall 900 completely rebuilt.
Temenos 5	1675–1650 B.C.	909–910	Enlarged courtyard temple built over edge of C embankment, streets 3–1. Silos built on embankment.
Temenos 6	1650–1600 B.C.		Fortress-temple 1-a, wall A and Northwest Gate.
Temenos 7	1600–1550 B.C.		Fortress-temple 1-b with small *massebahs* on either side of entrance. Altar base with marl-brick edging. Wall B on east and north. East Gate. Destructions (1500–1540 B.C.) and gap in occupation (1540–1450 B.C.).
Temenos 8	1450–1200 B.C.		Fortress-temple 2-a, new brick altar, first phase of podium, repair, and reuse of all fortifications. *Massebah* 1 erected in this period or the next.
Temenos 9	1200–1100 B.C.		Fortress-temple 2-b, marked by raising of floor and new stone altar. All three sacred standing stones in use. Destruction and end of sacred area.

the era of the monarchy. In early clan lists the city is included in the territory of Manasseh (Numbers 26 : 31, Joshua 17 : 2, 7, I Chronicles 7 : 19). In the new Solomonic district of Mount Ephraim (I Kings 4 : 8), it was probably the governor's headquarters. After the major interruption in the city's life with the destruction of the Bronze Age city, the period of United Monarchy marks the city's return to vigorous life. Strata XII–XI appear to belong to this period, the latter being destroyed by Pharaoh Shishak in 918 B.C. or shortly before. A small shrine in stratum XI with an unfinished *massebah* appears to have been rebuilt from the preceding city. Stratum X is a hasty and unsubstantial reconstruction of the city after its destruction by Shishak, and it was quickly replaced by the much more solidly built stratum IX-b. This stratum was destroyed by either an earthquake or enemy attack, perhaps by the Aramaeans in the time of Ben-Hadad (960–953 B.C.) as related in I Kings 20. Stratum IX-a was probably destroyed by Hazael, about 910 B.C., after which city VIII continued until the middle of the eighth century B.C.

Shechem evidently was a tax collection center during the eighth century B.C., as is attested by a large granary with thick plastered floor (stratum IX-a or VIII), which was built on the ruins of the temple in the second half of the ninth or during the eighth century. As the old religious center of Israel, the city was the site of the convocation which rejected Rehoboam and made Jeroboam king of the northern part of the divided kingdom (I Kings 12). Jeroboam repaired the Bronze Age fortifications, and made it his capital for a short time. On the north and west sides of the mound, Sellin found the remains of a casemate wall, but whether they belong to the time of Jeroboam or are later cannot be ascertained with certainty. With the construction of Samaria by the Omri dynasty, Shechem lost its central position, retaining only its religious importance. When Samaria was destroyed by the Assyrians in 724–722 B.C., Shechem, too, was violently destroyed (stratum VII). Stratum VI represents the poor resettlement of the city under Assyrian domination. It has two phases, both of which were violently destroyed by burning in the seventh century B.C., possibly by Josiah in his attempt to unify the country. Judging from Jeremiah 41 : 5, there was a village there in the early sixth century, but whether this belonged

to stratum VI or V is unknown. In any case the town of V must have continued until about 480 B.C., for Greek pottery with a range of approximately 525 to 475 B.C. was uncovered. During the subsequent 150 years the site was deserted.

Shechem's last major city lasted from about 330 to 100 B.C. A rich collection of coins from the end of the fourth to the end of second century B.C. attests to the date. Four different occupation levels have been distinguished during that period. The city was extensively rebuilt, and the Middle Bronze Age fortifications carefully reconstructed (except for wall A on the east, which was covered with a glacis), though leaving a sunken gateway (stratum IV). During the third century, disaster again befell the inhabitants who were forced to undertake widespread repairs, including a new glacis on the east side (stratum III). When Palestine was taken over by the Seleucids during the first decade of the second century, Shechem again suffered damage. Only its houses were subsequently rebuilt and apparently not the old fortifications (stratum II). In about 110–100 B.C., the site was finally destroyed and abandoned (ending stratum I). Afterward the northern area, where the city sloped steeply southward, was leveled, and huge amounts of earth from the mountain slopes were piled against and over wall A in the western and northern sectors. However, whatever was planned was never completed, for the mound itself was never reoccupied.

In correlating these data with the complex and much debated written sources for the era, it is possible to arrive at the following historical conclusions:

In spite of the fact that Josephus has badly confused the events from the end of the fifth and the fourth centuries, it is very probable that the Samaritans did come to terms with Alexander the Great and that his anti-Samaritan source is correct in informing us that the chief city of the Samaritans "at that time was Shechem, which lay beside Mount Garizein . . ." (cf. also Ben-Sira 50 : 26). The shift of the Samaritan capital from Samaria to Shechem can perhaps be understood by the statement of Quintius Curtius, History of Alexander (IV. v. 9) that the Samaritans had for some reason burned Alexander's governor alive, while Alexander was in Egypt (during the winter or spring of 331 B.C.). The latter hastened back to Palestine and punished the guilty parties. Eusebius, Jerome, and Syncellus also relate that Alexander took Samaria, and turned it into a pagan city by giving it to Macedonians who occupied it as a garrison. While the last-mentioned information is often doubted, it seems that it should be regarded as the reason for Samaritan reconstruction of Shechem on such a large scale after centuries of abandonment. It is not known why the reconstructions of strata III, II, and I were necessary, but it is very likely that the final destruction of the city was brought about by John Hyrcanus during his conquest of Samaria (about 107 B.C.; cf. Antiquities XIII, 372 ff.). The coins found on the mound cease at about 110 B.C. The Maccabean destruction of Shechem marked the end of a long series of events which culminated in the split between the Jews and Samaritans. Hereafter, the Samaritans' way of writing, and presumably also their traditions, showed no further contact with Jerusalem.

G. E. WRIGHT

BIBLIOGRAPHY

Report of the Austrian and German Expeditions: E. Sellin, *Anzeiger d. Kais. AD. d. Wiss. in Wien,* Phil-hist. Klasse 51 (1914), Nr. 7, 35–40, Nr. 17, 204–07: *idem, ZDPV* 49 (1926), 229–36, 304–20: 50 (1927), 205–11, 265–74: 51 (1928), 119–23 • G. Welter, *Archäologischer Anzeiger* (1932), 3–4, 289–314 • E. Sellin–H. Steckeweh, *ZDPV* 64 (1941), 1–20.
Cuneiform Tablets: F. M. T. Böhl, *ZDPV* 49 (1926), 320–27 • W. F. Albright, *BASOR* 86 (1942), 28–31 • E. F. Campbell, in: G. E. Wright, *Shechem, The Biography of a Biblical City,* New York–London, 1965, Appendix 3.
Arsenal: F. W. Freiherr von Bissing, *Mededelingen der Koniklijke Akademie Van Wetenschappen,* Amsterdam Afd. Letterkunde, Deel 62, Serie B (1926), 1–24.
Report of the American Expedition: G. E. Wright et al., *BASOR* 144 (1956), 9–26: 148 (1957), 11–28: 161 (1961), 11–54; (1963), 1–60; 180 (1965), 7–41 • E. F. Campbell, *BA* 28 (1965), 18–27: *idem, IEJ* 18 (1968), 192–93 • G. E. Wright, in: D. W. Thomas (ed.), *Archaeology and OT Study,* Oxford, (1967), 355–70 • J. A. Soqqin, *ZDPV* 83 (1967), 183 ff. • F. Zayadine, *ADAJ* 12–13 (1967–1968), 77–80 • G. R. H. Wright, *ZDPV* 83 (1967), 199–202: 89 (1973), 188–96: *idem, ZAW* 80 (1968), 1–35; 82 (1970), 275–78: *idem, PEQ* (1969), 34–36 • R. G. Boling, *BA* 32 (1969), 82–103: *idem, RE* 76 (1969), 419–21 • Horn-Moulds, *Andrews University Seminary Studies* 7 (1969), 17–46 • K. M. Kenyon, *Archaeology in the Holy Land,* London, 1970, 326–27 • E. F. Campbell et alii, *BASOR* 204 (1971), 2–17 • J. D. Seger, *BASOR* 205 (1972), 20–35; *idem, Levant* 6 (1974), 117–30: *idem, EI* 12 (1975), 34–38 • W. G. Dever, *IEJ* 22 (1972), 156–57, 239–40: 23 (1973), 243–45; *idem, RB* 80 (1973), 567–70.
Studies: Y. Yadin, *BASOR* 150 (1958), 34 • G. E. Wright, *ibid.,* 34–5; 167 (1962), 5–13 • S. H. Horn, *JNES* 21 (1962), 1–14 • N. Lapp, *BASOR* 175 '1964), 14–26 • G. R. H. Wright, *PEQ* (1965), 66–84 • G. E. Wright, *Shechem, The Biography of a Biblical City,* New York–London, 1965 • B. Mazar, *IEJ* 18 (1968), 65–97 • A. Malamat, in: *World History of the Jewish People* 3, Jerusalem, 1971, 148 ff., 319 f.

SHEMA' KHIRBET

IDENTIFICATION AND EXCAVATIONS. Khirbet Shema', situated in upper Galilee, has been known since at least late medieval times as the burial place of Shammai, the contemporary of Hillel. Situated some 760 meters above sea level just south of the Meiron Valley on a foothill of Mount Meiron, opposite the ancient settlement of Meiron, the ruin has been identified with Tekoah of Galilee by S. Klein and M. Avi-Yonah. The joint expedition, which dug at the site from 1970 to 1972 under the auspices of the American Schools of Oriental Research and under the direction of E. M. Meyers, found no direct evidence to support this theory. Excavations of the Great Mausoleum, which is still venerated as a holy place by pious pilgrims, produced no evidence for dating, as its foundations were completely disturbed. Other tombs excavated on the site indicated secondary burial to be the dominant mode of inhumation in a variety of tomb types: loculi, grave-type arcosolia, and variations and mixtures thereof. Coins and pottery indicate the main period of use to have been the fourth century A.D., contemporary with the settlement.

The Synagogue. The major discovery at Khirbet Shema' was the synagogue. Nineteenth-century surveys had noted the remains of a substantial building and had described the eagle incised in the doorpost of what turned out to be the western wall. The synagogue of Khirbet Shema' is not the usual kind of Galilean basilica. Two rows of four columns oriented eastward, with a bema situated on the south wall facing Jerusalem, provide a novel adaptation of the basilica as a broad house. The Shema' synagogue would seem to be the product of an architectural eclecticism, which may in fact be dependent upon a number of Palestinian building types rather than upon Greco-Roman forms. The bema, of which several phases were preserved, was the focal point of worship throughout the period of its existence. Both the pedestals and the capitals which stand before it are the most elaborately decorated of the eight, all of which differ from one another. A five-branched menorah fragment on a lamp base, found in the fill just above the floor level, leaves little doubt as to the identity of the building.

The mausoleum, looking north.

Other unique features of the building are these: a frescoed room in the western wall, probably intended to house a portable shrine; an adjoining storage room cut into bedrock and preserved under the staircase which connects the western entryway with the main level of the sanctuary; a woman's gallery built into the western wall; a terrace which forms an approach to the northern entryway; benches along the walls; and an underground cistern (?) in the northeast corner of the synagogue. Pottery and coins suggest a beginning date of early fourth century A.D. since 70 to 80 percent of all the coins date either to Constantine I (A.D. 324–337) or his immediate successors, especially Constantius

(A.D. 337–361). The synagogue was apparently destroyed in the sixth century in a natural catastrophe as most of the architectural fragments were discovered at floor level.

Major soundings were also conducted in the town itself, exposing a number of granaries, private houses, cisterns, and at least one ritual bath. Work conducted by a team of environmental scientists unearthed evidence of a flourishing olive industry, its major architectural remains being preserved just north of the mausolum.

Though a number of Byzantine, Arab, and Crusader coins were found together with pottery of these periods, these later settlements were more modest

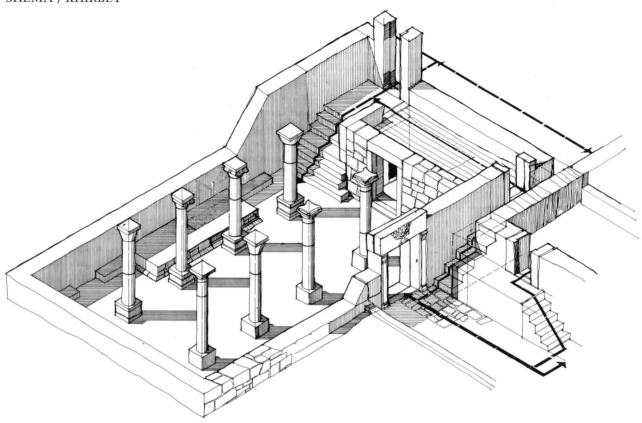

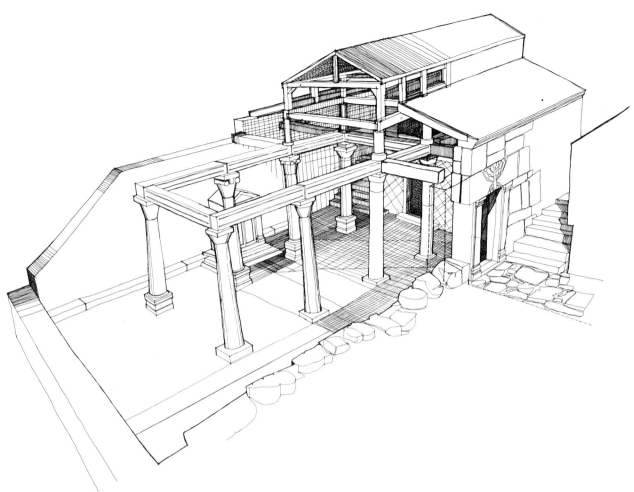

Both pages clockwise from bottom left: View of the synagogue (reconstructed), looking southwest; Isometric view of synagogue with bema of later phase on south wall; Perspective cutaway drawing of synagogue, showing basilica and ark of the Law on south wall; Ritual bath, looking south.

than the Jewish settlement which apparently flourished in the fourth and fifth centuries A.D.

The evidence from Khirbet Shema' is especially important when viewed with that of the other Jewish settlements in Galilee. The fact that just a few hundred meters across the valley in ancient Meiron is found a standard basilica-type synagogue with the familiar facade and heart-shaped columns suggests a great fluidity in synagogue typology. The closest parallels to the Shema' synagogue come from Eshtemoa and Susiya in the Hebron area, neither of which, however, have internal columnation.   E. M. MEYERS

BIBLIOGRAPHY

Conder-Kitchener, *SWP,* 1, 246–47 • Guerin, *Galilee,* 2, 433–34 • D. G. Dalman, *ZDPV* 29 (1906), 195–99 • S. Klein, *The Land of Galilee, Jerusalem,* 1946, 130 (Hebrew) • Z. Vilnay, *Holy Monuments in Eretz Israel,* Jerusalem, 1963, 289 ff. (Hebrew) • M. Avi-Yonah, *The Macmillan Bible Atlas,* New York, 1968, 141, 183 • E. M. Meyers et al., *BA* 35 (1972), 2–31; idem, *Qadmoniot* 18 (1972) (Hebrew); idem, *Perspectives in Jewish Learning* 5 (1972); idem, *AASOR* 42 (1976).

SHILOH

IDENTIFICATION. The location of Shiloh was already known in the Middle Ages through the investigations of Eshtori ha-Parḥi and others. In 1838, E. Robinson identified the site with the Arab village of Sailun (map reference 178162), about 30 kilometers (18.5 miles) north of Jerusalem, which preserved the ancient name of the site. The Bible contains a very instructive topographical description of the place: "Behold, there is a feast of the Lord in Shiloh yearly in a place which is on the north side of Beth-el, on the east side of the highway that goeth up from Beth-el to Shechem, and on the south of Lebonah" (Judges 21 : 19). The city also appears in later sources. Eusebius notes that Shiloh is twelve miles from Shechem (Onomasticon 156, 28). It is also mentioned by Jerome (Epistle 108, Commentary on Zephaniah, 1) and is noted on the Medeba map. All these sources confirm the accuracy of the identification.

The mound is oval in shape and thirty-five dunams in area. It lies between Wadi Sailun and the road

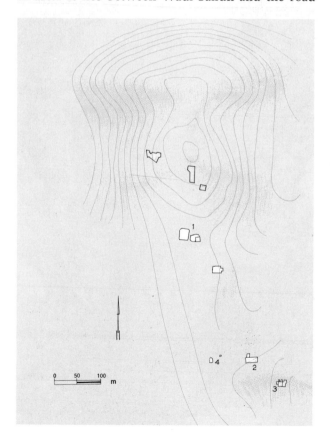

to the village of Quriot. The Roman–Byzantine settlement was built mainly on the southern slope.

HISTORY

According to biblical tradition, Shiloh was the amphictyonic capital of the tribes during the period of the Israelite settlement. The tabernacle was set up at Shiloh, and there the land was divided among the tribes and the Levitical cities were distributed (Joshua 18 : 1, 8–10; 21 : 2). The religious leadership in Shiloh conducted the negotiations between the tribes of Israel when a division in the league threatened (Joshua 22 : 11–12), and it led a defensive war against a common enemy (I Samuel 4). Religious festivals were held at Shiloh every year (Judges 21 : 19). Two important biblical figures, Eli and Samuel, are connected with Shiloh. The house of Eli led the war against the Philistines. At the battle of Aphek the tribes of Israel suffered a severe defeat, and in consequence the Philistines conquered Shiloh, as is mentioned in Jeremiah 7 : 12–14 and Psalms 78 : 60. Traces of this destruction were discovered in the excavations. Even after its ruin, Shiloh was apparently still considered a holy site, and a small number of inhabitants may have remained there to guard the ancient cult place. Ahijah the Shilonite was known in the days of Jeroboam, and from Jeremiah it is evident that even in his time the place was not forgotten. After the destruction of the First Temple, the people of Shiloh came to Jerusalem to offer sacrifices (Jeremiah 41 : 5).

HISTORY OF EXCAVATIONS.

In 1915, A. Schmidt conducted trial soundings at the site and dug several test pits. In 1926–29, systematic excavations were carried out under the direction of H. Kjaer with the participation of Schmidt and the architects C. Christensen and S. Beck. The archaeological adviser was W. F. Albright.

EXCAVATIONS

In the first season the finds were mainly of the later periods. The top stratum was a Crusader settlement apparently destroyed by Saladin. Beneath this stratum were discovered remains of the Hellenistic period.

The second season was a longer one, and the excavators, following Albright's suggestion, concentrated their activities along what they called the city wall (found to date to the Roman–Byzantine period and used also in the Early Arab period). On the western slope of the mound, an area 25 by

20 meters was excavated, which was found to consist of two main blocks: 1. house A and room B, the early structures in the area; and 2. houses C, E, rooms H, J, and adjoining buildings — the late structures.

Room B, of unclear stratigraphy, contained sherds of juglets, lamps, bowls, and other potsherds, which apparently belong to the Middle Bronze Age II-A. It appears that the room was initially constructed in that period. House A was erected later (Iron Age I) and partially covered room B, perhaps even utilizing the stones of its walls.

House A (4 by 3 meters) is attributed to the Iron Age I. In its northeast corner was a stone oven. The finds in the house included six collar-rim store jars typical of the Iron Age I-A and B. Their presence in the destruction level of house A dates the Philistine conquest of Shiloh to the middle of the eleventh century B.C. The "city wall" passes above house A and the adjoining buildings. Although some collar-rim jars were found near the wall, later material from the Iron Age II, Persian, and Hellenistic periods was found as well. The wall was apparently built at a late date, but the evidence does not allow exact dating.

Potsherds of the Iron Age II and the Persian period indicate that some sort of settlement existed there, although no clear structures were found. Buildings remains of the Hellenistic period were uncovered mainly in the trenches made in 1926 south of the mound. Pottery and coins of this period were also found. Shiloh was reoccupied at the beginning of the Hellenistic period and again became a large settlement. Remains of walls and buildings from the Roman period were in continuous use up to the Arab period.

From Byzantine times, two churches of the fifth and sixth centuries A.D. were exposed at the foot of the mound in the southeast. The excavators called the first church the pilgrims' church, and the second, the basilica.

The Pilgrims' Church. The plan of the pilgrims' church (about 11.7 by 25 meters) is not wholly clear, because it was incorporated into a later building. It seems to have had an internal apse, and a bema with a chancel screen, raised two steps above the nave of the church. Two rooms north of the nave were identified by the excavator as the prothesis and the diaconicon. Remains of several rooms, probably later ones, were exposed to the

Opposite page: General plan and areas of excavation 1926–1929. 1. Weli "yatin". 2. Basilica. 3. Weli "sitin". 4. Open-air weli and winepress next to it. This page, below: IA collared rim jars in situ. Bottom: Church. Mosaic pavement in the prothesis.

west. The church apparently had a narthex and an atrium with a mosaic floor in the center of which were traces of three columns. North of the atrium was a cistern to which water was conveyed through a channel from a source north of the church. Remains of small rooms (of unclear plan) were found near the cistern. They included a burial chamber hewn out of the rock.

THE MOSAIC FLOOR of the apse was decorated with vine leaves and bunches of grapes, but the floor of the nave displayed only geometric designs. The mosaic floor of the prothesis was the finest and most richly ornamented. It consisted of squares and a central panel, in which is depicted a pomegranate tree flanked by two deers. Behind each deer is the image of a fish. The excavator interpreted the deer as a reference to the passage "As the hart panteth after the water brooks, so panteth my soul after thee, O God" (Psalms 42 : 1). On the floor of the prothesis is a Greek dedicatory inscription in five lines in a circle inscribed in a square. It mentions the brothers Profirius and Jacob.

The Basilica. The basilica (15.1 by 18 meters) is closer to the mound than the pilgrims' church, and apparently served as a church. It consists of a nave and two aisles, and a narthex on its west side. The mosaic floor of the nave is decorated with geometric designs of intersecting squares, circles, shells, and various floral motifs. It bears a remarkable resemblance to the floor in the crypt of the Church of Elijah at Medeba, and it is very likely that the same artist was responsible for both. The basilica and the pilgrims' church were destroyed during the Arab conquest. Parts of them were dismantled and reused in Arab buildings.

The mound also contains numerous remains of the Arab period. Most of the houses east of house A also continued in use in the Arab period. Special importance was attached to the Muslim holy places.

In 1926, the expedition discovered an open-air *weli*, which in the opinion of the excavators represents the place of worship known as Jama Settin (the Mosque of the Sixty), a site considered holy prior to the period of the Arab conquest. This mosque, which was abandoned by the time of the excavations, was examined in several spots. Among its scanty finds are many Arab lamps from the Middle Ages. The columns and capitals of the mosque were taken from the Byzantine basilica.

The building is square (8.75 meters each side) and has a small niche in the southern wall which apparently served as a mihrab in its latest phase. The building may originally have been a synagogue which was later turned into a mosque, an assumption based on the fact that the niche faces Jerusalem. Remains of a lintel were found among the ruins of the mosque.

Burials. Two burial caves were excavated. One, of the loculi type, had its beginnings in the Second Temple period and was later converted into a reservoir. The second burial cave — el-Assad — was a cistern that was turned into a burial cave only in the Roman period. The excavators noted three layers of burial. The earliest is Roman, the middle Byzantine, and the latest is Arab. Many complete pottery vessels, scores of human skeletons, and some animal bones were discovered in the cave from all the three periods.

SUMMARY

Shiloh was the religious center of the federation of Israelite tribes during the period of their settlement. After the defeat at Aphek and the capture of the Ark of the Covenant, the Philistines ruled the central mountain region and their first act was to destroy Shiloh. This event, alluded to in the Bible, was confirmed by the excavations.

Shiloh evidently did not possess a time-hallowed tradition as a religious center, because with the change in the historical circumstances — i.e., with the decline of the tribal federation and the rise of the monarchy — the Ark of the Covenant was not returned to Shiloh, which was displaced as a religious center. Despite its destruction in the eleventh century, however, Shiloh was inhabited during the entire Israelite and Persian periods and also later. The settlement retained its sacred tradition. In the Byzantine period and the Middle Ages, Shiloh was one of the sites of pilgrimage, and based on memories of the past, it became a holy place for both Muslims and Jews.   A. KEMPINSKI

BIBLIOGRAPHY

W. F. Albright, *BASOR* 9 (1922), 10 f. • H. Kjaer, *PEF Qst* (1927), 202–13; idem, *JPOS* 10 (1930), 87–174; idem, *PEF QSt* (1931), 71–88 • W. F. Albright, *ibid.* 157–58 • H. Kjaer, *I det Hellige Land, de Danske udgravninger i Shilo*, K benhaven, 1931 • J. Starr, *BASOR* 57 (1935), 26–27 • O. Eissfeld, *VT* suppl. 4 (1957), 138–47 • Marie-Louise Buhl — S. Holm Nielsen, *Shiloh, The Danish Excavations at Tall Sailum, Palestine, in 1926, 1929, 1932 and 1963. The Pre-Hellenistic Remains*, Copenhagen, 1969 • Y. Shiloh, *IEJ* 21 (1971), 67–69.

SHIQMONA, TEL

IDENTIFICATION. The mound lies on the coast, about 1.3 kilometers southwest of the Carmel cape. It has an area of more than eight dunams, and prior to excavation its highest point was 12.74 meters above sea level. The Byzantine town spreads over the flat fields around the mound. Its average height is 5 meters above sea level. The area of dense ancient remains begins on the north adjacent to the sea near the mound, and spreads on the east to the slopes of Mount Carmel, and on the south to the modern French road. Isolated remains are found also farther south. The maximum extent of the town in Byzantine times was about 220 dunams. The cemetery of the city is situated to the east on the slopes of Mount Carmel, and extends along the slope from Elijah's Cave at the cape to the southern boundary of the town. Elijah's Cave itself is part of the sacred precincts situated at the Carmel cape. Although there is no convenient port on the site for shipping, there may have been an anchorage south of the town, adjacent to Kafr Samir in the sandy coastal belt.

In 1895, G. Schumacher reported that the cemetery of Shiqmona had been systematically plundered over a two-year period before the Turkish authorities intervened. A Byzantine monastery, which seems to have been located outside the built-up area of the town, was excavated in 1951 by M. Dothan on behalf of the Department of Antiquities (see Monasteries: Sha'ar ha'Aliyah). During the 1950's, several additional discoveries were made in the area of the town, including a bronze plaque bearing a Hebrew inscription.

Archaeological excavations on the site were begun in 1963, under the direction of J. Elgavish on behalf of the Haifa Municipal Museum of Ancient Art, and are still continuing.

The Persian period strata were examined mainly in the 1963–64 seasons. Remains of the Byzantine town were uncovered in the fields surrounding the mound mainly in the 1965–66 seasons. The cemetery was excavated in 1967–68. The Iron Age II strata were studied especially in 1968–70. An underwater survey off the site was conducted in 1969–70.

The grotto known popularly as Elijah's Cave was examined in 1966 by A. Ovadiah, on behalf of the Archaeological Survey of Israel.

THE MOUND

An area of about 800 square meters was cleared, stretching along the southern edge of the ridge and down the southwestern slope. Excavations were deepened here in 1970, and reached tenth-century B.C. strata. The lowest floor level found was 6.7 meters above sea level. There was undoubtedly also a Late Bronze Age settlement on the site. Several objects from that period, including a clay bulla with a seal impression of the Egyptian Pharaoh Seti I, were found in later strata.

No remains from earlier periods have yet been found on the mound, but a Middle Bronze Age II-B tomb was uncovered in the cemetery.

The excavations reveal the following sequence: 1. an almost continuous settlement of four occupational strata from the Iron Age II; 2. a Phoenician town of the Persian period; 3. three successive fortresses, Persian, Hellenistic, and Roman; 4. two occupational strata containing private dwellings from the Byzantine period.

Iron Age II

TOWN A. The destruction of this town is to be dated at the tenth century B.C. A casemate city

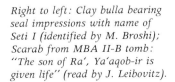

Right to left: Clay bulla bearing seal impressions with name of Seti I (identified by M. Broshi); Scarab from MBA II-B tomb: "The son of Ra', Ya'aqob-ir is given life" (read by J. Leibovitz).

Below: both pages left to right: Cooking pot with incised sign ⋀⋀, 10th century B.C.; Head of terra cotta figurine of woman; Terra cotta figurine of woman with drum, from tomb B, IA II, late 9th or early 8th century B.C. Bottom, both pages left to right: Town A. Street in center, the palace, at left, casemates of city-wall, in background. IA II, 10th century B.C., looking south; Town B. Oil press, IA II, late 9th or early 8th century B.C.

wall was uncovered for a stretch of some 60 meters near its southern corner. Within the town, two streets and four houses were cleared. Two of the houses are identical in plan and consist of two long rooms separated by a wall of stone pillars, and an additional room running along the width of the house. A third building, 11 by 15 meters, was undoubtedly a palace of the open-court type, with rows of rooms along two of its sides. The city wall was destroyed in a conflagration. Many pottery vessels were found in the casemates. All the cooking pots are of the type lacking handles, with the rims marked with various signs. One store jar bears an inscription in red: *lmlk'l,* ''[Belonging] to Malk[i]el.''

TOWN B. This town met its end in the ninth or possibly the beginning of the eighth century B.C. The fortifications have not been located. Within the town, three oil presses were found. These are large installations with storerooms containing store jars and other vessels. The actual presses consisted of a

*Above: Abecedary incised on sherd, stratum Pb
(read by N. Avigad). Below: Wine jar with Phoenician
inscription written in ink: "Ben Matton, twenty-five
royal (measures)/vintage wine of Gat Carmel"
(read by F. M. Cross), from fortress of stratum Pb,
end of 4th century B.C. Opposite page, top: Bronze
figurine of a Byzantine empress (?) 6th century A.D.
Bottom: Residential quarter of Byzantine town,
south of mound, looking east. The mosaic pavement
has been removed.*

stone mortar in which two stones revolved and crushed the olives. The olives were then pressed on a stone drum, 1.3 meters in diameter, which was found nearby.

A drain conveyed the oil to a sunken store jar.

A terra-cotta figurine of a goddess seated on a chair was found in this stratum, as well as a large number of figurines of horsemen and girl musicians.

TOWN C. This phase was destroyed in the second half of the eighth century B.C. Several dwellings of the town have been uncovered, two of them with storerooms containing store jars. One building comprising one room and two courts appears to have been a workshop.

TOWN D. This town was destroyed in the seventh or early sixth century B.C. Few remains of it were uncovered. The mound in this phase seems to have been sparsely settled.

Persian Period

STRATUM P. After a clear gap in occupation, the mound was again inhabited in the beginning of the sixth century B.C. and the town of this stratum was destroyed in the first third of the fifth century B.C.

The dwellings of the town were built on the ridge and on a series of terraces on the slopes of the mound. The stratum was relatively well preserved. Two intersecting stone-paved streets were found built of broad stairs. Three houses were excavated almost in their entirety. They consist of a court and three rooms, with the entrance from the street through the paved court, which also contained an oven for baking. The room near the court served as a kitchen and included an oven and a large plastered basin, possibly for soaking foods. One of the rooms, on the floor of which were found fifty-three intact vessels, appears to have been a shop for the sale of perfumes and pottery, or the storeroom of such a shop.

FORTRESS — STRATUM PB. The remains of only three rooms of this stratum from the late fourth century B.C. were found. The rooms appear to have belonged to a hastily constructed fortress. From this period on, the residential quarter was apparently situated in the surrounding fields. It can be assumed that the fortress was Tyrian or Persian, and was built around the mid-fourth century B.C. Its destruction is to be ascribed to the struggle which broke out among Alexander's heirs over control of the region. One of the rooms uncovered was a sub-

terranean storeroom, containing scores of vessels of various types, including four store jars bearing Phoenician inscriptions of an official character. The destruction of this stratum seems to have been violent. The site was looted, and the pottery deliberately smashed at the doorway of the room.

Hellenistic and Roman Periods

HELLENISTIC FORTRESS — STRATUM H. The destruction of stratum H is dated to about 130 B.C. A court and three rooms of a building were cleared (as yet only partially excavated), and the remnants of seven other rooms. These remains — perhaps of a fortress — were destroyed largely by later constructions.

Three of the rooms were large storerooms, filled with amphorae and other vessels. Two of the amphorae bear inscriptions in Greek. A locally produced amphora was also found, the handles of which bear seal impressions recording the *agoranomos* and the year 180 of the Seleucid era (131 B.C.—of the same type found in the excavations at Jaffa.

ROMAN FORTRESS — STRATUM R. This fortress

*Colorful mosaic pavement
from Byzantine town, one of
the pavements in the
public building south of
the mound. Length of
floor: 6.8 m.*

was erected in the second half of the first century A.D., in connection with the First Jewish Revolt. It existed on the site till the mid-third century A.D. The date and historical circumstances of the end of the fortress still require study. In the area cleared, thick, deep-set foundations were found, and several adjoining plastered pools. A cistern was also found, containing a layer of sherds and vessels of the second century A.D.

Byzantine Period

Part of a large dwelling, 9 meters long, and several houses, either dwellings or shops, were uncovered on the slopes of the mound. They were razed in a sudden destruction around the mid-fourth century A.D. These structures belonged to the town extending over the fields around the mound. In the sixth century, a large villa surrounded by a garden stood on the summit of the mound. Some 95 square meters of its area, including five rooms, have been cleared. The objects on the floors indicate that the building was of an official nature. It was destroyed at the start of the seventh century A.D.

Arab Period

Over the remains of the Byzantine villa were found the foundations of a building of the Arab period, with a paved approach leading from the foot of the mound. The date of this structure is not clear. It was undoubtedly an isolated building. No remains later than the seventh century A.D. were found on the surface of the town in the fields around the mound.

The Area Around the Mound

Of the Byzantine town in the fields surrounding the mound, an area of two dunams was thoroughly excavated south of the mound, adjacent to the seashore. Trial soundings were also carried out in another area of 1.5 dunams and northeast of the mound in an area of one dunam.

A single stratum was found, with the majority of its structures built during the sixth century A.D. Several buildings, however, date from the fourth century A.D. and continued in use with various modifications till the final destruction of the town, which occurred at the beginning of the seventh century A.D. In one of the trial soundings, Hellenistic remains were found close to bedrock.

A wealthy residential quarter was excavated south of the mound. Two almost complete dwelling units were cleared. Each covered an area of about 170 square meters and consisted of a long corridor,

Engraved pendant of a lady; 6th century A.D.

three or four rooms, a kitchen, a large court, and a nymphaeum. Two of the rooms were paved with mosaics in colorful geometric patterns, and the others were paved with stone flags. The walls were plastered and painted. Up to 1972, more than thirty mosaic pavements had been uncovered. On the floors were scattered various household objects — in pottery, bronze, and ivory — all witnesses to the abrupt end of the town. Cooking pots were found still standing on stoves. Plaques decorated with menorahs were found, as were bronze crosses. A large industrial building was erected in the fourth century A.D. It measures 13 by 14 meters and included a row of pools of various sizes. It is not clear what industry is involved here, but in the sixth century A.D., the building was adapted for dwelling purposes.

A public building — possibly a church — was also uncovered. It has an overall length of at least 51 meters and consists of a series of courts and a hall, terminating in an apse.

The streets, which divide the quarter into almost perfect squares, are stone paved. Beneath the pavements are enclosed channels. Public cisterns are also located on the streets, and a widespread subterranean network of channels carried rainwater into them. Sections of this network were examined at various spots.

Shops and workshops were situated in the area northeast of the mound. One workshop contained a collection of iron tools. In one of the shops was found a set of glass and bronze weights, from

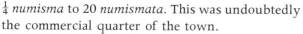

$\frac{1}{4}$ *numisma* to 20 *numismata*. This was undoubtedly the commercial quarter of the town.

The Cemetery

Within the cemetery, twenty-one tomb caves were cleared, nineteen of them close together inside the area of the Histadrut Park. This area was completely excavated down to bedrock. All of the tombs, with the exception of one, are of the third and fourth centuries A.D., as are the majority of the finds. Many of the tombs continued in use till the early seventh century A.D. Tombs with typical

Jewish symbols and tombs with typical Christian symbols were found side by side. The tombs are of two types:

1. A square court leading to a hall with arcosolia. These tombs were closed by rolling stones which fitted into a slot, and square stones above sealed the opening.

2. A deep shaft with arcosolia on two sides; the shaft was closed by rectangular slabs of stone.

One of the tomb caves dated from the Middle Bronze Age II-B. It contained a shaft 2.5 meters

Both pages, clockwise from left: Opening of tomb cave closed with a rolling stone, 3rd–4th centuries A.D.; Zoomorphic vessel in the form of a ram, from the 4th-century A.D. tomb; Zoomorphic vessel in the form of a harnessed ox, 6th century A.D.; Bronze figurine of a woman, Hellenistic period. Found on the sea bed by the Underwater Survey.

deep and two burial chambers. Burial was on benches and shelves hewn in the rock. A seal was found here bearing the Hyksos name "Ya'aqob-har."

A tomb cave with loculi in which were placed pottery coffins was found at nearby 'En-Yam. It is ascribed to the second century A.D.

Underwater Survey

The construction of a breakwater off the Carmel Beach in 1968 caused a considerable movement of the sand just offshore. Many objects, mainly of bronze and silver, are being discovered on the now exposed clay seabed. Various chemical factors have led to the fine preservation of the metal finds. An underwater survey uncovered objects from the Late Bronze Age to the Byzantine period. They include a bronze mirror bearing pictographic script, from the late Bronze Age or Iron Age I, and a porphyry plaque incised "Dux," the title of the commander of the occupation troops of the Byzantine province.   J. ELGAVISH

BIBLIOGRAPHY

J. Elgavish, *An Archaeological Trip into the Past of the City Through Excavations at Shikmona*, Haifa, (1967); *idem*, Archaeological Excavations at Shikmona, Field Report No. 1, The levels of the Persian Period, Haifa, 1968 (Hebrew); *idem*, *IEJ* 19 (1969), 247–48; 20 (1970), 229–30; 22 (1972), 187; 23 (1973); 117–18; (1974), 283–84; 25 (1975), 257–58; 27 (1977), 166–67; *idem*, Qadmoniot 3 (1970), 90–93 (Hebrew); *idem*, Archaeological Excavations at Shikmona, II, The level of the Hellenistic Period, Haifa, 1974 (Hebrew).

SHUQBA CAVE

IDENTIFICATION. The cave of Shuqba lies on the right bank of Wadi en-Natuf (one of the upper affluents of the Yarkon River) in the western part of the Judean Hills, about 14 kilometers (8.5 miles) northeast of Lod (map reference 154154). Here were discovered for the first time the remains of the Natufian culture, which was named after the wadi.

A. Mallon discovered the cave in 1924. It was briefly explored by Dorothy Garrod in 1928. The Shuqba cave opens into a central chamber (18 meter in diameter) with a chimney in the roof, and three side chambers. Before excavation, blocks of breccia containing Middle Paleolithic flints and bones adhered to the walls of the cave up to a height of 2 meters. More than half of the central chamber was excavated and a sounding was also made in the middle lateral chamber. The sequence of deposits is as follows (from top down):

Layer A : Early Bronze Age to recent.
Layer B : Upper Natufian.
Layer C : Redeposited artifacts from layer D.
Layer D : Upper Levallois-Mousterian.

Like many caves, Shuqba is the result of karstic activity. The excavator found that the chimney in the roof of the cave continues in a sinkhole in the rock floor of the chamber down to an unknown depth, and the natural floor of the cave was therefore irregular. Water erosion intensified after the deposition of layer D, and flints were redeposited. At this level parts of the surface hardened and turned into breccia under the action of waterborne calcium carbonate. Parts not turned into breccia or preserved because of special conditions (such as a band of soft red cave earth or a hearth with gray ashes) suffered damage from the water. For this reason implements redeposited in the red clay of layer C are abraded, whereas contemporaneous layer D implements are not. In the side chamber, it was found that this redeposition of material had not occurred at one time. In layer C, there were two beds with abraded implements. In this chamber also, breccia adhered to the vault. A similar phenomenon of water action on Upper Levallois-Mousterian layers was observed in the cave of el-Wad, where D. Garrod attributed it to the action of a source flowing inside the cave.

Garrod regarded this as a generalized process and related it to a period of increased rainfall.

THE ARTIFACTS

In layer D, some four hundred flint implements were collected, half of them side scrapers. The remainder of the tools are points, retouched flakes, a few disks and hand-axes, and a group of typically Upper Paleolithic burins. This industry is strongly reminiscent of the last stage of the Levallois-Mousterian of Mount Carmel, where narrow flakes and blades are also found in great number. With regard to fauna, a measure of similarity with el-Wad is claimed by Dorothy Bate, despite the scarcity and poor condition of the remains (see Carmel Caves). Hippopotamus and rhinoceros, the characteristic mammals of the pre-"faunal break" period (placed by D. Bate between the Lower and the Upper Levallois-Mousterian), are absent.

Between layers D and B, there is a long gap. Layer B was made up chiefly of black earth with traces of ashes and was classified as Upper Natufian by D. Garrod. A number of human burials were found, most of them poorly preserved. Seven of them were of children, and one, buried in the typically Natufian contracted position, lay over a large hearth filled with black ashes. The lithic assemblage recovered by D. Garrod at Shuqba was previously unknown in Israel. She therefore named it "Natufian" after the wadi in which the cave is situated. Natufian industries have since been discovered at several other sites in Israel (see Carmel Caves, Naḥal Oren, 'Eynan, Yonim Cave).

As the material was examined and published after the report of the Carmel Caves, D. Garrod was able to correlate layer B with the Upper Natufian at el-Wad (layer B-1). In the flint industry, lunates and sickle blades display less frequently the Heluan-type retouch. Conspicuous by its absence is the microburin, which is a characteristic feature of the Natufian culture. D. Garrod attributes this to the small quantity of tools collected (about 1,350) and the restricted area excavated. Of the sixty-one bone tools, the majority are points or fragments of points and awls. There are also a few needles and an engraved rib.

The fauna was described by Dorothy Bate. It is chiefly represented by cattle, deer, wildcat, and abundant gazelle remains.

In an attempt to reconstruct the process which led to the sequence of deposits in the cave, D. Garrod pointed out that when human occupation began in Levallois-Mousterian layer D, the pit in the cave floor must have been almost filled, i.e., layer D reached a height of 2 meters and filled chamber III. Only later did the water that seeped through the hole in the vault begin its activity, hardening parts of the layer into breccia. Then, due to increased rainfall, parts of layer D were eroded, implements were abraded, and redeposited, causing the formation of layer C. Water again, by underground drainage, caused the very deep cavity in the rock floor of the cave.

The first Natufian inhabitants found an irregular surface to settle on, but in a short time their occupation filled up the hollows in the ground. At the same time, some subsidence occurred in the pit, and the layer sank in a hollow. From then on, rock debris fallen from the roof filled all the hollows, leveling the surface of the deposits.

O. BAR-YOSEF

BIBLIOGRAPHY

D. A. E. Garrod, *PEF, QSt* (1927), 182 ff.; idem, *Journal of the Royal Anthropological Institute* 62 (1932), 257–69; idem, *Proceedings of the Prehistoric Society* NS 8 (1942), 1–20.

Shinjeh cave: The seal of the Governor of Samaria. Its legend reads: [yasha]yahu son of [San]ballat governor of Samaria" — 4th century B.C. (Photo by courtesy of the Israel Department of Antiquity and Museums).

SHINJEH CAVE (Wadi Daliyeh)

THE SITE AND FINDS. In 1962, Bedouins discovered a number of papyri in the Mugharet Abu Shinjeh in Wadi Daliyeh. The cave was cleared in 1963 by P. Lapp. The finds include more than two hundred skeletons of men, women and children, jewelry, 128 seals of documents, and a number of legal documents from Samaria, dated from 375 (or 365) to 335 B.C. The documents mention Yashayahu son of Sanballat (II), the (hereditary) governor of Samaria, and the prefect Hananiah. They mention the sale of slaves (including one Nehemiah to the Samaritan noble Yehonur). The occupants of the cave appear to have sought refuge there during the Samaritan revolt against Alexander and apparently perished in a Macedonian attack.

M. AVI-YONAH

BIBLIOGRAPHY

F. M. Cross, Jr., *BA* 26 (1963), 110–21; *idem, Harvard Theol. Review* 59 (1966), 201–11; *idem*, in: D. N. Freedman–J. C. Greenfield (ed.), *New Directions in Biblical Archaeology*, New York, 1971, 45–69 • P. W. Lapp, in: *Archaeologie und Altes Testament, Festschrift für Kurt Galling*, Tübingen, 1970, 180–81; *idem, The Tale of the Tell*, Pittsburgh, 1975, 66–76; *idem, AASOR* 41 (1974).

ṢIPPOR, TEL

IDENTIFICATION. Tel Ṣippor (Tell et-Tuyur), a small mound about half a dunam in area, is situated about 3 kilometers northwest of Kiryat Gat. The mound rises to a height of 5 meters above a surrounding terrace of some 50 dunams. The discovery of a hoard of coins from the Hellenistic period, numerous terra-cotta figurines from the Persian period, and pottery from the Early Iron and Late Bronze Ages, which were uncovered on the terrace as a result of deep plowing, prompted a rescue excavation. During three short seasons in 1963–65, excavations were carried out at the site by A. Biran and Ora Negbi of the Israel Department of Antiquities and Museums.

EXCAVATIONS

Evidence was found of extensive settlement in the Middle Bronze Age I, Late Bronze Age II, and Early Iron Age. The excavations were concentrated on the mound. Of the three upper strata uncovered, two dated to the Early Iron Age and one to the Late Bronze Age (below which a Middle Bronze Age I level was encountered). The mound was not occupied beyond the eleventh or beginning of the tenth century B.C.

Philistine krater, from tel Ṣippor, stratum II.

Below: Stone statuette, stratum III. Both pages; left to right: Bronze figurine, stratum III. Chalice, stratum II.

STRATUM I. The remains of this stratum were preserved only a few centimeters below the surface of the mound. A thinly plastered floor, three clay ovens, and four plastered pits were found, as well as an abundance of Iron Age I pottery. Hand-burnished bowls, a degenerate form of the horizontal handles characteristic of Philistine vessels, and a flask all show the influence of Philistine pottery. Undecorated vessels, a stamp seal, and a scarab (depicting Ptah seated on a stool) can be dated to the eleventh century B.C., the time of the United Monarchy.

STRATUM II. A well-made plastered floor sloped down in a continuous line to a shallow pit in which was found a complete Philistine krater. Nearby, fragments of a similar krater lay on the plastered floor, together with an intact painted chalice. Spouted jugs, flasks, stirrup vases, and more Philistine kraters and bowls were found on the floor and in pits. They were decorated with the distinctive geometric designs of Philistine ware. Decorated sherds, which make up about 28 percent of the pottery in stratum II, can be dated to the mid-twelfth–mid-eleventh centuries B.C.

STRATUM III was sealed by the floor of stratum II. A small paved area and a large plastered floor were uncovered. A storage jar, bowls, cooking pots, juglets, imported Cypriot and Mycenaean vessels, a group of three lamps, a bronze figurine, and a

SOREK, NAHAL

IDENTIFICATION. From archaeological surveys carried out in the lower course of Naḥal Sorek (the River Rubin), in the area bordered on the east by the Jaffa–Gaza highway and on the west by the coast, it was ascertained that this region was settled during most of the prehistoric and historic periods. In this district, bounded to the north and south by extensive sand dunes, are found two large mounds with remains from the Bronze and Iron Ages, Tel Maḥoz (Tell es-Sultan, map reference 125147) in the east and Ḥorvat Yavneh Yam (Tell Minat Rubin, map reference 121147) on the coast.

Although Tel Maḥoz has not yet been excavated, some information on its history in the Middle and Late Bronze Ages can be deduced from excavations conducted in nearby cemeteries.

THE SURROUNDINGS OF TEL MAḤOZ

On the northern bank of Naḥal Sorek, about 200 meters north of Tel Maḥoz, in the area called el-Jisr, four burial caves from the Middle Bronze Age I–II, dug into the *kurkar* rock, were cleared. One was examined in 1925 by L. A. Mayer, and the others were excavated in 1940 by J. Ory. Two of the caves, which were found destroyed, are ascribed to the Middle Bronze Age I (examined by J. Ory). The third burial cave, dated to the Middle Bronze Age II-A, consists of a chamber reached by a flight of six steps. This chamber opens onto two additional burial rooms. Some forty-five pottery vessels and one of alabaster were uncovered in the cave (examined by L. A. Mayer). The Middle Bronze Age II-B contents of the fourth burial cave (excavated by J. Ory) are of special interest. Aside from pottery and alabaster vessels, there were also weapons, jewelry, scarabs, a basalt mortar and pestle, and an undamaged ostrich egg and thirty-six bone inlays carved in the form of human figures and animals. Although clear Egyptian influence can be discerned in these objects, especially in the male figures and their dress, they are rare examples of Canaanite carving, and show a higher artistic standard than the usual bone carvings of the Hyksos period.

Another cemetery (of sixty-three burials) was cleared by J. Ory in 1942 about 1.5 kilometers northwest of Tel Maḥoz on a height known as

stone statuette were found. The pottery assemblage is typical of the last phase of the Late Bronze Age and the beginning of the Iron Age. The figurine represents a seated Canaanite deity, his right hand raised in benediction and his left hand holding some attribute (a scepter?) unfortunately broken off. The statuette depicts a Canaanite king or god sitting on a throne. The head is missing but part of the elaborate Egyptian headdress is clearly visible. He wears a Syrian cloak and holds a drooping lotus in his left hand. The right hand rests on the knee. In view of the mixed Egypto-Syrian style, it can safely be assumed that this unusual statuette is of Canaanite origin.

No identification for Tel Ṣippor has been proposed, but it was apparently a small gathering place or cult center. The site shows a continuity of occupation from the thirteenth to the eleventh centuries B.C. with no evidence of total destruction. There also seems to be cultural continuity although new elements — Philistine and Israelite — were introduced in the twelfth and eleventh centuries, respectively.
                                                A. BIRAN

BIBLIOGRAPHY

Ora Negbi, *IEJ* 14 (1964), 187–89; idem, *'Atiqot* 6 (1966) • A. Biran and Ora Negbi, *IEJ* 16 (1966), 160 ff. • L. Y. Rahmani, *Schweiz. Münzbl.* 16 (1966), 129–45; idem, *EI* 7 (1964), 33–38 (Hebrew).

these tombs are all jugs of the *bilbil* type. In one tomb only Mycenaean ware was found. This is the only built tomb among those cleared in this cemetery (of the cist type).

Besides pottery, the four tombs contained faience vessels, glass and ivory perfume phials, jewelry, scarabs, and two bronze mirrors.

YAVNEH-YAM – See separate entry.

Two Late Bronze Age II cemeteries, situated north and south of Yavneh-Yam, were partly excavated by the Department of Antiquities. The northern cemetery, discovered on the coast on the lands of Kibbutz Palmahim, consisted of built cist tombs. Two graves were cleared in 1961 by A. Kempinski and S. Lifshitz, and thirteen others were examined during 1967–69 by R. Gophna and S. Lifshitz.

The cist graves were built of hewn *kurkar* slabs and contained single burials. Most of the funerary offerings in the graves were pottery vessels, a large number Cypriot, and some Mycenaean.

The southern cemetery was discovered 500 meters south of Yavneh-Yam. There A. Kempinski and S. Lifshitz examined in 1961 two tombs hewn in a *kurkar* hill. These were kidney-shaped shaft tombs. In each tomb, to the left of the entrance, was a niche for a lamp. Cypriot and Mycenaean pottery was also found in these tombs.

During 1968–71, a Chalcolithic and Early Bronze Age I cemetery and settlement were investigated by R. Gophna and S. Lifshitz in a *kurkar* quarry, 2 kilometers northeast of Yavneh-Yam. Ten tombs were cleared. Most of them contained Ghassulian pottery and stone ossuaries and pottery vessels. A copper mace head and three fishing hooks were also found. Outstanding among the Ghassulian finds were two pottery bird-shaped vessels. The tombs were re-used during the Early Bronze Age I. Among the pottery vessels of that period were typical vessels of the Early Bronze Age I painted style.

R. GOPHNA

Below: Lower Nahal Sorek, archaeological sites.
Opposite page: Khirbet Humra, Ivory inlays, MBA II-B.

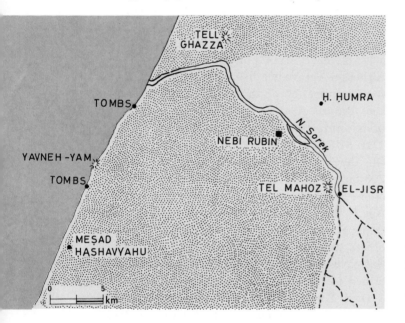

Khirbet Humra (Dhahret el-Humraiya, map reference 125149). Most of the tombs excavated there date from the Middle Bronze Age II-B, and a few belong to Late Bronze Age II-A–B. All the burials are in pits, except for one which is a built tomb. In addition to abundant pottery, typical of this period, some of the Middle Bronze Age tombs also contained Cypriot ware of the white-painted IV type. Most of the bodies were buried in a flexed position, the head toward the east. The bones of goats were found in three of the graves. Domestic animals were sometimes buried at the head or foot of the deceased. Among the other finds from this period are alabaster and faience vessels as well as bronze daggers and knives, and jewelry.

Four of the tombs examined belong to the Late Bronze Age II-A–B. In these tombs, the bodies had been placed with extended extremities, the head toward the west. The Cypriot pottery found in

BIBLIOGRAPHY

L. A. Mayer, *BPM* 2 (1926), 2–7 • J. Ory, *QDAP* 12 (1945), 34–42, Pls. 1–42, Pls. 1–2; 13 (1948), 75–89, Pls. 29–33 • M. Dothan, *IEJ* 2 (1952), 104–17 • H. J. Kantor, *JNES* 15 (1956), 158 • N. Glueck, *BASOR* 153 (1959), 35–38 • G. E. Wright, *The Bible and the Ancient Near East*, London 1961, 107, note 69 • A. Kindler, *Israel Numismatic Journal* 1 (1963), 3 • R. Gophna, *'Atiqot* 5 (1969), 80 (Hebrew) • Ruth Amiran, *The Israel Museum News* 12 (1977), 65–69.

SUBEITA

IDENTIFICATION AND HISTORY. Subeita, (in Hebrew — Shivta, Sobata — in antiquity), a town in the central Negev, is situated about 40 kilometers (25 miles) southwest of Beersheba (map reference 114032). It was founded in the Roman period, and flourished mainly in the Byzantine period. Subeita is the only Byzantine town in Israel to have been cleared almost in its entirety. The ancient name of the site is preserved in the Arabic Subeita. It is known also from two papyri from Nessana, dating from the end of the seventh century. The meaning of the name is obscure. F. M. Abel considered it a Semitic-Nabataean name, which is most likely correct, but there is no confirmation for his proposed interpretation of the name, "small tribe."

Occupation at Subeita began in the Middle Nabataean period. The settlement was founded on a link road connecting Eboda, Sobata, and Nessana, by way of a chain of small Nabataean settlements, which have not yet been identified. Nabataean Subeita was established in the early part of the reign of Aretas IV (9 B.C.–A.D. 40), or perhaps even earlier in the later years of Obodas II (30–9 B.C.). During this time, and especially in the Late Nabataean period (end of first–second centuries A.D.), the city enjoyed a period of prosperity. It was quite large, occupying about one third of the built-up area of the subsequent periods. The history of the city in the late second and third centuries A.D. is not known, but in the second half of the fourth century A.D., the first church of the town, the South Church, was erected. This was followed shortly afterward by the construction of the large North Church, possibly a center of pilgrimage, and the adjacent monastery. Like the other towns in the west part of the central Negev, Subeita continued to exist for two hundred years after the Arab conquest. The excavators, on the basis of the Arab glazed ware and the pottery cast in a mold, have been suggested that the Arab settlement there did not cease until the thirteenth or fourteenth century A.D. The earlier date of the eighth–ninth century seems more reasonable, however. At that time settlement ended also at Nessana and Elusa.

EXPLORATION

The ruins of Subeita were described for the first time in 1870 by E. H. Palmer, and the first general plan of the city with its most important buildings was drawn by A. Musil in 1901. Musil's plan, however, is not exact, because he failed to notice that the streets of the city were slightly curved. In 1905,

the site was visited by an expedition of the Dominican Ecole Biblique in Jerusalem, with the participation of A. Jaussen, R. Savignac, and H. Vincent, who discovered the location of the Byzantine cemetery and several tombstones with inscriptions from the end of the sixth century A.D., as well as a short Nabataean dedicatory inscription found among the ruins of the city. In 1914, C. L. Woolley and T. E. Lawrence drew a more accurate plan of the town, as well as plans of the churches, and of several houses. In 1916, the Committee for the Preservation of Monuments of the German-Turkish Army Staff sent an expedition to Subeita under the direction of T. Wiegand. Its main value lay in the fine air photographs they took. In 1934–38, the first large-scale excavations were conducted at Subeita on behalf of New York University and the British Archaeological School at Jerusalem, under the direction of H. D. Colt. The results of these excavations, however, were never published. From 1958 to 1960, the buildings and streets of the city were cleared by the National Parks Authority under the supervision of M. Avi-Yonah.

During several surveys of the site carried out in 1970–76 by A. Negev, the site and plan of the Nabataean town were studied, and a new chronology of the churches of the town was evolved.

HISTORY

Early Roman Period. In an early survey a Nabataean dedicatory inscription to Dushara from the time of Aretas IV was discovered. The Colt Expedition located a Nabataean dump southwest of the city, which contained typical Nabataean and Early Roman pottery. This material was published by Grace Crowfoot, who erroneously dated it to the second and third centuries A.D. The Nabataean settlement was founded on the northern bank of Naḥal Lavan. It flourished in the Middle and Late Nabataean periods.

Late Roman Period. The history of Subeita in this period is not well known. The town may have been resettled at the end of the third century A.D., when the central Negev was fortified by Diocletian and his heirs, who erected fortresses at Eboda and Nessana and the city wall at Kurnub. However, no positive evidence of their activities has been found at Subeita.

Byzantine Period. Unlike Nessana and Eboda, there was no fortress at Subeita. But abundant evidence was found of the practice of agriculture

Opposite page: North church. This page, below: General plan. 1. North church. 2. Central church. 3. South church. 4. Reservoir. Bottom: South church complex. 1. Church. 2. Narthex. 3. Chapel. 4. Court. 5. Tower. 6. Baptistery.

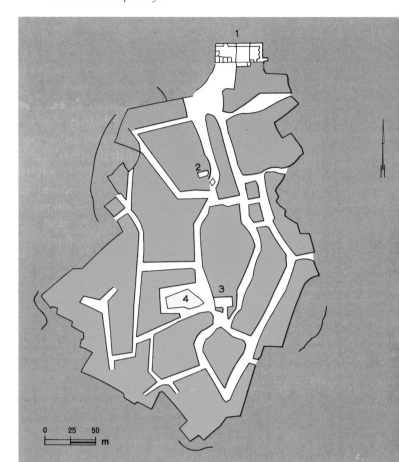

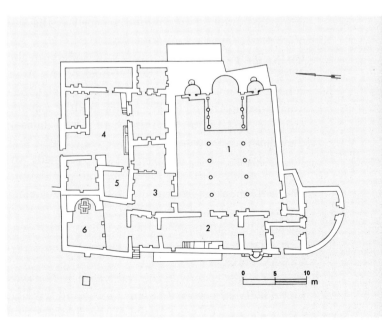

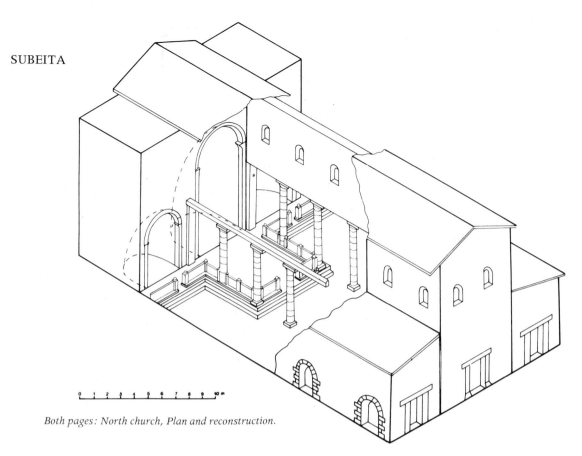

Both pages: North church, Plan and reconstruction.

in the immediate surroundings of Subeita and in the area of Naḥal Lavan, which attests to the fact that Subeita was a civil agricultural settlement. Near the city in Naḥal Lavan were discovered the remains of a large plantation and several individual farms. Additional information regarding the production and management of the individual farms is provided by archaeological finds at Eboda and Nessana and by the Nessana Papyri, many of which deal with water rights and land distribution. Subeita also seems to have been an important monastic center in this period, as well as the site of regional Christian pilgrimages.

Early Arab Period. The history of Subeita in the Arab period is obscure. At the time of the Arab conquest, the Christian population here, as at Nessana, was not harmed. The Arabs built a mosque near the South Church, taking care not to damage the adjoining baptistery. In all events, it seems that the existing Christian community lived side by side in peace with the new Muslim population. The settlement at Subeita probably did not exist longer than that of its neighbor Nessana. It was apparently abandoned in the eighth or ninth century A.D. at the latest.

EXCAVATIONS

A large water cistern of the Nabataean period was found halfway between Mitspe Shivta and Subeita. Inside the cistern were traces of the characteristic Nabataean technique of stone dressing, while the pilaster of the cistern has niches symbolizing Dushara.

Inside the Nabataean town itself, which occupies the southern and southwestern parts of the site, a large double reservoir was constructed on the northern fringes of the built-up area. Rainwater was collected from the gently sloping terrain by means of an intricate network of channels. South of the reservoir was a staircase tower, resembling the one at Nabataean Kurnub. To the southwest, the Colt Expedition excavated a building containing a stable of the Late Nabataean period, similar to the stable in building XII at Kurnub, but it did not establish its date or function.

Plan of the Byzantine City. The Byzantine city, covering an area of about 115 dunams, 460 meters from north to south, and 50 meters from east to west, lay on the shoulder of a ridge that slopes gradually to the southwest in the direction of Naḥal Shivta. The city was not walled, nor did it have a fortified citadel, but the houses and the walls of the courtyards and of the gardens are built in a continuous line, terminating in nine street ends. At the end of each street was a gate that could be locked. The houses were not built close together, the courtyards are spacious, and in the opinion of the excavators, there were also gardens inside the city. The streets are quite wide (average

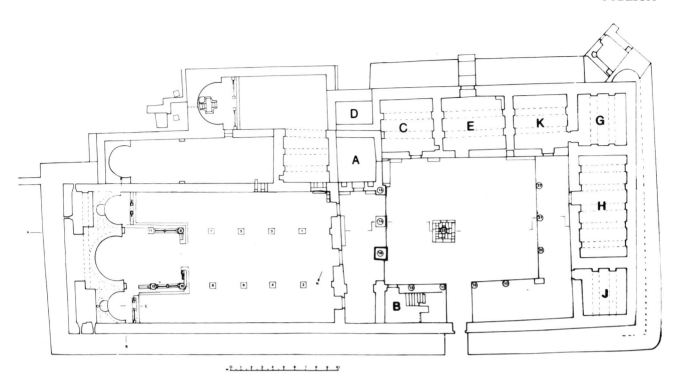

width 4 meters), and there were also several city squares.

All explorers of Subeita believed that the city with its streets turning and twisting was built without a definite plan. However, this does not seem to been for lack of a plan, but that the builders of the town intentionally limited the number of streets opening onto the area outside the city, the fields, and the cisterns. Inside the built-up area itself, there were numerous lanes leading to all parts of the town and ending at the doors of the houses on the border of the town. Water supply being the major problem, the town planners chose to use the streets for conveying rainwater to the two large reservoirs in the center of the town and to the numerous cisterns scattered throughout it. The layout of the streets seems to have been adapted to this need, and in this matter the builders of the Byzantine town followed the plan of the Nabataean town. The streets thus ran along the course of the ancient channels, some of which can still be traced in the lower part of their course in the vicinity of the reservoirs. The need to cope with the collection of water also explains the unusually large number of open squares and the width of the streets.

The construction of the Byzantine town, sometime in the fourth century A.D., began with the erection of the South Church, whereas the population itself must have lived in the older Nabataean houses, which, if contemporary Kurnub can serve as an example, required little repair. Irregularities in the plan of the South Church, such as the absence of a proper atrium, and the disharmony between the eastern and western parts of the church, attest to the fact that this building had been squeezed into an already built-up area. The same problem of inserting new buildings into an existing town plan also faced the builders of the two churches at Kurnub. At about the same time the North Church and the monastery were built in the northern extremity of the town, beyond the water-catchment area, so that they would not interfere with the proper functioning of the water-supply system. It was only later, possibly from the fifth century onward, that the central and northern quarters were built.

In building the houses, three different kinds of stones were used: hard crystalline stone for the foundations and lower parts of the walls, softer crystalline stone for the lintels and doorposts, and soft and brittle limestone for the upper parts of the walls. The narrow doors have lintels, while the wider ones are arched. The rooms are roofed with arches resting on engaged pilasters and paved with stone slabs. On the street side the walls have either no windows at all or very narrow ones. The wall cupboards are built of stone, only the shelves being of wood.

The houses are of the courtyard type, common in the East. They are entered through a small entrance hall which leads to the courtyard, from which all the rooms were entered. In the courtyard was located the opening of the cistern in which the rainwater running off the flat roofs was collected, and sometimes it was connected with a channel carrying runoff water from the adjoining street. The stairway leading to the second story was also situated in the courtyard.

The Reservoirs. The two large reservoirs of Nabataean construction were reused in the Byzantine period and formed the link between the older Nabataean town and the newer central quarter. The reservoirs, irregularly shaped polygons, were interconnected and built of stones set in mortar and coated with waterproof plaster. Steps led down to the bottom. The southern reservoir has a capacity of about 700 cubic meters, and the northern one about 850 meters. It was the duty of all the citizens to clean the reservoirs, and according to information contained in ostraca, this obligation was indeed fulfilled.

CHURCHES

South Church. From the excavations carried out by the Colt Expedition, only the plan of the South Church has thus far been published. Since the church was erected after the construction of the two reservoirs south of it, the builders, for lack of space, were unable to provide it with an atrium, as in the other two churches and had to suffice with a narthex only, which did not serve as a vestibule linking the church directly with the outside. The monumental entrance of the church is

located in the southwest corner of the narthex from which two entrances only lead into the church proper. The church is built on a nearly square plan (17.6 meters long and 18.2 meters wide) and is divided into a nave and two aisles by two rows of six columns each. The four eastern columns form part of the chancel screen erected on the bema. In front of the northwest corner of the bema stands the square base of the ambo. The excavators assumed that this church, like the two others at Subeita, was of the triapsidal type. A recent study by A. Negev, however, proves that this was not the case. The church was originally built as a monoapsidal structure with two rectangular rooms, one on either side of the apse, similar to the plans of the earlier churches at Kurnub, Eboda, and Nessana (North Church), all of which most probably date to the second half of the fourth century A.D. In a later stage, probably in the early sixth century, the rectangular rooms were blocked up and replaced by the small lateral nichelike apses. They held the remains of stone-built reliquaries, attesting to a cult of martyrs to which the churches were dedicated. It is not known whether this cult was also practiced in the early phase of the church. The central apse is twice the height of the lateral apses, above which there were chambers, probably entered from the upper story. The back walls of the lateral apses had niches. The three apses were not built on the same axis, and the southern wall of the church deviates slightly southward. The nave is paved with marble slabs, and the aisles with limestone slabs. The apses are plastered and decorated with paintings of religious subjects.

North of the church stood a chapel and a baptistery. They were entered from a small room north of the narthex, which leads to an open square in front of which is a small exedra with two columns. A cruciform baptismal font (the length of each arm is 1.5 meters) was cut out of a monolith and set inside an apse built of ashlars. Inside the font, on the east and west ends, are steps leading down to its bottom. North of this large baptismal font is a smaller one for infant baptisms, also cut out of a monolith. Southeast of the baptistery is a tower, which may have been the earliest annex, and also a small court surrounded by rooms.

Two inscriptions were found in the church compound. The earlier one, from Sobata of the Byzantine period, is engraved on a lintel, and attests to the construction of an annex to the church as early as A.D. 415/430. The other inscription appears in the floor of the southern aisle, and states that the pavement was laid in A.D. 640.

North of the baptistery was erected a mosque. Its mihrab is built against the north wall of the baptistery, and it seems that the builders of the mosque took special care not to damage the adjoining Christian establishment. The floor of the mosque is laid with limestone slabs.

The Central Church. No plan of this building has been published. Due to its position in the town plan, this church, facing one of the main streets of the central quarter, has no proper atrium, but only a narthexlike corridor. The Central Church has three apses, a type rare in the central Negev, the only other churches of this type being the South Church at Nessana (A.D. 601), and possibly a church at Ruheibah, now being excavated. The Central Church at Subeita most probably dates to the late sixth or early seventh century A.D.

The North Church lies on the boundary of the city, leading the excavators to assume that it was the latest church constructed at Subeita. This, however, is not the case. The walls of the church are supported by strong retaining walls, preserved to

Opposite page: Winepress.
Below: South church. Baptismal font.

a considerable height. Although in the opinion of the excavators these walls were meant to strengthen the structure and turn it into a stronghold, such retaining walls also support other buildings in the town, and it therefore appears that their purpose was to consolidate walls that were damaged by an earthquake in the fifth or beginning of the sixth century A.D. The building complex of the church comprises the church proper, a baptistery, chapel, and monastery. The church was entered from a small square south of the atrium, where there is a small exedra supported by three heavy piers. Above the exedra was a passage leading from the monastery to the church, this being the only link between them. The atrium (26 by 19 meters) was larger than the church proper. It was entered through a single gate pierced in its southern wall. Along three of its walls (west, north, and south) were rooms with walls supported by arches. In the west part of the atrium is a large cistern. In the middle of the atrium is a stump of a column enclosed in a rectangular frame. This was probably the memorial of a stylite who lived there, and was later sanctified and venerated in this church, which became a center of pilgrimage. This would account for the unusually large atrium, which has a parallel only at the above-mentioned church at Ruheibah, and the presence of the large paved square in front of the church, south of the atrium.

Originally the church was probably entered directly from the atrium, the eastern colonnade of which forms a kind of narthex. Later the columns of this colonnade were surrounded with wide pilasters, and thus a true narthex was formed. Three entrances lead into the church from the narthex. The church (20 by 13 meters) is divided into a nave and two aisles by two rows of six columns each, the western columns being attached to the doorposts of the central entrance. The church was originally of the monoapsidal type. The single apse was flanked by a rectangular room on either side, roofed over by arches, and provided with Negev-type slot windows. At a later stage, as in the contemporary South Church, were added the small nichelike apses with additional small niches in their center. Above them were small chambers. This church too was dedicated to the cult of martyrs, one of whom was probably the resident stylite.

The excavators distinguished two stages in the ornamentation of the church. Initially the walls were plastered and covered with paintings. Later they were faced with marble slabs up to half their height, and the floor was paved in its entirety with marble. A door in the southern aisle leads to the chapel, which is paved with mosaics laid in geometric patterns. A lengthy dedicatory inscription was also laid in the mosaic, but the date mentioned in it has not been preserved. A further door in the southern aisle leads to the baptistery, which is connected with the chapel to its south. The baptismal font is cut out of a monolith. The western half of the baptismal chapel was occupied by a small hypethral graveyard, in which members of the local clergy were interred (one of which was a Pharanite).

South of the church is a large complex of buildings, consisting of numerous courtyards and dozens of rooms. The excavators believed this complex was a monastery, but others consider it an area of workshops.

A large number of inscriptions were found in the church complex, most of them on gravestones. Most important is the inscription dated September 30, A.D. 506, which possible commemorates the dedication of the church, in which participated the most illustrious Flavius son of John, son of Stephen, *vicarius primi ordinis,* one of the high officials of the eastern Byzantine provinces, under whose auspices the renovation of the church was carried out. The mosaic pavement was apparently laid in the southern chapel in A.D. 518, under the auspices of Bishop Thomas. Burials here began on March, A.D. 506, several months before the official dedication, when a man, who probably died in an accident, was buried in the atrium. However, burial in the atrium as a regular practice did not begin before the winter of A.D. 542, at the time of the great plague which afflicted the whole of the Byzantine Empire, and claimed numerous victims in the other towns of the Negev. The latest burial of a layman in the atrium took place as late as A.D. 646. The clergy was buried in the graveyard in the baptismal chapel, between the years A.D. 614 and 679. Of great interest is a stone inscribed with the names of Abraham, Isaac, Jacob, Moses, David, Solomon, and Job, each with his most characteristic feature appended.

Winepresses. In the buildings adjoining the North Church and at two other locations in the town were discovered installations which the Colt Ex-

*Khirbet Susiya. Section of mosaic floor from
the synagogue's hall
Below: The inscription in the narthex*

pedition identified as bathhouses and Wiegand defined as tombs. Each installation consisted of two parts, one of which was a square floor paved with limestone slabs and surrounded by a low wall. In the center of the floor is the mouth of a channel running beneath the floor to the second part of the installation, situated on a lower level. This was a large, round, rock-cut tank, with a small depression in the bottom. The tank is completely coated with waterproof plaster. A comparison with similar installations discovered at Eboda indicate that these without doubt were winepresses. The grapes were crushed in the upper part, the juice running down the channel into the tank where the skins settled in the depression cut in the bottom.

It is interesting to note the difference between the winepress in the northern monastery and the southern winepress which was probably not connected with a church. The southern winepress has small cells around the treading platform, similar to those around the winepresses in Eboda. No such cells are found, however, in the winepress in the monastery. It seems that the southern winepress was used by private farmers of the city who stored their own baskets of grapes in the cells, whereas the monks, who worked their land in common, had no need of such storage facilities.   A. NEGEV

BIBLIOGRAPHY

E. H. Palmer, *PEF QSt* (1871), 29–30 • Musil, *Arabia Petraea* 2, 36–45 • A. Jaussen, R. Savignac, and H. Vincent, *RB* N. S. 2 (1905), 256–57 • T. Kühtreiber, *ZDPV* 37 (1914), 5 f. • C. L. Woolley and T. E. Lawrence, The Wilderness of Zin, *APEF* 3 (1914–15), 72–93 • T. Wiegand, *Sinai*, Berlin-Leipzig, 1920, 62–83 • A. Alt, *Die Griechischen Inschriften der Palästina Tertia Westlich der Araba*, Berlin und Leipzig, 1921, 43–44 • T. Canaan, *JPOS* 2 (1922), 139–44. F. M. Abel, *Byzantion* 1 (1924), 57 • R. Tonneau, *RB* 35 (1926), 583–604 • A. Mallon, *JPOS* 10 (1930), 224–29 • T. J. Colin-Baly, *PEQ* (1935), 171–81; Report *BSAJ, PEF QSt*, (1935), 9–11, 168–70 • W. F. Albright, *AJA* 39 (1935), 143; 40 (1936), 160–61 • G. M. Crowfoot, *PEQ*, (1936), 14–27 • F. M. Abel, *JPOS* 15 (1935), 7–11 • H. C. Youtie, *AJA* (1936), 452–59 • G. E. Kirk, *JPOS* 17 (1937), 209–17 • T. J. Colin-Baly, *QDAP* 8 (1938), 159 • J. W. Crowfoot, *Early Churches in Palestine*, London, (1941), 70–71 • H. D. Colt, *Archaeology* 1 (1948), 84–91 • Y. Kedar, *IEJ* 7 (1957), 178–89 • C. J. Kraemer, Jr., *Excavations at Nessana* 3 (Non-Literary Papyri), Princeton N.J., 1958, 227–33 • P. Meyerson, *BASOR* 153 (1959), 19–31; idem, *Proceedings of the American Philosophical Society* 107 (1963), 160–72 • A. Negev, *Cities in the Desert*, Tel Aviv, (1966) • N. Glueck, *Rivers in the Desert*, New York, 1968, 264–69 • M. Evenari, L. Shanan and N. Tadmor, *The Negev*, Cambridge, Mass., 1971, 168–71 • R. Rosentahl, *The North Church and the Monastery at Sobota* (Shivta), doctoral thesis, Jerusalem, 1974. A. Negev, *RB* 81 (1974), 397–420.

SUSIYA, KHIRBET

IDENTIFICATION. Khirbet Susiya is situated some 750 meters above sea level on the peak of a hill bounded on the north and east by Naḥal Maraje, in an area containing scattered ruins of the ancient settlements of Eshtemoa, Juttah, Ma'on, Carmel, and Kafr Aziz. The site was surveyed almost a century ago on behalf of the Palestine Exploration Fund. Although A. Reifenberg and L. A. Mayer, who excavated the synagogue at nearby Eshtemoa, mention the existence of a synagogue at Susiya, they give no further details as to its location. During an extensive survey carried out by the Israel Survey Society under the direction of M. Kochavi, the synagogue was rediscovered. It was again examined in 1969, in a survey by S. Gutman, who also conducted trial excavations under the auspices of the Area Command of Judea and Samaria. With the uncovering of the narthex of the synagogue, it was decided to clear the entire synagogue. Excavation and restoration work continued from January, 1971, until mid-1972 under the direction of S. Gutman, E. Netzer, and Z. Yeivin, on behalf of various Israel Archaeological Societies.

The Synagogue

The synagogue is situated on the southeast slope of the hill on the west side of Khirbet Susiya. It includes a court on the east side, which was paved with stone slabs and surrounded on three sides by porticoes roofed with stone arches supported by square columns. The entrance to the court was through the north and east porticoes. The south portico was paved with a mosaic floor with a dedicatory inscription at one end. Two small rooms in the northeast and southeast corners of the court were apparently used for storage. Because of the topography of the site, the floor of the court was 1.5 meters lower than that of the synagogue, and a flight of five steps, extending along the eastern facade of the synagogue, led up to the narthex. In the floor of the court were two pits. One stored rainwater drained from the court, and the other pit led into a series of caves, which had possibly first served as quarries and later as storerooms. The synagogue building consists of a narthex in the east, a long, narrow wing in the south, and a hall 9 by 16 meters in the north. Steps in the southern end of the narthex led to a second story stretching above the southern wing and possibly over the narthex as well.

The facade of the building was apparently two stories high and was crowned by a pediment. In its center was a porch with a row of Late Corinthian columns. Two of the columns and all but one of the bases were found in position. The missing base, the rest of the columns, two capitals, and parts of the architrave were found re-used as building stones in a mosque which was probably erected in the tenth century A.D. The column base had been placed into the stone floor top side down to seal the opening of the cistern, which was then no longer in use.

The south wing was divided into two rooms. The larger east one was entered through a doorway in the narthex, and the west room from the outside through a doorway in the south wall. A partition wall with an entrance cut into it separated the two rooms. The east room had a flagstone pavement similar to the one in the court. There were stone benches along the west, south, and east walls. A window in the north wall connected the east room with the hall. At a later stage, a flight of stairs was installed in the west room. The steps were built above a small vaulted storage chamber.

Three ornamented entrances, the middle one the largest, led from the narthex into the hall. Built against the northern wall of the hall, which was twice the thickness of the other walls, were two bemas (podiums). Because of the extensive damage on the spot, no remains were found of the niche in the wall above the main bema, though there were definite traces of its existence.

As in the synagogue at Eshtemoa, here too there is a certain disharmony between the general east–west orientation of the long-room building and its northern orientation toward Jerusalem, a fact that transforms it into a broad-room building. However, whereas a single bema was discovered at Eshtemoa, at Susiya there were two bemas. The main bema stood slightly west of the center of the northern wall. The smaller bema east of the latter is one of the major innovations of the synagogue at Susiya. Three tiers of benches, along the south, west, and north walls, extended up to the main bema.

The west wall of the synagogue was built of ashlar on both faces, while the other walls were constructed of ashlar only on the outside, and their inner face was of ordinary fieldstone. The building was roofed with tiles, as is indicated by the numerous tile fragments found in the debris of the hall.

The main bema, in its initial stage, was formed mainly by several tiers of white plastered benches — similar to those surrounding the hall — with steps leading to the niche above it. At a later stage, a ledge and additional benches were built in front of it, as well as columns and a chancel screen. During the zenith of the building, the entire bema was faced with gray marble, and semicircular flights of steps were placed on either side. Most of the columns of the screen and fragments of the screen itself were found in secondary use. The screen was decorated with a menorah, the tree of life surrounded by lions, and a palm tree surrounded by eagles. Several of the columns and the screen itself bore dedicatory inscriptions.

The small bema was roughly square in shape. It also underwent various alterations. In one of its corners, a carved stone of a column was found in situ, indicating the probable existence of a canopy above it.

MOSAICS

The remains in the area of the main bema show that the hall was originally paved with a plain white mosaic. However, already at an early stage it was replaced by a multi-colored mosaic consisting of a "carpet" in three panels extending the entire length of the hall. In the west were depicted three scenes: a hunt, a scene apparently depicting Daniel in the lions' den, and a third scene, too badly damaged to identify. In the central panel was a large circle divided into sectors apparently representing the zodiac. It was surrounded by a wreath containing a geometric pattern alternating with a bird or plant. The eastern panel was made up of interconnected octagons surrounded by birds, but nothing depicted within the octagons could be identified.

In front of the smaller bema was another panel depicting a tetrastyle Ark of the Law with a menorah between each pair of columns. A ram stood at either end of the panel. The position of this mosaic indicates the importance of the smaller bema, which probably served in the reading of the Scriptures. In the northern corners of the hall were two small panels decorated with geometric designs. The zodiac, of which only a very small fragment has

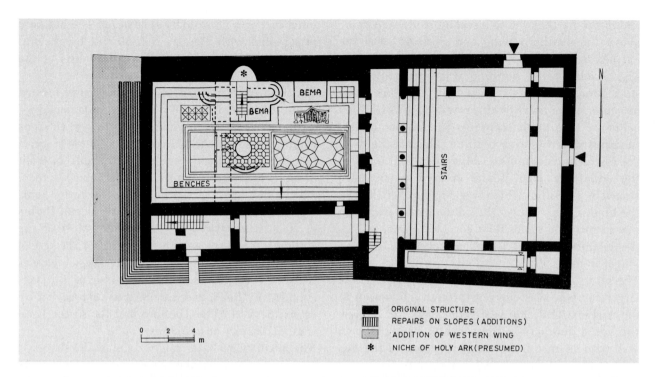

ORIGINAL STRUCTURE
REPAIRS ON SLOPES (ADDITIONS)
ADDITION OF WESTERN WING
* NICHE OF HOLY ARK (PRESUMED)

Both pages, counterclockwise from this page, below:
Reconstruction of the synagogue; Plan of the synagogue;
General view of the building; The southern wing;
Inscription No. 3, in the mosaic pavement.

survived, was later replaced by a geometric pattern with a rosette in the center. Numerous repairs were made in the mosaic over the years, mostly in coarse white tesserae, though occasionally the original colored stones were employed. Of particular interest is the geometric design in the center of the mosaic of the narthex made of tiny colored tesserae and enclosing an inscription.

Four inscriptions, two in Aramaic and two in Hebrew, were found in the mosaic floor, and several others were found incised on the chancel screen and its posts. Two of the inscriptions were found in the narthex, one in the center of the mosaic panel and the other near the north wall. A third inscription was just inside the central entrance in the hall, and a fourth was located in the southern portico of the court.

DATING

Evidence of coins and the building remains point to a date at the end of the fourth – beginning of the fifth century A.D. for the foundation of the synagogue. It continued in use until at least the ninth century. During this period, the synagogue underwent numerous repairs, which also attests to the continuous use of the building. There is no evidence of the synagogue's destruction in a sudden catastrophe, and it seems more likely that it gradually went out of use until it was finally abandoned in the ninth or tenth century A.D.

S. GUTMAN, E. NETZER, Z. YEIVIN

BIBLIOGRAPHY

S. Gutman, E. Netzer and Z. Yeivin, *Qadmoniot* 5 (1972), 47–52 (Hebrew) • Z. Yeivin, *IEJ* 24 (1974), 201–09.

Menorah mosaic pavement with small bema above it.

SYNAGOGUES

HISTORY. The origins of the synagogue are to be sought in the Diaspora, where Jewish communities, dispersed among the nations, felt the need for common public worship and meeting places. The first synagogues may have made their appearance as early as the Babylonian Exile and the Persian period. In any event, they certainly existed in the Hellenistic age, and there may even have been synagogues in the smaller settlements of Palestine prior to the destruction of the Second Temple (growing out of the institution of the priestly divisions, which had crystallized around the three annual pilgrimages). In Jerusalem itself, the need for a social-religious meeting place was felt more strongly by foreign pilgrims and the lower classes, such as freed slaves, than by native Jerusalemites, for whom the Temple represented the focus of their religious life. The first archaeological evidence of a synagogue is an inscription from Shedia, near Alexandria, from the time of Ptolemy III Euergetes (246–221 B.C.), which mentions the proseuche — Προσευχή, "house of prayer" — of the Jews. Later evidence stems from an Alexandrian inscription (37 B.C.) and an inscription of Theodotus son of Vettenos of Jerusalem (first century A.D.). In the third-century synagogue in the Roman port of Ostia, fragments of a second-century A.D. inscription were discovered, which may indicate that a Jewish house of worship had existed on the site during the reign of the emperor Augustus. It is also likely that the public buildings dated to the first century B.C. at Caesarea and the first century A.D. at Tiberias, which have been unearthed at the foundations of Palestinian synagogues, may themselves have served a similar purpose. But this is difficult to prove since clear evidence of the nature of these structures is lacking. In excavations at Masada (q.v.) a building was exposed, which was possibly a synagogue erected by the Zealots inside an older structure during the siege of A.D. 66–73. The first unmistakable remains of synagogues in Palestine (Galilee), Asia Minor (Miletus, Priene, Sardis), and Ostia, near Rome, date from the third century onward. The evolution of the various types of synagogue buildings can be traced mainly in Palestine where structures from the third to the eighth centuries have been found. These buildings can be divided into three types: 1. early synagogues; 2. transitional type; 3. late synagogues. The half-dozen or so synagogues discovered in the Diaspora are generally similar to the types found in Palestine.

THE EARLY SYNAGOGUES

These were constructed wherever possible on the highest point of a town (thus following Tosefta, *Megillah* 4) or on the shores of seas or banks of rivers. The synagogue consisted of a square or rectangular hall containing three rows of columns set on pedestals — two rows perpendicular to the entrance wall and the third running parallel to it. The dimensions of the buildings were from 360 square meters (Capernaum) to 150 square meters (ed-Dikkeh and Umm el-Qanatir, see below), the usual ratio between the building's length and width being 11:10. Four main features are characteristic of the early type of synagogue: 1. the facade oriented toward Jerusalem is richly ornamented; 2. the wall opposite the entrance is straight and has no apse; 3. there is a transverse row of columns; 4. the floor is paved with flagstones. The single architectural embellishment inside the hall is the column capitals. A (women's) gallery was apparently situated above the columns, judging by the remains of stairways and fragments of columns smaller than those in the hall and from pieces of railing screen. Some scholars are of the opinion that the splendidly carved friezes were also part of the gallery decorations.

The synagogues had three entrances in the facade, the middle entrance larger than the flanking ones. The entrances and windows were decorated in a special manner. Above the main entrance was a semicircular window, which served both to admit light and to remind the worshippers of the direction of Jerusalem. The entrances had carved doorposts and lintels, with the central lintel extending beyond the doorposts on either side. The facade teminated in a pediment with an arched base (the type known as the Syrian gable). Smaller windows were set above the side doors and perhaps even higher up to illuminate the gallery. In some synagogues, there was a portico outside the facade (Kefar Bir'am, Umm el-Qanatir) or a flight of steps (Capernaum, Chorozain). Several early synagogues had adjacent courtyards surrounded by porticoes. The one at Capernaum provided shelter from rain and sun for wayfarers and the poor. These various stylistic details were influenced by contemporary artistic trends, mainly Syrian (especially the regions of Hauran and Bashan). Some architectural elements were taken from the classical style (e.g., Corinthian capitals, Attic bases, and friezes with floral motifs), and the ornamentation also contained forms borrowed from the classical world (Hercules, Medusa, griffins, sea-horses, etc.) and, usually above the

Map of synagogues discovered in Israel.

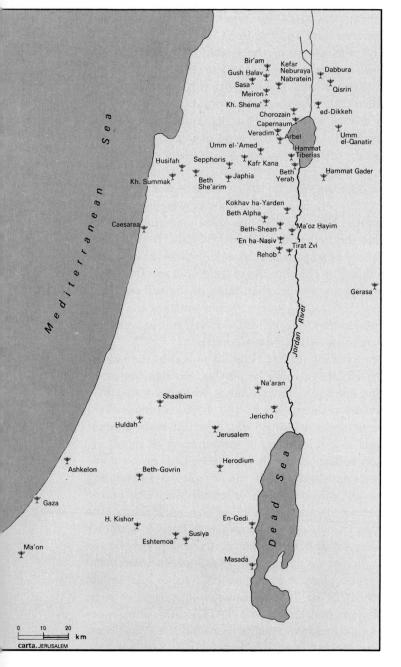

windows, wreath-bearing figures of Winged Victories. In the workmanship of these ornaments, however, one could distinguish the hand of the local artist, steeped in the tradition of the East. Many religious symbols appear among the decorative motifs (menorah, Ark of the Law, etc.), symbols of "good fortune" such as the hexagram (Shield of David) and the pentagram (Seal of Solomon), as well as symbols of fertility (the "seven species" of Palestinian agricultural products). The inscriptions are for the most part in Aramaic with a few in Greek. As a rule the inscriptions mention donors who had some part of the synagogue built at their expense or contributed towards its construction. The usual formula appearing in these inscriptions begins with the words "Remembered be for good" such and such who built or contributed (here the specific part of the building is recorded). The inscription concludes with the blessing "May his lot be among the righteous. Amen."

The interior of the structure was bare and contained only a bench running along the walls and an ornamented seat ("cathedra of Moses"). The location of the Ark of the Law and the direction in which the worshippers prayed were strongly disputed in the past. Most scholars today are of the opinion that, in the early synagogues, the worshippers prayed facing the facade (perhaps they entered through side doors and did not turn around after entering through the facade, although in Ostia there are indications to the contrary — that they did, in fact, make an about turn in the direction of the fixed ark). In Palestine, the ark was movable and must certainly have been placed by the entrance.

THE TRANSITIONAL-TYPE SYNAGOGUES

After finding the plan of the early synagogues inconvenient, the builders made alterations in the interiors from the middle of the third century (at Dura-Europos on the Euphrates) and throughout the fourth century (in Palestine). During this time, the plan of the buildings was not yet crystallized, and the old and new elements appear together in such a way that each synagogue stands as a type by itself, and it is difficult to point to any typical features of these synagogues as a whole. Nevertheless, it is possible to distinguish the innovations introduced in the plans of the early synagogues. The building was now adapted to a congregation which prayed facing in the direction of Jerusalem.

At Eshtemoa (q.v.) the synagogue was built as a broad house with a niche set in the wall facing Jerusalem, and the entrance was in one of the short sides. Although at Beth-She'arim the bema was first placed on the north side of the hall, the middle entrance facing Jerusalem was later blocked up. At Arbel a niche was cut out of the rock wall on the side facing the Holy City, and a congregants, entrance was opened on the north side. The entrances were eventually moved to the side opposite the wall facing Jerusalem, as, e.g., at Hammath-Tiberias and Ḥusifah. At first there were no apses or fixed altars facing Jerusalem at Hammath-Tiberias (phase II) or Ḥusifah, but these were later installed, together with columns and lintels (Hammath-Tiberias — phases I, II). Once the Ark of the Law was fixed in the wall, it was necessary to proceed one step further and to eliminate the transverse row of columns, which separated the worshippers from the Ark. And indeed this row of columns appears only once more, on the side opposite the apse at Hammat Gader.

Another innovation is the replacing of the flagstone pavements by mosaic floors. These have been found at Apemea in Syria (end of the fourth century) and at Hammath-Tiberias (mid-fourth century?). Of Rabbi Abun, who lived in the mid-fourth century, it is recorded in the Palestinian Talmud ('Avodah Zarah 3:4, 42d), according to the Leningrad manuscript: "During the days of Rabbi Abun, they began to draw figures in mosaics, and he did not protest against them." Additional confirmation may be found in the Targum Jonathan, Leviticus 26:1. At Apamea, Sardis, and Caesarea (the early building), the mosaic floors were decorated exclusively with geometric patterns, and it appears that they took pains not to employ pagan motifs. At Hammath-Tiberias II, on the other hand, where the pavement was laid at the initiative of a high official of the patriarchs, they did not hesitate to invite gentile craftsmen from Antioch (or a Jew ignorant of Hebrew) to decorate the floor. The artist portrayed lions on either side of the entrance, the signs of the zodiac with the seasons in the four corners, and prominently displayed in the center of the zodiac is the figure of the god Helios riding his chariot.

Typical synagogue plans. 1. Umm el-'Amed. 2. Eshtemoa. 3. Beth Alpha.

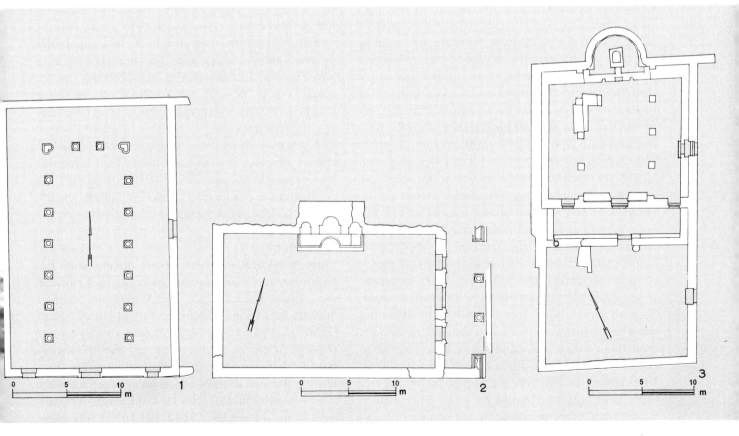

He also depicted the Ark of the Law flanked by menorahs. Apart from a biblical scene, one encounters in this early floor all the elements of the standard mosaic decoration of the late-type synagogues. In the basilica (non-apsidal) synagogue at Ḥusifah, the menorahs were set near the entrance, and at the far end the mosaic showed the signs of the zodiac. In the center is a vine trellis and a pair of peacocks (and cf. Ma'on).

THE LATE SYNAGOGUES

After the period of modifications and experimentation of the fourth–fifth centuries, a new type of synagogue style had developed by the end of the fifth century (Geresa). The late synagogue is a basilica structure with a court (containing a cistern in its center) opening onto a narthex. Three doorways in the narthex led into the basilica hall, which was divided by two rows of columns or pillars into a nave and two aisles. Above the aisles, there was apparently a women's gallery. There was a prayer-platform or sunken prayer area by the wall opposite the entrance, which contained an apse into which the Ark of the Law was placed. The floor of the apse had a depression (genizah) for storing worn-out or damaged sacred texts or the synagogue treasury. The apse stood in the wall facing Jerusalem, and the entire structure was built along a central axis running from the entrance to the apse. In this functional aspect, the synagogue plan corresponds to the plans of contemporary churches. As in the churches, the area in front of the bema (platform) may be separated from the rest of the hall by a step and a screen made of pillars and carved panels. Aside from the column capitals and chancel screens, the late-type synagogues contained no architectural ornamentation. The decoration of the building was concentrated in the mosaics, which almost without exception covered the entire floor (at Ma'on the nave only). In these pavements is seen for the first time an emphasis on lavish ornamentation, which in its most complete form incorporated the following four elements: 1. the entranceway decorated with lions or other figures; 2. a biblical scene of salvation depicting the devout being delivered by divine providence, e.g., Noah's Ark, the Offering of Isaac, Daniel in the lions' den, etc.; 3. the zodiac; 4. the Ark of the Law flanked by two seven-branched menorahs and other ritual objects flanked by lions. This pattern varies from place to place. In the course of time,

there is a clear tendency against the representation of human figures. At Ma'on, where the mosaic pavement closely resembles church floors in both plan and style, and also at Ḥammat Gader (q.v.), no human figures are portrayed. The mosaics at Jericho and the late synagogue at Hammath-Tiberias, also contain purely geometric ornaments.

Adjoining the various synagogues, additional chambers were built for study and teaching purposes, as well as storerooms and the like.

Palestinian synagogues attest to the struggle between two schools — those tending toward a strict observance of the religious prohibitions and those adopting a more liberal approach. The latter permitted the representation of human and animal figures in relief. (Three-dimensional sculpture had always been forbidden inside the synagogue; only at Chorozain and Kefar Neburaya have fragments of lion statues been found.) This freedom also reigned from the mid-fourth century where floor mosaics were concerned, but it gradually lessened in the first third of the sixth century onward. With the increasing opposition to pictorial representation came a concomitant increase in acts of mutilation of artistic works. While it is true that the Galilean synagogues underwent restoration in the sixth century (see Kefar Neburaya), all the human forms appearing on reliefs were apparently chipped away. At Na'aran the removal of images and figures (iconoclasm) is also evident in the mosaic floors as well, where the forms of living beings were eliminated carefully so as not to damage the inscriptions.

The destruction of the synagogues was caused in almost all cases by enemy action. This is clearly borne out by the remains, especially the signs of conflagration found on the mosaic floors. On the ruined synagogue at Gerasa, a church was erected in 530.

EXPLORATION

Various Jewish scholars, among them Estori ha-Parḥi, knew of the existence of synagogue ruins in the Galilee. The scientific world, however, learned of them first from E. Robinson (1852) and E. Renan (1864). C. Wilson and H. H. Kitchener carried out surveys of the synagogues during the 1870's, on behalf of the Palestine Exploration Fund. The foremost explorers of the early-type synagogues were the German archaeologists H. Kohl and C. Watzinger (1905). During the 1920's and 1930's, the synagogues at Na'aran and Gerasa were discovered. Jewish archaeologists began synagogue research in the 1920's. N. Slouschz excavated at Hammath-Tiberias and E. L. Sukenik unearthed the synagogues of Beth Alpha, Ḥammat Gader, Shaalbim, and Japhia. L. A. Mayer and A. Reifenberg excavated the synagogue at Eshtemoa and B. Mazar the one at Beth She'arim. N. Makhouly and M. Avi-Yonah cleared the synagogue at Ḥusifah. Since the establishment of the State of Israel, synagogues have been brought to light at Ma'on (S. Levy, L. Y. Rahmani, and M. Avi-Yonah, q.v.), Beth-Shean (N. Tzori, D. Bahat, q.v.), Hammath-Tiberias (M. Dothan), Caesarea (M. Avi-Yonah, q.v.), Ḥuldah (J. Ory and M. Avi-Yonah, see below). Samaritan synagogues have been uncovered at Shaalbim and Beth-Shean (qq.v.). A special publication, the *L. M. Rabinowitz Bulletin,* issued by the Institute of Archaeology of the Hebrew University of Jerusalem, is devoted to synagogue exploration.

BIBLIOGRAPHY

M. Avi-Yonah and S. Yeivin, *The Antiquities of Israel,* Tel Aviv, 1955, 220–36 (Hebrew) • Wilson–Kitchener, *Special Papers,* 294–305 • Kohl–Watzinger, *Synagogen* • Sukenik, *Ancient Synagogues* • Watzinger, *DP,* 2, 107–16 • Goodenough, *Jewish Symbols,* 1, 178–264 • F. Hüttenmeister and G. Reeg, *Die antiken Synagogen in Israel,* Wiesbaden, 1977 • J. Naveh, *On Stone and Mosaic, The Aramaic and Hebrew Inscriptions from Ancient Synagogues,* Jerusalem 1978 (Hebrew).

SYNAGOGUES NOT DISCUSSED IN SEPARATE ARTICLES

This section will deal only with those synagogues known from their building remains, and not merely through architectural fragments or inscriptions which were removed from their sites. The synagogues are listed alphabetically.

ARBEL. The ruins of this synagogue are first mentioned by Jewish travelers of the thirteenth–fourteenth centuries. C. Wilson carried out an exploratory dig at the site, and H. Kohl and C. Watzinger excavated there in May, 1905. The facade of the

Left: Arbel. Plan of the synagogue. Right: Arbel. Synagogue remains.

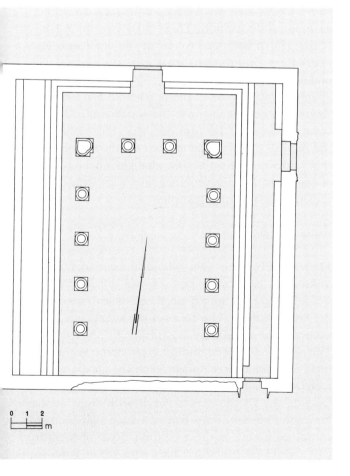

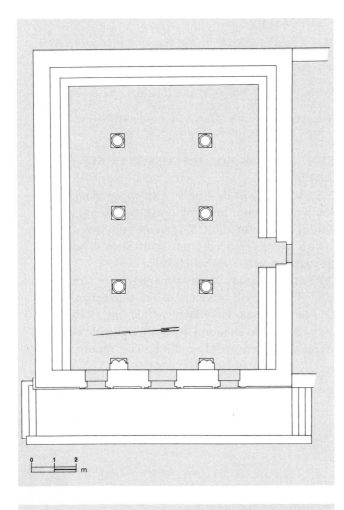

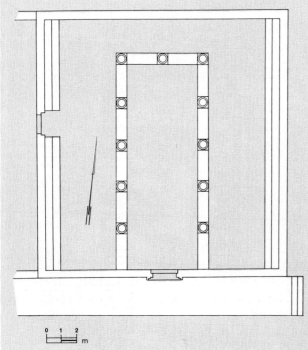

synagogue is oriented to the south, and its lower part is hewn out of the rock. The interior (external measurements 18.65 by 18.2 meters) is divided by two rows of four columns each into a nave (7.35 meters wide) and two aisles (each 3.8 meters wide). Between the two corner pillars with heart-shaped cross-section is a transverse row of two columns. Benches run in a south–north direction along the walls. In front of the benches is a 1.88 meters wide space from which three steps descend to the center of the hall. The two lower steps also extend along the northern wall. Both the nave and the aisles up to the steps were paved with flag-stones. A doorway with a threshold was found in the eastern wall, and at the eastern end of the southern wall there was another entrance (possibly leading to the upper gallery). A kind of stone ark (1.18 meters high and .8 meter deep) was located in the eastern wall. The architectural remains are few: Corinthian and Ionic capitals, attached pillars of the gallery, a cornice fragment ornamented with egg and dart and cyma reversa, an ornamented triglyph fragment and two pilasters attached to a stone block, one with straight fluting, the other with spiral decoration. These pilasters and a gable with a conch belonged to one of the windows. The excavators found signs that the synagogue had undergone modifications at a later date. A new opening was pierced in the north wall and an oval-shaped niche was cut into the south wall. The excavators were of the opinion that the niche was the mihrab of a mosque erected on the site, but all the evidence indicates that changes characteristic of the transitional-type synagogue were introduced into the early synagogue plan.

Kohl–Watzinger, *Synagogen*, 59–70 • Goodenough, *Jewish Symbols*, 1, 199.

ED-DIKKEH. This site, whose ancient identity is unknown, is located east of the Jordan, about 4.5 kilometers (3 miles) north of its entrance into the Sea of Galilee. The ruins of the synagogue were investigated in 1905 by H. Kohl and C. Watzinger. The small, elongated building (15.3 by 11.92 meters) contained three entrances in the facade which faced west, since the site lay east of the Jordan. Outside the facade was a porch with steps at the far end. The hall, only half of which was cleared, contained a row of three columns (two of them in situ, while of the third only the stone base re-

*Opposite page: Plans of synagogues, top: in Ed-Dikkeh, Bottom: in Gush Ḥalav.
This page: Gush Ḥalav. Decorated lintel from the synagogue.*

mained). No trace of a transverse row of columns was found, and the excavators surmised that no such row had existed. By the western wall were discovered the foundations of two engaged pillars, which may have been piers supporting arches between the wall and the columns, or intercolumnar arches. Remains of an arch were in fact discovered in debris on the site. A double tier of benches which run around the entire hall was well preserved in the northeast corner. The architectural ornamentation of the ed-Dikkeh synagogue was elaborate. Its remains include the lintel of the main entrance with Winged Victories holding garlands, a frieze decorated with a stylized vine trellis above the side entrances, while vine, bead, egg-and-dart patterns adorned the arches. In the Ionic capitals in the corners of the facade, the classical elements were separated (volutes in the corners and a frieze of egg and dart). Remains of two ornamented windows were also found, one with a pair of colonettes on either side, and the other with single colonettes on either side. There were conchs above the window openings, and the corners of the gable were ornamented with birds, dolphins, and bunches of grapes. A cornice was found displaying floral as well as egg-and-meander motifs.

Kohl–Watzinger, *Synagogen*, 112–24 • Goodenough, *Jewish Symbols*, 1, 205–06.

GUSH ḤALAV (GISCALA).

At least two synagogues have been discovered at Gush Ḥalav located approximately 8 kilometers (5 miles) northwest of Safed. One synagogue, whose ruins were observed by V. Guérin as early as 1863, stood at the top of the hill on which is built the present-day village of el-Jish. The village church now stands on the site of the synagogue, leaving few remnants of the ancient structure. Another synagogue was uncovered by H. Kohl and C. Watzinger on the slopes above the Gush Ḥalav brook, not far from the village spring. The structure (16.3 by 15.4 meters) apparently had only one doorway in the facade, which is oriented to the south (the synagogue is built on a north–south axis). There may have been an additional entrance in the western wall. The entire extent of the facade was fronted by a balcony with a flight of steps on the side. The interior was divided into a nave (4.67 meters wide) and two aisles (each 4.65 meters wide) by two rows of five columns each (no remains of the corner columns have survived). A transverse row consisted of three columns. The long side walls on the east and west appear to have contained a double tier of benches. The doorpost of the main entrance was molded, and above it was a rounded frieze decorated with a garland. In its lower part, the lintel depicts an eagle in the center, holding a long garland in its beak. Several of the capitals discovered were simple Ionic. Also found was a fragment of a wall frieze decorated with a rosette and a flat bowl enclosed by a stylized twisting vine. E. Renan found an inscription on one of the pillar drums: "Jose son of Nahum made this [pillar]. May he be blessed."

Kohl–Watzinger, *Synagogen*, 107–11 • Goodenough, *Jewish Symbols* 1, 205.

ḤULDAH. In 1953, J. Ory excavated on behalf of the Department of Antiquities a rectangular structure (12.7 by 7 meters) consisting of two rooms (4.6 and 5.3 long). The entrance was in the south side. In the floor of the first room was a circular depression (2.5 meters in diameter) with steps descending inside and another square-shaped depression (1.1 square meters) connected to it. The second room had two niches in each of the three outer walls. Both rooms were paved with mosaics. In the floor in front of the entrance was a rectangular panel in which was represented a seven-branched menorah, the branches thin lines decorated with yellow knobs. The foot of the menorah is triangular. The candles are square with red flames issuing from them. To the right of the menorah is depicted a shofar, and to the left a censer, ethrog, and lulab. Between the lulab and the menorah are the Greek words: Εὐθογιά τῷ λαῷ ("Blessing on the people"). To the right of this panel is a circular medallion (1.16 meters in diameter) within a square border. The medallion contains a Greek inscription (in black tesserae but with names in red): "Good fortune to Eustochios and Hesychios and Evagrios the founders."

Since the Ḥuldah mosaic floor contains representations of Jewish ceremonial objects, the building has been included here with the synagogues, but the orientation and plan of the structure are not those of a synagogue, and it may very well have been a miqve.

M. Avi-Yonah, *Rabinowitz Bulletin* 3 (1960), 57–60 • Unesco, *Israel Ancient Mosaics,* New York, 1960, Pl. XXVIII (Introduction by M. Shapiro and M. Avi-Yonah).

KAFR KANA. In this village about 6 kilometers (3.5 miles) north of Nazareth, part of a mosaic pavement was discovered in 1901 near the altar of the Franciscan Church. The pavement bore a fragmentary guilloche design and an inscription in five lines: "Remembered be for good Jose son of Tanḥum, son of Botah, and his sons, who made this tablet. May they be blessed. Amen." Nearby was a fragment of a second inscription. These are the only remains of the synagogue erected on this site.

C. Clermont–Ganneau, *PEF QSt,* 1901, 251, 374–89; *ibid.,* 1902, 132–34 • S. Klein, *Corpus,* 74–76.

SUMMAK (OR SUMMAKA), KHIRBET. The site is located approximately 2 kilometers south of Daliat ha-Carmel (map reference 154231). H. Kohl and C. Watzinger cleared here part of a building. In excavating a section of the facade which faced east, they exposed the north and middle doorways as well as part of the south one. They also uncovered part of the northern and western walls and could consequently establish the dimensions of the building (19.3 by 14.8 meters). As in the other ancient synagogues on Mount Carmel (see Ḥusifah), the facade of the building also faced east. Apparently all synagogues considered as situated on the seashore were oriented to the east, toward Jerusalem. Since only a limited area of the building was excavated, the basilica plan of the structure could not be fully examined. Inside the hall, a single column base of the southern row was found, and another column shaft still stood in position in the same row. Kohl and Watzinger concluded that the hall had contained two rows of six columns each (the distance between the columns being approximately 1.93 meters). No signs of a transverse row were noted, and considering the short distance between the rows (about 4.5 meters), no such row had apparently existed. The nave and aisles were of equal width. Two or three courses of the facade masonry were still intact in 1905, and the doorpost of the middle entrance still stood to a height of 2 meters. There were two pilasters remaining in the northern entrance and one in the southern entrance (1.99 meters high), all with simple capitals and Attic bases. The side entrances were 1.07 meters wide, and the middle doorway was 1.52 meters wide. On the lintel above the side entrance, two lions flanking a goblet (or calf's head?) were carved on a *tabula ansata.*

Conder-Kitchener, *SWP* 1, 318 ff. • L. Oliphant, *PEF QSt,* 1884, 41 • E. G. von Mülinen, *ZDPV* 31 (1908/9), 158 ff. • Kohl–Watzinger, *Synagogen,* 135–37 • Goodenough, *Jewish Symbols* 1, 208.

TIRAT ZVI. Near the mound of Kefar Karnaim, approximately 8 kilometers (5 miles) south of Beth-Shean (map reference 19942037), a fragment of a mosaic floor was exposed, on which was represented part of a menorah with branches made of knobs and ovals. A line extends along the top of the branches, and above it are circular candles and red flames. A shofar is represented next to the menorah.

M. Avi-Yonah, *Antiquity and Survival* 2 (1957), Fig. 14, opposite page 269.

Left, top: Umm el-'Amed. Synagogue inscription.
Bottom: Umm el-'Amed. Below: Umm el-Qanatir.
Plan of the synagogue.

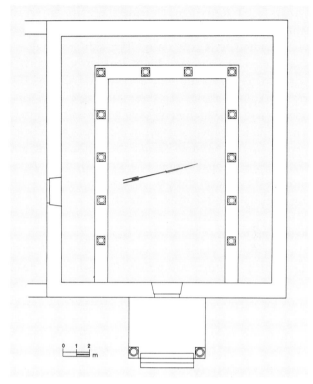

UMM EL-'AMED (Khirbet ha-'Amudim) on the east edge of the Beth Netopha Valley. An upright corner column marked the site of the synagogue when it was cleared by H. Kohl and C. Watzinger in 1905. A rectangular building (18.75 by 14.1 meters) was exposed with a flagstone pavement and a facade containing three doorways facing Jerusalem. The interior is divided into a nave (6.21 meters wide) and two aisles (each 3.15 meters wide) by two rows of seven columns set on pedestals. A transverse row of columns, consisting of two double corner columns with heart-shaped section with two columns between them, separated the nave from the inner porch running parallel to the entrance. An additional entrance was on the east side of the building. There was no sign of a fixed place for the Ark of the Law. On the lintel of the main entrance, two lions were carved with their bodies in profile and their faces toward the onlooker, each lion resting a forepaw on a calf's head. Between the lions is an amphora. The side door lintels have a guilloche border and are divided into three panels: the side ones containing rosettes, and the middle one the figure of an animal almost completely defaced. The Attic bases of the column rest on low pedestals (.41 by .38 meter). The shaft itself is 3.35 meters high. The capitals are of the Ionic order and of crude workmanship. Also discovered were capitals of engaged pillars, which the excavators believed may have belonged to the rear wall of the women's gallery. An inscription cut in stone was also found. It read: "Yo'ezer the ḥazan and Simeon his brother (made) [contributed] this gate of the Lord of Heaven."

Kohl–Watzinger, *Synagogen*, 71–79 • N. Avigad, *BIES* 19 (1954/5), 183–87 (Hebrew); idem, *Rabinowitz Bulletin* 3 (1960), 62–64.

UMM EL-QANATIR. Located on the eastern slope of Wadi esh-Shabib, a tributary of Wadi es-Samak in the Golan, within the confines of Hippos. The town's aqueduct drew its water from nearby springs. H. Kohl and C. Watzinger uncovered a building on this spot (approximately 18.8 by 13.8 meters) with a facade oriented to the east. In the interior of the building were two rows of five columns each (without double corner columns), and a transverse row of two columns between the end columns of the perpendicular rows. The south wall contained a side entrance while the main entrance was in the facade in the east, so that the worshippers prayed turned to the west rear wall, which faced Jerusalem. Outside the main entrance was a small paved porch with two columns, which was reached by three stairs. The columns, whose shafts were 2.44 meters high, had corbeil capitals with Attic bases and foiled corners. Among the architectural remains are these: an eagle with outspread wings, which may have adorned the lintel a stone lion, crudely carved, which may have been placed in the window frame above the front entrance; the gabled frame of a side window decorated with a floral design; two pillar capitals with egg-and-dart and dentils. Beneath the window was carved a band with a stylized vine trellis alternating with an egg-and-dart motif. According to H. Kohl and C. Watzinger, the synagogue is later in date (fifth century A.D.) than the other Galilean synagogues. However, judging from its plan (the transverse row of columns), lack of apse, and pavement, the synagogue must be ascribed to an earlier period. In spite of the fact that the facade is oriented to the east and thereby differs from the rest of the early-type synagogues in Transjordan, where facades faced either west or south in the direction of Jerusalem, worshippers at the Umm el-Qanatir synagogue prayed with their backs to the east (facade) wall. It is possible that the Ark of the Law was kept in a niche in the west wall.

M. AVI-YONAH

Kohl–Watzinger, *Synagogen*, 125–34 • E. L. Sukenik, *JPOS* 15 (1935), 172–74 • Goodenough, *Jewish Symbols* 1, 206–07.

BIBLIOGRAPHY

M. Avi-Yonah and S. Yeivin, *The Antiquities of Israel,* Tel Aviv, 1955, 220–36 (Hebrew); idem, *Rabinowitz Bulletin* 3 (1960), 57–60; idem, *Antiquity and Survival* 2 (1957), Fig. 14, opposite page 269 • Wilson-Kitchener, *Special Papers,* 294–305 • Kohl-Watzinger, *Synagogen,* 59–79, 107–24, 125–37 • Sukenik, *Ancient Synagogues* • Watzinger, *DP,* 2, 107–16 • Goodenough, *Jewish Symbols,* 1, 178–264 • Unesco, *Israel Ancient Mosaics,* New York, (1960), Pl. XXVIII (Introduction by M. Shapiro and M. Avi-Yonah) • C. Clermont-Ganneau, *PEF QSt,* (1901), 251, 374–89; ibid. (1902), 132–34 • Conder-Kitchener, *SWP* 1, 318ff. • L. Oliphant, *PEF QSt* (1884), 41 • E. G. von Mülinen, *ZDPV* 31 (1908/9), 158ff. N. Avigad, *BIES* 19 (1954/5), 183–87 (Hebrew); idem, *Rabinowitz Bulletin* 3 (1960), 62–64 • E. L. Sukenik, *JPOS* 15 (1935), 172–74 • B. Lifshitz, *Cahiers de la Revue Biblique* 7 (1967) • S. J. Saller, *A Second Revised catalogue of the Ancient Synagogues of the Holy Land,* Jerusalem, 1972 • F. Hüttenmeister and G. Reeg, *Die antiken Synagogen in Israel,* Wiesbaden, 1977 • J. Naveh, *On Stone and Mosaic, The Aramaic and Hebrew Inscriptions from Ancient Synagogues,* Jerusalem, 1978.

TAANACH

IDENTIFICATION. There has never been any doubt that biblical Taanach is located at Tell Ta'annek (map reference 171214). It is an impressive 45-dunam mound rising more than 40 meters above the Plain of Jezreel on the southwest flanks of the Irron Hills, 8 kilometers (5 miles) southeast of Megiddo. The maximum north–south limit of this pear-shaped mound is 340 meters. Its widest east–west limit is 110 meters. Passes entering the Jezreel Plain are guarded by Jokneam, Megiddo, and Ibleam. Taanach is not at the head of a major pass but lies between Megiddo and Ibleam on a northwest–southwest route. By the tenth century B.C., Taanach was an Israelite administrative and religious center. It may have served the same function during the Bronze Age.

HISTORY

In non-biblical literary sources, the earliest reference to Taanach is in the fifteenth-century B.C. Karnak inscription describing Thutmose III's first military campaign into Asia. To reach the enemy encamped at Megiddo beyond the northern hills of Manasseh, one of the three routes to the Jezreel Plain was a road along the Wadi Abu Nar, past modern Yabad, through the Burqin Pass, which debauches into the plain 4 kilometers (2.5 miles) south of Taanach. Both Thutmose III in 1468 B.C. and Shishak I in 918 B.C. list Ta'anach as a city captured by their forces. Knudtzon's restoration of "Taanach" (Ta-ah-[nu-k]a) in the early fourteenth-century Amarna letter 248:14 is unlikely on both archaeological and paleographic grounds. Eusebius' *Onomasticon* (ed. Klostermann, 100, 7–10) indicates that in the third century A.D. "Thaanach" was a "very large village," three Roman miles from Legio-Maximianopolis (near Megiddo).

In biblical tradition, Taanach first achieved eminence as the site of the battle of Israel, mustered by Deborah and Barak, against the Canaanites, led by Sisera (Judges 5:19). Though the king was reported taken by Joshua (Joshua 12:21) and the city assigned to Issachar and Asher, it was later given to Manasseh (Joshua 17:11, I Chronicles 7:29) who, however, failed to occupy Taanach because of the strength of the Canaanites (Judges 1:27). In time, probably not before the tenth century B.C., "Israel was strong, that they put the Canaanites to tribute" (Judges 1:28) and occupied (ruled) the site. In the same century Taanach seems to have become a Levitical city (Joshua 21:25) as well as the headquarters of Baana, administrator of Solomon's fifth district which included all of the Jezreel Plain to just beyond the Jordan River (I Kings 4:12).

EXCAVATIONS.

Tell Ta'annek was first excavated between 1902 and 1904 by E. Sellin of the University of Vienna. In three campaigns (with a total of four months of actual excavation) he employed between 150 and 200 workers to open long trenches on the mound. He was first assisted by G. Schumacher and later, after the discovery of an archive of Akkadian cuneiform tablets, he was joined by F. Hrozný. Sellin's two major reports were published by 1905, and although they lacked adequate plans and photographs of buildings and pottery, Sellin was nevertheless a perceptive observer and prompt reporter. Two years later H. Thiersch critically reviewed the results.

The second excavation of the site was the work of a joint American expedition of the American Schools of Oriental Research and the Graduate School of Concordia Seminary, St. Louis, Missouri, directed by P. W. Lapp. In three major seasons of almost six months in 1963, 1966, and 1968, a staff numbering from seventeen to thirty, with from 125 to nearly 200 workers, excavated four areas in the southwest quadrant of the mound. The aim of the excavations was to clarify the fortifications, domestic and industrial installations, public buildings, and cult.

EXCAVATION RESULTS

Sellin's long diagonal trenches were planned to locate the city defenses as well as any major architecture. By the end of the third season, he was certain that "there is . . . no sizable building to be found on the mound." In his final report, the plans of only five buildings are included, all designated "fortresses." No other structures are described. Sellin located more than fifteen cisterns.

Sellin found no city defense walls and concluded that the site was defended by a series of fortresses. The earliest fort was a modest structure with sub-

View of Taanach from the Jezreel Plain, looking south.

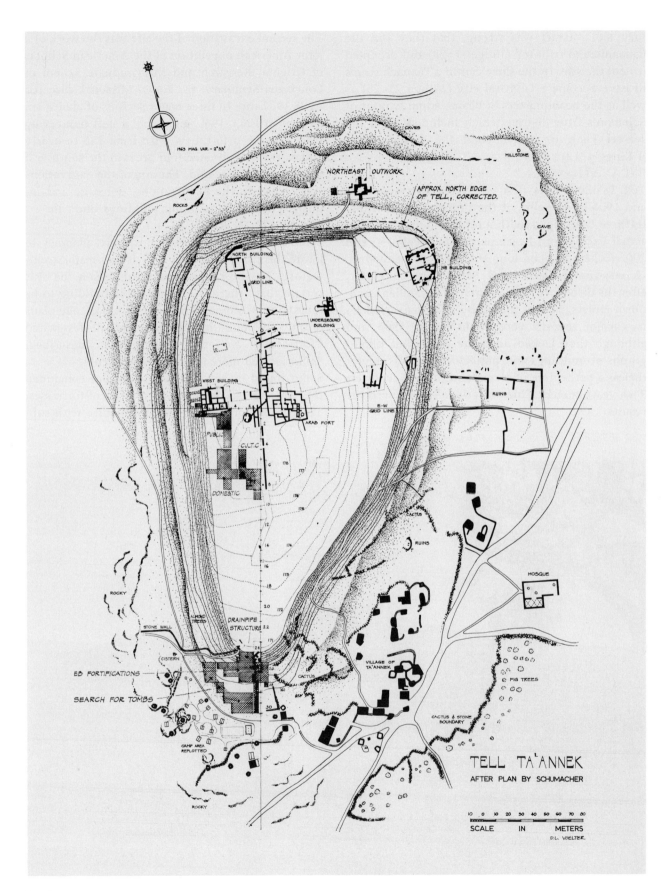

TELL TA'ANNEK

AFTER PLAN BY SCHUMACHER

SCALE IN METERS

D.L. VOELTER

Opposite page: Plan of Taanach showing Sellin's trenches mostly in the north; and areas of the new excavation in the southwest quadrant. This page, below: Ugaritic cuneiform tablet, from the 12th century B.C. *destruction level. Bottom: Cult building, 10th century* B.C.

Cult stand from the tenth century B.C.

terranean rooms in the north center of the mound, dating to between 1500 and 1350 B.C. W. F. Albright later interpreted the structure as an Early Bronze Age funerary chamber similar in construction to Third Dynasty Egyptian tombs. Later the structure was reused as a cistern, according to Sellin. In the debris above the upper level of this building, he discovered an archive of twelve Akkadian cuneiform tablets, eight letters, and four name lists. At the south end of a long central trench, he uncovered fragments of a Canaanite cult stand 90 centimeters high. When restored, it showed four tiers of modeled lions on each side of a windowed facade capped by a basin. On the upper left panel, a youth in relief strangles a serpent. On the front of the lowest panel, there is a tree of life with ibexes on either side. Both the tablets and the cult stand are today in museums in Istanbul.

Sellin identified four major strata of occupation, each with two sub-phases. The revised dates from his second report are as follows: 1. fifteenth–fourteenth centuries B.C., including the cuneiform archives, its building, as well as the subterranean structures, followed by the West Building; 2. thirteenth–ninth centuries B.C., including the east fortress and its outbuilding as well as most of the burials; 3. eighth–sixth centuries B.C., when the buildings founded in period two and the "incense altar" were both destroyed, the period of Greek influence; 4. eleventh–twelfth centuries A.D., the Arab fortress-palace on the center plateau of the mound.

The thirteen Akkadian tablets from Taanach (including the new TT 950) are either letters to the local king (eight) or administrative name lists (five). Two of the four readable letters (the other four are fragmentary) are from Amanhatpa, an Egyptian administrator posted in Gaza but probably writing from Megiddo. He requests chariots and men for his garrison, and that prisoners of war, as well as tribute, be sent to him. Another correspondent is Ahiyami, who orders a bow, bowstrings, chariot wheels, and a copper javelin. Also, wishing to be married, he seeks brother-in-law-ship. A third writer is Ehli-Teshub, who promises to repay fifty shekels of silver, asks for wood and myrrh, and advises that a servant girl be sold or married. Though written in Akkadian, the syntax and morphology of these letters have many West Semitic features. Five tablets, including TT 950, are name

lists. The letters and lists contain some ninety names. About 60 percent are Northwest Semitic and 20 percent are Indo-Aryan or Hurrian-Anatolian. The name of the prince of Taanach, the addressee, is written RI.WA-shur. The first element may be read ri/e- or tal-. The second may be wi/e- or ya. Albright took the initial sign to be Egyptian, thus reading the name as Rewashur. According to a recent collation, the copies published by Hrozný in the Sellin reports are generally more trustworthy than Albright believed.

The second excavation conducted in the 1960's clarified and elaborated Sellin's work at many points. Although mainly limited to the southwest quadrant of the mound, the excavation nevertheless confirmed the general impression gained from Sellin, that in no period was the city occupied by wall-to-wall architecture as at other important sites. However, the discovery of massive defenses on both the south and west showed not only that the site was protected by city walls in all major periods, but also that the earliest city dates to Early Bronze Age II–III (about 2700–2400 B.C.). An Early Bronze Age occupation had already been suggested by Albright on the basis of pottery published by Sellin.

Four phases of the Early Bronze Age defenses were exposed on the south slope by the Concordia-ASOR expedition. The earliest fortification wall (1) resting on bedrock is fronted by a rectangular tower (2). An east wall of a second tower (3) is fragmentary. In the second phase the same city wall serves as the founding base for a new wall (4) which diverges 19 degrees northwest from the line of the first wall. In the third phase this wall is fronted by a stepped revetment (5) almost 4 meters wide. Between the city wall (4) and the revetment (5) a tipped fill (6) provided the base for a ramp or room adjacent to an entrance into the city not yet discovered. In the fourth and final phase, a huge rectangular tower (7) surmounted the wall. A plastered glacis surface covered all earlier walls and towers.

After a long gap in occupation, a campsite from the Middle Bronze Age (from about 1700 B.C.) is found on the mound, and it is followed by extensive but poorly constructed domestic architecture and fortifications. The West Building discovered by Sellin was redated to about 1600 B.C. and interpreted as a patrician dwelling that was part of a substantial rebuilding of the Middle Bronze Age II-C city.

Facade of incense stand discovered by Sellin. Now in the Arkeolji Muzeleri in Istanbul — 10th century B.C.

Right: Small cooking pot filled with weights from destruction layer at end of the twelfth century B.C. *Below: Solid copper baboon from pot of weights.*

The so-called Late Bronze Age I Building was found to be a large block of small rooms in the center of the mound between the west city and a north–south street founded in the early seventeenth century ("Domestic" area). Associated with the later Middle Bronze Age II-C phases, which became the Late Bronze Age I Building, was a casemate wall. Parallels from Hazor and Shechem now show that this style of city wall construction predates the Israelite monarchy. Below the floors and in the walls of Middle Bronze Age rooms were found sixty-four burials, of which about 90 percent were of children entombed in store jars. Selective destruction marks the end of the Middle Bronze Age on the site.

Taanach continued to be a substantial city into the Late Bronze Age I, suffering a major catastrophe at the hands of Thutmose III in about 1468 B.C. In the modest occupation that followed this destruction was found an Akkadian cuneiform tablet (TT 950). It is dated to about 1450 B.C. as is the archive discovered by Sellin. Though most of the limited quantity of Late Helladic pottery dates to the Mycenaean III-A–2 period (fourteenth century B.C.), there is no significant occupation between

Looking west over the south slope fortifications. The meter stick rests on the west wall of the tower projecting from the first phase city wall which rests on bedrock.

the mid-fifteenth and the late thirteenth centuries B.C. Substantial houses with numerous installations on both of the south (Drainpipe Structure) and west edges of the mound date to the twelfth century and were completely destroyed in about 1125 B.C. Some Iron Age defenses noted on the west were also dated to the twelfth century B.C. In the north center of the southwest quadrant ("Public" area), a Canaanite cuneiform tablet (TT 433) turned up in the early twelfth-century destruction of a large building. The two-line inscription registers the receipt of a shipment of grain. A slight eleventh-century occupation is followed by a larger tenth-century presence, destroyed by Shishak about 918 B.C.

To this period belongs a structure related to the local cult. A heavy ash layer on the floors contained nine iron knife blades, 140 pig astragali, some eighty restorable vessels, fifty-eight "loom weights", many querns, rubbing stones, pestles, three small stelae, and a figurine mold. In an associated cistern, an elaborate cult stand emerged not far from where Sellin had found the "incense altar." Standing less than two feet high, the cult stand is built up of four superimposed hollow clay squares topped by a ridged basin. The lion and human faces protruding above animal legs on the corners of the three panels are each accompanied by winged leonine bodies in relief along the side panels. These animals represent demons protecting the deity symbolized by the stylized winged sun disk between volutes and above an equid in the top panel.

Evidence for later occupation is limited to a tower dating to the ninth century B.C. (Sellin's Nordostburg) located on a terrace below the north end of the mound, and to some fifth-century B.C. Persian pits and two rooms. In Late Abassid times, tenth–eleventh centuries A.D., an elaborate palace was constructed at the highest point of the mound. A cemetery on the south slope over the Early Bronze Age defenses seems to date from the early seventeenth century A.D.   A. E. GLOCK

BIBLIOGRAPHY

Preliminary Reports: E. Sellin, *Mittheilungen und Nachrichten des deutschen Palästina-Vereins* (1902), 13–19, 33–36; (1903), 1–4; 1905, 33–37; *PEF QSt* 1902, 301–04; 1903, 34; 1904, 98, 187, 297, 388–91; 1905, 176, 284; 1906, 115–20; *RB* 11 (1902), 596–97; 12 (1903), 646–47; 14 (1905), 114–18; 270–71; 15 (1906), 287–92 • P. W. Lapp, *BASOR* 173 (1964), 4–44; 185 (1967), 2–39; 195 (1969), 2–49; *idem, BA* 30 (1967), 2–27; *idem, RB* 71 (1964), 240–46; 75 (1968), 93–98; 76 (1969), 580–86; *idem, The Fall of the Tell*, Pittsburgh, 1975, 91–103.
Final Reports: E. Sellin, *Tell Ta'annek*, Wien, 1904; *Eine Nachlese auf dem Tell Ta'annek in Palästina*, Wien, 1905 • A. E. Glock, (ed.) *Taanach I* (in press, 1976).
Studies of Cuneiform Tablets: A. Gustavs, *ZDPV* 50 (1927), 1–18; 51 (1928), 169–218 • B. Maisler (Mazar), *Klausner Festschrift*, Tel Aviv, 1937, 44–66 (Hebrew) • W. F. Albright, *BASOR* 94 (1944), 12–27 • A. Malamat, *Scripta Hierosolymitana* 8 (1961), 218–27 • D. Hillers, *BASOR* 173 (1964), 45–50 • A. E. Glock, *BASOR* 204 (1971), 17–30.
Studies of Cult Stands: E. Mader, *Biblische Zeitschrift* 10 (1912), 351–62 • M. Lods, *Revue de l'histoire des religions* (1934), 129–47 • P. W. Lapp, *Qadmoniot* 2 (1969), 16 (Hebrew).
Reviews: H. Thiersch, *Archäologischer Anzeiger, Beiblatt zum Jahrbuch des kaiserlich-deutschen archäologischen Institut* 22 (1907), cols. 311–57 • H. Vincent, *Canaan d'après l'exploration récente*, Paris. 1907, 52–63, 181–82 • Aharoni, *LB*, 156–57.

Basin in cult area, 10th century B.C.

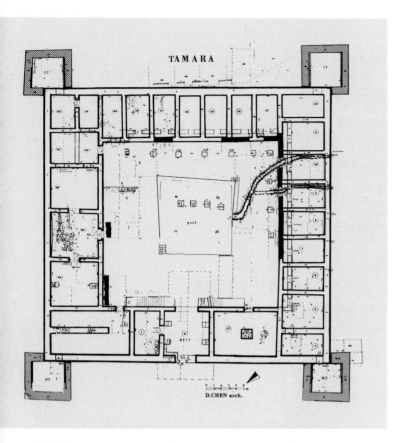

TAMARA

IDENTIFICATION AND EXPLORATION. Meṣad Tamar is a Late Roman castellum on the Limes Palaestinae (map reference 17300485). Its ruins were first described by F. Frank in 1930 and were later visited by G. E. Kirk in 1938. Its Arabic name, Qasr el-Juheiniye, gives no indication of its identification. A. Alt identified the site – basing his interpretation on such sources as Ptolemy, Eusebius, the *Tabula Peutingeriana,* etc. – with Tamara, a castellum also mentioned in the *Notitia Dignitatum,* the Madeba map, and the Beersheba edicts. Although Roman Tamara was certainly not the site of biblical Tamar, as has been correctly pointed out by Y. Aharoni, this identification for the Roman site has been generally accepted.

After a preliminary survey and sounding in 1971, Tamara was excavated during three seasons in 1973, 1974, and 1975, by the Division of Classical Archaeology, Tel-Aviv University, in conjunction with the Saalburg Museum of Bad Homburg. Ex-

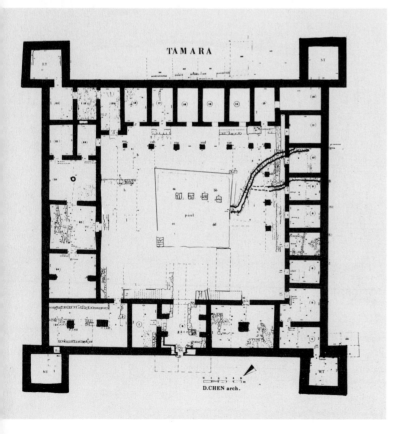

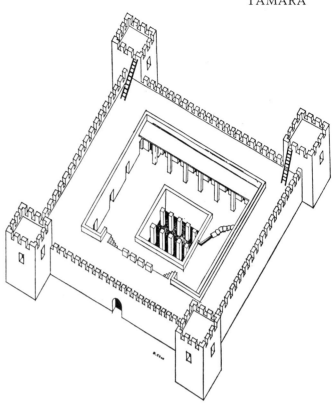

cavations revealed the greater part of the castellum proper, as well as one of the watchtowers situated on the hill to its south. The civil and agricultural remains and burials have not yet been investigated sufficiently.

HISTORY

The first period of settlement at Tamara was in Nabataean times. Although no structure has as yet been definitely attributed to the Nabataeans, the wealth of pottery as well as Nabataean ashlars in secondary use make the occupation of the site in that period a certainty. It probably served at that time as a road station on the highway from biblical Moab by way of Zoar to Kurnub. Like Kurnub, it may have been taken over by the Romans immediately on their acquisition of Nabataea in A.D. 106. And like many other Negev sites, it was held up to the time of Hadrian. The excavations ended before it was possible to establish which of the following two alternatives is correct:

1.) The Nabataean structure survived until it was rebuilt in the Late Roman period, when, having vanquished the short-lived Palmyran Empire of Queen Zenobia, the Illyrian Emperors began, after A.D. 270, to reorganize the East.

Both pages, counterclockwise from opposite page, top: Tamara fort, phase one: Black: excavated. Underlined: assumed. Dotted: phase Ia; Tamara fort, phases two and three: Black: excavated. Underlined: phase three; General view: The barrack blocks (strigae), in foreground. The bakery (pistrina), on the left. The South Tower, on the right. The cistern, in the center, looking east; Isometric reconstruction of the castellum.

2.) The Nabataean structure is now largely buried under the new metaled highway adjacent to the castellum, which was erected by the Illyrians (Aurelian or Probus). In this case, the traces of an elongated building that are visible in early air photos may be attributed to the Nabataeans. Above its southern salient was erected the northern corner tower of the castellum, the only part in which a

Below: Southern corner of the courtyard showing remains of phase one walls, pillars of the portico (phase two), water channels and staircase — looking east. Opposite page, top to bottom: Painted inscription, probably instructions of the master builder; Principa. The regimental shrine (sacellum), in foreground. The commander's private quarters (praetorium), in background — looking east; The gate. The reduced width of the entrance (phase three) — in left background. Staircase, in foreground seen from the southeast.

clear Nabataean layer was noted by the excavators. Whether as a new structure or a reoccupied one, the castellum served as a border fortification from the second third of the third century to the Arab conquest. Its inner portions were once completely rebuilt, and the many repairs point to damage caused either by the then frequent earthquakes or by hostile tribes, possibly in Sassanid pay. From sometime in the fourth or fifth century, the regular army unit *(auxilia)* stationed at Tamara became an armed border-militia, and the castellum combined new administrative and economic functions with its military ones. The Persian (Sassanid) invasion of 614 wrought much havoc, and the castellum was rebuilt in a rough way to meet the Arab onslaught. Some of the families of the militia men must have sought refuge in this final stage within the walls of the castellum, and additional living space was created for them by partitioning rooms. Even if the castellum had been captured, it was not demolished, but the Limitanean families seem to have disappeared gradually in the century after the conquest with the cessation of government-supported agriculture and commerce in these regions.

EXCAVATIONS

Tamara is a typical τετραπύργος, a square fort, 38 by 38 meters, with four protruding corner towers, 6 by 6 meters, a single entrance, and all the internal structures built leaning on the curtain walls. The middle of the great central courtyard is occupied by a large square cistern.

These features were preserved throughout the three main phases of the castellum's existence: 1. last third of the third century A.D. to the latter half of the fourth century or later; 2. second half of the fourth century A.D. (?) to the Persian conquest of 614; 3. from the reconquest of Heraclius in about 624 to the Arab invasion in about A.D. 635. In phases 1 and 2, and probably initially in phase 3 as well, the interior arrangements of the castellum were as follows:

Two barrack blocks (strigae) on the southwest and southeast sides. The northeast tract comprised the regimental shrine (sacellum) with adjacent side rooms that housed the offices, and together making up the unit headquarters (principia). In the eastern corner was the commander's private quarters (praetorium) with direct access to the headquarters. On the northwest side, the gate was flanked in the north by a guardroom with a stone bench, and behind it, a large storeroom, the roof of which was supported by two central pillars. This was either a grain store or armory *(horreum* or armamentarium). West of the gate, the great bakery *(pristina),* with ovens and basalt mill, again had a roof supported by a central pillar.

The flat roofs that served as extensions to the battlements could be reached by three stone-built staircases from inside the courtyard, two flanking the gateway and one in the southern corner.

The exact number of *contubernia* (section rooms) could not be definitely established, but all evidence points to there having been six, as in phase 2, which leaves two rooms for the officers of the presumably senior sub-unit *(centuria)* that was housed in the southwest barracks, and one room as officers' quarters in the southeast barracks.

At least parts of the rooms were whitewashed with plaster, and the plaster in the principia and the praetorium was decorated with bichrome frescoes of geometric design.

The inner dimensions of the strigae were 3.8 by 5.5 meters, allowing each soldier about 2.1 square meters of living space in his *contubernium,* if each section contained ten soldiers.

The main constructional change between phases 1 and 2 was the rebuilding on a reduced scale of the two barrack blocks, either because of an earthquake or an enemy attack. They now measured only 3.8 by 4.5 meters, but each one was equipped with a porticus 3 meters wide, built in front, and affording each *contubernium* a shaded space at its entrance.

Also sometime during phase 2 some of the *contubernia* were converted into workshops or storerooms, indicating that their former inhabitants had moved out of the castellum and become Limitanei (militiamen).

The rebuilding carried out in phase 3 was rough in the extreme, and no major constructional changes were introduced. Rooms in the northeast administration tract were partitioned for refugee(?) dwellings.

The curtains were built of ashlar in two faces with a rubble core, to a width of 1.1. meters. Their minimum height, including the parapet, must have been 3.8 meters, with the towers rising a minimum of 3 meters above them. Access to the towers was gained by wooden ladders (no stone staircases were found). Since all towers were leaning on the

curtains and not engaged, the possibility of a later addition of the towers during phase 1 cannot be ruled out. (If the castellum as it stands goes back to a first-century Nabataean origin, phase 1-b, the phase marked by the addition of the towers, might be that of the Late Roman refurbishing).

The towers and other structures were roofed by wooden beams. The shelf formed by a recessed upper wall to hold these beams has been preserved in all the towers.

The gate also retained its initial plan throughout, but during the third phase, the width of its entrance was reduced from 2.8 meters to 1 meter. Its plan was that of a straight passage, 6 by 6 meters, which was narrowed and compartmented by two pairs of opposing piers that jutted out about 1 meter into the gateway. Whether these were merely supports for the roof beams, or served also for fortification purposes and to check an enemy charge, is not clear.

The main source of water in these barren parts must have been the 2-kilometer-distant spring and various water catchment installations in the vicinity. To ensure an emergency supply of water, the castellum was erected in the lowest spot of the defile to which the rivulets of winter rains converged. Channels conveyed the water through the walls into the cistern, which measured 10 by 10 by 3.8 meters. Square ashlar pillars carried the grid of wooden beams, on which the lightweight limestone roof slabs rested, mainly to prevent evaporation. In rainless winters, the cistern was filled by animal train from the above-mentioned sources.

Undecipherable abbreviations, written under the wall plaster in red paint, most probably were the master-builder's instructions.

The watchtower above the castellum was a simple square structure, 3.8 by 3.8 meters, preserved to the height of 3 meters. Ceramic evidence beginning with Late Nabataean pottery indicates that its history is contemporary with that of the castellum.

M. GICHON

BIBLIOGRAPHY

Identification: F. Frank, ZDPV 57 (1934), 257 ff. • A. Alt, ibid., 58 (1935), 34 ff. • T. Abel, GP, 2, 181 • M. Avi-Yonah, The Historical Geography of Eretz Israel, Jerusalem, 1949, 165 (Hebrew) • G. E. Kirk, PEQ 1938, 221–25.
Excavations: M. Gichon, Qadmoniot 6 (1974), 144 ff. (Hebrew); idem, Tamara (1973–74), Vorbericht der Grabungen, Limes Studien (1974), Beih. B. Jhrb. 1976; idem, IEJ 25 (1975), 176–77; 26 (1976), 188–194; idem, Three Years of Excavation at Mezad Tamar (Tamara), Saalburg Jahrbuch (1976).

ET-TANNUR, KHIRBET

IDENTIFICATION. Khirbet et-Tannur is situated on top of Jebel et-Tannur (550 meters above sea level, map reference 217042), an isolated mountain between Wadi el-Ḥesa (Zared) and Wadi el-'Aban. The site is approached from the southeast by a single path provided with ancient banking and cut in the rock near the top. It may also have had a flight of steps in its upper part. The top of Jebel et-Tannur is fairly flat. The temple, situated on the east side, is the only building on it.

EXCAVATIONS

In March–April 1937, excavations were carried out at the site by a joint expedition of the American Schools of Oriental Research and the Jordan Department of Antiquities under the direction of N. Glueck. Several outside rooms and walls remained unexcavated.

The Temple. An approach cut in the rock leads by way of broad steps to the gateway in the east wall of the outer court of the temple. The walls flanking the entrance of the gate were adorned with an engaged column and a pilaster, topped with Nabataean capitals. The east (outer) court is square (15.6 square meters) and on the north and south had porticoes with the columns standing on podiums two steps high. Part of the paving of the court on the east and west sides has been preserved. Shallow channels leading from the northeast and southeast corners of the court drained the rainwater through apertures in the outer east wall. The floor of the temple slopes to the southeast. An altar stood on the north side of the court near its east end, and an unpaved area of the court may have held a ritual pool.

THE SANCTUARY was oriented to the east. It was approached by four steps which led to a gateway. The steps in the facade are flanked by engaged columns and corner pilasters. On each side of the gateway, between the column and pilaster, was a shallow niche, crowned by an architrave, and above it was a pediment with a denticulated ornament. On the architraves are three triglyphs separated by two rosettes, the whole set between two female busts carved in relief. Over the main doorway was a bust of Atargatis, represented as a goddess of foliage and fruit. On her forehead, neck, and bosom are leaf decorations, which however do not conceal the features. Two side panels, which together with the centerpiece form a semicircular panel, are decorated with vine, leaf, and fruit (pomegranate and fig) motifs. Above the head of the goddess may have originally been the relief of a large eagle. A pediment apparently topped the entire entablature. The walls of the sanctuary, with the exception of the eastern one, had two pilasters between corner pilasters. The engaged columns and pilasters have Attic bases which rest on solid stylobates. Their capitals, which were originally Nabataean, were replaced at a later period with Corinthian capitals. Near the east end of the south wall of the sanctuary was a doorway, probably used by the priests and temple servants.

THE INNER COURT of the sanctuary was paved but open to the sky. In its center stood an inner shrine (4 by 3.6 meters) oriented almost exactly

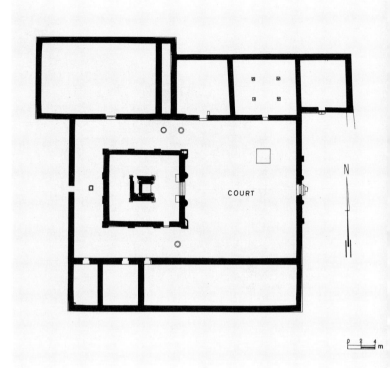

Below: View of the Nabataean temple. On the right: Plan of the temple.

Above: Atargatis as vegetation goddess. Opposite page: Air view of the top of Jebel Tannur.

due east. A staircase on the west side of the shrine led to the presumably flat roof on which probably stood an altar. The east facade of the shrine was ornamented with pilasters with quarter columns. They were built of stone courses, four and possibly five of which were ornamented with busts in relief of Atargatis either as "dolphin goddess" or as "grain goddess." The bust of the dolphin goddess is carved on a soft white limestone block, 36 centimeters wide, 27.8 centimeters high and 34 centimeters thick. The head and body project from the front of the block. The wavy hair, which is covered with a headcloth, is parted in the middle, clasped on either side by a shell and falls in two thick braids on either side of the face. Two strands of hair are plastered down each cheek. The groove between the full lips and the sunken areas around the eyeballs show clear traces of red paint. On the headdress two dolphins are realistically portrayed, with their mouths meeting. The entire bust is carved against the background of a shell.

At the corners of the west (back) wall of the shrine are two square pilasters which support a large architrave decorated with rosettes, egg-and-dart motifs, and vine and leaf patterns.

THE INNER SHRINE was built on top of an earlier one, which also had steps along its western side, two of which were preserved in situ. The upper four courses of the pilasters of the east facade of this earlier shrine are decorated with rosettes and vine patterns. This decoration is replaced in the third course of the pilaster at the north end by a small niche (to hold lamps). The pilasters are set on Attic bases, and their capitals bear the thunderbolt motif. An architrave decorated with rosette designs and niches was set over an arch resting on the jambs of the pilasters. In the shallow niches below the arch, two cult reliefs were apparently set, one of the god Hadad, the other of Atargatis. Hadad was represented sitting. He is carved in almost three-quarter relief on a stone block, approximately 1 meter long and 45 centimeters wide. His body, which is disproportionally small (three quarter length), measures 35 centimeters. The head, on the other hand, is life size (29 centimeters long). The hair is waved and curled, and the beard and the ends of the flowing moustache are set in snail curls. The high-girdled chiton is fastened by a brooch at the neck. A fold of it is thrown over the left shoulder. Beneath the lower end of the fold appears the left hand, with the palm turned inward and upward and the fingers turned inward, grasping the right ear of a young bull. The top of the head seems to have been crowned by a low polos. The forehead is low, with two horn-like (?) locks above the center of the forehead. Around the neck the god wears a torque, the ends of which consist of lions' heads. Attached to the fold of the chiton

over the left shoulder is a thunderbolt, which runs from above the left elbow to the palm of the hand, its arrowhead pointing toward the head of the young bull. The bull was represented with its two forelegs free of the slab. Its horns were small, and its head realistically portrayed. A small lion's head, part of its body, and a single foot with traces of its mate are indications that a relief of Atargatis was carved besides that of Hadad. On top of the earlier shrine, there was also an altar, most of the remains of which have been recovered. Among them are four corner pilasters with tiny female heads ornamenting the tops. It is possible that this altar and the reliefs of Hadad and Atargatis were reused in the later shrine.

THE SECOND SHRINE was built around a smaller, cruder one, which was the original shrine of the site and the nucleus around which arose the entire temple complex.

In front of the east pilasters of the shrine are two small subterranean chambers. They were covered by paving blocks, one of them found in situ, which could be lifted by inserting one's finger or a hook in the center of the outside edge of each block. A similar concealed chamber was found in the rear of the shrine. These chambers were evidently receptacles for the remains of offerings, for their contents consisted of ashes, charred animal bones, and grains of wheat.

On the north and south sides of the inner temple area and the outer court are a series of well-paved rooms, with a high benchlike platform running along three sides of each room. The roofs of these chambers were supported by square pillars, each course of which is composed of three triangular stones. The chambers may have served as lodgings and dining rooms for priests and pilgrims.

An altar with a thunderbolt motif was found in situ outside the west wall of the inner temple area.

THE SCULPTURED OBJECTS found during the excavations include a large, crude head of Hadad, revealing Hellenistic–Parthian influence, a stone water basin on the front of which is a lion realistically carved in high relief, whose mouth was the waterspout. A Winged Victory (Nike), which was found after the excavations and belongs to the zodiac described below, had her right upper arm raised horizontally at shoulder level. The upper part of the left arm is also held horizontally at shoulder level, while the forearm (the right one is missing) is raised perpendicularly above the elbow, with the hand and fingers supporting the zodiac above the goddess' head. In the center of the zodiac is a relief of Tyche. On her head she wears a mural crown covered with a hood. To the right of her head is carved a moon crescent, to the left a scepterlike symbol. It is composed of a torch bound together with a wand, which ends in a broken crescent moon. Encircling this outer relief is a panel containing the figures of the zodiac, counterclockwise from the top center: 1. Aries, represented by a Minerva-like (?) figure; 2. Taurus; 3. Gemini; 4. Cancer; 5. Leo; 6. Virgo carrying a sheaf; clockwise from the right top of the center 7. Libra; 8. Scorpio; 9. Sagittarius; 10. Capricon; 11. Aquarius, with his bucket upside down; and 12. The new fragment discovered after the close of the excavations. The order of the signs seems to indicate that one New Year began with the spring and another New Year began with autumn.

Several fragments were also found of the winged Tyche, carrying aloft in each hand a cornucopia. There was also an almost intact incense altar, with a central panel containing a relief of Hadad, and two side panels with reliefs of Winged Victories (Nike). On the altar was a Greek dedicatory inscription reading: [ΑΛΕΞ]ΑΝΔΡΟΣ ΑΜΡΟΥ.

THE POTTERY found included rouletted ware, sherds of terra sigillata of Pergamene type and

*Both pages clockwise from above: Typical
Parthian head; Zeus-Hadad seated on throne;
Atargatis as dolphin goddess (two views); Atargatis as
grain goddess; Tyche of the Zodiac.*

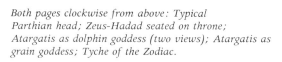

Counterclockwise from above: Fragment of decorated
Nabataean bowl; Bunch of grapes carved in
acanthus frame; Incense altar. On the right the figure
of Hadad–Zeus. On the left — Winged Victory;
Altar with the name of its donor: mati'l.

fine eggshell Nabataean sherds. The last are definitely associated with the earlier levels on the site.

The excavators distinguished three building periods at the site. The first has been dated to the first century B.C. The second can apparently be dated by a Nabataean inscription to the second regnal year of Aretas IV (7 B.C.), although W. F. Albright has suggested that the stone was originally part of a nymphaeum at the source and was later used in building or repairing the temple. The last phase, which includes most of the sculptures, is dated to the beginning of the second century A.D. The temple was probably destroyed by an earthquake in the second century A.D. when the site was abandoned briefly. During the Byzantine period it was occupied sporadically by squatters.

THE ART of Khirbet et-Tannur is evidence of the swift development of Nabataean civilization, especially between the second century B.C. and the second century A.D., when Nabataea was incorporated by Trajan in A.D. 106/07 into his Provincia Arabia. The influence of this art is subsequently seen in Byzantine art of the Negev, Coptic art of Egypt, and Umayyad art, as at Khirbet Mafjar in the Jordan Valley and Qasr el-Heir in Syria. The art and architecture of the Nabataeans were distinctive, but they nevertheless had much in common with their Syrian, Parthian, Arabian, Egyptian, and Mediterranean neighbors. An entire pantheon of Nabataean deities was discovered at et-Tannur, with Atargatis their main deity, appearing either as dolphin goddess, goddess of vegetation, grain, or tutelary divinity. Thunderbolt-carrying Zeus-Hadad was her consort. The deification of the seven planets characterized their theological system. This was a fertility religion, strongly influenced by Hellenistic culture, but in its essential character predominantly Semitic. The details of the fertility cults were adopted by the Nabataeans from the civilizations with which they came in contact.

N. GLUECK

BIBLIOGRAPHY

N. Glueck, *BASOR* 65 (1937), 15–19; 67 (1937), 6–16; *idem, AJA* 41 (1937), 361–67 • R. Savignac, *RB* 46 (1937), 401–16 • R. B. Freeman, *AJA* 45 (1941), 337–41 • N. Glueck, *BASOR* 85 (1942), 3–8 • M. Avi-Yonah, *QDAP* 10 (1944), 114–18 • N. Glueck, *BASOR* 126 (1952), 5–10; 141 (1956), 22–23 • M. Avi-Yonah, *Oriental Art in Roman Palestine*, Rome, 1961, 49–50 • N. Glueck, *EI* 7 (1964), 40* f.; *idem, Deities and Dolphins*, New York, 1965.

TEL AVIV

SURVEY. The archaeological survey conducted by J. Kaplan in January, 1950, in the Yarkon Plain and the hill range to its south disclosed many previously unknown sites. Soon after the completion of the survey, Kaplan began a systematic excavation of these sites and others discovered in the adjoining urban areas of Bene-Berak, Ramat Gan, Giv'atayim, and Bat Yam. Excavations have continued for over twenty-five years and have yielded finds dating from the fifth millennium B.C. onward. A good part of these finds are exhibited in the Museum of Antiquities, Tel Aviv–Yaffa.

NEOLITHIC, CHALCOLITHIC, AND EARLY BRONZE AGE SITES

Ha-Bashan Street. The site is located 500 meters from the south bank of the Yarkon along the rising ground in the east part of Bodenheimer Street, between Pinkas (formerly ha-Bashan) and Louis Marshall Streets.

In three seasons of excavations conducted by J. Kaplan between 1950 and 1952, three occupation layers were exposed, all without building remains. The earliest occupation layer (III), lying above the alluvial virgin soil, belongs to the Neolithic period. Its pottery is identical with the pottery of the Yar-

Map.

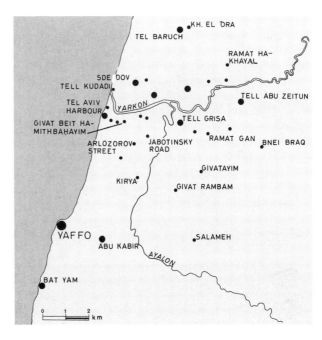

Above, left to right: Nordau Blvd. Cup and saucer lamp — EBA I; Ha-Bashan St. — Neolithic fertility statuette. Below, both pages left to right: Pinkas St.— Open section of MBA I tomb. The upper part is a shaft that leads to that tomb chamber; Jabotinsky St. — Chalcolitic churn.

mukian culture discovered a year earlier at Sha'ar ha-Golan. The remains of occupation included a thin layer of whitish ashy soil as well as pits and depressions in the virgin soil. This occupation layer contained potsherds, animal bones, and flint implements. At the bottom of one of the pits a human burial was found in a flexed position covered by a few stones and ringed by a circle of stones and two large Yarmukian sherds. In another pit were found fragments of a large burnished bowl with small, triangular-shaped ledge handles. A pile of stones in a shallow depression showed signs of burning in its upper part and yielded bones, burned animal horns, fragmentary clay fertility figurines, and polished *kurkar* stone statuettes. This stone pile was apparently a cultic site. One of the clay figurines — its lower part was missing — had a mask covering the face similar to figurines later found at Sha'ar ha-Golan and Ḥorvat Minḥa.

The pottery included all types of the Sha'ar ha-Golan repertory, including vessels decorated with a herringbone design between red-painted incised lines. The herringbone decoration surrounded the body of the vessel in zigzag lines, and a horizontal band passed round its neck. Alongside typical Yarmukian objects, the flints also showed a number of Pre-Pottery Neolithic types. It may thus be assumed that long before the arrival of the Yarmukian people, this had been a temporary camp site (Kathleen Kenyon's Pre-Pottery Neolithic B).

Above layer III, a strip of ashy earth, layer II, was brought to light. It contained potsherds, a small amount of flints, and animal bones, as well as baked-clay loom weights. The remains belonged to the Chalcolithic period. Its pottery is virtually identical with the pottery uncovered by J. Garstang in stratum VIII at Jericho, except for the black-burnished ware, which is absent at Jericho. The same Chalcolithic assemblage was also found in larger quantities on the south bank of Wadi Rabah, and has been named the Wadi Rabah culture by the writer.

Layer I above layer II dates to the Early Bronze Age II. Here, too, the finds included numerous potsherds, flint implements, animal bones, and baked-clay loom weights.

CONCLUSIONS. The exposure of an Early Bronze Age II stratum at the ha-Bashan Street site was not unexpected, but what makes this site important is finding here a second Yarmukian settlement, far from the discovery site — Sha'ar ha-Golan. This implies that the Yarmukian culture may have been distributed throughout the country. The material from this second site facilitated the identification of the characteristic Yarmukian objects. The most important discovery at ha-Bashan Street, however, was stratigraphic: It placed the Wadi Rabah culture (a kind of prototype of Jericho VIII) later than the Yarmukian.

Jabotinsky Street (Jamasin). The site is on a commanding *kurkar* hill about 1 kilometer west of Naḥal Ayalon. In 1950–51 and in 1961, three seasons of excavations were conducted at the site by J. Kaplan. Although the major part of the site had been destroyed by *kurkar* quarrying, excavations in the remainder yielded abundant material. On the east side of the quarry three shelter pits were cleared (the largest was 2 meters in diameter and 1.5 meters deep), and north of these pits was a beaten clay floor, perhaps of a tent or hut. The pits

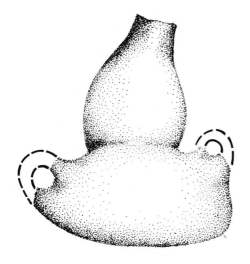

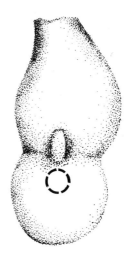

Above: Sde Dov. Hollow used as a dwelling. MBA II. Below, Tel Aviv harbor — plan of the double cave tomb, MBA II. Opposite page, top: Sketch of Jannaeus' fortifications line, sector from Antipatris to the hill country (based on Josephus' description). Bottom: map of Jannaeus line.

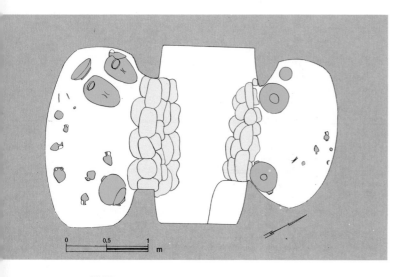

contained a large quantity of ashes, potsherds, flints, and animal bones. One of the pits yielded the second complete example of a type of pottery vessel previously found only in a fragmentary state at several Ghassulian sites. In the excavator's view, these vessels were used for churning, and he therefore suggested calling them churns. A number of grinding stones lay face down around the site.

In 1961, excavations were resumed after two shaft pits (diameter .9 meter) filled with ashes, potsherds, flints, and animal bones had been discovered at the western edge of the site. Work in the first pit was stopped at a depth of 11 meters, and in the second pit at a depth of 20 meters. The finds in the pit indicated that the lowest part had probably been a

burial cave, but due to its great depth the bottom could not be reached.

THE POTTERY. The pottery is Ghassulian and includes many examples of the rich repertory of shapes and decorations of this ware. The characteristic bowl is flower-pot shaped. Also found are hole-mouth jars, jugs, pithoi, horn-shaped beakers and "egg-cups," and perforated and knobbed handles. Decorations are impressed or incised—thumb-indentations, nail slashes, short oblique lines, and applied thumb-indented bands. The bases often bear mat impressions. Painted decorations are also present. Rims and occasionally other parts of the vessel are colored red, dark-red, or violet.

OTHER FINDS. The flint material included axes, adzes, sickle blades, blades and bladelets, scrapers, and lithic-industry waste. The bone material pointed to sheep and cattle raising. It also included the bones of animals hunted in the Ayalon and Yarkon valleys.

CONCLUSIONS. The excavations at Jabotinsky Street indicated that the site had been used as a temporary station by a Ghassulian clan in its seasonal wanderings after grazing its cattle and sheep.

Giv'at Beth ha-Mitbaḥayim. The mound of the former Municipal Slaughter House (Giv'at Beth ha-Mitbaḥayim) is located on the bend of the Yarkon River, where it turns from east–west to west–north. The mound overlooks both the Yarkon Valley and the coastal plain. Because of its location, it served at various times as a camping and burial site for caravans and armies passing through the country. The sites on the mound are named after the streets in which they are found.

Yanai Street. In Yanai Street, Chalcolithic and Early Bronze Age remains were exposed on the eastern margin of Giv'at Beth ha-Mitbaḥayim.

The excavations, conducted in 1950–52 and 1955 by J. Kaplan, on behalf of the Museum of Antiquities of Tel Aviv–Jaffa, concentrated in seven loci, all caves and pits cut in the *kurkar* rock during the Chalcolithic period. In two caves were found Chalcolithic burial remains, fragments of clay ossuaries and human bones. Also found was a fragment of an ossuary coping with a relief decoration of two snakes. The other caves were used as shelters or silos.

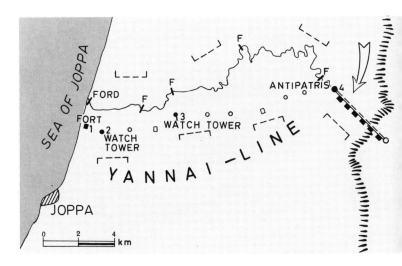

Only part of cave 1 was excavated. The cave is 5.5 meters long, and its ceiling was supported by one or two pillars cut from the solid rock. The cave was linked by short underground passages to smaller caves in the vicinity. The ceiling of the cave had collapsed, burying the occupation remains beneath its debris. Cave 1 revealed a most interesting stratification. Its sequence is as follows:

STRATUM A. 0–.2 meter, humus earth mixed with Persian and Middle Bronze Age II sherds.

STRATUM B. .2–.45 meter, light-brown earth, Middle Bronze Age II sherds.

STRATUM C. .45–2.65 meters, large stones from ceiling debris in the upper part and below them a layer of reddish earth with Early Bronze Age I and a few Chalcolithic sherds.

STRATUM D. 2.65–2.9 meters, Early Bronze Age I sherds, flints, and animal bones, powdery gray-black earth.

STRATUM E. 2.9–3.3 meters, Chalcolithic sherds, flints, and animal bones.

In April, 1974, stratum C was examined by Ḥaya Kaplan, who found that its lower part forms a

Museum Haaretz Center. Winepress, Byzantine period.

separate stratum, with pottery dating to the Early Bronze Age I. The collapse of the ceiling occurred at the end of this phase.

93 Nordau Avenue. This site is the continuation of the Early Bronze Age I remains on the south side of cave 1 and also of the Early Bronze Age I burial cave south of cave 4. The latter was robbed of its contents in 1950, the only object rescued being a high loop-handled juglet now in the Museum of Antiquities of Tel Aviv–Jaffa. Although the cave at 93 Nordau Avenue was damaged by a bulldozer, many Early Bronze Age I vessels as well as burned and scorched human bones were found at its base. A notable find was a lamp of the cup-and-saucer type.

Salameh. On the bottom of a collapsed burial cave at the corner of Hatayasim and Lod Streets were found pottery vessels and burned human bones. The material was dated to Early Bronze Age I.

MIDDLE BRONZE AGE

No Middle Bronze Age I occupation remains were discovered in Tel Aviv, but rock-cut shaft graves of this period have been found, usually as a result of building and road works. These graves are found in groups. Only a few have been excavated. One small graveyard was excavated near the Ramat-Aviv–Natanya Road petrol station. Another graveyard is located slightly to the northwest, near the east fence of the Sde Dov airport, another in Pinkas Street between Yad Lebanim and Shikun ha-Tsameret. There was apparently a graveyard also in Ramat Heḥayal, where a grave with a Middle Bronze Age I burial was found beneath a Middle Bronze Age II-A burial. An isolated Middle Bronze Age I grave was found in Yanai Street, north of the Chalcolithic cave 1.

Sde Dov–Middle Bronze Age II-A. A temporary squatters' dwelling of a clan of Amorites (?) excavated near the Sde Dov airport is the first dwelling of this type discovered in Israel.

The site, dating to the Middle Bronze Age II-A, was exposed during building operations. It was excavated in October–November, 1969, by Haya and J. Kaplan, on behalf of the Museum of Antiquities of Tel Aviv–Jaffa.

The site is an elliptical hollow dug in the *kurkar* rock and measures approximately 20 by 9 meters. It was filled with thin layers of drift sand and clayey soil. Between these layers could be distinguished thin occupation strata containing many potsherds and animal bones, including those of goats, sheep, turtles, various field animals, and also the complete skull of a donkey. In a higher section were found the remains of ovens and hearths. The hollow was probably roofed over with a goat hair tent similar to the Bedouin tents of today. The pottery dates the site to the Middle Bronze Age II-A.

A small graveyard was also exposed in the Exhibition Gardens (Ganei ha-Ta'arukha), and seven of its graves were excavated. Individual graves are also known in Hadar Yosef and Ramat Heḥayal.

Excavations near Tel Aviv Harbor. Near the southern fence of Tel Aviv Harbor, approximately 30 meters from the shoreline, a small cemetery with eighteen Middle Bronze Age–Late Bronze Age tombs was excavated by J. Kaplan in 1949–51. The tombs were in the form of rectangular rock-cut shafts, about 1.6 meters deep. On the long side of each tomb was a vaulted burial niche in which the body was placed. The openings of these niches were blocked with clay-sealed stones. In all, the remains of twenty-five adult and infant burials were found. The dead were buried fully clothed, adorned with their jewelry and scarab seals and with their personal belongings placed nearby. The funeral equipment consisted as a rule of two large jars, dipper juglets, bowls, carinated bowls, and cosmetic juglets. Among the twenty-four scarab seals found is one which, according to J. Leibovitch, is incised with the first name of the Egyptian queen Hatshepsut (1503–1482 B.C.).

CONCLUSIONS. There are two dating possibilities for the cemetery:

1. The period ranging between the latter part of stratum D at Tell Beit Mirsim to the end of stratum IX at Megiddo, about 1550–1480 B.C.

2. A period of one generation during the reign of Queen Hatshepsut.

Hill Square. In the western part of Hill Square, a pottery kiln and a tomb cave, both dating to the Middle Bronze Age II-B, were exposed. In Shimon Hatarsi Street was found a destroyed cemetery dating to the Middle Bronze Age II-C–Late Bronze Age I.

IRON AGE

Iron Age remains in the Tel Aviv area occur mainly

Courtyard of a catacomb from the ancient Jewish cemetery at Abu Kabir — Roman period.

at the following mounds: Kudadi, Qasile, Jerishe Jaffa, and Abu-Zeitun. Eighth-century B.C. remains without buildings, found at Hill Square, on Giv'at Beth ha-Mitbaḥayim, and in areas bordering on Yehoshua Bin Nun and John Hyrcanus Streets, may have belonged to military camps and are possibly connected with Sennacherib's campaign against Hezekiah. It is known that on his way to Judah, Sennacherib conquered Jaffa, Beth Dagon, Azor, and Bene-Berak, all cities of Sidqa, king of Ashkelon, who was Hezekiah's ally. It is therefore possible that, at this strategic position on Giv'at Beth ha-Mitbaḥayim, there was a forward camp of the allies.

PERSIAN PERIOD

The only Persian period remains in the Tel Aviv area were found at Giv'at Beth ha-Mitbaḥayim. Sections of walls and large quantities of pottery were excavated at various points of the site. The upper part of a faience statuette showing Egyptian influence, which was found in Hill Square, dates to the Persian period.

HELLENISTIC PERIOD

The Hellenistic sites in the Tel Aviv area are of two kinds: remains of agricultural estates dating from Ptolemy II's time (285–246 B.C.), and remains dating from the Hasmonaean period, from the second half of the second century to the second half of the first century B.C. The remains of buildings and two winepresses belonging to an agricultural estate were excavated on Giv'at Rambam (today within the city limits of Giv'atayim). Similar remains were found at the eastern limit of the Kiriya (formerly Sarona), west of Naḥal Ayalon, but excavations there were limited in scope. In addition, such remains were also excavated at the corner of Yehuda Maccabi (formerly 556) Street and Netanya Road. At all these sites pottery and bronze coins were found.

In the Hasmonaean period, most of the coastal cities in the Yarkon Valley and the Sharon Plain were conquered and annexed to Judea. Among Hasmonaean remains in Tel Aviv are a winepress dating to Alexander Jannaeus' time, excavated in Ḥevrah Ḥadashah Street, and parts of Jannaeus' defense line.

Excavation of the Jannaeus Line. In 1949, Has-

Opposite page: Museum Haaretz Center.
Greek mosaic inscription: "Blessing and peace on Israel and on this place, Amen".

monaean remains were excavated in Tel Aviv for the first time at two sites located in front of the Hilton Hotel in Hayarkon Street and at the intersection of Arlosoroff and Blokh Streets. The foundations of a rectangular structure (13.5 by 9 meters) were exposed at the first site (Hayarkon Street), while at the second (Arlosoroff Street) part of a structure with hexagonal plan was excavated. The finds at the two sites date to the Hellenistic period and include a coin of Alexander Jannaeus found in Hayarkon Street. The two sites are probably part of the fortification line, which Josephus reports was built by Alexander Jannaeus "from the mountainside above Antipatris to the sea coast of Joppa" (*Antiquities*, XIII, 390). It is assumed that the main section of this line (its right eastern flank) ran from the Rosh ha-'Ayin springs to the mountains in the east, while the remaining section (its left western flank) was the Yarkon River, which formed a natural defense trench. It appears therefore that military camps were erected at regular intervals along the southern bank of the Yarkon and had fortified posts in front of them. The two excavated structures may be such fortified posts and belong to the western sector of the line. In 1961, a further section of the line was discovered at Pardes Katz, near Bene-Berak, where the foundations of a hexagonal structure were also exposed. This structure is smaller than the one excavated in Arlosoroff Street. It also dates to the Hellenistic period and here too a coin of Jannaeus was found.

END OF SECOND TEMPLE PERIOD

Remains from this period include a settlement of Khirbet Hadra located on a high mound (near the Shanghai Immigrants Housing Estate) across the Yarkon, and a number of tombs, one of which (in Shikun Dan) contained a limestone ossuary with a rosette decoration. Other tombs of this period were found at the edge of the Herzliya School in Blokh Street.

Across the Yarkon, remains of agricultural settlements of this period are found at Khirbet Hadra and Khirbet el-Ora on the northern municipal boundary near Tel Barukh. The principal Roman–Byzantine remains include the Jewish cemetery at Abu-Kabir, extending from Herzl Street to Kibbutz Galuyot Street, the graveyard (near Tel Barukh) west of Khirbet el-Ora, and the remains in the area of the Museum Haaretz Center which belong to the settlement at Tell Qasile.

ROMAN-BYZANTINE PERIOD

Abu-Kabir. In 1872, C. Clermont-Ganneau explored at Abu-Kabir the ancient Jewish cemetery of Jaffa from which about seventy marble tombstones have been recovered to date. Most of them reached various museums in Europe. The funerary inscriptions are mostly in Greek, and only a few are in Hebrew or Aramaic. They provide many details on the origin and trades of the Jews of Jaffa in the Roman–Byzantine period.

Since 1951, eight tomb caves were excavated by J. Kaplan. Except for human bones (usually not in situ), these tombs were empty and had probably been plundered by the local Arab population. However, in the courtyard of two caves, a tombstone was found near the entrance. Most of the caves have loculi, but several had loculi and arcosolia.

Cemetery near Tel Barukh. The cemetery lies 1.5 kilometers north of the railway bridge on Rishpon Street. In 1951–52, excavations carried out on the site revealed burial caves dug in the rock and a pit full of animal bones. Each cave had a courtyard with steps and one or two burial chambers (2.5 by 2 meters). Often there were benches along the walls of the courtyards and depressions for draining rainwater from the floor. The entrance generally was sealed by a round slab, which fits into a narrow groove on its short side. The cave was opened by rolling the stone aside. Both loculi and arcosolia were cut in the walls of the burial chambers. There were indications that most of the burial chambers and also the floors had been reused several times at various periods. Numerous offerings were found: glass and pottery vessels, lamps and bronze, iron and glass jewelry. There were also iron nails, indicating that the dead were buried in wooden coffins. In some tombs, bronze coins were found, and in one cave there was a hoard of about one hundred coins, mostly from the fourth century A.D. An isolated pit with cattle and sheep bones is noteworthy. This may be early evidence (fifth century A.D.) of the Jewish custom of burying every firstborn of a ritually clean animal within or near human graves.

Excavations in Museum Haaretz Center. Near the main entrance of the Museum Center, a section of a floor mosaic was exposed. Excavations showed that the section preserved is about a third of the original mosaic, which apparently belonged to a Samaritan synagogue.

Parts of three pillars from a double row supporting the ceiling as well as rubble-stone foundations of the south wall were exposed. The building is oriented east–west, with its opening facing east. It had a wide central nave flanked by two narrow aisles. The excavations showed that the synagogue was situated outside the main settlement at Tell Qasile. It was erected above a large pottery kiln. Such kilns were usually placed outside the city.

The mosaic is beautifully executed in four basic colors and intermediate shades, in a pattern of plant motifs intertwined with geometric designs. The mosaic contains three inscriptions, two in Greek and one in Aramaic in Samaritan script. The latter definitely proves that the building was a Samaritan synagogue. One Greek inscription reads, "Blessing and peace on Israel and on this place, Amen." The second Greek inscription, placed near the synagogue threshold, lacked half of its right side and two lines at the end. It was apparently the dedicatory inscription of the synagogue builders, who were Christianized Samaritans, as indicated by the four-line Samaritan inscription.

The pottery and single bronze coin found in the excavation indicate that the building was erected at the end of the sixth or the beginning of the seventh century A.D.

Samaritan Settlements in Tel Aviv. From the evidence of two Samaritan amulets, one found in a fourth-century A.D. tomb near Khirbet Hadra and the other in a grave of the Tel Barukh cemetery, as well as from the synagogue remains in the area of Museum Haaretz Center, it can be concluded that these sites were once occupied by Samaritans. These were not, however, the only Samaritan sites in the area, since Samaritan communities are also known in the Byzantine period at Rishpon (Appolonia) and in the Petah Tikva area.   J. KAPLAN

BIBLIOGRAPHY

S. Tolkovsky, *The Gateway of Palestine*, London, 1924, 168–73 (Abu-Kabir) • Frey, Corpus 2 • J. Kaplan, *EI* 2 (1953), 157–60; *idem, The Neolithic and Chalcolithic Settlements in Tel Aviv and Surroundings*, Tel Aviv, 1954, (Hebrew); *idem, BIES* 18 (1954), 91–92 (Hebrew); *idem, 'Atiqot* 1 (1955), 1–13; *idem, IEJ* 8 (1958), 149–60; *idem*, in: M. Gichon, *Roman Frontier Studies 1967*, Tel Aviv, 1971, 201–05; *idem, IEJ* 17 (1967), 158–60; *idem, Bull. Museum Haaretz* 11 (1968), 8–9; 13 (1971), 18–22; *idem, RB* (1971), 422–23; *idem, BA* 35 (1972), 66–95; *idem, PEQ* 97 (1975), 144–52; *idem, IEJ* 25 (1975), 157–59.

TELL ESDAR

IDENTIFICATION. Tell Esdar is a loess hill, approximately 20 dunams in area, situated on the west bank of the Aroer Valley, midway between Beersheba and Dimona (map reference 14750645). The remains of several periods of settlement are visible on the surface of the hill. The site attracted settlers because of the presence of underground water in the bed of the nearby valley. Tell Esdar was first discovered by N. Glueck in 1956.

EXCAVATIONS

A salvage excavation was conducted at the site in December–January 1963–64 under the direction of M. Kochavi, on behalf of the Department of Antiquities. The remains on the surface were examined, and a trench was dug on the south side of the mound. Five periods of settlement were distinguished: stratum I — Roman-Byzantine period; stratum II — Iron Age II-A; stratum III — Iron Age I-B; stratum IV-a — Early Bronze Age II; stratum IV-b Chalcolithic period.

IN STRATUM IV-b were found the remains of silos, some built and some dug into the ground, as well as ashpits and living floors. The stratum belongs to the Beersheba culture of the Chalcolithic period, as was indicated by the painted pottery, fragments of churns, flint axes, and an agate pendant.

STRATUM IV-a contained a collection of large fan scrapers, about 20 centimeters in diameter, which were decorated with various incised patterns. Scrapers of this type and similar incised decorations are known from Early Bronze Age sites. The ledge handles and rims of hole-mouth jars found are typical of the Early Bronze Age II. Stratum IV was encountered in all excavated areas on the mound, either as a single stratum of remains, or beneath the Iron Age strata.

STRATUM III represents the most important stratum on the mound. It was the first village excavated that dates from the period of Israelite settlement in the Negev. The houses were built on the summit of the hill in a circle about 100 meters in diameter. Eight houses were cleared, and the remains of another two were distinguished on surface level. The houses were built close together and apparently also served as a defensive wall. All the doorways were on the inside, facing the center of the circle.

Below: Plan of building 90 — stratum III — 11th century B.C.; Plan of building 38 — stratum II — 10th century B.C.

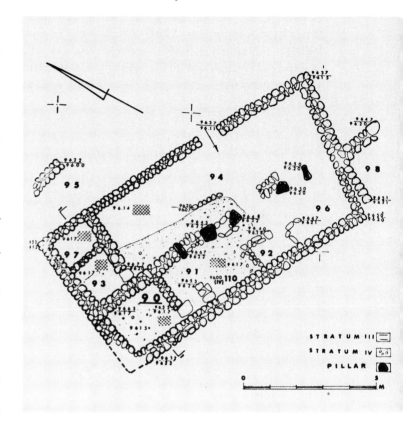

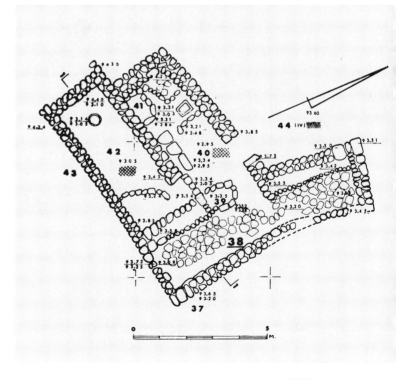

The remains of these houses had lain exposed since the time of their destruction, and they were severely damaged by erosion and agricultural activities. The plan of only one of the buildings was intact. It consisted of three areas, with a court separated from the living and working rooms by a row of pillars. Smashed domestic vessels lay on the stamped clay floors of the dwellings — testimony to the sudden destruction of the settlement. Among the typical finds of this stratum were thirty-six store jars, with high collar and pointed base, chalices found together with lamps, suggesting that the chalices served as stands for the lamps, large jugs with trefoil mouths, and shallow carinated cooking pots with handles. The pottery showed no sign of slip, burnish, or decoration. This stratum was attributed to the second half of the eleventh century B.C.

Below: Plan of the mound and areas of excavation. Opposite page: Incised flint scraper, stratum IV — Chalcolithic period.

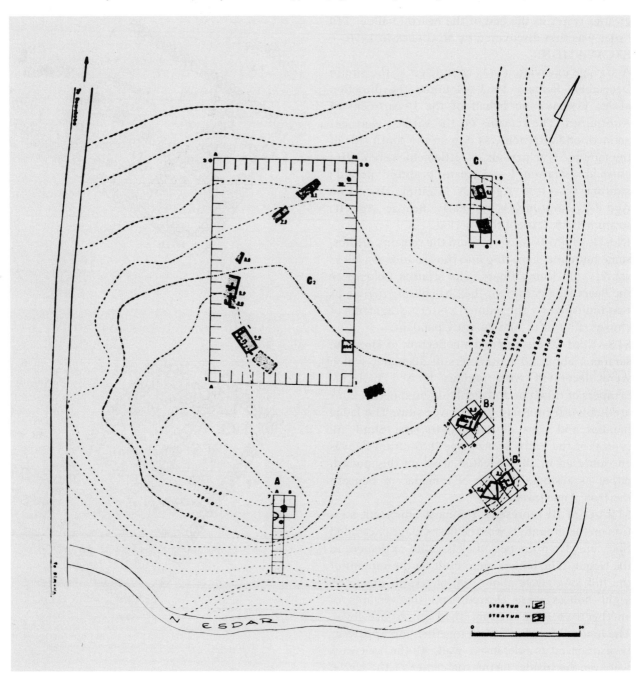

STRATUM II was found only on the southern slope of the mound, where a three-room house was uncovered with stone floors and silos and two subsidiary buildings. The pottery with slip and burnish and the differences in the form of the bowls, store jars, cooking pots, jugs, and juglets distinguish this settlement from its predecessor. The settlement was dated to the tenth century B.C.

TO STRATUM I were ascribed terraces used in agriculture and Roman–Byzantine potsherds found scattered over the surface of the mound.

SUMMARY

The earliest settlement at Tell Esdar (stratum IV), is one of the many Chalcolithic sites of the Beersheba culture found in the northern Negev. After a gap in occupation, the site was again inhabited in the Early Bronze Age II (stratum IV-a), a period of prosperity in the Beersheba Valley, the Negev, and Sinai. Only in the Iron Age, 1,500 years later, was occupation resumed on the mound. This settlement, stratum III, was apparently founded by the Israelite tribes, as part of their intensified efforts to settle the Negev in the eleventh century B.C. The sudden destruction of the settlement may have been caused by a surprise raid of the Amalekites, with whom Saul fought to protect the southernmost settlements of the Israelite tribes (I Samuel 15). In the tenth century B.C., Tell Esdar was a farm (stratum II), one of the ḥaṣerim, which took root in the Negev of Judah during periods of relative calm, as in the days of David and Solomon.   M. KOCHAVI

BIBLIOGRAPHY

N. Glueck, *BASOR* 145 (1957), 14 (site 308) • M. Kochavi, *'Atiqot* 5 (1969), 14–48 (Hebrew).

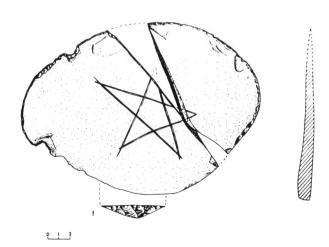

TIBERIAS

IDENTIFICATION. The area which extends from the southern part of the modern city of Tiberias to Hammath-Tiberias is generally identified as the Roman city of Tiberias. It stretches along the foot of the mountain range on the west and the coast of the Sea of Galilee on the east over an area of about 1,200 by 250 meters. Systematic excavations were conducted in this area in 1973 and 1974, on behalf of the Israel Department of Antiquities, the Institute of Archaeology, Hebrew University, and the Israel Exploration Society, under the direction of G. Foerster.

Earlier, large-scale excavations had been carried out in this area, but no results have yet been published. The principal finds uncovered include a Byzantine bathhouse with a magnificent mosaic pavement, a marketplace (?) of the Early Arab period, a colonnaded street (the cardo) to the west, and a large Late Roman building, apparently a basilica, to the east.

EXCAVATIONS

The 1973–74 excavations were concentrated south of the previous excavations, in the vicinity of the southern walls (area C) and farther south (areas A, B, and B-1). The area north of the walls was also investigated (areas D-1 and D-2). Judging from the latest coins and from the ceramic evidence, it appears that the city ceased to prosper in the second half of the eleventh century A.D., and the areas examined were abandoned with the Crusader conquest and never resettled. The city was thereafter confined farther north within the limits of the modern city of Tiberias, covering a much smaller area than its predecessors.

In areas A, B, and B-1, the remains of a number of spacious, well-built houses were uncovered. They were built on virgin soil. Some of them were built in earlier cemeteries. Two phases of repairs were distinguished in them. The walls were constructed of plastered unhewn stones and were well preserved, in some cases to a height of 2–3 meters. The buildings yielded a rich variety of pottery, metal and glass objects, and coins, which attest that the area south of the walls enjoyed an era of prosperity in the three centuries between the eighth and the eleventh centuries A.D.

Area A. This area is situated near the shore of the Sea of Galilee. Three buildings were partly excavated here, two of them containing staircases leading to a second story. The walls were built of unhewn stones laid without mortar. The corners strengthened with well-dressed ashlars were preserved to a height of some 3 meters. Traces of plaster have survived on the walls. The floors were mainly of beaten earth, and the courts were paved with slabs of stone or basalt or with unhewn stones. One room had a white mosaic pavement. A fine network of drainage and sewage channels, some of them made of pottery pipes, was found beneath the rooms.

The buildings had been constructed on rich agricultural soil, which contained potsherds of the Roman-Byzantine period, although no building remains of this period were found in the area. Beneath some of the houses were graves which were attributed, on the basis of the stratigraphy and pottery, to the end of the Byzantine period or beginning of the Early Arab period. No objects were found in the graves.

Area B. In this area, which lay some 100 meters west of area A, parts of three or four large buildings were excavated. Like the buildings in area A, these too had staircases leading to a second story. They were built of unhewn stones and ashlar masonry was occasionally employed in the corners and the piers. An interesting discovery in this area (which also appeared in other areas as well) were walls which were not bonded. This method of construction was probably designed to withstand the earthquakes which frequently struck the region. In the western sector of the area was found a group of rooms of uniform size. They were probably used

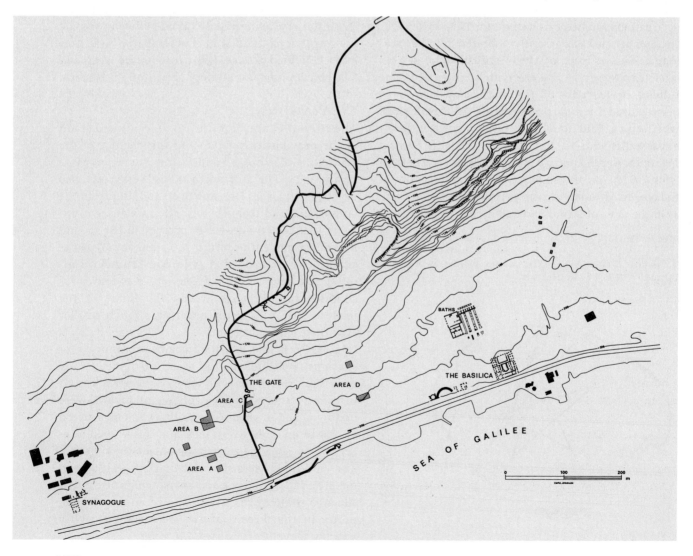

as shops. They faced the road leading from Hammath-Tiberias in the south to the city gate and the cardo of Tiberias, partly excavated many years ago, farther to the north. One of the rooms contained an interesting assemblage of delicate pottery vessels which may have been used in the spice trade. These buildings were also constructed on virgin soil, and beneath them a complex network of drainage and sewage channels was uncovered. The only earlier remains in this area was a terracotta coffin, which apparently came from the cemetery which was noted both in area A and farther south near Hammath-Tiberias.

Area B-1. This was the most extreme area in the south investigated. The remains of well-built houses were uncovered, but virgin soil was not reached. The excavations south of the line of the walls and the gate revealed that in the Roman and Byzantine periods the area between the twin cities of Tiberias and Hammath-Tiberias was uninhabited. In the latter city were excavated two synagogues and settlements from the Hellenistic, Roman, and Byzantine periods (see below). It seems that it is this unoccupied area that is referred to in the Talmud when it states that the distance between Tiberias and Hammath-Tiberias was one mile (Tosefta, *Megillah* 4, 3). This source confirms that there was indeed an open area between the two cities, although the distance appears to be exaggerated. In the Byzantine period some of this area served as a cemetery. Although it was settled only in the eighth century and abandoned some three centuries later, the two cities were nevertheless considered as one.

Area C. This was the main area of excavation. The aim here was to ascertain the nature and date of the series of walls and of the gate in the southern part of the city. They had previously been considered Roman by some remains visible on surface level and two Roman inscriptions found here in secondary use.

In the center of the area stood the gate and the cardo leading from the gate to the center of the city in the north. The gate, built of well-dressed basalt stones, was the earliest construction in this area. Round towers, 7 meters in diameter and projecting to the south, flanked the gate. The lower

part of the towers and the gate building were carved with a cyma profile. Two niches flanked the entrance inside the gate building. Two pedestals were set between the round towers and the door jambs in front of the gate. The pedestals supported columns and were decorated with rhombuses in relief.

The road which ran northward from the gate was paved with square basalt slabs, and the area of the entrance was paved with rectangular slabs laid parallel to each other. Farther north the slabs were laid obliquely, as was customary in Roman streets in both the Eastern and Western parts of the empire. Soundings made in several points revealed that the walls are later than the towers, and thus than of the gate itself, which is banded to the towers. The gate complex was supported by massive foundations composed of small stones and mortar, which solved the problems caused by the heavy soil on the banks of the Sea of Galilee.

Judging from the stratigraphy and the architectural evidence, the gate was probably constructed with the founding of the city. A sounding made in the street, after the removal of several heavy basalt

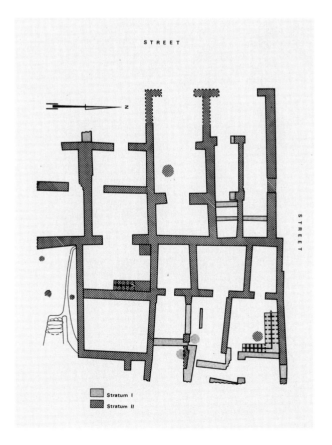

STREET

N

STREET

Stratum I
Stratum II

Opposite page: Plan of the areas of excavation. This page: Area B. Residental building.

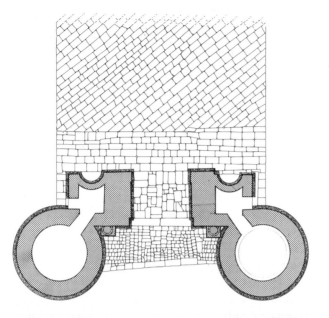

slabs, revealed pottery of which the latest sherds were attributed to the first century A.D. and provide a post quem date for the construction of the gate and the street. The plan and ornamentation of the gate point to the same date, probably at the foundation of the city in the second decade of the first century A.D. Soundings conducted east and west of the area of the gate yielded no remains earlier than the sixth or seventh centuries, and it can be assumed that in the Roman period the gate and towers stood isolated and served as a kind of outer gate having no connection with the walls in that period. Although there is no definite proof that the Roman city was fortified, this possibility should not be totally dismissed. Allusions to a wall in this period are contained in the literary sources

and several Talmudic passages also hint at the existence of a gate outside the city of Tiberias.

According to the stratigraphic evidence, the gate complex and the street thus represent the earliest constructions (stratum V) in the excavated area. In the Byzantine period, in the sixth or seventh century (stratum IV), a wall 2.7 meters wide was built up to the gate and the towers. Other remains of building activity in this period were found in the area of the gate and east and west of it, but since they lay mostly beneath later remains, the plan of the structure adjacent to the wall could not be traced. In the eastern tower were found a large number of "incendiary bombs" from stratum IV, which probably belonged either to the defenders of the city or to the attackers. The major building activity east and west of the gate and in the gate itself belong to the eighth to the tenth centuries A.D. (strata III and II). To the east of the gate was uncovered part of a large structure built against the wall and above it and narrowing the wall at that spot. The building continued to exist in strata II and I. The floors were raised, but no other significant alterations were made in the plan when the wall ceased to serve a defensive purpose, and openings were made in it on the south side to accommodate the city's expansion in the eighth and ninth centuries (areas A and B). The walls of the

building have been preserved to a height of about 3 meters.

To the west of the gate was a very large well-built structure, which had a beautiful paved court with a small garden in its center. It had two stories, like most of the other buildings uncovered. Doorways led to the area of the gate at a lower level where various buildings, mostly shops, were erected. Shops also stood along the side of the cardo, considerably narrowing it. Most of the doorways were on the north side of the building, indicating that there was probably a street perpendicular to the cardo. In this period changes were also made in the gate. Openings were pierced in the niches decorating the interior of the gate and led to the towers and other areas of the gate. The narrowing of the street was accompanied by a marked reduction in the width of the entrance, which in strata II and I was only 1.5 meters wide. Strips of metal and nails belonging to the doors were uncovered. The floor levels were also raised and a stone paving, about 1.5 meters above the Roman street, was found in the latest stratum.

Opposite page top: Area C, drawing of the Roman gate and floor. Bottom: Area C, Roman City gate covered by muslim structures. Below: Plan of the Gate's area.

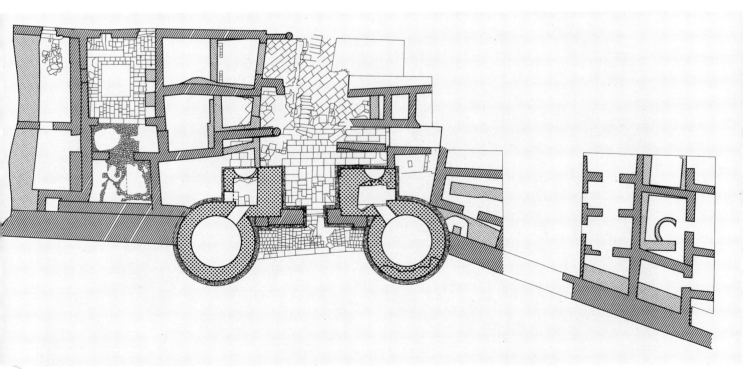

Below: Area C. Domestic building — 11th century C.E.
Bottom: Area C. Domestic building — 8–9th centuries C.E.
Opposite page: Area D. hoard of coins and jewllery —
11th century C.E.

The gate's present location inside a wadi is most likely the result of changes in the course of the wadi which originally flowed south of the gate, since it is hardly conceivable that a gate would be placed in the bed of a wadi. A series of walls was built inside and close to the western tower to protect it from flood water, but part of it was nevertheless completely destroyed.

Areas D-1 and D-2. These areas were situated some 200 meters north of area C. A workshop from the eighth to the eleventh centuries, possibly for dyeing, was found in area D-1. It yielded a hoard of coins and jewelry from the tenth and eleventh centuries. A drainage system of the Early Roman period ran beneath this installation. It contained Early Roman pottery, marble fragments, and coins. No building remains from this period were found in this area.

In area D-2 a series of retaining walls was preserved to a height of about 7 meters. The foundations of a very large building were also found but its nature and date are not yet clear.   G. FOERSTER

BIBLIOGRAPHY

G. Foerster, *RB* 82 (1975), 105–109: *idem, Qadmoniot* 10 (1977), 87–91 (Hebrew).

TIBERIAS, HAMMATH

IDENTIFICATION. The remains of Hammath-Tiberias extend from the hot springs (al-Ḥammam) to the southern boundary of ancient Tiberias. In the Talmud the place is identified with Hammath (Joshua 19 : 35), a fortified city of the tribe of Naphtali: "Hammath-Hammatha" (Palestinian Talmud *Megillah* 1, 70). This identification is not certain, however, since the excavations and the survey of the Hammath area uncovered no remains earlier than the Hellenistic period. Hammath is mentioned many times in the Mishnah. Tiberias and Hammath were originally two separate cities, each surrounded by a wall of its own ("R. Jeremiah said . . . from Hammath to Tiberias — a mile" [*Megillah* 2, 2]) but

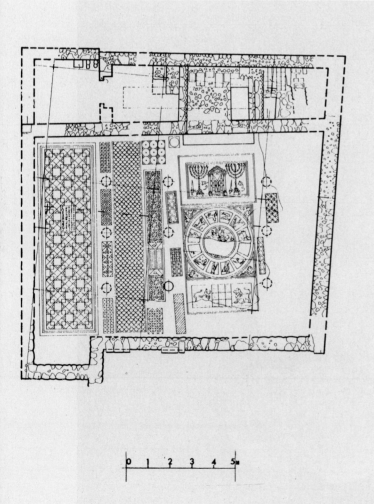

they were subsequently united into a single city, apparently in the first century A.D.: "Now the children of Tiberias and the children of Hammath again became one city" (Tosefta, *'Erubin* 7 : 2, 146). Tiberias was known as Maziah after the priestly order that had settled in Hammath (Tiberias was forbidden to the priests because it contained a cemetery). When Tiberias became the seat of the great Yeshivah and the Sanhedrin in the third century A.D., and the spiritual center of the Jews of Palestine and the Diaspora, the suburb of Hammath shared its prominence. With the abolition of the Patriarchate in A.D. 429, Hammath began to decline, but it continued to exist as a city, supporting itself by its profitable hot springs. The Jewish community remained in the city throughout the Arab period until its decline in the Middle Ages.

EXPLORATION OF THE SITE

Two excavations were carried out at the site. The first was undertaken in the year 1921 (two seasons) under the supervision of N. Slouschz (the first excavation by a Jewish resident of the country and the first on behalf of the Palestine Exploration Society and the Department of Antiquities) and the second (two seasons, 1961–62, 1962–63) under M. Dothan, assisted by I. Dunayewsky and S. Moskowitz, on behalf of the Israel Department of Antiquities. The site was earlier explored by the Department of Antiquities of the Mandatory Government in 1947.

SLOUSCHZ'S EXCAVATIONS

About 500 meters north of the city's southern wall, a synagogue was uncovered in the form of a square basilica (12 by 12 meters), divided by two rows of columns into a nave and two aisles. The three entrances to the building were on the north. East of the building was a courtyard which was entered from the east, and from there a doorway led to the eastern aisle. At the southern end of the nave was a partition consisting of four small columns. The enclosed area behind it probably held the Ark of the Law. In the eastern aisle stood the "seat of Moses" (cathedra). The various levels of pavements, the mosaics, and the alterations in the structure indicate that there were several phases in the construction of the synagogue, although the excavators did not succeed in tracing them. In the opinion of H. L. Vincent, there were two building phases. In the first phase, the entrance to the building was on the south, in the side facing Jerusalem. Two build-

Opposite page: Plan of the synagogue of level II A. This page, left: Synagogue. Aramaic inscription, level II A. Bottom: Synagogue, mosaic of the Ark of the Law, level II A.

ing phases are also confirmed by the pavements, one of which is a stylized mosaic.

Slouschz identified the synagogue with "the synagogue of Hammath" and assigned it to the Early Roman period. Vincent, however, disputed this identification, on the basis of a comparison with other ancient synagogues and the small dimensions of the building. In his opinion the main, late phase of construction should be attributed to the fourth–

fifth centuries A.D. Synagogue research since the time of Slouschz' identification attributes this synagogue, which lacks an apse but has an entrance on the side facing Jerusalem, to the fourth century A.D. Near the synagogue the excavators uncovered part of a cemetery containing sarcophagi of the third and fourth centuries A.D. with the names of the deceased written in Greek — Isidorus, Symmachus son of Justus — as well as several graves dating

from the Early Arab period. Among the finds are a capital decorated with a menorah, a fragment of a chancel screen with a menorah in relief, and a seven-branched menorah carved in limestone. In addition to the investigations of Slouschz, M. Narkiss and Z. Eshkoli published architectural details and a number of objects found in the area of the synagogue and in its vicinity.

DOTHAN'S EXCAVATIONS

An area of approximately 1,200 square meters was excavated near the hot springs, about 150 meters west of the Sea of Galilee. The ancient remains had been erected on an artificial terrace running parallel to the seashore from southeast to northwest, closely following the contours of the terrain. Beyond the southern limit of the main excavation area were uncovered the remains of the city wall and one of its towers. These were found to date not earlier than the Byzantine period, although they appear to rest on the remains of walls of an earlier city. Three main construction levels were uncovered, dating from the first century B.C. to the eighth century A.D. The numismatic evidence showed that remains from the first century B.C. lay beneath level III. The main building in level III dates from the first century or first half of the second century A.D. This building (60 by 40 meters), only half of which was excavated, consists of a central court with halls and rooms along at least three of its sides. Two entrances to the building were found on the south side. Its plan resembles that of a public building, such as a gymnasium, and it may have already been

Below: Synagogue, level II, in the background. Level III in the foreground (after removal of the mosaics).

a synagogue in that early period, since no plans of Palestinian synagogues of the first to the second centuries A.D. are known, and furthermore, all the later structures above the building (except perhaps those of the intermediate phase III–II) were synagogues. Noteworthy among the meager finds in this building is a unique glass goblet in the shape of a centaur silvered on the inside and outside and decorated with floral reliefs below the rim.

LEVEL III seems to have been destroyed in the middle of the second century, and the few remains above it (intermediate phase III–II) do not apparently belong to a public building. Synagogue II was erected on these remains. The last stage of the synagogue (II-A), which was the better preserved, is based for the most part on the earlier phase, II-B. It is a broad house (15 by 13 meters), oriented southeast–northwest and is separated from the other structures around it. Three rows of columns, each containing three columns, divide the building into four halls, the widest of them (the second from the west) is the nave. Attached to the building on the south is a corridor paved with mosaics with an entrance on the east side. Although no other entrances to the building have been preserved, there may have been more than one. On the north side of the building was a room which may have contained stairs leading to the roof or to a second story.

Building II-A (see plan) does not differ greatly from its predecessor. The corridor, however, was divided into cells and closed off as a passage. The direction of the entrance to the synagogue was also changed. Henceforth the entrance seems to have been through three openings situated in recesses in the northern wall. The stairwell was no longer in use, and access to the second floor seems to have been from a small room adjoining the corridor. From the southern end of the nave, a step led to a raised niche in the corridor where the Ark of the Law, which in the previous stage had no permanent place, was probably kept. The walls of the building were decorated with colorful wall paintings, remains of which were found in the debris.

The nave and aisles were paved with magnificent mosaics in thirty hues, which have survived in a fine state of preservation. The most important is the mosaic pavement of the nave, which is divided into three panels. In the southern panel is depicted the Ark of the Law, flanked by burning seven-branched menorahs and a lulab, ethrog, shofar, and incense shovel. The middle panel represents the zodiac surrounding the figure of the sun god Helios riding in his chariot (the chariot was partly destroyed when the wall of level I was built). Helios is depicted with a halo above his head, one hand raised in benediction and the other holding a globe of the universe. The corners of the panel display female busts, each with a Hebrew name by its side, symbolizing the four seasons of the year. The northern panel contains a dedicatory inscription in Greek of the founders of the synagogue. It is flanked by two lions. The two eastern aisles contain mosaics in geometric design and three inscriptions, one in Aramaic and two in Greek.

The main builder of the synagogue, according to the Greek inscription, was Severus who is called "the pupil of the most illustrious patriarchs," evidently the title bestowed on high officials in the court of the presidents of the Sanhedrin in Tiberias ("Severus . . . completed [the work of construction]. Praise be to him and to Julius the parnes [synagogue official]"). Another Greek inscription

mentions Profuturos who built one of the porches. The Aramaic inscription refers to the place as "a holy site," that is, a synagogue.

The remains of the floors, as well as the coins and lamps, date the synagogue to the fourth century A.D. This is also confirmed by the plan of the building, which is of the broad-house type, divided into four halls, and differs from all the known synagogues of the second–third centuries A.D. It combines features derived from the third century (absence of an apse) and from the fifth century onward (entrance in the wall facing Jerusalem and a permanent place for the Ark of the Law).

The artistic level of the mosaics surpasses all that has so far been uncovered in the early synagogues in Israel. In the individual treatment of the figures, they strongly resemble the Constantinian mosaics at Antioch. Evident here is the strong influence exerted by Hellenistic-Roman art of the beginning of the fourth century on the Jewish capital at Tiberias (the sages of Tiberias permitted the representation of images in mosaic, as is attested by the written sources). The free artistic expression

Remains of synagogues I and II, looking west.

Below: Capital from the synagogue.
Bottom: Stone carved menorah, 3rd century C.E.

displayed in the nude representations of the signs of the zodiac, the frequent use of Greek, as well as the various finds, all accord with the spirit that prevailed in the period when the heads of the Sanhedrin flourished in Tiberias, and confirm a date in the first half of the fourth century A.D. for the construction of synagogue II-A.

LEVEL II-A was evidently destroyed in the fifth century and the great synagogue I-B was erected in its place. The new synagogue was oriented in the same direction as its predecessors but, unlike them, it was not isolated from the other buildings, which were attached to it on all but the east and west sides, where streets skirted the building. The synagogue was built in the form of a basilica as was common in synagogue and church construction of the fifth and sixth centuries A.D. It was divided by two rows of columns into a nave and two aisles. A third row of columns divides the nave transversely, thus creating an entrance hall (pronaos). The three rows of columns supported a gallery on the second story that ran along three sides of the building. The three main entrances were on the north side of the building. Three steps led from the nave to an interior apse. East of the apse was a room with stairs ascending to the second story, and to the west was another room where "the treasury" of the synagogue was hidden in the floor. From the western aisle, three doorways opened onto a courtyard paved with flagstones. Its walls are well preserved. A small apse was discovered on the southern side of the courtyard and beyond it were plastered rooms which served as cisterns *(miqve)*. The mosaic in the hall was made of tiny colored tesserae and the preserved fragments indicate that they depicted figures of animals in addition to geometric and floral designs. Level I-B was apparently destroyed in the first half of the seventh century, perhaps at the time when the Byzantines reconquered the country from the Persians. The new synagogue (level I-A), probably built at the beginning of the reign of the Umayyads, is not markedly different from its predecessor except that the small apse was no longer in use. Part of the courtyard was covered with a roof, supported by a column, thus creating a room in which one of the stairs of the apse served as a bench. This may have served as a *beth-midrash*. A new mosaic pavement was laid decorated mainly with geometric designs but at the

Mosaic pavement in synagogue, the season Tishri, *level II A.*

entrance to the nave there were other motifs such as a menorah. The rich finds included pottery of the type found at Khirbet Mafjar. Many clay lamps were discovered, some bearing Arabic inscriptions. A long Aramaic inscription on a jug has been partly deciphered. It concerns a gift of oil from Sepphoris.

In this level a segment of a paved street was also found (which began in level I-B). It ran from the city gate along the western wall of the synagogue's courtyard. The evidence furnished by the coins makes it clear that all the structures of this level were destroyed at the beginning of the Abbasid period, in approximately the middle of the eighth century, and never rebuilt. The ruins served as dwellings and silos for squatters in the eleventh to the fifteenth centuries.

SUMMARY

1.) At Hammath several superimposed synagogue buildings were found, and beneath them was a public building whose function is not clear. The construction of the synagogue went through four phases, beginning in the fourth century and terminating in the middle of the eighth century A.D.

2.) A new type of synagogue was uncovered here, a broad-house type of four rooms (II-A, B), with the entrance on the side facing Jerusalem (II-B) and having a permanent place for the Ark of the Law. This was a rectangular room which preceded the apse in Palestinian synagogues (II-B).

3.) The mosaic pavement in synagogue II-B is constructed in the spirit of the Hellenistic-Roman art of the fourth century. The zodiac depicted in the mosaic is the earliest found in the country.

4.) The Greek inscriptions of the builders of this synagogue are the first to mention the patriarchs of the Sanhedrin and contribute greatly to the knowledge of Judaism of the fourth century A.D. in Tiberias.

5.) The uppermost synagogue (I-A) is an instructive example of Jewish architecture at the beginning of Arab rule in Palestine and sheds light on a number of customs practiced in synagogues in those days.

M. DOTHAN

BIBLIOGRAPHY

N. Slouschz, *Koveṣ PJPES* 1 (1921), 5–37; 49–52 • A. Z. Eshkoli–M. Narkis, *ibid.* (1935) (Sefer Mazie), 175–96 (all Hebrew) • M. Dothan, *IEJ* 12 (1962), 153–54; idem, *Qadmoniot* 1 (1968), 116–23 (Hebrew); idem, *EI* 8 (1966), 183–85 (Hebrew).

TIMNA'

IDENTIFICATION. The Timna' Valley (Wadi Mene'iyeh) lies alongside the Wadi 'Arabah, some 30 kilometers (18.5 miles) north of the Gulf of Elath-Aqabah. It is a huge semicircular erosion formation of about 70 square kilometers, open on the east toward the 'Arabah, and containing four valleys, running from the 300 meter high Timna' Cliffs into the Wadi 'Arabah. Along the foot of the Timna' Cliffs, within a white sandstone formation, are found copper ore nodules which consist of up to 25 percent of malachite mixed with azurite, cuprite, and chalcocite. These are the copper ores which were exploited in ancient times. Clear signs of mining activities, including shafts and galleries, as well as mining tools of various periods were found in this part of the Timna' Valley. Eleven camps, located in the center of the Timna' Valley, west of the Timna' Massif, several containing substantial slag heaps, testify to the existence of intensive copper-smelting activities. These remains belong mainly to the period of the New Kingdom (Late Bronze Age–Iron Age I). A Chalcolithic copper-smelting installation was excavated east of the modern copper works, and just north of the Timna' Valley an Early Bronze Age II copper smelting site was uncovered. South of the Timna' Valley, the center of Roman copper smelting in the western 'Arabah was located at Beer Ora.

HISTORY OF EXPLORATION

In 1845, the British explorer, J. Petherick identified in Timna' (Wadi el-Mahait) copper-smelting slag. In 1907, A. Musil found there "remains of dwellings." F. Frank located seven copper-smelting sites in Timna' in 1934. These were also described in 1935 by N. Glueck, who first dated the pottery found there to the Iron Age I–II, but in 1940 attributed the copper smelting in Timna' to King Solomon, calling the area King Solomon's Mines. In 1959–61, B. Rothenberg explored the Timna' Valley and in 1962 he published, together with Y. Aharoni and B. H. McLeod, a detailed description of its ancient mines and smelting camps. King Solomon's Mines were dated to several widely separated periods, from the fourth millennium B.C. to Roman times.

In 1964, Rothenberg founded the 'Arabah Expe-

Map of the Timna' Valley.

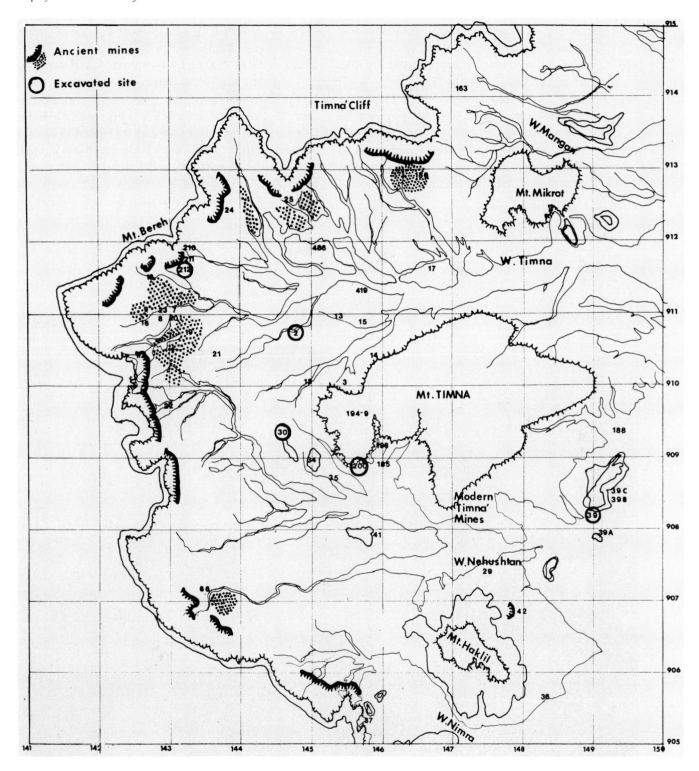

dition (Museum Haaretz, Tel Aviv) to conduct excavations in Timna'. The members of this research group included A. Lupu (extractive metallurgy), Technion, Israel Institute of Technology, Haifa, R. F. Tylecote (metallurgy), University of Newcastle-upon-Tyne (England), and H. G. Bachmann (chemistry and mineralogy), University of Frankfurt a.M. (Germany). The excavations were directed by B. Rothenberg. Since 1964 the following sites at Timna' have been excavated:

1964–66 Site 2, a smelting camp dated to the Ramesside period.

1965 Site 39, a primitive copper-smelting site from the Chalcolithic period.

1969 Site 28 (at Beer Ora, south of Timna') a second century A.D. Roman copper-smelting plant.

1969 Site 200, a mining sanctuary dedicated to Hathor and dated by inscriptions to the fourteenth–twelfth centuries B.C.

1974–76 Site 30, a smelting camp of the Ramesside period.

1974–76 Site 212, an area of shaft and gallery mining, Ramesside period.

1977 Site 201a, an Early Bronze Age II smelting site and settlement.

EXCAVATIONS

Site 39 (map reference 14909183). Site 39 is located at the top (39-b) and at the foot (39-a) of a 30 meter high hill, east of the modern Timna' works and just north of Nahal Neḥushtan.

SITE 39-a. The building remains at site 39-a con-

Air view of smelting site 2 with Wadi 'Arabah in background

sisted of an oval, wall-like configuration of rough field stones and three tumuli. The surface finds indicated that a smelting mixture of ores and fluxes was prepared here, probably for the smelters on top of the hill (39-b). Chalcolithic flint tools and pottery were also found. In locus 1 was excavated a structure 4 by 5 meters with rounded corners and its entrance on the west. Inside, small flat stones formed a roundish "floor" about 80 centimeters in diameter, with a small pit, full of charcoal, next to it. This arrangement resembles a group of pebbles at Chalcolithic Tell Abu Matar, near Beersheba, but, unlike it, the Timna' group bore no marks of any kind. Some bone fragments were found. This structure seems to have served as a dwelling. In loci 2–4 were found fireplaces built of stone circles and containing ashes. Stone hammers and mortars as well as a quantity of copper ores found here attest to a connection with the copper-smelting site 39-b.

SITE 39-b, on top of the hill, was the site of the copper smelting. Before excavation, small pieces of a peculiar rough slag and some flint implements and sherds had indicated a Chalcolithic smelter.

Chalcolithic smelting site 39a near the modern Timna' mines, in background.

A 3 by 5 meter area was excavated. About 10 centimeters below surface level, a heavily burned pit was found, about 45 centimeters in diameter and 30 centimeters deep, filled with burned material (containing 2.5 percent Cu) and bits of smelting slag. This was a copper smelting furnace of a primitive bowl type, which originally was some 60 centimeters high. A working surface with slag, charcoal, Chalcolithic flint tools, and pottery, was found in situ around the furnace. This is the earliest copper-smelting installation known so far. Of very primitive construction, it may indicate the very beginning of extractive copper metallurgy.

Site 2 (map reference 14489107). Site 2 is located in a small side arm of Naḥal Timna'. Smelting was indicated by the presence of slag heaps. The aims of the excavations at this site were the reconstruction of the ancient copper-smelting processes and of a large copper plant of the late second millennium B.C., as well as establishing a reliable stratigraphy for site 2, in order to clarify the chronology of Timna' and the 'Arabah. Site 2 was excavated during two seasons, in 1964 and 1966.

AREA A. Southeast of the industrial area and higher up the slope, a tumulus was excavated to bedrock, and two superimposed structures were uncovered. Structure I, built on bedrock, was a rectangular building, 9 by 8 meters, with its entrance on the east. On both sides of the entrance was a low stone bench, probably for offerings. A large, square, flat-topped monolith stood in the center and may have served as an altar. Around it was a large quantity of broken animal bones, ashes, and pottery. On the west side of the building stood a row of five large roughly dressed *massebahs*, with a large stone bowl, perhaps for libations, in front of them. A semicircular annex was built next to the entrance, another against the outer northern wall. Much ash and many broken bones of goats were found inside both annexes.

Structure I was a small place of worship, attached to the large smelting camp at the site. After its destruction, apparently by an earthquake, it was abandoned and completely covered by windblown sand. Structure II (3.5 by 2.5 meters) was erected on top of the sand-covered debris, its entrance was also on the southeast side, and its walls were 80 centimeters high. It contained only a few coarse sherds.

AREA B. At the east side of site 2 was found a large charcoal pile, 10 by 7.5 meters, used to manufacture charcoal from acacia trees. An adjacent furnace (40 by 40 centimeters and 80 centimeters deep) was uncovered, in which pellets of metallic copper, which had been extracted from the smelting slag, were melted in small crucibles prior to casting small copper objects. Near this melting installation, a small workshop was uncovered, 5 by 4 meters, with a deep, stone-lined ore pit and a solid, semicircular crushing platform. Stone crushing tools and a quantity of finely crushed copper ore was found in situ on this working platform.

AREA D–K. In this area, located at the northern end of site 2, a large building complex, approximately 400 square meters, was uncovered. It comprised a complete working and storage unit. Its walls were dry built in header-and-stretcher construction. In its center was a courtyard, 8 by 11 meters, with a very large, stone-lined storage pit for ores. Next to it was a stone platform, with many crushing and grinding tools and crushed copper ore in situ. This courtyard was a center for the preparation of the smelting charge. Two rooms built against the western wall of the courtyard, each had stone-lined storage pits along the walls. Attached to the eastern side of the courtyard, a two-roomed structure served as a workshop and perhaps living quarters. A small cooking stove was found outside.

In the north end of area D–K was a casting workshop, containing several superimposed working floors of furnaces, together with a large quantity of wood ash, charcoal dust, copper pellets, slag, and slagged crucible fragments. A large storage pit was also found here. The workshop was partly destroyed by an earthquake and subsequently reconstructed.

AREA C. An area of 10 by 6 meters was excavated, including part of a solid, 50-centimeter-high heap of heavy circular slag plates (35–50 centimeters in diameter). Next to the slag heap were found two smelting furnaces (FU III, FU IV). Furnace IV was in an excellent state of preservation. The actual smelting hearth was merely a hole in the ground, 40 centimeters deep and 45 centimeters in diameter, lined with a thick layer of clay mortar. Much slag was found adhering to the furnace walls. Two flanking stones protected a shallow pit dug in front of the furnace. This was a slag-tapping pit, dug at a lower level to guarantee the swift flow of the hot liquid slag through a tapping hole, drilled into the side of the furnace.

A clay tube found in situ penetrating the furnace wall opposite the tapping hole must have served as the tuyere for the bellows. There were probably more bellows entering the furnace wall from all directions as such a large furnace required several bellows. Many clay tuyeres were found scattered over site 2.

In area C three superimposed working floors were found separated by a thin layer of wind-borne drift sand, attesting to seasonal operations at the site. The pottery found on the floors belonged to the Iron Age I and was identical with the three types—Negev, Midianite, and ordinary ware, described below.

AREAS E AND G. Smelting furnaces (Fu I, II) were found in these areas next to large slag heaps. They are similar for the most part to furnace IV described above, except that they are stone built. They consisted of a semicircular wall of dolomite, its open side above the tapping pit, which was protected by two flanking stones. The wall and bottom were clay lined, with a clay tuyere piercing its back wall. Behind the furnace was a solid working platform of large flat stones.

Opposite page, top: Site 2. Massebahs and stone bowls. Bottom: Site 39b. Remains of Chalcolithic copper smelting furnace. This page: Site 2. Smelting furnace.

Five superimposed metallurgical working floors, with remains of smelting furnaces and metallurgical waste, were found in area G, the lowest floor resting on bedrock. Many small, bell-shaped pits, 20–40 centimeters deep, were dug in all the floors. In the lowest floor were found thirty-six pits, some of which contained date pits and bones of goats, donkeys, camels, and fish.

AREA F. About 70 meters west of the actual smelting area, on the summit of a hill, an oval-shaped tumulus, 4.8 by 3.1 meters and 50 centimeters high, was excavated, and a "floor" of carefully laid flat stones was exposed on solid rock. An unusually large quantity of sherds was found in area F, including numerous decorated sherds of Midianite ware as well as many beads of faience, carnelian, mica schist, stone, and glass, several very small copper spatulas and needles, many perforated Red Sea shells and ostrich-egg shells and remains of metallurgical activities. On the "floor" itself lay several goat horns, copper rings, two iron armlets, and many beads.

Because of its location, structures and finds, area F may be interpreted as a *bamah,* a high place, where small copper votive implements, such as were later found in the neighboring Hathor sanctuary, were cast. It seems that the small-scale metallurgical operations at area F were an integral part of the actual ritual and that the Midianites were the workshippers.

AREA I. A small working area with much metallurgical waste, but no clear structures. A large copper needle with its eye complete was found here.

AREA M. Inside a carefully built corbeled vault, a skeleton was found with its head on a flat stone as a head-rest. There were also remains of another skeleton. Both were of Proto-Boskopoid type of African origin (N. Haas).

Finds at site 2 included numerous saddle-backed red sandstone querns, flint, granite and sandstone hammer stones, mortars and pestles. Several copper implements were found, some in an "as cast" stage and unfinished. These implements were locally made.

A scarab found in area K belonged to the period of Ramses II.

In all areas, three essentially different kinds of pottery were found: ordinary wheelmade pottery, Negev type pottery, and Midianite pottery. On the basis of the ordinary pottery, site 2 was attributed to the Late Bronze Age–Iron Age I (thirteenth–twelfth centuries B.C.), a date confirmed in 1969 by the discovery of the Hathor sanctuary.

Site 200 — the Hathor Sanctuary of Timna' (map reference 14579090). Site 200, discovered in 1966 by B. Rothenberg, was a low mound, measuring 15 by 15 meters and 1.5 meters in height, leaning against one of King Solomon's Pillars. These pillars are huge, picturesque Nubian sandstone formations at the southwestern end of the Timna' Massif, located almost in the center of the ancient mining and smelting area of Timna'. It was excavated in March–June, 1969, and September–October, 1974.

STRATIGRAPHY. The mound's five strata consisted of sand, building remains, floors, and floor-like surfaces, destruction debris and many unrelated building stones — all these in a depth of less than one meter.

STRATUM I, the latest phase, represents the sanctuary's re-use during the Roman period (first century A.D.).

STRATUM II represents a period of great upheaval and destruction, a devastating earthquake, and a short revival of the Egyptian Hathor shrine by the Midianites. This final phase is dated not later than the middle of the twelfth century B.C.

STRATA III AND IV, the two main phases of the original Hathor sanctuary, are dated to the Nineteenth–Twentieth Dynasties, from the end of the fourteenth to the middle of the twelfth centuries B.C. with a short break in its occupation, apparently during or shortly after the reign of Queen Twosret.

STRATUM V, the earliest occupation of the site, is dated by pottery and flint implements to the Chalcolithic period.

The history of the Timna' Sanctuary

1. The earliest remains at the site included several shallow rock-cut pits, a few fireplaces, some undefinable building remains, and a number of Chalcolithic rope-decorated sherds and flint implements.

2. During the reign of Ramses II (1304–1237 B.C.) or perhaps Seti I (1318–1304 B.C.) of the Nineteenth Dynasty, an Egyptian shrine was erected on top of the Chalcolithic remains. An open court (9 by 7 meters) containing the *naos* (2.7 by 1.7 meters) of white sandstone, was built against the face of one of "Solomon's Pillars", into which an almost man-high niche was carved. Two well-dressed square bases have survived. These were apparently the foundations of two square pillars bearing sculptured representa-

Copper smelting camp (site 30) of the 19–20 dynasties of Egypt. It is surrounded by a defensive wall with two gate towers. The dark areas within the wall are smelting slags on the site of the copper furnaces. The rough stone remains of structures on the right are the remains of workshops. In the background are the Timna Cliffs with the ancient copper mines at their foot.

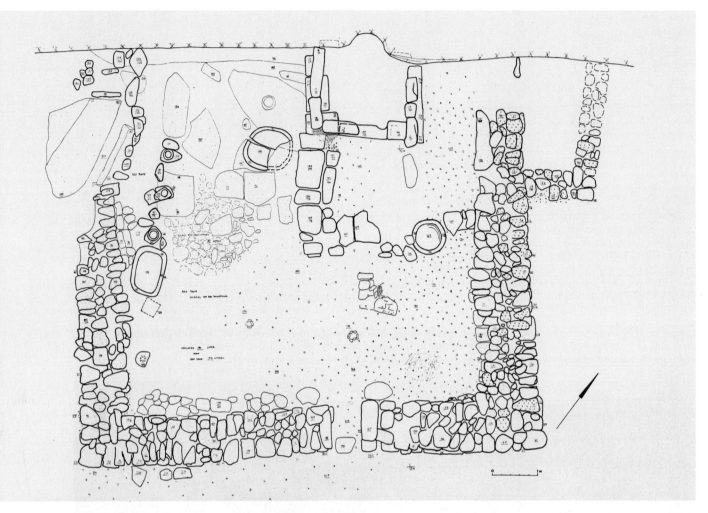

Above: Plan of the Timna' sanctuary in its last "Midianite" phase. Left: Site 2. Corbel-vaulted tomb containing remains of two bodies of Afro-Egyptian origin. Opposite page: site 200. The Hathor sanctuary in its last "Midianite" phase.

tions of the head of Hathor, which were found in the excavation. One end of a large stone architrave had rested on the Hathor pillars, and the other end rested in two niches cut in the rock face. Several square pillars bearing traces of hieroglyphic inscriptions lay around the *naos*. A number of Egyptian incense altars were found, as well as two flat, rectangular offering tables of white sandstone. The original shrine seems to have been deliberately destroyed, but there is no evidence to indicate by whom.

3. The shrine was repaired, re-using many parts and objects from the original structure. A new floor was laid of crushed white stone, perhaps debris from the original shrine. The walls of the court were repaired and expanded to 9 by 9 me-

ters. The *naos* was rebuilt with a lime plaster finish. A vestibule or pronaos of large flat stones was built in front of the *naos*. Inscribed objects found on the floor suggest that the second shrine may have been built by Ramses III. It was destroyed by an earthquake and the site was temporarily abandoned.

4. The shrine was again used for worship a short while after its destruction, after undergoing numerous alternations: an offering bench was built against the interior of the walls flanking the entrance. An additional chamber was built outside the east wall of the court, perhaps for the use of the priest. Along the west wall a row of *massebahs* was erected, consisting of monoliths and various Egyptian installations in secondary use, such as a Hathor pillar, standing on its head, incense altars, square pillars as well as a large basin, filled with a large granite boulder.

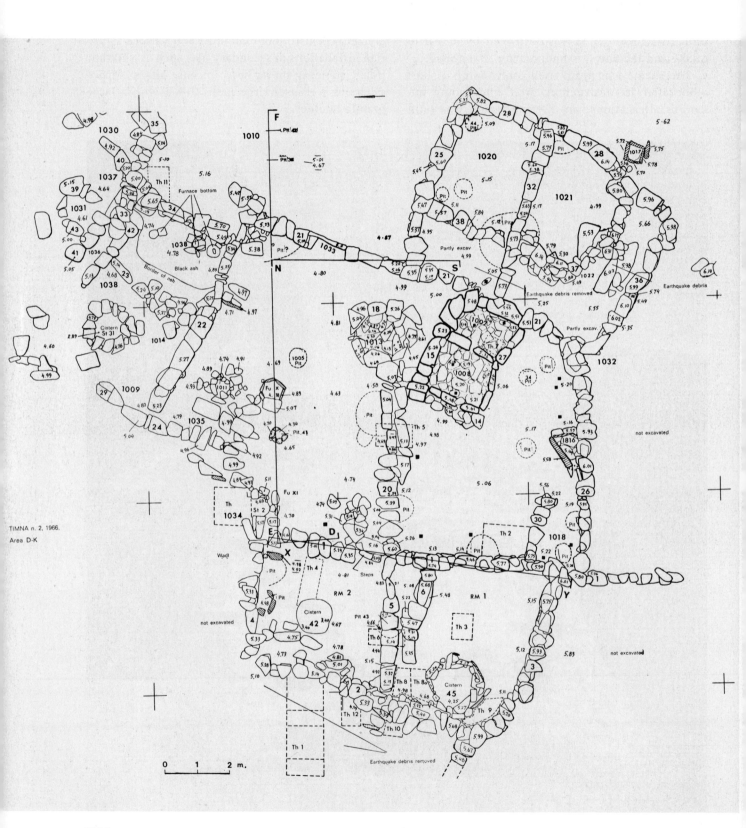

TIMNA n. 2, 1966.
Area D-K

0   1   2 m.

Opposite page: Site 2. Plan of workshops D-K.
Below, left to right: IA I bowls — 12th–11th centuries B.C.; Site 200. Faience ring stand with double cartouche of Ramses III. Bottom: "midianite"' ware, IA I.

Along the east and west walls of the court was uncovered a large amount of a heavy red and yellow cloth with beads woven into it. This cloth was part of a tent in the final phase of the sanctuary. There is convincing evidence for attributing this tent sanctuary to the Midianites, who returned to Timna' after the termination of the Egyptian copper-mining expeditions. The Midianites, in using Egyptian architectural elements, effaced all the Hathor representations and any visible hieroglyphic inscription. The central niche in the *naos* was left empty, but in the *naos* itself a Midianite copper snake with a gilded head was found in situ. This was the only votive object found in the *naos*.

THE VOTIVE OFFERINGS found in strata III–II of the shrine can be divided into two main groups:

1. Egyptian-made votive offerings, including pottery, stone and alabaster vessels, faience beads, wands, ringstands, menats, faience bowls, glass, gold ornaments, faience animal figurines, scarabs and seals, and several Hathor figurines and plaques. There was also a small sphinx, perhaps representing Ramses II.

2. Non-Egyptian, probably Midianite votive offer-

Site 200. Row of massebahs with secondary use of Egyptian pillar and altars as found in situ.

ings: a cast copper figure of a phallic idol, a copper sheep figurine, numerous rings, amulets, earrings, armlets, and many copper tools. There were also large numbers of shell beads from the Red Sea and much beautifully decorated Midianite pottery.

THE POTTERY found in the shrine was of the same three types as were found previously at site 2:

1. Ordinary, wheelmade pottery dating mainly to the Iron Age I with some Late Bronze Age sherds.

2. Handmade, primitive cooking pots and bowls of the Negev type, found previously in the central Negev and the 'Arabah.

3. Bichrome pottery, which did not appear in the first phase of the Hathor sanctuary. Its decorations included large birds, probably ostriches, and many sophisticated geometric designs. This pottery, found in Timna' for the first time in a stratified context and dated absolutely by inscriptions, is identical with pottery found by Parr-Dayton in Hedjaz (northwest Arabia) and is therefore called Midianite.

The pottery found in site 200 is dated by the inscribed Egyptian objects. There were many cartouches containing the names of Nineteenth Dynas-

Site 200. Square Hathor pillar. The face of Hathor seems to have been deliberately damaged.

ty pharaohs: Seti I (1318–1304 B.C.) (?), Ramses II (1304–1237 B.C.), Merneptah (1236–1223 B.C.), Seti II (1216–1210 B.C.), and Queen Twosret (1209–1200 B.C.) (?). Twentieth Dynasty names include Ramses III (1198–1166 B.C.), Ramses IV (1166–1160 B.C.), and Ramses V (1160–1156 B.C.). In the Roman period, the site of the sanctuary was again partly occupied for a brief period.

Site 28 (Beer Ora, map reference 14829032). Site 28 is located about 1 kilometer north of the well called today Beer Ora (formerly Bir Hindis). It consisted of two very large and several small heaps of large circular slag plates (60–80 centimeters in diameter) with cast-in hole in the center. Eight areas were excavated.

AREA A. A copper-smelting furnace (Fu I) was excavated in area A. This was a pit in the ground (60 centimeters in diameter) with a semicircular row of stones around the rim, to support the upper part of the furnace wall that rose above the level of the working surface. The furnace was 70 centimeters high, its interior clay lined. In front of the furnace was a slag-tapping pit.

AREA F. A second smelting furnace (Fu IV), similar to Fu I, was unearthed in area F. The original slag pit had been dug in the form of a wide ring, with a hard core left in the center for the casting-in of the center hole, found in all the slag circles of site 28.

AREA E. A shallow, oval-shaped melting-casting hearth, 60 by 45 centimeters and 30 centimeters

Site 30, surrounded by a wall with two gate towers. A large slag heap in its center makes this site a major copper production site. Wadi 'Arabah and Mountain of Edom, in background.

deep, was found full of wood ash. A row of small stones plastered with red clay enclosed its rim. A quantity of typical melting slag and casting waste was found here.

A crucible furnace, where copper was melted in crucibles prior to being cast, was also found in addition to the two copper-smelting furnaces, where metallic copper was produced from copper ores.

In the other areas excavated, storage pits lined with large slag plates, as well as workshops and a workers' kitchen, built of slag, were uncovered. Roman pottery of the second century A.D. was found in every area. There is reason to assume that site 28 was the central Roman copper-smelting site of the western 'Arabah, operated by the Third Legion Cyrenaica.

Site 30 (map reference 14479093). Site 30 is a large-walled smelting camp, 40 by 80 meters. The excavation of the entire camp is planned in order to study for the first time a copper extraction plant from the fourteenth–twelfth centuries B.C. Excavations were begun in 1974, and so far about 500 square meters have been exposed.

STRATIGRAPHY. Three strata (I–III) were distinguished. Strata III–II consisted of many super-imposed working floors, separated by wind- and water-laid sand, and the uppermost stratum, I, appears only in part of the site and was relatively short-lived.

In strata III–II, a number of rough enclosures were found, which served as workshops and contained

Site 30 at end of 1974 season of excavations.

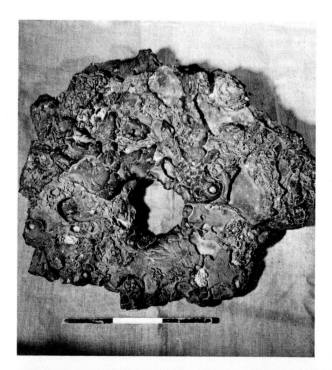

smelting furnaces. Large heaps of broken-up slag were piled up between the workshop enclosures. There were also a few more solid rectangular structures, stores, workshops, and perhaps dwellings.

Numerous small, mostly stone-lined pits were dug into the working flowers of III and II. The areas between the work enclosures, not occupied by slag dumps, were used for charcoal piles and clay heaps. Stratum I had only some very rough enclosures and shallow pits next to the smelting installations.

Most of the finds are directly related to the metallurgical character of site 30 — ores, slag, charcoal, stone implements, but also many bones of goats, camels, and fish, some beads, food remains, textiles, baskets, and ropes.

In strata III–II, a large quantity of mainly Iron Age I sherds was found, belonging to the same three kinds — Midianite, Negev, ordinary ware — found in the Hathor sanctuary. There was also much Egyptian pottery.

In stratum I, Iron Age I pottery was uncovered, but the exact date of this final stratum of site 30 is not yet firmly established.

METALLURGY. In strata III and II, small clay-lined, bowl-shaped smelting furnaces were found, dug into the ground, 30–40 centimeters in diameter and about 50 centimeters deep. There were no tapping pits, but the slag was apparently tapped out of the furnaces onto the ground and was then crushed to extract the metallic copper pellets entrapped in the slag. Many small tuyeres (about 10 centimeters in diameter) were found in the slag heaps and next to the furnaces. There were also several melting furnaces, with crucible fragments and melting-casting slag.

In stratum I, a new technology appeared: the furnaces were much bigger, pear-shaped, and lined with a thick layer of slag-tempered clay. There were also very large tuyeres (about 20–25 centimeters in diameter) made of the same material, and the slag was tapped into well-prepared tapping pits (without a cast-in hole). The fact that stratum I followed stratum II with no great lapse of time is interesting, as stratum I represents a new highly developed extractive metallurgical technique.

Strata III–II correspond well with the picture obtained in the excavations of site 2, with the exception of the tapping furnaces Fu I–IV, which represent the final development of the smelting technology at site 2 and are different from the furnaces of stratum I at site 30.

Mining Area, Site 212 (map reference 14329115). During the survey of the Timna' Valley by the 'Arabah Expedition (1959–61, 1967), shafts and galleries were discovered in white sandstone formations at the foot of the 300 meter high Timna' Cliffs. These were excavated in 1974–76 in collaboration with a specialized team of miners and mining surveyors of the Bergbau Museum Bochum, Germany. The excavations in

Opposite page, top: Site 28. Slag circle from a large slag heap — typical tapping slag. Bottom: Site 28. Roman smelting site near the well of Beer Ora. It has the largest slag heap in the 'Arabah. This page: Site 212. Entrance to underground LBA-IA I mining system. Horizontal galleries follow the horizon of copper mineralization.

Below: Site 212. Underground gallery. A shaft leads down into a second gallery system below. Bottom: Site 212. Rock-cut shaft, 21 meters deep, with niches for footholds cut into its sides. Opposite page, top: Map of underground workings of the Early Iron Age I mine, excavated in 1976. The upper level is on the left (shaded). The narrow shaded section running parallel to the gallery is the "ventilation shaft". Bottom: Plan of the Early Bronze Age mine. The shaded section is the upper level. Access was gained initially by shaft T31.

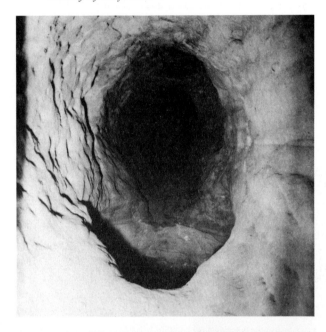

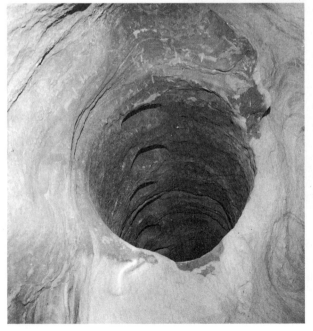

the mines were directed by B. Rothenberg and I. Ordentlich.

Three different elements of mining technology were revealed in the area investigated: 1. Deep shafts, some more than 20 meters deep, carved vertically into the cupriferous white sandstone formations. 2. Narrow galleries (about 70 centimeters wide and 1 meter high), driven horizontally into the white rock, branched and sometimes widened out underground. One system of galleries had two superimposed levels, or floors, connected by a narrow shaft. In one of the three gallery systems cleared in 1974, pottery of ordinary and Negev type was found, confirming the Iron Age I date of these systems. In another shaft-and-gallery system of a more primitive nature, excavated in 1976, shafted mining hammers were found together with Early Bronze Age pottery. This is the earliest shaft-and-gallery copper mining system known so far. It adds considerable importance to the excavation of an Early Bronze Age II smelting site in the 'Arabah (see below, site 201a) because these mines, found for the first time in Timna', represent large-scale, sophisticated enterprises and greatly alter many of the basic data of mining history and early metallurgy. 3. On many slopes above the cupriferous white sandstone layer, silt-filled saucer-like round areas (2–6 meters in diameter) had been noted since 1959 and interpreted as ore-dressing installations, where copper ore, mined nearby, was separated from the unwanted gangue. Investigations by a team of the 'Arabah Expedition in 1975, led by A. Bercovici and I. Ordentlich, established that these "plates" are in fact silt-filled mining shafts of many periods, dug through the upper conglomerate cover and into the copper ore-bearing sandstone, either for prospecting or as part of the shaft-and-gallery mining systems.

Finds of pottery, stone, and metal mining tools on the plate areas and in the mines indicate a Late Bronze Age–Iron Age I date for the major mining activities at Timna'. The exact date of the three different mining techniques and their interrelationship is still under investigation.

The discovery of Late Bronze Age–Iron Age I shaft gallery systems in Timna' is of great significance for the history of mining, as so far such sophisticated technology was known only in the Roman mines of Europe.

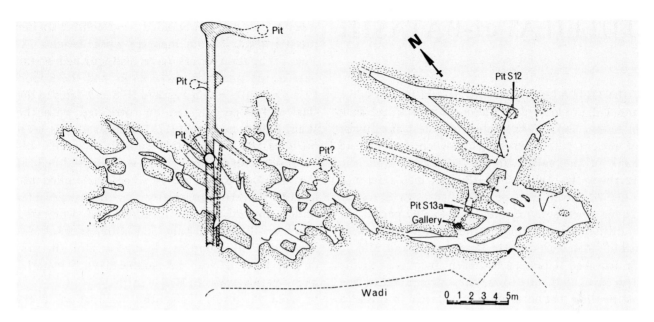

Site 201a (map reference 15109175)

Site 201a is located in the 'Arabah, about 3 km north of Timna'. It consists of a widely dispersed group of enclosures, one of which was excavated in 1977. It was found to be a habitation and workshop structure, typical of the Early Bronze Age II in the Negev and Sinai, and contained pottery and flint implements of this period.

A quality of small, crushed slag pieces was found in the excavation, but no smelting furnace has yet been uncovered. The slag is similar to the Chalcolithic smelting slag from site 39, but it shows the flow-structure of a typical tapping slag. This is the earliest evidence for the tapping of slag found so far and represents an advanced stage of extractive metallurgy.

The discovery of an Early Bronze Age copper smelting site in the Timna' area provides the first evidence of copper smelting in the 'Arabah in this period and proves that during this age of urbanization an extensive network of small settlements continued to exist also in semi-arid and arid areas and that all known deposits of copper ores in the area were mined and smelted by these Early Bronze Age II settlers on an industrial scale.

B. ROTHENBERG

BIBLIOGRAPHY

J. Petherick, *Egypt, The Soudan and Central Africa*...Edinburgh and London, 1861 • W. M. F. Petrie, *Researches in Sinai*, London, 1906 • Musil, Arabia Petraea, 2, 185–87 • F. Frank, *Aus der Araba* 1 *(ZDPV* 57), (1934), 233–34; 241–42 • N. Glueck, *Explorations in Eastern Palestine* 2 *(AASOR* 15, 1935), 42–45, 139; *idem, The Other Side of the Jordan*, New Haven, 1940, 77–79; 84 • B. Rothenberg, *God's Wilderness*, London, 1961; *idem, PEQ*, 1962, 5–71 • B. H. McLeod, *ibid.*, 68–71 • N. Glueck, *BA* 28 (1965), 70–87 • B. Rothenberg, *ZDPV* 82 (1966), 125–35; *idem, Museum Haaretz Bulletin* 8 (1966), 86–93; 9 (1967), 53–70; *idem, Negeb, Archaeology in the Negeb and the 'Arabah*, Tel-Aviv, 1967 (Hebrew); *idem, Museum Haaretz Bulletin* 10 (1968), 25–35; 12 (1970), 28–35 • A. Lupu, *Bulletin of the Historical Metallurgy Group* 4 (1970), 21–23 • A. Lupu and B. Rothenberg, *Archaeologia Austriaca* 47 (1970), 91–130 • P. J. Parr, G. L. Harding, and J. E. Dayton, *Bulletin of the Institute of Archaeology, London* 8–9 (1970), 193–242 • B. Rothenberg, *Midianite Timna*, London, 1971; *idem, Timna, Valley of the Biblical Copper Mines*, London, 1972; *idem, The New Timna Project, Auschnitt*, Bochum, 1976.

TULEILAT el-BATASHI

IDENTIFICATION. The two Batashi barrows (T-1 and T-2) are located on the north bank of the Vale of Sorek, about 7 kilometers (4 miles), northwest of ancient Beth-Shemesh. Nearby on the opposite bank of the valley, about 750 meters from the barrows, lies Tell Batashi (Betesh, map reference 142132), which may be identified with Ekron or Timna. Sherds dating from the Israelite period onward have been found on the mound, while Neolithic, Chalcolithic, Early Bronze Age, and Middle Bronze Age II pottery has been uncovered in the area around the barrows, thus strengthening the assumption that occupation first started in this area and later shifted to the site of the mound.

EXCAVATIONS. Excavations were conducted at the site during March and July–August, 1955, by J. Kaplan, on behalf of the Israel Exploration Society. The work was concentrated in three areas: A and B, near the large barrow T-1, and C, cutting through the northern part of the barrow itself.

Neolithic sherds of level IVa (identical with Jericho IX).

Area A, south of T-1, yielded two Neolithic shelter pits—level IV—contemporary with Jericho IX. Two occupation layers were distinguished at the base of the pits: the lower, IV-b, and the upper, IV-a. Level III, which overlaid IV-a and dates to the Chalcolithic period, can be correlated with the Wadi Rabah culture (q.v.). The finds of this level included several Neolithic Yarmukian sherds. Level II of the Early Bronze Age was exposed only in the northwest part of area A, where it is sunken into level III. Level I is represented by the remains of a Middle Bronze Age II pit, which had penetrated into level II. Isolated Late Chalcolithic remains (designated III-h), found in a limited area on the surface of level III, can be paralleled with material from Wadi Gaza, site H.

In **area B**, three Chalcolithic occupation layers were exposed. The two upper layers, III-a and III-b, contained Ghassulian pottery while the lowest layer, III, resting on virgin soil, included pottery identical to the Wadi Rabah culture.

In **area C**, the excavation cut across the large barrow and exposed two cells, numbers 1 and 2 (each measuring 1.7 by 1.9 meters), built of river cobbles. Behind these two cells to the south was uncovered part of a third cell (number 3). Round ovens of baked clay as well as Middle Bronze Age II-B–C pottery were found on the floor of the cells. The finds included a Hyksos scarab.

To the east of the cells were concentric walls, which decreased in height toward the edge of the barrow. The space between the walls was packed tightly with small stones. These concentric walls apparently served as clamps to hold together the small stones forming the barrow. The excavation showed the barrow to date to the Middle Bronze Age II-B–C. This type of barrow is so far unparalleled in Israel, but common in Western Europe where it is known as the "long barrow" type. The barrow, which is linked with the remains of level I in area A, was erected near the earlier remains of the Neolithic and Chalcolithic periods.

POTTERY

The pottery of the upper level IV-a is identical with that of Jericho IX and Kathleen Kenyon's Pottery Neolithic A. The dominant characteristic is the red-painted (incising being entirely absent) decoration of zigzags and triangles in bands around the vessel on a cream or pink burnished ground. The burnishing of the decorative bands, generally a glossy or dark red, is applied with a brush. Part of the un-decorated pottery is also burnished. A large number of objects are parts of vessels typical of the Jericho IX culture: various knobbed handles, small triangular or rectangular ledge handles applied near the rim of the vessel, as well as ring bases.

The pottery of level IV-b differs from that of IV-a mainly in its decoration, which is executed in a primitive finger-painting technique, in colors ranging from dark-red to blackish. Here, too, part of the undecorated pottery is burnished. Especially common are sherds of the "dark-faced burnished ware," first noted in the 'Amuq Plain and at Mersin.

The pottery of level III belongs to the Wadi Rabah culture. A rich assemblage of this pottery was found, including sherds of the distinctive black-burnished ware. The pottery of levels III-a and III-b does not deviate from the Ghassulian assemblage, and the same is true of the pottery of level II (Early Bronze Age II) and level I (Middle Bronze Age I).

CONCLUSIONS

1.) At Tuleilat Batashi a clear occupation layer (IV-a) identical with Jericho IX, was again discovered in Israel (the first such layer was found at Lod). Level IV-b, despite its proximity to IV-a, is wholly different, and yet it is not unlikely that IV-a developed from IV-b. Combining the new material from Batashi and Lod with the material from Jericho has permitted a correlation with Mersin, strata XXIII–XXIV.

2.) In area B, evidence was found for the second time in Israel of the priority of the Wadi Rabah culture in comparison with the Ghassulian.

3.) The meager Yarmukian material uncovered at Batashi together with the material from level III confirms the priority of Jericho IX compared with the Yarmukian culture, as in fact, was already established by J. Garstang and Kathleen Kenyon.

4.) To the varied types of Middle Bronze Age II burials known so far in Israel may now be added the long barrow, which is common mainly in Western Europe.

J. KAPLAN

BIBLIOGRAPHY

J. Kaplan, *IEJ* 5 (1955), 273–74; idem, *EI* 5 (1958), 9–25 (Hebrew), *83–*84 (English summary) • J. Naveh, *IEJ* 8 (1958), 166–70 • F. Hole, *Syria* 36 (1959), 154 • J. Kaplan, *BASOR* 156 (1959), 15–22; 159 (1960), 32–36; 194 (1969), 2–39; idem, *JNES* 28 (1969), 197–99.

TULEILAT el-GHASSUL

IDENTIFICATION. Tuleilat el-Ghassul is situated in the southern Jordan Valley, about 2 kilometers (1.5 miles) northeast of the Dead Sea. The site is very large, consisting of some dozen low mounds extending along the northern side of the Wadi Djarafa, on the gently sloping Plain of Moab, 850 feet below sea level. The importance of the site was recognized by A. Mallon, who noted the unusual equally abundant flint and ceramic surface finds. Excavations revealed the remains of some of the oldest known copper artifacts (adzes and a fish hook) found in Palestine. This discovery was to make the terms "Chalcolithic" and "Ghassulian culture" almost synonymous in the vocabulary of Palestinian archaeology.

EXCAVATIONS

Tuleilat Ghassul was excavated by the Pontificial Biblical Institute in Jerusalem, under the direction of A. Mallon and R. Köppel during seven seasons between 1929 and 1938 and by R. North in 1960. Later excavations on behalf of the British School of Archaeology and the University of Sydney, Australia, were undertaken by B. Hennessy in 1967 and 1975 (further campaigns are planned).

Stratigraphy of the Site. The unraveling of the stratigraphy of the small mounds of Ghassul proved extremely difficult for the excavators. A. Mallon and his collaborators made several deep probes down to virgin soil and distinguished four major levels of occupation in mound 1. R. Köppel excavated mound 3, uncovering level IV in 1936, and level III in 1938. Levels II and I have never been sufficiently exposed for definite conclusions to be drawn. The Hennessy campaigns have added further precision to the stratigraphic picture by distinguishing a (provisional) scheme of nine major building phases in the continuing work on the northern part of mound 1. Mallon's level IV-B–IV-A has been subdivided into phases A–D. The stratigraphy of Ghassul is complicated by the fact that all the neighboring knolls were probably occupied differently and matching the levels or phases can be accomplished only after a more detailed analysis of the finds has been made, and the evolution of types has been established.

Architecture. No evidence has been uncovered

Both pages, top left to right: Painted cornets, a typical form at Ghassul; Bases of pottery vessels with mat impressions. Bottom, left to right: Mound 1. View from the north; Mound 3.

that the large village of Ghassul was ever encircled by a protective wall. The buildings of Ghassul are of stone and mud-brick construction (sometimes only of the latter), with reed and mud roofs. The bricks are of flattened bread-loaf shape and size, frequently with finger impressions to catch the mud mortar. The houses are rectangular or squarish in shape, grouped without evident plan around small courtyards. Storage pits, silos, and stone rings are common features of the house interiors and courtyards alike. The latter also contain bake ovens.

It is difficult to estimate the population of Ghassul because of the problem of determining how much of the site was occupied at any one time. However, in its heyday it was the regional center, and its population must have numbered in the thousands. **Pottery.** Ghassulian pottery is of a distinctive type. It is generally well made, thin, and well fired. Despite earlier reports, there is no compelling evidence that even a slow wheel figured in its manufacture, although the tournette came into use during this period (as at Beersheba). The pots were

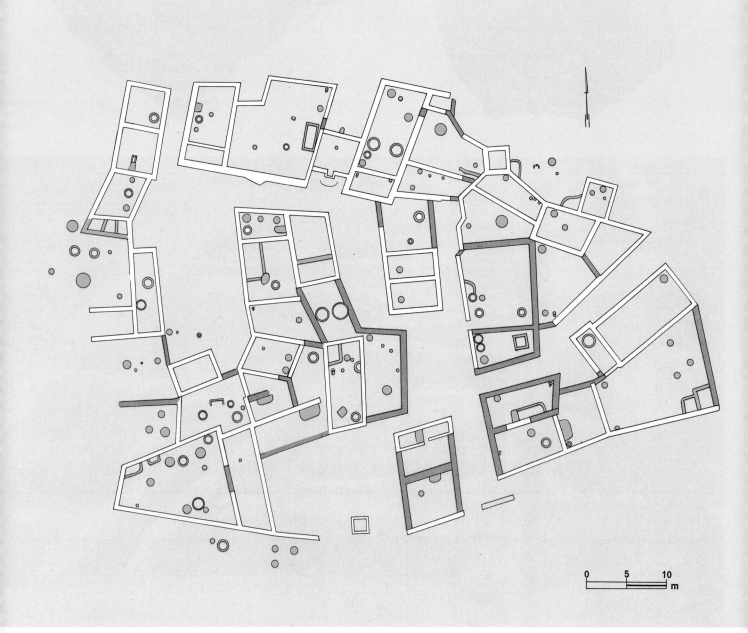

Opposite page: Mound 1. Stratum IV. This page, above: Sherd decorated with relief of snake. Right: Sherd with painted decoration of deer and bird. Below: Bird wall painting.

Tuleilat Ghassul. Wall painting, Chalcolithic period.

sometimes set out to dry on straw mats and picked up the mat impressions on the bases. The pottery of Ghassul is painted, molded, incised, and impressed. The repertory includes hole-mouth jars (an innovation), pithoi and storage jars of various sizes, V-shaped bowls, cups, particularly those of the distinctive cornet (cone) shape, churns ("bird vases"), strainer jars, and spoons. Loop and lug handles (often pierced), and applied rope molding decorated with finger impressions, incisions, or punctates are prominent features. Sometimes slips are used, and red-painted decoration is common in both geometric and naturalistic patterns.

Stone Industry. The Ghassulian stage is the last one in which flint artifacts assume a major importance in the economy, except for knives and sickle blades, which continue in use. For most other purposes, copper begins to replace flint. In general the flint assemblage displays a marked conservatism, containing many of the Near Eastern Late Neolithic traits. At Ghassul this includes hundreds of bifacially worked tools loosely called chisels (but which are more properly differentiated into categories of axes, adzes, gouges, and [true] chisels).

Many of these tools have ground and polished working edges. Backed, rectangular, truncated blades, commonly with edge luster, occur in large numbers. These must have been hafted for use as sickle tools, further proof of the importance of agriculture. One of the most common Ghassulian tools is the fan-shaped tabular flint scraper knife, probably used for skinning animals and scraping the hides. On some of these implements the bulb of percussion has been removed from the thin oval flake by secondary chipping. Projectile points are quite rare, indicating the importance of domestic flocks in providing milk, meat, hides, and bone. The flint assemblage also includes scrapers, knives, denticulates, double notches, perforators, and choppers. An additional artifact is the not uncommon small flint bladelet. Its use is unclear, since such bladelets are rarely retouched. The quite frequent occurrence of triherdal picks, along with the axes, adzes, and gouges may indeed indicate woodworking as a common pursuit (as well as a more abundant forest cover than is found today in the local area). Other stone finds are a single bladelet of obsidian, as well as limestone amulets, mace heads,

Fan-shaped scrapers.

cosmetic pallets, mortars, and a rare V-shaped bowl. One example of an alabaster bowl-rim fragment also occurs. Basalt, imported probably from the Galilee or Golan, is a common material for both fine and rough uses: fenestrated and V-shaped bowls (some with delicate incised decoration), mortars, pestles, querns, and hoe blades.

Bone, Shell, and Ornament. The bone industry of Ghassul is quite rich. Among the utilitarian objects found are awls, eyed needles, weaving shuttles, cloak pins, and gorges for fishing. Ornamental bone includes pendants, beads, and bangles. Worked shell is represented by beads and pectorals.

Murals. Perhaps the most distinctive feature of Ghassul is its own unique Palestinian art form — mural paintings. They occur in combinations of red, brown, black, yellow, and white mineral paints on both mud and (more commonly) lime-plastered walls, in both geometric and naturalistic designs. The best known example is the eight-pointed Star

of Ghassul which combines the geometric form with "spook" masks and imaginary creatures. Other paintings depict a tiger-like reclining figure, a procession of feet facing what remains of another figure with a star at his back, and a lovely painting of a very life-like and delicate figure of a dove-like bird.

Religious Practice. The most recent excavations may have provided the first real evidence of a religious installation at Ghassul. While the mural paintings have suggested religious cults, painting is too common in itself to be assigned a cultic function. The association of other elements does not help to assess the religious meaning, if any, of the Star mural. It has been suggested that the cornet drinking cups may have served a ritual function and that the fenestrated bowls in both basalt and ceramic were offering stands or incense burners. Small limestone fiddle-shaped figurines suggest the fertility or the mother-goddess cult, as do the numerous small clay animal figurines.

Domestication of Plants and Animals. At Ghassul, the domestication of plants and animals was well advanced, which helps define quite closely the course of the everyday life of the inhabitants, as well as their annual round of activities. It can be said that they were a horticultural and a pastoral people, not unlike those living in the area today. An analysis of the seed remains found in the excavations has revealed three categories of plants: fruits, cereals, and pulses. These are represented by carbonized olive pits *(Olea europaea)* and date pits *(Phoenix dactylifera),* barley *(Hordeum vulgare)* and wheat, and lentils *(Lens culinaris).* Flax was probably also grown, since fragments of linen were discovered in the excavations.

Animal bones recovered include only domesticated species, emphasizing the probability that little hunting was practiced by the Ghassulians. The rarity of projectile points suggests this, as well. Among the faunal remains are sheep *(Ovis? aries),* goat *(Capra hircus),* cattle *(Bos taurus),* and pig *(Sus scrofa).* A few bones of equids (horse and donkey) have also been identified.

Physical Anthropology. Some two dozen burials of infants, mostly interred in jar fragments, have been discovered beneath house floors. A study of the remains indicates that the population was tall, robust, and generally well-fed. The relatively small number of infant burials encountered in ten seasons of excavations, combined with the normally expected high mortality rate, indicates that, even for infants, jar burial was not the common method of disposing of the dead. The identification of the Adeimeh cist-grave area (several kilometers to the southeast) as the necropolis of Ghassul cannot be upheld on the basis of current information.

Carbon-14 Dating. Carbon-14 dates of this and other sites of the same archaeological horizon indicate that Ghassul and its sister-sites belong to the fifth, as well as the fourth, millennium B.C. Testing of a sample of wood charcoal from Köppel's 1938 level III has produced a date of 5500 $\pm$ 110 B.P. (4410 $\pm$ 120 B.C.). The several radiocarbon dates from the Beersheba sites average around a corrected date of 4000 B.C. The uppermost level of Ghassul, based on other comparative cultural elements, could probably be assigned a similar date.

Climate and Environment. During recent years evidence has been accumulating from archaeology and other scientific disciplines that the climate of the period of Ghassul and the Near East generally was less severe than it is today. During Sub-Boreal times, the rainfall regime was probably more conducive to a more luxuriant vegetation, either in the amount of precipitation or in its distribution, producing a more effective rainfall pattern. It would seem that a fluctuation of the climate, which produced a progressive dessication of the desert edges, made life at Ghassul progressively difficult, and eventually impossible.　　　J. R. LEE

BIBLIOGRAPHY

A. Mallon, R. Köppel, Annual Excavation Reports in *Biblica* (1930–1938) • A Mallon, R. Köppel, and R. Neuville, *Teleilat Ghassul I,* Rome, 1934 • R. Köppel, H. Senes, J. W. Murphy, and G. S. Maham, *Ghassul II,* Rome, 1940 • R. North, *Ghassul 1960 Excavation Report,* Rome, 1961 • B. Hennessy, *Levant* 1 (1969), 1–24 • J. R. Lee, *Chalcolithic Ghassul: New Aspects and Master Typology,* Ph. D. Thesis, Hebrew University, Jerusalem, (1973) (publication planned).

Opposite page: Infant jar burial. This page: Jar burial.

'UBEIDIYA

IDENTIFICATION. A prehistoric site on the west bank of the Jordan, 3 kilometers south of the Sea of Galilee, near Tell 'Ubeidiya, 205 meters below sea level (map reference 20242328). The site was discovered in 1959 during agricultural work when a bulldozer struck a stratum of limnic deposits, known as Melanopsis, and in the opinion of L. Picard, dating from the Lower Pleistocene. The bulldozer exposed remains of the culture of early man as well as fossilized bones of extinct mammals and another animals. Since 1960, an expedition for the Research of the Pleistocene and the Prehistory of the Jordan Valley has conducted excavations at the site on behalf of the Israel Academy of Science and Humanities in cooperation with the Wenner Gren Foundation, the American Philosophical Society, and the Swiss National Fund for Anthropological Research. The outcrop of the Melanopsis deposits extend over an area of 16 square kilometers, of which some 3.6 percent were examined in the excavations. In order to ascertain the nature of the deposits and the stratigraphy of the Pleistocene strata, eight trenches of various lengths (from 80 to 160 meters) were dug. These cross sections provided the excavators with valuable evidence of the stratigraphy and revealed strata containing remains of early man and fossilized animal bones.

EXCAVATIONS

Excavations were conducted at three sites, at a distance of 200 meters from each other, for a total area of 580 square meters. Two cultural assemblages were uncovered: a Pre-Abbevillian and an Abbevillian complex, both of them in a stable stratigraphic context. In addition, living floors of early man were discovered over an area of 120 square meters.

L. S. B. Leakey designated the Pre-Abbevillian assemblage discovered by him in the Lower Pleistocene beds in the Olduvai Gorge in Africa by the name of Olduwan Culture. The lithic complex discovered in Olduvai Gorge, bed II, is however not identical with it, and it was therefore called the Israel Variant of Olduwan II Culture.

Within the Israel Variant of Olduwan II, three cultural phases, I–III, are distinguished. In phase I,

Opposite page: Handaxe, chopper and spheroids.

Opposite page: Handaxe, chopper and spheroids.
Below: The site and its surroundings, geological cross section.

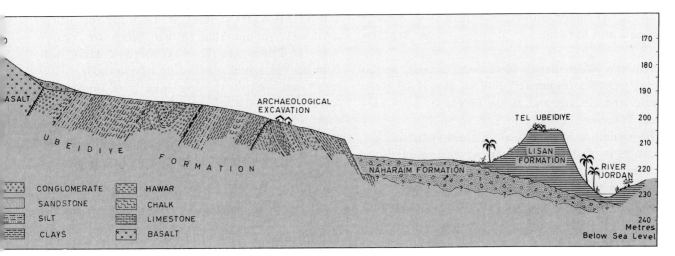

the technical capacities of man were very limited, and his tools are primitive. Phases II and III, however, show a definite advance and an increase in the number of types. All the tools were made of flint, basalt, or dolomite pebbles, collected on the spot. Among the implements are various kinds of tools, spheroids, polyhedrons, cores, flakes, and picks.

The following is the list of stone implements discovered at site A in phases II–III of the Israel Variant of Olduwan II (a summary of two excavation campaigns):

	PHASE II	PHASE III
Chopper tools	18	20
Polyhedrons	15	18
Spheroids	2	2
Picks	1	—
Cores	18	10
Cuboids	4	4
Flakes	91	63
Miscellaneous	21	26

At site B, a layer of conglomerate was found together with bones of big mammals and with various stone artifacts. Two cultural complexes can be distinguished in this layer. In the lower part were found stone implements belonging to the Israel Variant of Olduwan III, while the upper contained

mammal bones, chopping implements, and a large group of handaxes and picks of basalt. In technique this assemblage is similar to, but not identical with, the Abbevillian culture, and it is therefore called the Israel Variant of the Abbevillian Culture. The fossilized bones are those of elephant, rhinoceros, hippopotamus, giraffe, several species of gazelle, horse, rodents, tortoises, and fish. G. Haas has tentatively identified about eighty species of animals so far. Numerous fossilized mammalian bones were found broken or split lengthwise by man. Some showed signs of having been struck with stones in an attempt to dismember them or of having been scraped with flints to remove the flesh, etc. From the kitchen middens, it appears that man ate everything that was edible. Meat was an addition to his vegetarian fare which he collected in the close surroundings, filled with abundant vegetation.

The results of the excavations at this site so far have exposed a vertical cultural profile, comprising two early complexes, one the Israel Variant of Olduwan II with three phases, and the other the Israel Variant of the Abbevillian Culture. Both complexes belong to the Lower Pleistocene and were discovered in an undisturbed stratigraphic context.

The lithic assemblage found near 'Ubeidiya is the most ancient known outside the borders of Africa. The material culture found clearly shows the presence of early man, although it is not known what his physical type was (teeth and fragments of a human skull were found). Discoveries made in the Pleistocene beds of the Jordan Rift near 'Ubeidiya can aid in understanding the cultural development in Asia and Europe.   M. STEKELIS

With the aid of heavy machinery, several geological trenches (numbered I–V, K and K–a) were excavated (Picard and Baida 1966a, b; Bar-Yosef and Tchernov, 1972).

The structure as observed in these artificial exposures is of an anticline with several undulations accompanied by a few faults. The lowermost layers at the core of the anticline have not yet been reached, and therefore the base of what is defined as the upper part of the 'Ubeidiya formation is not known.

The numerous layers in the trenches were numbered from the earliest observed layer to the latest. They were divided into four cycles, two limnic and two terrestrial. This division is based on the interpretation of the different lithologies as follows (Picard and Baida, 1966a):

1.) The Li-cycle characterized by clays, silts and limestone, ends with laminated silts, rich in freshwater mollusks, and fish remains. One layer contained mammalian bones and some artifacts and provided the only pollen spectrum analyzed to date (Horowitz in Bar-Yosef and Tchernov, 1972).

2.) The Fi-cycle is made up of clays and conglomerates (mainly beach deposits). Most of the archaeological finds and faunal remains were obtained from this member.

3.) The Lu-cycle, the upper limnic member, consists of two parts. The lower one is basically clay and chalk, while the upper part is a white grayish-yellow silt series. Only a few artifacts were encountered in it.   O. BAR-YOSEF

BIBLIOGRAPHY

M. Stekelis, *BIES* 25 (1961), 115–18 (Hebrew); idem, *Archaeological Excavations at 'Ubeidiya, 1960–1963*, Jerusalem, 1966 • L. Picard–M. Baida, *Geological Report on the Lower Pleistocene Deposits of the 'Ubeidiya Excavations*, Jerusalem, 1966 • G. Haas, *On the Vertebrata Fauna of the Lower Pleistocene Site 'Ubeidiya*, Jerusalem, 1966 • P. V. Tobias, *A Member of the Genus Homo from 'Ubeidiya*, Jerusalem, 1966 • O. Bar-Yosef, *Mada* 15 (1970/1), 143–49 (Hebrew) • O. Bar-Yosef and E. Tchernov, *On the Palaeo-Ecological History of the Site of 'Ubeidiya*, Jerusalem, (1972) • O. Bar-Yosef, *Archaeology* 28 (1975), 30–37.

YAVNEH-YAM

IDENTIFICATION. The remains of the ancient coastal city Yavneh-Yam (Minât Rubin are located some 15 kilometers (9 miles) south of Jaffa, near Kibbutz Palmaḥim. According to one theory, Yavneh–Yam was the harbor suburb of the city of Yavneh situated 8 kilometers (5 miles) to the southeast, while according to another theory it was called מחוז = port ("Mukkazi" in Egyptian inscriptions), a name also attributed to Tell el-Sultan located 6 kilometers (3.5 miles) east of Yavneh–Yam. From the Hellenistic period on Yavneh–Yam was known by the name Ιαμνητων.....λιμήν, which persisted to the end of the Crusader period.

Fortifications. The most impressive remains in this area are those of a square enclosure bounded by freestanding ramparts. More than half of this enclosure has been eroded due to the slowly rising sea level since the Pleistocene. However, the entire east rampart and parts of the north and south ramparts are preserved. The length of the east

Plan of the enclosure.

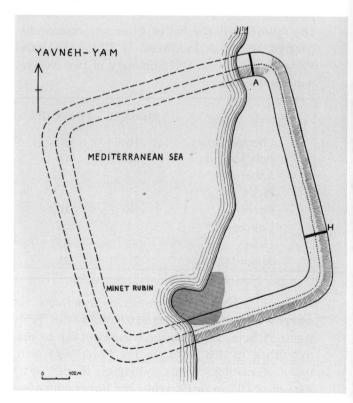

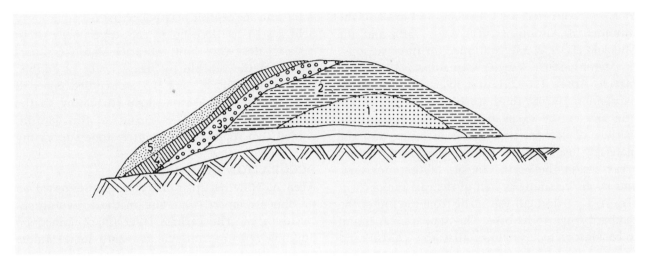

rampart is approximately 800 meters, and it can be reasonably assumed that the entire enclosure measured 800 by 800 meters, i.e., 640 dunams. A complete square enclosure of this type was first observed at el-Mishrefe in Syria. These enclosures were apparently intended to accommodate and shelter large numbers of troops with their families and herds.

No traces of occupation were uncovered inside the open enclosure, but building remains and graves were found in a strip along part of the inner rampart slope. Occupation remains were also revealed on and around the small mound located on the prominent headland of Yavneh–Yam (Minât Rubin).

EXCAVATIONS

The excavations of the fortifications at Yavneh–

Above: Schematic cross section of the fortifications. 1. Core of hamra. *2. Sheath of* hamra. *3. Glacis of* clay. *4. Covering layer of* Kurkar. *5. Stone glacis. Below: General view of the gate area — looking west.*

Yam were directed by J. Kaplan, on behalf of the Museum of Antiquities, Tel Aviv—Jaffa and the Museum Haaretz, and continued for three seasons: in March, 1967, August—September, 1968, and March—April, 1969. Haya Kaplan codirected the excavations in the third season.

The aim of the excavations was to examine the method of construction of the enclosure and the materials used. Work was concentrated in two areas: A, in the north rampart of the enclosure, and H, in the southern half of the east rampart. In area A, a vertical cut was made from the top of the rampart down to its base. The rampart was found to be constructed as follows: first, the whitish sand covering the virgin soil was leveled along the proposed alignment of the rampart. A layer of *khamra* (red clay soil of the coastal plain), 12 centimeters thick, was then laid as a bedding for the rampart core, constructed of light-brown, pounded earth, which in the final stage was cased by a sheath of *khamra,* built up from the base on both sides of the core toward the top. The glacis consisted of two layers, the lower, of heavy clay soil approximately 60—70 centimeters thick, extends from the top of the rampart down to virgin soil. A second, covering layer of crushed *kurkar* 50 centimeters thick was probably intended to prevent the damp clay soil from desiccating and pulverizing. At a later stage, an additional glacis was laid over the crushed *kurkar* layer. This new glacis was constructed in two parts: the lower, about 3 meters high, was in the form of a retaining wall inclined about 45 degrees, from which point and up to the top the rampart was paved with stone and raked approximately 30 degrees.

The Gates. The enclosure was assumed to have one entrance gate on each of its sides, by analogy with the el-Mishrefe enclosure. And indeed, three superimposed gates were exposed during excavations in area H, indicating that the enclosure was entered from the same spot during each of the periods of its use as a fortified stronghold.

The two lower gates (II and III) were built of sun-dried brick and were flanked by towers. The bottom gate III contained three pairs of gate-piers. The lower part of gate II, with only two pairs of gate-piers, was well preserved. One of the defensive towers of gate II was of a hitherto unencountered plan. The walls of the right-hand tower were 2.4 meters thick, and the narrow space between its

walls and its central massive structure apparently held a staircase leading to the upper story. Both earlier gates were built of brick and were protected on the outside by heavy walls of rubble. Above the ruins of gate II was exposed one half of a smaller rubble-stone gate (I), dating to the Late Bronze Age II. The remains of this gate included two rooms and an outer stone supporting wall.

OCCUPATION REMAINS

Area A. Nine occupation layers were exposed on the inner rampart slope and in the adjoining enclosure area. The earliest layer (9) contained no building remains, and yielded only some Middle Bronze Age II-A sherds. In layers 3—8 were found sherds and a few vessels dating from Middle Bronze Age II-B—C. Layers 1—2 contained Late Bronze Age I sherds, especially of "Tell el-'Ajjul" ware. In a trial pit dug near area A, a rubble-stone structure was found with a pithos of Tell el-'Ajjul style filled with pieces of pumice.

Area H. In a small area on virgin soil in front of gate III were found the remains of hearths. Inside and around them were Middle Bronze Age II-A sherds, fragments of an incense burner and a number of ivory plaques incised with designs. Middle Bronze Age II-A sherds were also found on the lowest floor of one of the chambers of the gate towers and in the foundation trench of one of the tower walls.

CONCLUSIONS

The Yavneh—Yam excavations have furnished information on the construction method of the terre piseé ramparts, glacis, and gate structures of the Middle Bronze Age II square enclosures. It is now evident that the square enclosure with the three-pier gates made its first appearance in the Middle Bronze Age II-A, between 2000 and 1800 B.C. The pottery found in small quantities in the two excavated areas indicate that the Yavneh—Yam enclosure was used intermittently, with alterations and repairs, throughout the Middle Bronze Age II. Only at the beginning of the Late Bronze Age I did the enclosure cease to be used as a fortification.

J. KAPLAN

BIBLIOGRAPHY

R. du Mesnil De Buisson, *Syria* 7 (1926), 289—325; 8 (1927), 277—301 • M. Dothan, *IEJ* 2 (1952), 104—17 • J. Kaplan, *IEJ* 17 (1967), 269; 19 (1969), 120—21: *idem, ZDPV* 91 (1975), 1—17.

YERUHAM, MOUNT

IDENTIFICATION. Ancient remains dating from the Middle Bronze Age I are located on the northeast spur of Mount Yeruham, above Nahal Revivim and Lake Yeruham, about 30 kilometers (18.5 miles) south-southeast of Beersheba. The site was first discovered and described by B. Rothenberg. It stretches over an area of about 5 square kilometers and includes a flat expanse of about four dunams, containing a cluster of densely built structures surrounded by a stone fence. Near this main settlement on another spur was a High Place consisting of a rock altar encircled by a stone wall. Around the main settlement was a field of tumuli and scattered structures.

EXCAVATIONS

Excavations were conducted on the site in 1963 by a joint expedition of the Department of Antiquities, the Israel Exploration Society, and the Hebrew University, in conjunction with the Fund for the Exploration of Ancient Agriculture in the Negev, headed by M. Evenari of the Hebrew University, the American Institute for Holy Land Studies in Jerusalem, and the Southeastern Baptist Theological Seminary of North Carolina. The expedition was headed by M. Kochavi.

The excavations were concentrated in the main settlement, where two Middle Bronze Age I levels were distinguished. In the upper level (I) were found traces of a poor and sparsely populated settlement of round structures, high-built tumuli (some built on the remains of level II), and large animal pens to the northeast. The settlement of level II was more densely built and contained various workshops — square structures built against the stone fence surrounding the entire settlement, and a public building with large rooms. Most of the tumuli were built in the form of circles filled in with stones.

The ceramic finds are typical of the Middle Bronze Age I and for the most part resemble contemporary finds from the settlements at Lachish, Jericho, and Jebel Qa'qir. The numerous grindstones and querns, flint scrapers and sickles found on the site indicate that seasonal agriculture was practiced nearby, probably in the adjacent Yeruham Basin, which has a high water table. Two animal figurines, unique for this period, one of clay and the other

Plan of the excavated areas.

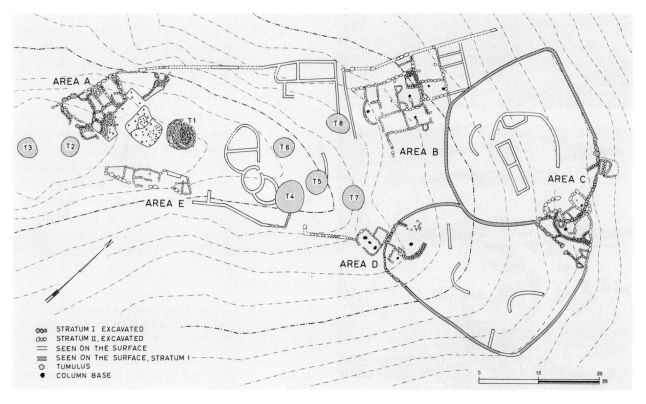

STRATUM I EXCAVATED
STRATUM II, EXCAVATED
SEEN ON THE SURFACE
SEEN ON THE SURFACE, STRATUM I
TUMULUS
COLUMN BASE

*Above, left to right: Pot found inside kiln;
Copper ingots. Below: Main settlement. Tumulus and
altar next to it, in foreground. Bottom: Public building.
Rooms on leveled rock.*

of stone, were found near a pottery kiln which still had a Middle Bronze Age I vessel inside it. In one of the dwellings was found a hoard of eighteen copper ingots of low lead content. These suggest the existence of a metal industry, which may have provided the means of exchange for trade with other settlements.

SUMMARY

The excavations at Mount Yeruḥam are of particular value because they have brought to light a settlement with clearly defined architectural remains and workshops of a period hitherto known mainly from tomb finds. The two occupation levels, both belonging to the same period, but different in character, appear to represent two separate but consecutive waves of settlement in the Negev. The Middle Bronze Age I occupants of the Negev were apparently seminomads who lived from hunting, grazing, and seasonal agriculture. They practiced their religious ceremonies at rock altars on mountain tops, and the single burials in tumuli indicate that they believed in a life after death.

M. KOCHAVI

BIBLIOGRAPHY

B. Rothenberg, *Tagliyoth Sinai,* Tel Aviv, 1958, 123–26 (Hebrew) • N. Glueck, *BASOR* 149 (1958), 10; 152 (1958), 22; *idem, Rivers in the Desert,* Tel Aviv, 1960, 78, 81–82 • M. Kochavi, *Mada'* 8 (1963), 8–15 (Hebrew); *idem, IEJ* 13 (1963), 141–42; *idem, Yediot* 27 (1964), 284–92 (Hebrew) • N. Glueck, *BASOR* 179 (1965), 11 • M. Kochavi, *Qadmoniot* 2 (1969), 39–40 (Hebrew).

YONIM CAVE

IDENTIFICATION. The Yonim Cave is located in a cliff on the right bank of the Meged Valley, a tributary of Naḥal Yiṣhar. It is located 35 meters above the valley bed and 250 meters above sea level (map reference 17072588). The cave consists of two chambers and the remains of two other chambers which had already collapsed in prehistoric times. The entrance to the main chamber faces southeast, and the second chamber faces southwest. Since the Yonim is the largest cave in the Western Galilee, and no previous prehistoric excavations had been conducted in this area, it was thought that its remains could throw light on the relationship between the famous sites of Mount Carmel and those of the Lebanese coast.

Excavations have been in progress since 1965 under the direction of O. Bar-Yosef and E. Tchernov on behalf of the Institute of Archaeology of the Hebrew University, Jerusalem.

STRATIGRAPHY AND FINDS
The stratigraphy of the excavated area reveals four complexes of levels. Bedrock has not yet been reached.

Layer A. Thin layers of black and white ash exposed to a depth of 1.5 meters. On the basis of sherds and a coin found at the bottom of the layer, it appears that the accumulation began during the second century A.D. and is mainly the result of fires made in the cave by shepherds in attempts to eliminate insects. Chunks of glass within the layer suggest that glass was produced here at one time.

Layer B. The exposed thickness of this layer varies from .1 to .9 meter. There are four interim stratigraphic units, the lower two representing phases of burials. These are covered by discontinuous floors, which are followed by a later burial. According to the lithic assemblage, the layer belongs to the Natufian culture. The burials were dug into earlier layers, some into the brecciated Mousterian deposits, and only the later burial is a constructed grave. In a total of nine graves were interred more than twenty-five individuals. Anthropological research was carried out by B. Arensburg of the Department of Anatomy, Tel Hashomer. Skeletons in the burials vary from one to many, and there are at least five couples, sometimes accompanied by

General view of Yonim Cave, looking west.

a child or infant burial, which suggest familial graves. Arrangement of the skeletons is extended, semiflexed or flexed. Most occur as primary burials, but secondary burials also exist. Associated with the burials are numerous *dentalium* shells which were used as beads. One female skeleton was adorned with a necklace of *dentalium* shells, bracelets on each arm, and a belt of bone pendants. Ground stone tools, broken mortars and bowls, pestles and mullers, were also encountered in association with the graves.

Among the numerous bone tools uncovered are broken sickle hafts, points, awls, gorgets, and spatulas. The flint assemblage included many burins and scrapers, some Heluan lunates, and sickle blades.

Layer C has been exposed only under layer B at the entrance to the cave. It has a total thickness of 1.2 meters. Its division into three sublayers was substantiated by the location of fallen blocks within sublayer C-b. Characteristic of the lithic assemblage are microliths, of which the obliquely truncated backed bladelet and a narrow curved micropoint predominate. Associated with these are scrapers and burins which define a Kebaran industry.

Layer D. Exposed under layer B inside the cave, with a total thickness of .3 to .45 meter, this layer was divided into four sublevels. Nosed and carinated scrapers, burins, and an absence of el-Wad points indicate that all four sublayers belong to the late Levantine-Aurignacian tradition. Two carnivore teeth pendants and a total of twenty bone points and awls were found in this division. This industry is known as phase IV in R. Neuville's division of the Upper Paleolithic.

Layer E is a complex of Mousterian layers numbering from E-1 to E-16, which vary in thickness from 5 to 15 centimeters. There is an unconformity between the top of layer E-1 and the overlying Aurignacian layer caused by erosion following the Mousterian occupation.   O. BAR-YOSEF

BIBLIOGRAPHY

O. Bar-Yosef and E. Tchernov, *Israel Journal of Zoology* 15 (1967), 104–40 • O. Bar-Yosef, *Qadmoniot* 3 (1970), 19–21 (Hebrew) • O. Bar-Yosef and E. Tchernov, *IEJ* 20 (1970), 141–50 • O. Bar-Yosef and N. Goren, *Paleorient* 1 (1973), 49–68 • P. Smith, *ibid.*, 69–72 • O. Bar-Yosef, B. Arensburg, and E. Tchernov, *Bema'aravo shel Hagalil,* ed. M. Yedaha (1974) (Hebrew).

Left: Grave No. 8. Two bodies laid in flexd position one above the other. In the right — a skull. Right: Plan of the cave, excavated area is dotted.

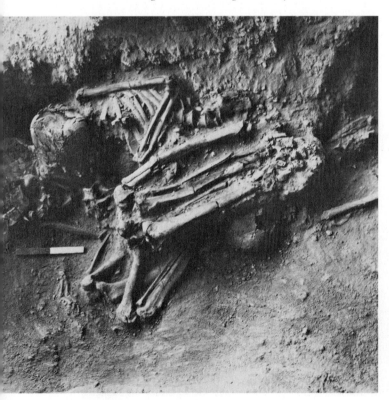
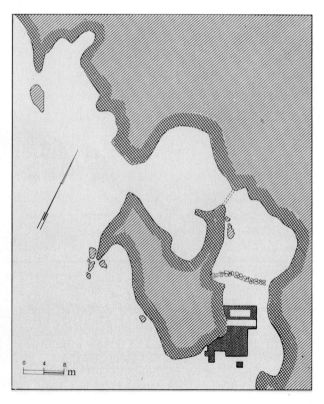

ZEROR, TEL

THE SITE AND ITS IDENTIFICATION. Tel Zeror (Khirbet et Tell Dhurur) is situated in the Sharon Plain, about .5 kilometer from the confluence of the 'Iron and Ḥavivah Brooks and the Ḥederah River (map reference 14762038). The largest of the chain of mounds on the western fringe of the Sharon, Tel Zeror's main importance in antiquity was its position near the river's ford on the western branch of the Via Maris.

The mound is composed of two promontories connected by a saddle. The northern height is smaller and steeper than the southern one, which is of greater breadth and more moderate slopes.

The mound is identified by B. Mazar with *d-r-r* in Pharaoh Thutmose III's list (No. 115) and by Y. Aharoni with *m-k-t-r* in the same list (No. 71, Migdal-yene in Amenhotep II's list). The excavations did not succeed in confirming the identification of the mound.

EXCAVATIONS. In 1928, J. Garstang spent a single day digging a trial trench at Tel Zeror. No other work was carried out at the site until the three seasons of excavations which were conducted from 1964 to 1966 by an expedition of the Japanese Society for Near Eastern Research under the direction of K. Ohata, with M. Kochavi acting as field director. A fourth season was held under the same auspices in 1974, with K. Goto as field director. The excavations were concentrated as follows:

1. **Area A,** the main excavation area, on the summit of the northern height and on its southern and eastern slopes, contained remains from the Middle Bronze Age II-A to the Roman period.

2. **Areas B and C,** on the summit of the southern height and on its southern slope, contained remains from the Middle Bronze Age II-A to the end of the Iron Age, and from the Mameluke and Arab periods.

3. **Areas D and E,** on the western slope of the saddle connecting the heights, contained remains of the Middle Bronze Age II-A urban settlement, as well as installations, pits, tombs, etc. from the other periods represented on the mound.

4. **The Cemetery,** situated on a low *khamra* hill, about 150 meters west of the mound, which was used as a burial ground at the end of the Late

Above: Typical pottery assemblage of the eleventh century B.C. — from a stone-built tomb.
Below: Philistine pottery rhyton, in the form of a lioness.
Bottom: Family tomb built of stone — eleventh century B.C.

Bronze Age, the beginning of the Iron Age, and the Hellenistic period.

Middle Bronze Age. The first settlers of Tel Zeror arrived at the site in this period. The occupation of the mound was limited to the first phase, of which four strata of settlement were uncovered, all of the Middle Bronze Age II-A. All the areas of excavations, with the exception of the cemetery, yielded remains of this period; the area inhabited is estimated at between forty and fifty dunams. Two superimposed city walls, up to 4.5 meters in width, and built of brick on stone foundations, were excavated. They were constructed on an earthern ramp, which included a moat, revealed on the western side of the mound. The discovery of the remains of the wall on three sides of the mound made it possible to trace its general course. A two-chambered tower projecting eight meters from the wall was erected on the western side of the mound. It had formed part of the earlier wall and was also constructed of brick on a very solid foundation of large field stones. The ramp, uncovered in all the excavated areas, consisted of layers of earth laid horizontally and tied together by vertical shafts filled with stones and earth. The sides of the moat were coated with a mixture of *khamra* and beaten *kurkar*. The moat was about ten meters wide, but the depth could not be determined since the excavators reached underground water 4.5 meters below the surface and it can be assumed that also in antiquity water filled the bottom of the moat.

The ceramic finds in the buildings connected to the walls and in the tower date to the early and middle phases of the period and have close affinities with pottery from other settlements of the same age in the Sharon, such as Tel Poleg, Tell Burga and Tel Mevorakh. No signs of destruction are evident from the end of this period, although there is a gap in the occupation of the mound from the eighteenth to the beginning of the fifteenth century B.C.

Late Bronze Age. No traces of fortifications were found from this period and the settlers apparently dwelled in an unwalled village. The majority of the Late Bronze Age remains were uncovered on the summit of the southern peak, in areas B and C. Part of a public building with walls one meter wide was cleared, and from the small section uncovered, it appears to have been a secular building, perhaps the palace of the local ruler. The building was abandoned at the end of the thirteenth century B.C.

Pottery Astarte figurine — beginning of the IA.

Throughout the Late Bronze Age a coppersmiths' quarter existed on the southern slope of the southern peak, where smelting furnaces, crucibles, clay bellows' pipes, and a quantity of copper slag were found. An unusual amount of Cypriot pottery uncovered in this area suggests a connection with Cyprus, which was the source of copper in that period. Evidence of the Late Bronze Age settlement was also uncovered in the other areas examined. The absence of fortifications suggests that the settlement, which spread over most of the mound, was under the protection of the acropolis on the southern hill.

The cemetery was first used for burial in the fourteenth-thirteenth centuries B.C., at which time interment was carried out in plain individual graves cut in the *khamra*. The body was laid in a supine position with the funerary offerings beside it and sometimes on the body itself. Another burial custom, mostly of children, was in pithoi or storage jars set together. The graves were oriented east-west with the heads on the west side. This cemetery bears a close resemblance to the one unearthed at Tell Abu Hawam.

Iron Age. Pits dug into the ruins of the Late Bronze Age II public building in area B, on the southern peak, represent the beginning of the Iron Age settlement. The pits contained refuse, such as animal bones of sheep and goats, and especially buffalo, and sherds of bowls, pithoi, and cooking pots typical of the period of the settlement of the Israelite tribes in the thirteenth-twelfth centuries B.C. In the eleventh century, a citadel with a casemate wall of large bricks was built on the northern height (area A).

In the cemetery a particularly rich assortment of finds are attributed to the eleventh and beginning of the tenth century B.C. Nine large cist tombs, built of stone and covered with large stone slabs, were uncovered. The tombs were dug in a south-east-northwest direction, and the bodies were laid in a supine position with the head pointing to the northwest. These were family tombs. The wealth of funerary offerings included Philistine pottery, some bronze bowls, and a socketed javelin head. Among the unique pottery finds here were lamps with closed nozzles and a figurine of a naked goddess.

Storehouses containing large numbers of stone jars from the tenth century B.C. were found above the ruins of the Iron Age citadel. In the ninth and eighth centuries, the village also spread to the southern height, which was left undefended while new fortifications were constructed on the northern height. Typical Israelite four-room houses on the northern height were surrounded by a thin wall, only 1 meter wide, which was strengthened on the interior with salients, .5 meter wide, set at 2 meter intervals. During these centuries, the Iron Age village suffered a series of destructions in the military expeditions of the Aramaeans and the Assyrians along the Via Maris. The upper part of a stone-lined cistern uncovered along the foot of the northern slope (area E) in the last season of excavations contained pottery which indicated that it was in use up to the end of the Iron Age, and it may even have been dug at that time.

Among the principal finds from this period is an ostracon incised on the base of a burnished bowl in a script which exhibits Aramaic influence: ... *b' l'lsmk;* a bronze figurine of a deity wearing a high hat and waving his hand; a steatite bowl with a palm of a hand scratched on its base; and a store jar with the Hebrew letter "mem" incised on its side.

Later Periods. Pottery from the Persian period (fifth century B.C.) was found on the summit of the northern height in large pits which penetrated through the ruins of buildings from the end of the Iron Age. In the third-second century B.C. a Hellenistic farmhouse stood on the northern hill together with a number of agricultural installations. A stepped watch-tower was erected on this hill in the Early Roman period. It apparently guarded the road to Caesarea. In the Byzantine period the settlement was located about 2 kilometers south of the mound. The Arab village Khirbet et Tell Dhurur on the southern hill dates back to the Mameluke period.

Hellenistic graves were found in area E and in the cemetery on the mound and Roman built tombs were uncovered in area D.

Summary. As the first mound to be excavated in the heart of the Sharon Plain, the investigation of Tel Zeror has shed light on the history of the entire area. The settlement on the mound reached its greatest period of prosperity in the beginning of the Middle Bronze Age II-A, the period of the urbanization of the Sharon and the coastal plain. After a period of abandonment in the Middle Bronze Age II-B and beginning of the Late Bronze Age, the mound was again settled with the revival of Egyptian rule in Palestine. A community of coppersmiths of Cypriot origin plied its trade on the mound during this time. At the end of the period the population apparently fled the unwalled settlement and sought refuge in the neighboring fortified cities, such as Gath and Yaham on the Via Maris. The Israelite tribes arrived at the central Sharon at the start of their settlement and the village they established on the mound resembles their other settlements which were discovered during the survey of the Sharon. The well-built citadel from the eleventh century B.C. and the contemporary cemetery may have belonged to the *T-k-r*, one of the Sea Peoples whose capital was at Dor, about 20 kilometers (12.5 miles) north of Tel Zeror. In the days of David the Sharon was restored to the control of Israel and the partly fortified Iron Age village continued in existence until the fall of the Israelite kingdom in 732 or 720 B.C.

M. KOCHAVI

BIBLIOGRAPHY

On the Identification: B. Maisler (Mazar), *ZDPV* 58 (1935), 78–48 • Y. Aharoni, *IEJ* 9 (1959), 110–22 .
Excavations and Finds: K. Ohata (ed.), *Tel Zeror* I–III, Tokyo, 1966–70 • M. Kochavi, *Ariel* 21 (1967/68), 65–70; idem, *Qadmoniot* 1 (1968), 128–30 (Hebrew) • K. Goto, *Orient* 5 (1969), 41–53 • H. Ogawa, *ibid.* 7 (1971), 25–48 • K. Goto, *ibid.* 9 (1973), 1–30.

CHRONOLOGICAL TABLES

The Prehistoric Periods in Palestine

PERIOD	CULTURE	ICE AGE IN EUROPE	GEOLOGICAL EPOCH	APPROXIMATE DATES
Lower Paleolithic	Lower and Middle Acheulian	Mindel	Middle Pleistocene (Quaternary)	700,000
		Mindel-Riss		to
	Upper Acheulian	Riss		120,000
Middle Paleolithic	Micoquian, "pre-Aurignacian"	Riss-Würm	Upper Pleistocene (Quaternary)	80,000
	Yabrudian and Mousterian	Würm I		
		Würm II		
Upper Paleolithic	"Emireh"	Würm III		35,000
	Emiran and other Paleolithic industries			
Epipaleolithic (Mesolithic)	Geometric Kebaran A			15,000
		Würm IV		
	Natufian	Post glacial	Holocene	8,000
Pre-pottery Neolithic	Phase A			
	Phase B			
Pottery Neolithic				5,500
Chalcolithic	Early phase			4,000 to
	Ghassulian phase			3,150

The Archaeological Periods in Palestine

Paleolithic (Old Stone Age)	700,000–15,000 BC	
Epipaleolithic (Middle Stone Age)	15,000–8,300	
Neolithic (New Stone Age)	8,300–4,500	
Chalcolithic	4,500–3,100	

Bronze Age
Early Bronze Age I A–C — 3150–2850
Early Bronze Age II — 2850–2650
Early Bronze Age III — 2650–2350
Early Bronze Age IV (IIIA) — 2350–2200
Middle Bronze Age I — 2200–2000
Middle Bronze Age IIA — 2000–1750
Middle Bronze Age IIB — 1750–1550
Late Bronze Age I — 1550–1400
Late Bronze Age IIA — 1400–1300
Late Bronze Age IIB — 1300–1200

Iron Age
Iron Age IA — 1200–1150
Iron Age IB — 1150–1000

Iron Age IIA — 1000–900
Iron Age IIB — 900–800
Iron Age IIC — 800–586

Babylonian and Persian Periods — 586–332

Hellenistic Period
Hellenistic I — 332–152
Hellenistic II (Hasmonaean) — 152–37

Roman Period
Roman I (Herodian) — 37 BC–AD 70
Roman II — AD 70–180
Roman III — 180–324

Byzantine Period
Byzantine I — 324–451
Byzantine II — 451–640

Early Arab Period — 640–1099

Crusader Period — 1099–1291

Selected List of Kings

Egypt

Pre-Dynastic Period	
4th and 3rd millennium	
Proto-Dynastic Period	
Ist Dynasty	*c.* 3100–2890 BC Narmer
IInd Dynasty	*c.* 2890–2686
IIIrd Dynasty	*c.* 2686–2613
Old Kingdom	
IVth Dynasty	*c.* 2613–2494
	Snefru
	Khufu
	Khafre
Vth Dynasty	*c.* 2494–2345
VIth Dynasty	*c.* 2345–2181
	Pepi I
First Intermediate Period	
VIIth Dynasty-Xth Dynasty	
Middle Kingdom	
XIth Dynasty	*c.* 2133–1991
XIIth Dynasty	*c.* 1991–1786
Amenemhet I	1991–1962
Senusert I	1971–1928
Amenemhet II	1929–1895
Senusert II	1897–1878
Senusert III	1878–1843
Amenemhet III	1842–1797
Amenemhet IV	1798–1970
Sebeknefrure	1789–1786
Second Intermediate Period — the Hyksos Period	
XIII–XVIIth Dynasties	
New Kingdom	
XVIIIth Dynasty	1567–1320
Ahmose	1570–1546
Amenhotep I	1546–1526
Thutmose I	1525–1512
Thutmose II	*c.* 1512–1504
Hatshepsut	1503–1482
Thutmose III	1504–1450
Amenhotep II	1450–1425
Thutmose IV	1425–1417
Amenhotep III	1417–1379

Amenhotep IV (Akhenaton)	1379–1362 BC
Smenkhkere	1364–1361
Tutankhamon	1361–1352
Eye	1352–1348
Haremhab	1348–1320
XIXth Dynasty	1320–1200
Ramses I	1320–1318
Seti I	1318–1304
Ramses II	1304–1237
Merneptah	1236–1223
Seti II	1216–1210
XXth Dynasty	1200–1085
Ramses III	1198–1166
Ramses IV–XI	1166–1085
End of New Kingdom	
XXIst Dynasty	1085–935
XXIInd Dynasty	935–730
Shishak I	935–914
Osorkon II	914–874
XXIIIrd Dynasty	817–740
XXIVth Dynasty	730–709
XXVth Dynasty	750–656
(Nubian or Ethiopian)	
Shabaka	716–695
Taharka	689–664
XXVIth Dynasty	664–525
Psamtik I	664–610
Necho II	610–595
Psamtik II	595–589
Psamtik III	526–525
XXVIIth Dynasty (Persian)	505–404
Cambyses	525–522
Darius I	521–486
Xerxes	486–466
Artaxerxes	465–424
Darius II	424–404
XXVIIIth–XXXth Dynasties	404–343

Assyria

Shalmaneser I	1274–1245 BC
Tiglath-Pileser I	1115–1077
Ashurnasirpal I	1049–1031
Shalmaneser II	1030–1019
Tiglath-Pileser II	966–935
Adadnirari II	911–891
Ashurnasirpal II	883–859
Shalmaneser III	858–824
Adadnirari III	810–783
Shalmaneser IV	782–772
Tiglath-Pileser III	745–727
Shalmaneser V	726–722
Sargon II	721–705
Sennacherib	704–681
Esarhaddon	680–669
Ashurbanipal	668–631

Neo-Babylonian Kingdom

Nabopolassar	626–605 BC
Nebuchadnezzar II	605–562
Amel-Marduk	562–560
Nabunaid	556–539
Nergal Sarussur	560–556

Persia

Cyrus	559–530 BC
Cambyses	530–522
Darius I	522–486
Xerxes	486–464
Artaxerxes I	464–423
Darius II	423–404
Artaxerxes II	404–359
Artaxerxes III	359–338
Arses (Xerxes II)	338–336
Darius III	336–331

The Kings of Judah and Israel

THE UNITED KINGDOM

Saul	ca. 1020–1004 BC
David	1004–965
Solomon	965–928

JUDAH		ISRAEL	
Rehoboam	928–911	Jeroboam	928–907
Abijam	911–908	Nadab	907–906
Asa	908–867	Baasha	906–883
Jehoshaphat	867–846	Elah	883–882
Jehoram	846–843	Zimri	882
Ahaziah	843–842	Omri	882–871
Athaliah	842–836	Ahab	871–852
Joash	836–798	Ahaziah	852–851
Amaziah	798–769	Jehoram	851–842
Uzziah	769–733	Jehu	842–814
Jotham	758–743	Jehoahaz	814–800
Ahaz	733–727	Jehoash	800–784
Hezekiah	727–698	Jeroboam	784–748
Manasseh	698–642	Zechariah	748
Amon	641–640	Shallum	748
Josiah	640–609	Menahem	747–737
Jehoahaz	609	Pekahiah	737–735
Jehoiakim	609–598	Pekah	735–733
Jehoiachin	597	Hoshea	733–724
Zedekiah	596–586		

The Hasmoneans

Jonathan	152–142 BC
Simeon	142–134
John Hyrcanus	134–104
Aristobulus	104–103
Alexander Jannaeus	103–76
Salome Alexandra	76–67
Aristobulus II	67–63
Hyrcanus II	63–40
Matthias Antigonus	40–37

The Herodians

Herod (the Elder)	37–4 BC
Archelaus	4 BC–AD 6
Herod Antipas	4 BC–AD 39
Philip	4 BC–AD 34
Herod Agrippa I	AD 37–44
Agrippa II	53–100(?)

The Procurators

Coponius	*c.* AD 6–9
M. Ambibulus	9–12
Annius Rufus	12–15
Valerius Gratus	15–26
Pontius Pilatus	26–36
Marcellus	36–37
Cuspius Fadus	41–46
Tiberius Alexander	46–48
Ventidius Cumanus	48–52
Antonius Felix	52–60
Porcius Festus	60–62
Albinus	62–64
Gessius Florus	64–66

Seleucid Kings

Seleucus I Nicator	311–281 BC
Antiochus I Soter	281–261
Antiochus II Theos	261–246
Seleucus II Callinicus	246–225
Seleucus III Soter	225–223
Antiochus III the Great	223–187
Seleucus IV Philopator	187–175
Antiochus IV Epiphanes	175–164
Antiochus V Eupator	163–162
Demetrius I Soter	162–150
Alexander Balas	150–145
Demetrius II Nicator	145–140
Antiochus VI Epiphanes	145–138
Antiochus VII Sidetes	138–129
Demetrius II Nicator	129–125
Cleopatra Thea	126
Cleopatra Thea and Antiochus VIII Grypus	125–121
Seleucus V	125
Antiochus VII Grypus	121–96
Antiochus IX Cyzicenus	115–95
Seleucus VI Epiphanes Nicator	96–95
Demetrius III Philopator	95–88
Antiochus X Eusebes	95–83
Antiochus XI Philadelphus	94
Philip I Philadelphus	94–83
Antiochus XII Dionysus	87–84
Antiochus XIII	69–64
Philip II	67–65

The Ptolemies

Ptolemy I Soter	304–282 BC
Ptolemy II Philadelphus	285–246
Ptolemy III Euergetes	246–221
Ptolemy IV Philopator	221–204
Ptolemy V Epiphanes	204–180
Ptolemy VI Philometor	180–145
Ptolemy VII Neos Philopator	145–144
Ptolemy VIII Euergetes II	145–116
Ptolemy IX Soter II	116–107
Ptolemy X Alexander I	107–88
Ptolemy IX Soter II (restored)	88–81
Ptolemy XI Alexander II	80 BC
Ptolemy XII Neos Dionysos	80–51
Cleopatra VII Philopator	51–30
Ptolemy XIII	51–47
Ptolemy XIV	47–44
Ptolemy XV	44–30

Overlapping dates usually indicate co-regencies.

Roman and Byzantine Emperors

Augustus	27 B.C.–A.D. 14	Septimius Severus	193–211	Aurelian	270–275	Valens	364–378
Tiberius	A.D. 14–37	Geta	211–212	Tacitus	275–276	Theodosius I	378–395
Gaius Caligula	37–41	Caracalla	211–217	Probus	276–282	Arcadius	383–408
Claudius	41–54	Macrinus	217–218	Carus	282–283	Honorius	383–423
Nero	54–68	Diadumenianus	218	Carinus	283–284	Theodosius II	402–450
Balba	68–69	Elagabalus	218–222	Numerianus	283–284	Valentinian III	425–455
Otho	69	Alexander Severus	222–235	Diocletian	284–305	Marcian	450–457
Vitellius	69	Maximian I	235–238	Maximianus Herculius	286–305	Leo I	457–474
Vespasian	69–79	Gordianus I	238	Constantius I	293–306	Anthemius	467–472
Titus	79–81	Gordianus II	238	Galerius	293–311	Zeno	474–491
Domitian	81–96	Balbinus	238	Severus	306–307	Anastasius I	491–518
Nerva	96–98	Pupienus	238	Maxentius	306–312	Justin I	518–527
Trajan	98–117	Gordianus III	238–244	Licinius	308–324	Justinian I	527–565
Hadrian	117–138	Philip Senior	244–249	Maximinus II	308–313	Justin II	565–578
Antoninus Pius	138–161	Philip Junior	247–249	Constantine the Great	308–337	Tiberius II	578–582
Marcus Aurelius	161–180	Trajanus Decius	249–251	Constantius II	337–361	Tiberius Maurice	582–602
Lucius Verus	161–169	Trebonianus Gallus	251–253	Constans	337–350	Focas	602–610
Commodus	180–192	Hostilianus	251	Julian	361–363	Heraclius	610–641
Pertinax	193	Volusian	251–253	Jovian	363–364	Constans II	641–668
Didius Julianus	193	Valerian	253–260	Valentinian I	363–375		
Pescennius Niger	193–194	Gallienus	253–268	Gratian	367–383		
Clodius Albinus	193–197	Claudius Gothicus	268–270	Valentinian II	375–392		

INDEX TO NAMES

INDEX TO PLACES